Oracle SQL and PL/SQL Handbook

Oracle SQL
and
PL/SQL Handbook

A Guide for Data Administrators, Developers, and Business Analysts

John Adolph Palinski

♠♦Addison-Wesley

Boston • San Francisco • New York • Toronto • Montreal
London • Munich • Paris • Madrid
Capetown • Sydney • Tokyo • Singapore • Mexico City

Many of the designations used by manufacturers and sellers to distinguish their products are claimed as trademarks. Where those designations appear in this book, and Addison-Wesley was aware of a trademark claim, the designations have been printed with initial capital letters or in all capitals.

The author and publisher have taken care in the preparation of this book but make no expressed or implied warranty of any kind and assume no responsibility for errors or omissions. No liability is assumed for incidental or consequential damages in connection with or arising out of the use of the information or programs contained herein.

The publisher offers discounts on this book when ordered in quantity for special sales. For more information, please contact:

Pearson Education Corporate Sales Division
201 W. 103rd Street
Indianapolis, IN 46290
(800) 428-5331
corpsales@pearsoned.com

Visit Addison-Wesley on the Web: www.awprofessional.com

Library of Congress Cataloging-in-Publication Data

Palinski, John (John Adolph)
     Oracle SQL and PL/SQL handbook : a guide for data administrators, developers, and business analysts / John Adolph Palinski
         p. cm
     Includes bibliographical references and index.
     ISBN 0–201–75294–8 (alk. paper)
       1. SQL (Computer program language) 2. PL/SQL (Computer program language) 3. Oracle (Computer file) I. Title.

QA76.73.S67 P35 2002
005.75'65—dc21

                                                                                                    2002023208

Pearson Education, Inc.
Rights and Contracts Department
75 Arlington Street, Suite 300
Boston, MA 02116
Fax: (617) 848-7047

ISBN 0–201–75294–8
Text printed on recycled paper
1 2 3 4 5 6 7 8 9 10—CRS—0605040302
First printing, August 2002

I would like to dedicate this book to my mother, Catherine Semin Palinski. No one had a more energetic and loving mother than I. After my father passed away in 1967, she took over support of the family. My sisters and I never wanted for anything of importance. Without her support through my early years, I would not be where I am today.
I love you, Mom.

Contents

Acknowledgments   xvii

Introduction   xix

About the Author   xxxiii

CHAPTER 1   Understanding Relational Databases   1

Entities and Attributes   3

Entity Relationship Diagram Concepts   7

    Ordinality and Cardinality   9

Keys and Joins   10

Creating an Entity Relationship Diagram   12

    Identifying the Major Entities   12

    Defining the Identifiers   14

    Defining the Relationships, Cardinality, and Ordinality   14

    Defining Descriptive Attributes   15

    Creating the Entity Relationship Diagram   16

Converting the Entity Relationship Diagram
to a Relational Model   17

    Conversion to the Relational Model   18

    Normalization   19

The Data Schema Diagram   22

Table Relationship Diagram   23

Employee Database Table Relationship Diagram   26

What's Next?   28

Practice   28

CHAPTER 2   Building the Database with the Data Definition Language   31

Logging on to SQL*Plus   32

    Entering a Command   33

Using the SQL*Plus Editor   36

    Menu Commands   37

Database Objects That Store Data   39

    The Desk Analogy   39

    Tablespaces   40

    Creating and Modifying Tables   44

    Indexes   51

    Maintaining the Integrity of the Database   53

    Synonyms and Other Nice Things   62

Oracle Object-Oriented Features   68

    User-Defined Data Types   69

    Collection Types   70

TOAD   73

What's next?   74

Practice   74

CHAPTER 3   The Data Control and Data Manipulation Languages and the Data Dictionary   77

Creating User Accounts   77

Data Control Language (DCL)   79

    Roles   80

    Revoking Privileges   81

    Privileges   82

    Granting Access to Your Tables and Database Objects   87

Data Manipulation Language (DML)   88

    Using the INSERT Command   88

    Inserting Records from Another Table   90

    Using the UPDATE Command   91

    Deleting Records   92

    The COMMIT and ROLLBACK Commands   93

    The TRUNCATE Command   93

Oracle's Data Dictionary   94
    The User_objects and All_objects Views   96
    Reviewing PL/SQL Code Blocks with User_source   97
What's Next?   99
Practice   99

CHAPTER 4   Retrieving Database Records Using SQL: The Select, Where, and Order By Clauses   101

Identifying Table and Column Names   101
Making a Simple Database Query   103
    Components of a Simple SELECT   104
    Examples of Simple SELECT Statements   104
    Creating Character Values in the SELECT Clause   106
    Computing Numeric Values in the SELECT Clause   107
Limiting the Database Records Retrieved   109
    Evaluation Operators Used in the WHERE Clause   110
    Using the Equal (=) and IS Operators   111
    Using the Greater Than (>) and Less Than (<) Operators   112
    Using the IN Operator   113
    ANY, SOME, or ALL Keywords   114
    Using the BETWEEN Operator   115
    Using the LIKE Operator   116
    Using AND or OR to Document Multiple Conditions   120
    Mixing AND and OR in the WHERE Clause   121
Ordering Records   123
    Ascending/Descending Order   124
    Using Expression Numbers as the Names of Sort Columns   126
Printing the Results of Your Query   127
What's Next?   128
Practice   128

CHAPTER 5 Retrieving Records Using SQL: The FROM, GROUP BY, and HAVING Clauses   131

The FROM Clause   131
    Retrieving Records from Multiple Tables   131
    How to Combine or Join Tables   132
    What to Do with Join Columns with the Same Name   133
    Join Types   134

Joining Tables When the Value Exists in Only One Table:
The Outer Join   135
Nonequijoins   138
Self Joins   139
Cartesian Joins   141
Computing Group Values   142
Group Functions   143
Counting the Group's Record Instances   143
Summing the Values in a Group   144
Averaging the Values in a Group   145
Determining the Minimum Value   145
Determining the Maximum Value   146
Using the Group Functions on Smaller Groups   146
Limiting Selected Records by Using a Group Function   148
What's Next?   149
Practice   149

CHAPTER 6   Creating New Values with Character Functions   151

Character Functions   151
The INITCAP Function   151
The INSTR Function   153
The LENGTH Function   154
The LOWER Function   155
The LPAD Function   156
The LTRIM Function   156
The REPLACE Function   157
The RPAD Function   158
The RTRIM Function   159
The SOUNDEX Function   160
The SUBSTR Function   161
The TO_CHAR Function   162
The TRANSLATE Function   162
The TRIM Function   163
The UPPER Function   164
The DECODE Function   165
Case Expressions   167
Using Functions in the WHERE Clause   169

What's Next?   170

Practice   170

CHAPTER 7   Creating New Values with Numeric and Date Functions   171

The MOD and TO_NUMBER Functions   171

Using the NVL and the NVL2 Functions   173

The ROUND Function   175

The TRUNC Function   176

Dates and Date Functions   177

Date Pictures   178

Changing the Date Picture   178

Date Functions   181

The ADD_MONTHS Function   181

The LAST_DAY Function   183

The MONTHS_BETWEEN Function   183

The NEXT_DAY Function   184

The ROUND and TRUNC Date Functions   185

The TO_DATE Function   186

What's Next?   188

Practice   188

CHAPTER 8   Using Set Operators, Subqueries, and Variables   191

Set Operator Rules   192

The UNION and UNION ALL Operators   192

The MINUS Operator   195

The INTERSECT Operator   196

Subqueries   196

Multiple-Row Subqueries   198

Multiple-Column Queries   202

Correlated Subqueries   203

Variables   205

Using the Single-Ampersand Substitution Variable   205

Using the Double-Ampersand Variable   207

Defining User Variables   209

What's Next?   212

Practice   212

CHAPTER 9   Analytical Processing with SQL   215

ROLLUP   216

CUBE   218

The GROUPING Function   220

Ranking Functions   222

    The RANK Function   222

    The DENSE_RANK Function   225

    Top-N and Bottom-N Queries   226

    The PERCENT_RANK Function   227

    The CUME_DIST Function   229

    The NTILE Function   230

    The ROW_NUMBER Function   231

Windowing   233

    The Cumulative Aggregate Function   234

    Moving Averages   236

    The RATIO_TO_REPORT Function   238

    The LAG and LEAD Functions   239

Statistical Functions   243

What's Next?   246

Practice   246

CHAPTER 10   Using Database and Materialized Views   247

Administering Database Views   248

DML and Views   252

    The WITH CHECK OPTION Clause   253

    The WITH READ ONLY Option   254

    How to Update Records by Using a View That Can't Be Updated   255

Why Use Views?   258

Materialized Views   262

What's Next?   265

Practice   265

CHAPTER 11   Using SQL*Plus as a Report-Writing Tool   267

Title and Footer Settings   267

Formatting Columns   269

Breaks   274

Subtotals   277

Sending the Output to the Printer   280

SET Commands   282

What's Next?   288

Practice   288

CHAPTER 12   What You Can Do If Your SQL Does Not Perform   291

Indexes   292

   Which Columns Should Be Indexed?   293

   Multicolumn Indexes   294

   Index Types   295

Optimization   299

   The Rule-Based Optimizer   299

   The Cost-Based Optimizer   301

   Setting the Optimizer   302

   Another Word or Two on Access Paths   302

Join Operations   303

   Nested-Loop Join   303

   Sort-Merge Join   304

   Hash Join   304

EXPLAIN PLAN Statement   305

   PLAN_TABLE   305

   Populating PLAN_TABLE   307

   Reading the EXPLAIN PLAN Results   308

Dynamic Performance Views   312

Trace   313

   Running and Viewing the Trace Statistics   313

   Hints   318

Odds and Ends   321

What's Next?   322

CHAPTER 13   Using Business Objects   323

Data Warehouses   323

Business Objects   325

Drilling Down and Exceptions   331

Oracle Discoverer 4.0: The OLAP Tool of Choice   334

What's Next?   336

CHAPTER 14   The Basics of PL/SQL   337

Writing Your First Program   337

Executing the PL/SQL Program   339

Code Block Components and Block Labels   339
    Code Block Sections   340
    Block Labels, Labels, and the GOTO Keyword   341
    Comments   343

Declaring Variables and Assigning Values   343
    Defining Variables   343
    Character Definitions   344
    Numeric Definitions   344
    Other Definitions   345
    Constrained Definitions   345
    Aggregate and PL/SQL Record Definitions   346
    Assigning Values to Variables   347
    Using the INTO Assignment Keyword with PL/SQL Records   348

The IF-THEN-ELSE and ELSIF Structures   349
    The IF-THEN-ELSE Structure   350
    Nested IF-THEN-ELSE Structures   351
    The ELSIF/THEN Structure   353

Cursors   354
    Declaring the Cursor   354
    Cursor Commands   355
    Using Aggregate Variables with Cursors   356
    Cursor Attributes   358
    Differences between a Cursor and a SELECT/INTO Statement   360

Loops   360
    The LOOP Structure   361
    The WHILE Loop   363
    Using the %FOUND Cursor Attribute with Loops   364
    Nested Loops   366
    Locking Records with the FOR UPDATE Option   367
    The FOR UPDATE OF Option   369
    The WHERE CURRENT OF Option   370

FOR Loops   372
    Numeric FOR Loops   372
    The Basic Cursor FOR Loop   375
    Defining the Cursor in the Cursor FOR Header   376
    Nested FOR Loops   377
What's Next?   379
Practice   379

**CHAPTER 15   Handling Exceptions and Using
Named Procedures   381**

Exception Handling   381
    Predefined SQL Exceptions   382
    Handling an Exception with a Predefined Exception   383
    Defining Error Handlers   385
    The OTHERS Exception   386
    Using SQLCODE and SQLERRM   387
    Using the Exception Section for Your Own Processing   388
PL/SQL Records and Arrays   389
    PL/SQL Table Attributes   392
    Deleting PL/SQL Table Records   395
Named Procedures   396
    Creating or Changing, Executing, and Deleting a Named Procedure   397
    The Header Section   398
    Header Parameters   399
    Inputting Values by Using the IN Parameter Mode   401
    Calling a Procedure from a Procedure and Outputting Values by Using the OUT Parameter Mode   402
    Defining a Named Procedure within a Procedure   404
    Overloading   405
Functions   407
    Function Structure   408
    Creating and Using a Function   408
    Creating and Using a Function in a SELECT Clause   410
    Using a Function in an Assignment Statement within a Procedure   411
Packages   412
    Package Components   413
    Package Specification Template   414

Package Body Specification   414
Employee Package Example   415
What's Next?   418
Practice   419

CHAPTER 16   Advanced PL/SQL Topics   421
Cursor Variables   421
Processing Objects   424
Nested Object Tables   426
PL/SQL and Java   427
Creating and Using a Java Class within PL/SQL   428
Loading the Java Source Code into the Database   430
What's Next?   431

Appendix A   Glossary   433

Appendix B   Answers   441
Chapter 1   441
Chapter 2   442
Chapter 3   444
Chapter 4   444
Chapter 5   446
Chapter 6   447
Chapter 7   447
Chapter 8   448
Chapter 9   450
Chapter 10   452
Chapter 11   453
Chapter 14   453
Chapter 15   464

Bibliography   473

Index   475

Acknowledgments

I would like to acknowledge several people who have helped me write this book. The first person is my agent, Neil Salkind. He helped me get this contract and offered me words of encouragement throughout the writing. I would also like to acknowledge my friend Nick Steferos. Nick is an Oracle user whom I trained for several years. His relentless Oracle questions and his desire to push Oracle to its technical limits tremendously increased my knowledge of Oracle. I would also like to recognize my coworker and friend, Jim Hightower. Jim and I have spent years developing management reports and business objects. Most of my knowledge of this topic evolved from discussions with him. Finally, I would like to recognize my wife, Linda Gorzelanski Palinski. She was at my side every moment of the writing, offering me words of encouragement and making sure that I had my priorities set correctly. A person needs a best friend, and she is mine.

Introduction

Oracle SQL and PL/SQL Handbook: A Guide for Data Administrators, Developers, and Business Analysts is a book whose purpose is to teach you techniques that you can use to extract information from complex modern Oracle relational databases. The business world has constructed numerous online transaction processing (**OLTP**) systems, databases, and data warehouses over the past twenty years. Information from these databases is very important to the successful operation of businesses. Corporations have also discovered that it is important to have personnel who can understand and efficiently extract information from these databases. This is why developers, data administrators, and business analysts who can get information from complex databases are so valuable to their companies.

Structured Query Language (**SQL**), which is an ANSI standard language for interacting with relational databases, is the main tool for extracting the information. SQL is somewhat standard across most relational database products; however, this book covers only Oracle's version. Oracle is the largest database manufacturer in the world and has the most product installations. So this is a good place to start your education.

There are other tools you will need to know about in order to produce business information. This includes the ability to read and understand the database blueprint. This blueprint is the entity relationship diagram (ERD) or my own favorite tool, the table relationship diagram. You will also need to be aware of database objects such as views, synonyms, and indexes. After you learn how to extract the information, you will want to know how to extract the information quickly. This book contains a chapter that has some common techniques that can be used to enhance the performance of your SQL. This book also covers

PL/SQL, which is Oracle's programming language and is an extremely useful language for accessing object attributes and performing special calculations.

This book contains numerous examples of various SQL techniques. It also has practice questions at the end of most chapters. The questions will allow you to practice the skills immediately after studying them. Appendix B contains answers to the practice questions and provides you with another set of examples to study, copy, and adapt to your work.

The book is meant to be a basic reference book and a how-to manual that covers the most important and common Oracle database topics. It is not the ultimate reference book. It is very difficult to learn SQL from these types of books. This book can be used as a reference book, but it does not totally eliminate the need for true reference books that cover the mundane, once-used-in-five-years topics. The purpose of this book is to help you get the skills to analyze, understand, and efficiently extract information from an Oracle database. Developers, database administrators (DBAs), data administrators (DAs), and business analysts normally have a score of books in their work area. No single book can contain everything about all topics. *I want this book to be the first book you go to for answers about the Oracle database because it contains the most frequently used information.*

This book is based on courses I have taught at Iowa Western Community College and the University of Nebraska at Omaha and on-site seminars I teach at many major companies. During the past four years, I have helped many students understand the basics of Oracle SQL and the techniques used to extract information. The techniques I cover are the result of 15 years of experience producing business information from relational databases. Students say my books and seminar workbooks are "very practical." I believe in studying and identifying good design, copying it, modifying it, and calling it my own. Much of this good design is included in this book. I truly hope and believe that you will find the information in this book practical, and I hope you steal it and call it your own.

What Is Oracle?

Oracle is the largest database manufacturer and the second-largest software manufacturer in the world. The company began as a relational database manufacturer. In the beginning, Oracle touted its software as "being able to run on any platform." This openness has been most attractive to companies, and

Oracle has tried to maintain its image as an open product. Oracle was at a good place when industry became extremely interested in moving away from network databases and the mainframe.

By allowing companies to use the client/server paradigm, Oracle had a competitive advantage. It also identified the Internet as the future paradigm. Oracle remains the premier database manufacturer due to its foresight. Oracle continues to increase the power of its database. The current version is called Oracle9i. It's an object-relational database, which has features that allow developers to model objects within the database. The *i* in the name means that its database can also support the Internet. To this end, Java programming functions can be placed within the database. Oracle can understand applications using the Java functions. Oracle has recognized that Java is an open product and is one of the more important languages of the Web.

Oracle also has several other database products. Personal Oracle is a smaller version of the Oracle Enterprise edition. It resides on the client (your personal computer) and is designed primarily as a stand-alone database. Oracle also has a small database called Oracle Lite9i, which is designed for use on portable computers and handheld devices.

Oracle has very powerful application-development, report-writing, and database-analysis software. The application-development package is currently called the Internet Developer Suite. It consists of a number of products, two of which are Developer6i Form Builder and Report Builder. Developer6i Form Builder is Oracle's rapid application development (RAD) software. Report Builder is Oracle's main report-writing software.

Designer6i is Oracle's computer-aided software engineering (CASE) product. It is one of the best-selling CASE products in the country. In addition to performing database documentation and object creation, it can be used to generate forms (screens). It is integrated with the other Developer6i products. Even though it will not be covered in this book, Designer is used in many shops as a repository of database information. It is an important tool that can be used to develop and obtain ERDs and other database documentation.

The last remaining development software is JDeveloper. This is a Java-based application-development product somewhat similar to Developer6i Form Builder. It can be used to create Java-based applications, both client/server- and Web-based. Borland supplied the core technology for this product, which is why JDeveloper has a strong resemblance to Borland's Jbuilder. Oracle hopes that JDeveloper will someday be the dominant Web development tool.

Discoverer is Oracle's database-analysis product. It is an online analytical processing (**OLAP**) tool. It has a very easy user interface and is an extremely powerful tool for developing and analyzing business information. The success of this product is due to the ease of creating business objects for analysis, and to the end users' easy use of the product. I have actually had novice students using the product with less than two hours of training. It is a great tool for empowering your users and reducing the report-writing load of the programmers, DAs, and business analysts.

Finally, Oracle has an array of packaged products for businesses. One such product is Oracle Financials, an entity resource planning (**ERP**) application that companies use to document work requests, purchase the materials, maintain inventory levels, and manage their fixed assets, accounts payable, and other financial concerns. Oracle also has an array of other entity packages. As you can see, Oracle has a large number of tools and products.

Who Should Use This Book?

At Iowa Western and in my seminars, I allow anyone with Windows (or UNIX) experience to enroll in the courses. I would expect that this is the minimum technical criterion to use this book properly. This is an intro book and will cover most of the commonly used areas of Oracle SQL and PL/SQL. It will also have some elementary coverage of relational and object database components and terminology. This book will be of interest to the following people:

- Mainframe programmers wanting to upgrade or develop SQL skills
- Systems analysts, developers, or business personnel interested in data administration
- Students desiring the skills needed to enter the Oracle market
- Oracle developers looking for new techniques
- Developers interested in implementing business objects for analysis
- Business analysts interested in gaining the skills to analyze corporate databases

You would expect a book such as this to be of interest to readers who desire a technical career. Increasingly, however, it is of importance for accountants, financial analysts, and other nontechnical people to have SQL, database, and online analytical processing (OLAP) skills.

A case in point is the job description for accountants at the company at which I am employed. Accountant job descriptions request Oracle knowledge as a needed skill. With the proliferation of ERP-type databases such as Oracle Financials, SAP, or PeopleSoft, nontechnical personnel are having to derive information from these databases. Knowledge of SQL, PL/SQL, and Discoverer will greatly aid these people, giving them an edge over their coworkers. The worker who can furnish information to management is always a valuable asset. The worker who cannot is not as valuable.

Another class of developers who may reap benefits from this book are Microsoft Access developers. Access is a low-level database product that is highly automated. Over the years, I have received many comments that my courses on SQL and database-object creation help students understand what Access is actually doing.

How Is This Book Organized?

This book contains 16 chapters, a glossary appendix, and an answer appendix. It begins with a discussion of the logical data model, which is used to determine what the database represents, to identify data elements, and to identify the data linkages. This information is needed to extract business information effectively using SQL.

The book then discusses the various Oracle database objects. It is important for you to understand these objects, as many of them will affect the SQL that is written. However, it may not be necessary for you to read the latter portions of Chapter 2 until after the SQL chapters. Chapter 2 covers the use of the Data Definition Language (**DDL**), which is used to create and maintain database objects such as tables or views. The chapter also discusses how to log on to the Oracle database and enter commands. This section is important for the reader new to Oracle. I place the DDL section at the beginning of the book for the readers who want to understand the database engine components before running the engine.

Chapters 4–9 cover the SELECT command, the language used to extract information from the database. Chapter 10 discusses the use of views and sequences. Views are a really important tool for creating runtime virtual records.

Chapter 11 discusses commands that are contained within the database and that can be used to change the presentation of your information. The Oracle database has limited report-writing tools. There are more powerful tools available on the market, including some fine Oracle tools. However, if your company does not have any of these tools, you will always have the tools discussed in Chapter 11 available.

Chapter 12 discusses performance-tuning techniques, those that are common and often used. Chapter 13 discusses business objects, which are database objects that can be used for analysis or to increase the performance of reports. The final three chapters cover Oracle's PL/SQL language. This language is a must for the data administrator and can be used to create business objects and **entity** attributes of interest to the user. The language is also used in Oracle's Report Builder and Form Builder products.

Appendix A of the book is a glossary, providing you with definitions of important database words. Appendix B contains the answers to exercises that reside at the end of many of the chapters. These questions will allow you to practice the discussed topics. I strongly encourage you to perform the practice questions before checking the answers.

Conventions

There are two conventions that will be used throughout this book:

Bold Text.   Identifies the first occurrence of a keyword that will be defined in the glossary.

Italic Text.   Identifies places in a command-syntax template that will require a user-defined value.

Other Sources of Information

Despite the best attempts by the technical editors, copy editors, and me, errors and misunderstandings will exist in this book. It is extremely humbling for an author/teacher to have his students/readers interpret his writing differently from what he expected. I have tried to be as skilled a technical writer as possible; however, I am sure that I fail occasionally. To remedy this, I intend to maintain a Web site that you can use to raise questions and to view the answers to previous inquiries. The site will contain corrections, explanations, and clarifications. I believe this will be a valuable aid to you. The following is my home Web site: www.oracle-trainer.com.

Another valuable site is the Oracle Developer Tools User Group (ODTUG). This is an organization to which I have belonged for several years. The group has an annual conference, a quarterly newsletter, and a special site where members can post enhancement requests to Oracle. Of special importance are the organization's list servers, the access to which at the present time is free to everyone. The list servers allow you to post, answer, and receive advice about a variety of Oracle topics, including SQL.

I belong to the SQL, Java, Developer6i, and Discoverer list servers. I monitor the questions and answers all day, and so do a number of other highly skilled professionals (and authors). It is an excellent place to get the latest Oracle information or help with technical issues. The ODTUG site is at www.odtug.com.

If you are truly interested in Oracle, you must visit their Web site frequently. The home page (www.oracle.com) can be very complex and appears to change daily, but it is the source of new Oracle information. Following are some of the Oracle pages I recommend. Before trying to access the pages, you should know that many of them are available only to members of the Oracle Technology Network. This is a free membership, and you may join using Oracle's Web site. It will enable you to access a great deal of information.

- Oracle Store. This page is the site for purchasing CD packs of Oracle databases—Personal Oracle, one of these databases, can be used on your personal computer for course work—and for the Internet Development Suite. These tools include Developer6i, JDeveloper, Discoverer, and Designer. I strongly encourage you to purchase the database pack and install Personal Oracle—which runs on only Windows NT/2000 at the present time. You can practice all of the techniques discussed in this book. It is one thing to read about Oracle and another actually to employ the techniques. The current site for the CD packs is www.oraclestore.oracle.com/OA_HTML/ibeCCtpSctD spRte.jsp?section=11536&jfn=CAB2E7AB8B81E955A27B05. The database package is called Oracle(R) 9i Release 1 (9.0.1) CD Pack for Microsoft Windows.

- Oracle Certified Professional Programs. Oracle has a variety of certifications, which are a series of tests about Oracle topics. Two of the more popular are the DBA and Developer, which consist of five tests. The initial test for the DBA and Developer certifications concerns SQL and PL/SQL. This book is an excellent primer for this exam. To learn more about Oracle certifications, visit www.oracle.com/education/certification/.

- Oracle Certified Professional Assessment Test Download. It is possible to download sample certification exams. You might be interested in how you would perform on a certification exam before and after reading this book. Visit www.oracle.com/education/certification/index.html?sts.html to obtain the sample exams.

Installing the Practice Database and Tools

Oracle offers evaluation copies of their products for *free (or at a nominal price)*. Many of my students would like to practice their skills at home. I recommend that they visit the Oracle site and obtain the latest evaluation production.

The students sometimes find that the most difficult part of learning Oracle is installing the Oracle products and the practice database. This is usually because the student is not familiar with the Oracle products, has ordered the wrong products—Oracle can change the names of products—or has problems with versions, or there may be a variety of other reasons. I encounter this problem every semester. The installation process can seem like a daunting task, but I think these instructions will help you get the products loaded and will get you on your way to learning Oracle.

What Software to Get

First of all, you need to acquire the following product:

Personal Oracle   This is the personal-computer version of Oracle. It has all of the features you need for this book. It is a much smaller version than the Oracle9i Enterprise edition. The Enterprise Edition may also be used with this book, but it requires Windows NT, 2000, or XP.

If you work for a company that has Oracle installed, you might want to use your company's installation to practice. Your company will likely have a version of the Enterprise edition of Oracle. This product can also be used, and everything within this book applies to the Enterprise edition.

Versions have differences that might be of interest to the experienced Oracle user. The differences in the SQL basics are not generally substantial, and the version differences are not as important for the new student. If you have access to older versions of Oracle, they can be used with this book. However, I would try to acquire the latest database and product versions.

How to Get the Software

At the time of this writing, Oracle offers several options, the best of which is to purchase the Oracle Database CD Pack or the Oracle Tools CD Pack (which is not covered in this book). Each of the packs currently costs $39.95 and contains the full range of Oracle databases and tools.

Individual Oracle products may also be downloaded from the Oracle Tech Network (www.otn.oracle.com/software/content.html). You must register, but the registration is free. The only disadvantage of the download process is that files are very large, and you will need a high-speed connection. If you do not have access to such a connection, the CDs are your only option. The products on the CDs and from the Oracle Tech Network are evaluation copies. They are licensed for a 30-day evaluation. However, this small period of time will help you develop skills that can be used in the workplace. In my opinion, the evaluation products are an excellent tool for the student.

In my opinion, the easiest method to obtain the software is to purchase the CD packs. However, several other sources are available:

- I have had students contact the local Oracle sales representative. This can be an effective mechanism when you have trouble ordering the CD packs.
- Oracle has a program known as the Oracle Academic Initiative, which allows any qualified academic institution to purchase all Oracle products for $500 per year. It also allows the institution to copy the software for its students. If you are attending an institution enrolled in this program, you should be able to get the software through the school's IS department.

Setting Up Personal Oracle

The first product to install is the Oracle database. This is an automated process. Simply place the proper CD into the CD-ROM and follow the instructions. I have seen student installations go relatively easily, and I have seen their installations be very difficult. The difficulty has varied with the different releases of the product. The students did not cause the problems. Incorrect load scripts from Oracle caused the problems. If you encounter difficulties, don't get frustrated; join the large crowd of new users who have had problems and overcame them. One thing you can do is check my Web site (www.oracle-trainer.com), where I will attempt to have additional instructions or advice available. Another good source is the list server at the Oracle Developer Tools Users Group (www.odtug.com) site. Of course, the best source is Oracle itself.

After installing the database, you must check to see if the database is operational. The following instructions pertain to Oracle 9i.

1. Before the database can be used, it must be started. When the database is installed, settings are made that start the Oracle database whenever Windows is launched. To determine if the database has been started, check the OracleserviceORCL service. You can view this service by using the Services menu option on the Control Panel, which will display a Windows dialog box. Starting Oracle causes some of your computer's memory to be used. If you are not using Oracle all the time, you may want to stop the database. This can be done on the Service dialog box.

2. Launch SQL*Plus. Instructions are contained in Chapter 2. There are two default user IDs and passwords:

   - scott/tiger   This is a default Oracle training ID. It contains the normal privileges allowed for a developer. Your practice database will be installed on this user ID.

   - system/manager   This is the default Oracle master ID. It has the ability to perform all database functions.

If you cannot log on to SQL*Plus, you might not have started the database, you might have entered an incorrect user ID/password, or you might not have installed the Oracle database properly.

Installing the Practice Tables

After you are ensured that Personal Oracle is installed and started, you can install the practice database. The necessary files reside in the Introduction directory of this book's CD-ROM. The following is a description of the files:

- move.bat This file creates a directory, called tab_cre, on your drive C. It will also cause each of the following files to be moved into this directory.

- install.bat This batch file will create the necessary tables on the scott/tiger user ID and will load the data into the tables.

- tabl_cre.sql This file contains the scripts that will create the tables.

- loaddept.ctl This file is an **SQL*Loader** control file. It contains the loader specifications and the data for the Department table.

- loademp.ctl This file is an SQL*Loader control file. It contains the loader specifications and the data for the Employee table.

- loadglas.ctl This file is an SQL*Loader control file. It contains the loader specifications and the data for the Glasses table.

- loadtool.ctl This file is an SQL*Loader control file. It contains the loader specifications and the data for the Emp_tools table.

Follow these steps to install the practice tables (after moving the above-mentioned files to your personal computer):

1. Ensure that the Oracle database is started.
2. Launch the install.bat file in the Introduction directory on the CD-ROM.

Files can be launched in three ways:

1. Locate the file, using My Computer. Double-click the desired file.
2. Locate the file, using Windows Explorer. Double-click the desired file.

3. Click Run from the Start menu. Type the names and full file paths of the batch files (e.g., d:\intro\move.bat, c:\tabl_cre\install.bat).

If the root drive of your computer is not C, your CD-ROM drive is not drive D, or you are not using the Personal Oracle8i (8.1.5), you might have to perform additional work.

If your CD-ROM drive is not drive D, perform the following steps:

1. Move the files to your hard drive. The move.bat file on the CD-ROM is designed to move files if the CD-ROM drive is drive D. Move this file to your computer. Edit the file in Notepad. Change the drive D designation to the appropriate drive. (You may also use My Computer or Windows Explorer to move the files.)

2. Move the files to the tabl_cre directory. (The move.bat file should create this directory. If you are not using the move.bat file or if your root directory is not drive C, you must manually create the tab_cre directory on your computer.)

3. Ensure that the files can be edited. You may have to change the Read Only file property of each file. You may use Windows Explorer to locate the file, and the right mouse button to open the file's Properties dialog box, which can be used to change the properties of the target files.

4. Use Notepad to change the drive designation (e.g., C, D, E) in the install.bat file.

5. Follow the load instructions in the Readme file.

If you are not using Personal Oracle8i (8.1.5), you might have to edit the install.bat file, which uses the Oracle executables Plus80w.exe and Sqlldr.exe. The former executable launches SQL*Plus and is used to create the tables. The latter executable launches SQL*Loader, which is used to populate the tables. Oracle generally changes the names of these files and their locations with each major upgrade of the database.

To locate the location and name of SQL*Plus, follow these steps:

1. Open the Find All Files dialog box from the Windows Start menu.

2. Type plus*.exe in the Name box.

3. Locate the executable.

To locate the location and name of SQL*Loader, follow these steps:

1. Open the Find All Files dialog box from the Windows Start menu.
2. Type sqlldr*.exe in the Name box.
3. Locate the executable.

After locating the names and locations of the executables, follow these steps:

1. Move the files from the CD-ROM to your computer, using the instructions for modifying drive paths.
2. Open Install.bat in Notepad or any other suitable text editor.
3. Change the names and locations of the executables, and ensure that the referenced drives are correct. Listing Intro. 1 illustrates the install.bat file and the items to change.

Listing Intro.1 *MS-DOS Commands for Creating and Populating the Database*

```
sqlplusw scott/tiger @d:\practice_database\tabl_cre.sql
sqlldr scott/tiger control=d:\practice_database\loaddept.ctl
log=c:\ld.log bad=c:\ld.bad
sqlldr scott/tiger control=d:\practice_database\loademp.ctl
log=c:\le.log bad=c:\le.bad
sqlldr scott/tiger control=d:\practice_database\loadtool.ctl
log=c:\lt.log bad=c:\lt.bad
sqlldr scott/tiger control=d:\practice_database\loadglas.ctl
log=c:\lg.log bad=c:\lg.bad
sqlldr scott/tiger control=d:\practice_database\loadtaxes.ctl
log=c:\ltax.log bad=c:\ltax.bad
```

I hope these instructions do not scare you off. They are designed to be informative because computers and product versions vary. Most students install the practice database painlessly. These instructions, however, do not address problems with the Oracle software; Oracle must address those. If you are having problems with the practice-table installation, I am very confident that my instructions will help. If they do not, feel free to post a question through my Web site (www.oracle-trainer.com). I will post revised instructions for all unique questions.

What's Next?

The next chapter will introduce you to relational database terminology and theory. The chapter will discuss entity relationship diagrams, table relationship diagrams, and the principles of normalization. The chapter is important in that it will help you understand how to identify needed data items within a relational database. If you cannot locate the database components you need, you will certainly not be an effective user of SQL.

About the Author

John Palinski is a supervisor of computer applications at the Omaha Public Power District. He has developed and implemented numerous Oracle systems for the district. He has also spent countless hours writing SQL for reports and business analysis. John is a Certified Oracle Developer Release 1. He has taught SQL, PL/SQL, and Developer 2000 at Iowa Western Community College. He currently teaches prerequisite courses for the Master's in MIS program at the University of Nebraska at Omaha. John is the author of *Oracle Database Construction Kit* (QUE, 1997) and has written numerous articles for *Oracle Internals* magazine. He has also developed a variety of Oracle curricula that he teaches for corporations nationally. He may be reached through his Web site: www.oracle-trainer.com.

Understanding Relational Databases

The Entity Relationship Diagram, Data Schema Diagram, and Normalization

The Oracle product that is discussed throughout this book is Oracle's **database** product. Databases store data and **metadata**. Data are the individual facts that are used to derive information. Metadata describe the content, quality, condition, availability, and characteristics of data. Database management software (DBMS) is used to modify the data. For the purposes of this book, *database* will refer to the data stored in a database product such as Oracle9i.

Over the years, there has been a variety of database types: sequential files, hierarchical databases, network databases, and relational databases. The latest type of data storage is an object-relational database such as Oracle9i. An object-relational database is essentially a relational database that has some object properties.

Business has overwhelmingly adopted the relational database as its database of choice. The conversion from network databases to relational databases has been occurring for the past 15 years. It really accelerated in the late 1990s due to the Y2K concerns. Relational databases became popular because of their ease of use. They consist of a series of independent but related tables called a schema. A table is similar to a spreadsheet; it consists of rows and columns. In a table, each of the columns has a name.

Relational databases became popular because it was easy to modify the schema. It is very easy to add tables and columns to the schema, and doing so does not affect the remainder of the schema and, more important, does not affect the applications that access the database schema. Therefore, the database easily adapts to changes in the business. Older databases required the databases to be restructured and the applications to be modified. Avoiding database and application maintenance is an important benefit and the reason for the switch.

Initially, relational databases had some poor features. Performance of early relational databases was poor. They were not nearly as fast as network databases. Relational databases were not effective for large databases or for databases with heavy transaction volume. Over the years, Oracle technology has eliminated these problems. Another problem remained.

Relational databases consist of independent tables. Relational database management software (RDBMS) does not know how the records in the tables are related. For example, our practice database has an Employee table that consists of unique attributes about an employee. It also contains an Employee Tools table that consists of unique attributes about a tool purchase. The tables are independent but related. Oracle does not know how they are related. In order to retrieve the attributes from the tables, the data administrator must identify the tables that contain the attributes and define within an SQL command how the table records are related. As you will see in this book, this can be very difficult. In fact, without a database blueprint, it is almost impossible. I will introduce you to mechanisms that will help you perform this.

The most recent database upgrade was an attempt to eliminate the latter problem. The upgrade was the addition of object properties into the Oracle database. Network databases knew related records because of pointers. A pointer identifies the location of the related record. Oracle9i now employs pointers. Their use allows the developer to define attributes within one object. For example, rather than having a series of tables that are used to store employee attributes, an object that can store all of the employee attributes can be created. Using this technique, the data administrator can access the desired attributes by simply knowing the object name and the name of the attributes. This is a potentially simpler approach.

The problem with Oracle's object technology is the difficulty in designing the objects. It takes a great deal of effort to design these objects properly. Object databases are also not effective for high-transaction systems or large numbers of users. Overwhelmingly, industry is still relying on the relational paradigm. Neither Oracle nor any other major database manufacturer is going to move entirely away from the relational database until they see a large shift. It hasn't happened to date. Despite the use of C++ and Java (object-oriented languages), industry does not appear to be moving rapidly toward the object-relational database. This book will primarily focus on Oracle's relational features, especially because Oracle is primarily a relational database. It will have some coverage of the object features, in the event that you should encounter an object database.

The intent of this chapter is to introduce you to the basic relational database terminology and concepts. Before you can use SQL to create business information, you must have the skills that will enable you to locate and extract the required data. You must be able to discern the names of the interested data items, where they are located, and the path needed to extract the data. To this end, this chapter will contain the following topics:

- Definitions of key relational database terms
- How to model a database using the **entity relationship diagram (ERD)**
- How the ERD is translated into a relational model
- How the relational model is designed to store data efficiently through the use of **normalization**
- What a data schema diagram represents
- How to create a table relationship diagram
- How a **table relationship diagram** can help you as a business analyst or data administrator

Entities and Attributes

A database is a representation of a real-world thing called an **entity**. Examples of entities are vehicles, employees, customers, fish, buildings, and even things such as baseball teams. The database stores facts about the entity in an organized framework, **model**, or schema. These facts are called **attributes**.

An **instance** is one occurrence of an entity. Figure 1.1 illustrates three instances of the entity Student. The facts about the student entity are its attributes. As you can see, we know that one of the students is named Matt and plays baseball (not shown is that he was 9-1 his senior year and won the Nebraska Class B state championship game).

A database is a model or representation of one or more entities. It stores an entity instance's attributes in an efficient manner. This type of model is different from a visual model, but it is just as effective. For instance, architects often create smaller-scale models of the bridges or buildings they design.

The figure contains a panel reading:

—Entity—
Student
—Attributes—

Name	Matt
Height	6 feet
Weight	155 lbs
Course	Algebra
Course	Physics
Sport	Baseball
Sport	Basketball

Figure 1.1 *Three instances of the entity Student and attributes for the instance Matt*

Visual models help a client see that the represented building has features such as granite facing, will be 40 stories tall, and has a penthouse. If these facts are stored electronically in a database, you can use SQL to give the same information to your client. The entity model is one of the blueprints that describe how the facts are stored. Thus it is vital that you understand how to read (and create) the database blueprint.

Relational databases are comprised of a set of tables that contain the entities' attribute values. The best way to visualize a table is to think of a spreadsheet. A spreadsheet contains rows and columns. Each **column** is one of the entity's attributes. An entity instance is comprised of the set of columns in the **table**. Thus each instance of the Student entity's name, weight, and height attributes would form one row or record in the table.

Most databases are very complex. They contain many different tables to store an entity's attributes effectively. This is done in order to store the attributes more efficiently. For example, the Student entity depicted in Figure 1.1 has two repeating sets of attributes: courses and sports. It would not be efficient to store these attributes in the same table as the student's name, weight, and height attributes. A student can take one course or an infinite number of courses. If you placed 50 course columns on the same row as the name, weight, and height attributes, you would have a lot of wasted space. If you added columns whenever they were needed, you would have to modify the table continually. That is not a good situation. It is better to store repeating attributes in a structure that eliminates these problems. This structure is a related table that contains a record for each instance of the courses. If the student does not take a course, no records are stored. If the student takes 50 courses, 50 records are stored.

Databases also contain descriptions of other attributes. For example, each course a student can take has a name. A course I often teach is called the "Introduction to the Oracle Database." If we put this course name in the same table as the courses that students have taken, you would see this course name repeated many times. Good database design eliminates the need to place descriptive attributes in the same record as the described attribute. Descriptive attributes are placed in related tables. Each time the description is needed, the related table is referenced.

Databases are further complicated in that entities can be related to other entities. For example, Substation is an entity that has various pieces of electrical equipment within it. The substation can have a transformer, circuit breaker, switch, and a score of other entities. Each of these entities can have many related entities of its own. For example, a transformer can have oil-test results, electric-test results, and inspection results.

I hope that you are getting a sense that databases can be complex. SQL can retrieve the various attributes from the tables. However, you need to know a number of things:

- The database name of the desired attribute
- The name of the table in which the attribute resides
- The paths that are used to extract the attributes
- The keys that determine which records are related

The documents that represent the database schema can determine these facts. The documents that can be used are entity relationship diagrams and, more important, database schema diagrams. These diagrams are the blueprints of the database and are essential for your understanding. Figure 1.2 depicts the entity relationship diagram for a Relay entity database that I developed. The diagram is hard to read, but it does depict what I want to show: the complexity of a relatively simple database. Notice the number of entities or tables.

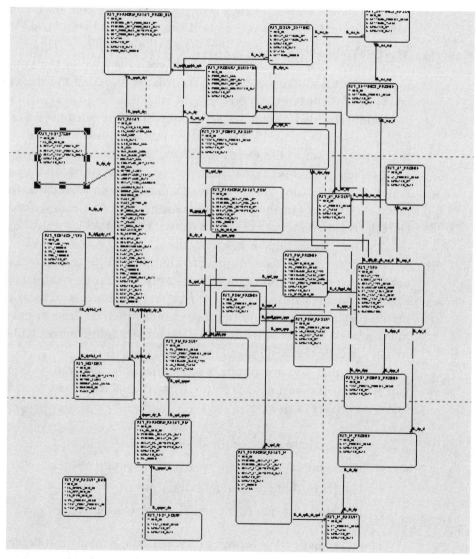

Figure 1.2 *Relay entity relationship diagram*

The Figure 1.2 database schema is relatively simple, yet look at the diagram. It fills most of a page. ERP databases that businesses are using, such as Oracle Financials, People Soft, or SAP, are tremendously more complex. These databases can contain thousands of tables. Imagine trying to determine where the desired attributes reside in such a database. Need I say more about the need of a database schema blueprint?

Entity Relationship Diagram Concepts

Entity relationship diagrams (ERDs) are the second major document (the first is the data flow diagram) that is developed when using the traditional approach to system analysis and design. When designing a new system, the systems analyst first identifies all of the processes and data needed within a system. The system processes, the flow of data between the processes, the **data stores**, and the external entities are captured in a **data flow diagram** (DFD).

Data moving through a system is depicted on a DFD by **data flows**. Each data flow contains a variety of data items. These are the bits of data that are the inputs to a process and the outputs from a process. When these bits of data are at rest, they are contained in a data store, which is a database when in electronic form.

The DFD shows you how the bits of data flow. It does not show you how the bits of data are structured in the database. The ERD is the tool used to perform this task. I often think of the unstructured data as bits of material in outer space. The pull of gravity eventually combines the materials into worlds. The data identified for a system is the same: The bits of data will eventually gravitate toward an entity.

The first step in designing a database is to identify the entities that the database represents. As we have seen previously, databases usually consist of a number of entities. A database may have a Student as the main entity. However, the database may also have related entities that may or may not be totally dependent upon the main entity, such as Courses Taken, Sports Played, or Organizations Belonged To.

The second step is to gravitate the database attributes to the appropriate entity. An entity can have a few attributes or a large number of attributes. Each entity must have an **identifier**, which is one or more attributes that make each entity instance unique from any other instance. The identifier should contain a value that does not change. Examples of identifiers are student IDs, payroll numbers, or social security numbers. If the entity does not have an attribute that can be used as an identifier, an artificial identifier can be created. The identifier of an entity is often called a **primary key**.

The third step is to describe the **relationships** between the entities. Relationships are important because they describe the interconnectivity between entities. They are the paths that need to be followed to extract the desired database attributes. There are three types of relationships, which are depicted in Figure 1.3. The following are their descriptions:

Unary   This relationship indicates that an entity is related to itself. An example of this type of relationship would be an Employee entity that has a Manager attribute. The value in the Manager attribute is an Employee ID (which is the identifier of the Employee entity). Thus the Employee entity is related to itself through common values in its Employee ID and Manager attributes.

Binary   This relationship indicates that an entity is related to only one other entity. This is the most common type of relationship and requires common attributes in each of the related entities.

Ternary   This relationship indicates that several entities are related to each other.

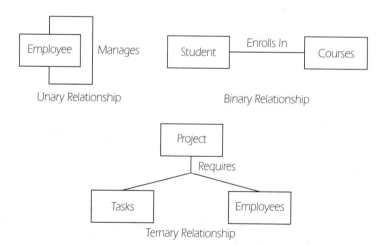

Figure 1.3 *Relationship symbols*

Ordinality and Cardinality

Ordinality and **cardinality** are two very important database properties. Cardinality is a relationship property that indicates the number of related instances an entity may have. An entity may have zero, one, or many related entity instances. This property helps the analyst identify whether more than one related instance exists. This can have an effect on calculations and the number of records that may be displayed. After you gain a better understanding of SQL, you will better understand the use of this property.

Figure 1.4 depicts several relationships that show cardinality. There are two different sets of symbols that are used to show cardinality. When a related entity can have only one instance, this is depicted by the numeral *1* or by a pipe symbol (|). Cardinality that is One-to-Many is depicted by the character *N* or by a crow's-foot symbol (⅄).

Ordinality is a property that indicates whether an entity instance is mandatory. The analyst is extremely interested in this property. It determines whether an outer join should be used when extracting attributes from the

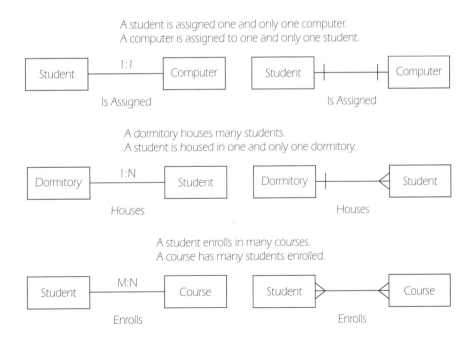

Figure 1.4 *Relationships displaying cardinality*

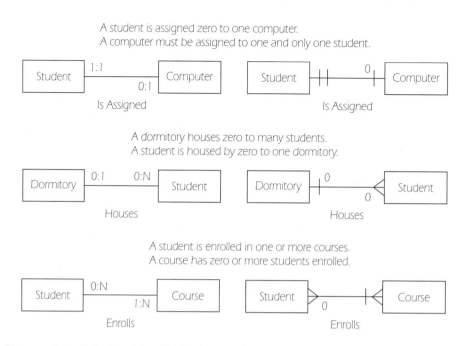

Figure 1.5 *Relationships displaying cardinality and ordinality*

two entities. An **outer join** is an SQL tool that allows an entity instance to be extracted even if a related instance does not exist. If an outer join is not used, neither instance will be returned. You will learn more about outer joins and the importance of this property during the discussion of joining tables, in Chapter 5. Suffice it to say, many analysts get incorrect results from their SQL statements when they ignore this property.

The numeral 1 or the graphic pipe symbol depicts mandatory ordinality. Optional ordinality is depicted by the numeral 0. Ordinality is shown in the ERD on both sides of the relationship. Figure 1.5 illustrates some examples for relationships showing both ordinality and cardinality.

Keys and Joins

In the previous discussions, I used terms such as *primary key* and *join*. These are important database terms. As you know, a database consists of a series of related entities. These entities will model the tables that will hold the data.

The attributes that you will extract from the database will most likely be contained in several tables. A join is the process of matching records from one table to another. The entity relationships show you the entities (tables) that can be joined.

The database keys are the tools used to match the records from two different tables. Records are matched by having a common value(s) in one or more columns in the related tables. For example, suppose that the database has two tables: Departments and Employees. These tables are related, and the ERD shows that each employee must work in one and only one department.

When the Department and Employee tables are created, common columns must be placed in each of the tables. The Department entity identifier is Department. This is a code for each department instance (record). Each code is unique and will exist once as an instance or record. The Department attribute (column) is the primary key to the table.

The Employee table must also have a department code column. This is the column that is used to relate records from the Employee table to records in the Department table. Thus we can determine which department instances correspond to an employee's by using the common department code columns in the Employee and Department tables. The department code column in the Employee table is a **foreign key**. A foreign key is a column that exists as a primary-key column in another table. Database records are matched (joined) through the use of primary and foreign keys.

An important and mandatory property of every database table is that it contains a primary key. Related or child tables often require more than one column to make the record unique. This means that the primary key will consist of more than one column. An example of a child table is an Employee Tool Purchase table. This table stores instances of employee tool purchases. It is related to the Employee table. It is an optional relationship that says an employee may have zero to many tool purchases. The primary key to the Employee table is the Payroll_number column. In order to relate the Employee table to the Employee Tool Purchase table, the latter table must contain a Payroll_number column as a foreign key. What do you think the primary key of the Employee Tool Purchase table is?

It would seem that Payroll_number might be the primary key of the table because the tool purchase is really a repeating attribute of the Employee entity. However, if the Payroll_number column is made the primary key of the table, only one tool purchase could be made for each employee because the primary key must make the record unique. It's obvious that this cannot be the primary key. The table has a column containing the date of the purchase, which satisfies the relationship when combined with the Payroll_number column. An employee can purchase many tools; however, the employee may make only one tool purchase per day. If this meets the business rules of the database user, the primary key can consist of the two columns. If it does not, another column may be needed.

Child tables or tables that require a parent table (e.g., Employee) almost always have primary keys that consist of multiple columns. In addition, one of the columns is a foreign key to the primary key of the parent. Primary keys that contain multiple columns are called **composite** or **concatenated keys**.

One of the first things an analyst must do in order to retrieve data from the database is to identify the primary and foreign keys. These are needed to join records. This is one of the weaknesses of an ERD. They do not show foreign keys, which means they do not show the entire composite keys of child tables. We will see later in this chapter that ERDs' other weaknesses are eliminated through the use of a data schema diagram that is created from the ERD.

Creating an Entity Relationship Diagram

This section portrays a real example of the creation of an entity relationship diagram (ERD). I don't intend that this discussion be all-inclusive of this topic; however, I would like you to see the basic steps that are taken in the event that you need to create one:

1. Identify the entities.
2. Define the identifiers.
3. Define the relationships.
4. Determine cardinality and ordinality of the relationship.
5. Determine descriptive attributes. Move these to related entities.
6. Create the ERD.
7. Review and refine the ERD.

Identifying the Major Entities

The attributes of the database are contained in the flows of the system's data flow diagram (DFD). The analyst reviews this set of data, identifies the major entities, and gravitates the attributes to their respective entity. To illustrate this step, I will use the attributes from this book's practice database, which is representative of an employee and contains the following attributes:

Department Name	Payroll Number	Last Name
First Name	Social Security Number	Street
State	Current Position	Employment Date
Birth Date	Wages	Gender
Eyeglasses Purchase Date	Optician	Eyeglasses Cost
Eyeglasses Check Number	Tool Purchase Date	Tool Name
Tool Cost	Payroll Deduction Indicator	Payment
Last Payment	First Payment Date	Absences

The attributes pertain mainly to the Employee entity. However, some of the attributes will repeat for each employee instance. These are the attributes that describe eyeglasses and tool purchases and can, in theory, be shown with the Employee entity on an ERD as multivalued attributes. They will eventually turn into tables of their own in a later design process; therefore, it is better to show them as their own entity. Entities that are based on repeating values are called weak entities. The following are my recommended entities and associated attributes:

Entity	Employee	Eyeglasses Purchase	Tool Purchase
Attributes	Payroll Number	Eyeglasses Purchase Date	Tool Purchase Date
	Department Name	Optician	Tool Name
	Last Name	Eyeglasses Check Number	Eyeglasses Check Number
	First Name	Eyeglasses Cost	Payroll Deduction Indicator
	Social Security Number		Payment
	Street		Last Payment Date
	State		First Payment Date
	Current Position		
	Employment Date		
	Birth Date		
	Wages		
	Gender		
	Absences		

Defining the Identifiers

Each entity must have an identifier, which is the attribute that differentiates each instance from any other instance within the entity. It is sometimes very easy to identify these, sometimes difficult. In the case of the Employee entity, two possible identifiers are evident: Payroll Number and Social Security Number. While both of the attributes contain values that can be unique to the database, only one can be an identifier and primary key. When this happens, the analyst must look at business rules.

With respect to this database, in rare occasions the social security number of the employee is not known when the employee instance is created. The new employee might have forgotten the number or has not received one. When this occurs, the employee must furnish the social security number before the first day of work and after the employee instance is created. The payroll number is always assigned when the employee instance is created. Based on the database user's business rules, Payroll Number is the better identifier.

The Eyeglasses Purchase and Tool Purchase entities are weak entities. As such, they cannot stand on their own. An instance of these entities may exist only in relation to the major entity: Employee. These entities will have the Employee entity identifier as part of their identifier. This is a repeating attribute (an employee can have many purchases); therefore, other attributes will be needed to create a unique identifier for these entities (e.g., Eyeglasses Purchase Date and Tool Purchase Date). The effect of this will be that an employee can make only one eyeglasses purchase per day and only one tool purchase per day. If the business rules of the database user conform to this requirement, the attributes can be used. If not, additional attributes must be used (or an artificial key created). For the purposes of this discussion, Eyeglasses Purchase Date and Tool Purchase Date will be used as identifiers. The following are the entities and their identifiers:

Entity	Employee	Eyeglasses Purchase	Tool Purchase
Identifier	Payroll Number	Payroll Number Eyeglasses Purchase Date	Payroll Number Tool Purchase Date

Defining the Relationships, Cardinality, and Ordinality

The third step is to identify the relationships between the entities. Three entities have been identified thus far. In reviewing the entities, we can determine that an employee may purchase many pairs of eyeglasses and tools over his or her career. There appear to be two relationships between these entities:

> An employee purchases a tool.
> *and*
> Tools are purchased by an employee.

> An employee purchases glasses.
> *and*
> Glasses are purchased by an employee.

Business rules or practices determine ordinality and cardinality. There are employees who have purchased many tools. There are also many employees who are clerical and have not purchased any tools. This same practice is true for eyeglasses purchases. The cardinality for the eyeglasses purchase and the tool purchase end of the relationship is "many." The ordinality of the relationships is "optional" because the employee does not have to purchase eyeglasses or tools.

The cardinality of the other end of the relationships is "one." Only one employee may make a specific purchase of eyeglasses or tools. Multiple employees may not purchase a single tool or pair of eyeglasses. Only employees can purchase eyeglasses and tools. They cannot be purchased by customers or by someone who is not an employee. This means the ordinality for this end of the relationship is "mandatory." The following are the relationship descriptions, including the ordinality and cardinality properties:

> One and only one employee can purchase zero to many tools.
> *and*
> A tool must be purchased by one and only one employee.

> One and only one employee can purchase zero to many pairs of eyeglasses.
> *and*
> One and only one employee must purchase a pair of eyeglasses.

Defining Descriptive Attributes

Databases often contain descriptive codes. Codes are a shorthand means to describe an attribute. For example, the employees in our practice database can be in one of several departments. These departments have names such as *Treasury Department, Interior Department,* or *Welfare Department.* These names are lengthy, and errors can easily occur when the user types the value into the database.

It is common to assign codes to attributes such as department name (e.g., TRE, INT, and WEL). It is much easier for the user to type these values than the full value of the attribute they describe. Codes also have the benefit of saving database space. Department Name is one of the attributes for the Employee entity. If a department code can be recorded, rather than the full department name, space can be saved. For example, the value *Welfare Department* consumes 18 bytes. The code *WEL* consumes 3 bytes. This is a saving of 15 bytes. Multiply this saving by each employee instance, and the space savings can be substantial.

Identifying these types of attributes occurs in this step. It would be beneficial to the overall design of the database to place Department Name into its own entity along with the department code it describes. The following describes the relationship between the new Department entity and the Employee entity:

A department can employ zero to many employees.
and
One and only one department must employ an employee.

Creating the Entity Relationship Diagram

The last two steps are to draw and redefine the ERD. The diagram can be hand drawn using the symbols presented earlier in this chapter, or it can be drawn using an automated tool. There are a variety of tools that can be used, but my preference is Oracle's Designer6i, which is a computer-aided software engineering (CASE) product that allows the developer to design, document, and generate the database objects.

Figure 1.6 illustrates the final ERD for the book's practice database. You might notice that Designer uses symbols that are different from those outlined in the previous sections of this book. Each automated tool has slight variations in the symbols. Oracle is no exception. However, you can rest assured that the concepts are the same, and it is easy to identify the symbol differences. Figure 1.6 illustrates the Designer version of the employee database using Designer symbols.

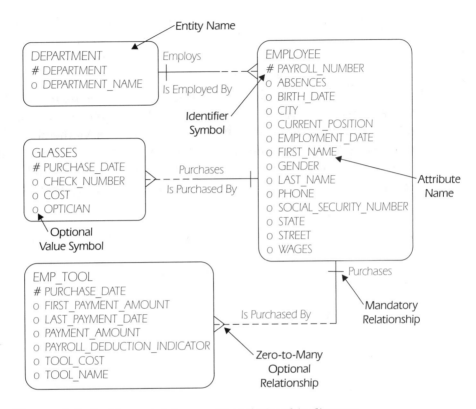

Figure 1.6 *Employee database entity relationship diagram*

Converting the Entity Relationship Diagram to a Relational Model

The entity relationship diagram has some limitations as to its use in extracting information from the database. It is useful for the analyst to see how data are related and to see the available attributes; however, it has the following limitations for the analyst writing SQL:

- The names of the entities may not match the names of the tables.
- The names of the attributes may not match the names of the table's columns.
- Foreign-key columns are not shown.

Database tables can be represented by relationships or as an attribute rather than as an entity. Examples are multivalued attributes and Many-to-Many relationships that may have associated attributes.

The best tool to use is the data schema diagram, which accurately represents the database and is based on the entity relationship diagram (ERD). The differences occur because two procedures are applied: the conversion of the ERD to the relational model, and the normalization procedures. The procedures can be applied at the time the ERD is created, but they are not mandatory. However, they must be applied before the database objects are created.

Conversion to the Relational Model

An ERD can be converted into a relational model by performing the following steps:

1. All entities become a relation (e.g., table).
2. All weak entities become a relation.
3. Create a relation for all multivalued attributes.
4. Add a foreign key to one of the members of a binary One-to-One relationship. It is also possible to combine the members of a One-to-One relationship into one entity.
5. Add a foreign key to one of the members of a binary One-to-Many relationship.
6. Create a relation or link table for all binary Many-to-Many relationships.
7. Create a relation or link table for all ternary relationships.

The first three steps are similar to the suggestions that have been made throughout this chapter. Each entity should become a table. All multivalued attributes should be placed in their own table. You will see this task mentioned again when the normalization discussion occurs. The fourth step bears some discussion.

Step 4 says that entities that are in binary One-to-One relationships may be combined. This makes sense. If one entity instance can have one and only one related entity instance, and vice versa, why place the attributes in two entities? The only reason I am aware of is if the related entity contains attributes for a small subset of the other entities' instances. Creating an instance for only this subset can save space in the database. Whenever you see a binary One-to-One relationship, consider combining the entity attributes.

The sixth and seventh steps are important. It is common for databases to have entities that have Many-to-Many relationships. Here are some examples:

A student can enroll in many courses.
and
A course can have many students enrolled.

Projects can have many employees assigned to it.
and
An employee can be assigned to many projects.

This type of relationship causes problems. Entity instances or table records are matched by common values in their respective primary and foreign keys. The needed foreign keys exist as attributes (or columns). How many attributes should be placed in the Student entity to hold Course foreign-key values? This question cannot be answered because we don't know how many courses a student will take. A second problem occurs when we try to match column values. Is the primary-key value compared to foreign-key value 1, foreign-key value 2, foreign-key value 3, or foreign-key value 4?

For these reasons, a relation or link table should always be created in order to coordinate the entity instances. This table should contain the primary-key values of the related entities. These two values will be the identifier and primary key of the relations. Each instance in this relation can then be matched to instances of the original entities. Figure 1.7 illustrates a typical Many-to-Many relationship before and after the **relation** has been added.

Normalization

Normalization is the last database-design process to be discussed. The purpose of this design is to ensure that the tables within the database are space efficent and performance efficient. This is really a database-optimization process. The effect will be the elimination of database redundancy and content consistencies.

This process consists of a series of steps that group the database attributes. These steps are called normal forms. Three steps are generally taken. However,

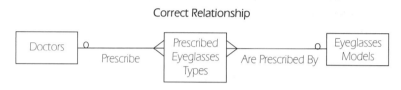

Figure 1.7 *Example of a Many-to-Many relationship*

it is possible to perform more steps. These steps actually have the same effect as the steps identified for the creation of the ERD and the conversion of the diagram to the relational model. I have designed many databases by simply performing this process without using the other tools. I do not recommend skipping the other processes, as documentation is important; however, it can be done.

The following are the steps to normalize a database to the third normal form:

Zero Normal Form	Each of the relations (tables) has a unique identifier (primary key).
First Normal Form	Separate the repeating groups of attributes or multivalued attributes into a relation of their own. Be sure to form composite keys.
Second Normal Form	Establish full functional dependency by separating out attributes that are not fully dependent on the full primary keys.
Third Normal Form	Remove transitive dependency by separating attributes that are dependent on a nonkey attribute.

If you have performed the techniques discussed in the previous sections of this chapter, your database should be in the first normal form. The relations should have identifiers, and the repeating attributes should be removed into relations of their own. Placing the database into second normal form requires some discussion.

Second normal form establishes full functional dependency within the database. This requires the analyst to review each of the attributes in the database. The analyst must determine whether this attribute is dependent on the primary key of the relation. If it is not, the attribute should be moved to a relation in which it is dependent on the primary key. I find that descriptive attributes often fall in this category.

Returning to the earlier section that described how to create an ERD, notice the Employee entity. The entity has a Department Name attribute. Does this attribute depend on the Employee Payroll Number attribute, or would it be better suited to exist in a relation (table) that contains attributes that describe a department?

The department attributes might consist of department number, department manager, or company division. It's evident that Department Name is functionally dependent on the primary key of the Department relation. If one does not exist, it's often good design practice to create such a relation, even if a code value must be developed as a primary key, as described earlier in the chapter.

Third normal form occurs as the last step in the normalization process. This step requires the analyst to review the attributes and determine whether any of the attributes are dependent on a nonkey attribute. Assume that the Employee entity has two department attributes: Department Code and Department Name. In this situation, the department name is dependent on the department code. This is a transitive dependency, and the attributes should be moved to their own relation.

At this point, the database should be optimized and ready to be created. There are fourth and fifth normal forms, but they are seldom used and will not be discussed.

The normalization process discussed in this section is always used when designing a relational database. With its Oracle8i release, Oracle added object features into the database. These features consist of varrays and nested object tables (discussed in detail at the end of Chapter 2). This changed Oracle into an object-relational database, which means that Oracle can be used as an object database or a relational database. The normalization process is not used when designing object databases. Object design is concerned with placing attributes into one object. If the object attributes repeat, they are placed into a varray or a nested table that resides in the master object table rather than related tables. This violates the first normal form, but is correct for object design.

Relational databases are the industry norm, and they conform to the rules of normalization. However, in the industry there is an object school of design that prefers to use the object database design. If you encounter an object database, you need to remember that normalization is used only in relational design.

The Data Schema Diagram

After the relational model has been created, the information needed to write SQL is available. If this information was documented in Oracle's Designer6i tool, a data schema diagram can be developed, which is the document of choice to determine the information needed to write your SQL. If you do not have Designer6i available, you can create a document that I call a table relationship diagram. I will discuss this in the next section.

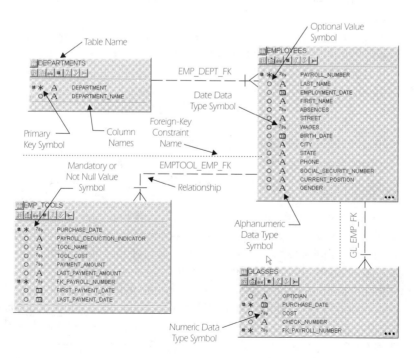

Figure 1.8 *Designer6i data schema diagram of the practice database*

Figure 1.8 illustrates a database relationship diagram based on the entity relationship diagram depicted in Figure 1.6. At first glance, the two documents look similar, especially because the entities shown in Figure 1.6 have been normalized. However, there are some important differences:

The diagram represents tables rather than entities.

Table names, rather than entity names, are displayed.

Column names, rather than attribute names, are displayed.

Foreign-key columns are displayed. They are not displayed in the entity relationship diagram.

The diagram shows the full composite key.

Table Relationship Diagram

If you don't have Designer6i or another CASE tool, you can develop your own SQL documentation. Sometimes I prefer to develop the documentation I use to write SQL by hand. Databases are often very complex and can have many tables. Yet, the majority of the queries I write come from a small subset of the database tables. I create a document that contains just the needed subset of the database tables. I place only the tables and relationships in the diagram in which I am interested. This special document is a useful device called a table relationship diagram.

The document is similar to a data schema diagram. It is a physical model of the relational tables within the database and contains all of the information necessary to understand and extract information from a database. Table relationship diagrams contain the following:

Name and graphical representation of each table

Name of each field in the table

Bold primary-key fields

Italic foreign-key fields

Table relationships that depict how two tables are related.

Table relationships describe how two tables are related, which is usually illustrated by a depiction that consists of graphic lines between the two tables. There are a number of different types of relationships, and the relationships are similar to those used in other diagrams depicted in this chapter.

Figure 1.9 *Table relationship symbols used in the author's table relationship diagram*

However, because this is a personal diagram, any symbol you understand can be used. Figure 1.9 illustrates the symbols that I like to use.

The symbols must be linked together, showing how the tables are related. The relationships are the path to the desired attributes. There are a number of relationships, as we have seen earlier in the chapter. The relationship that follows is One-to-One Not Optional. If a record exists in one of the tables, a corresponding record must exist in the other table. This is not a typical rela-

One-to-One Not Optional

tionship. As said earlier, if it is encountered, the developer should consider combining the tables.

The One-to-One Optional relationship that follows means that the left table can contain a record, but a corresponding record does not have to exist in right table. It also means that records that exist in the right table must have

One-to-One Optional

a corresponding record in the left table. An outer join may be needed when writing SQL against the right table.

One-to-Many Not Optional

The following One-to-Many Not Optional relationship means that the table on the left contains one record, and the table on the right must contain multiple records. This is a very rare relationship.

The One-to-Many Optional relationship is the most common relationship. It means that the table on the left must contain a record if the table on the right contains a record. If the table on the left contains a record, the table on

One-to Many Optional

the right can contain many corresponding records but does not have to contain any corresponding records. An outer join may be needed when writing SQL against the right table.

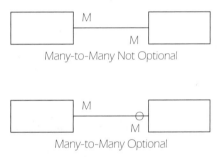
Many-to-Many Not Optional

Many-to-Many Optional

The depictions of the Many-to-Many Not Optional and Many-to-Many Optional relationships follow. These relationships mean that many records in one of the tables have many corresponding records in the other table.

This last relationship should be avoided if possible. If the developer

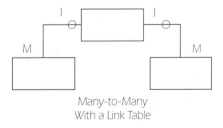
Many-to-Many
With a Link Table

encounters this relationship, a link table containing One-to-Many relation-

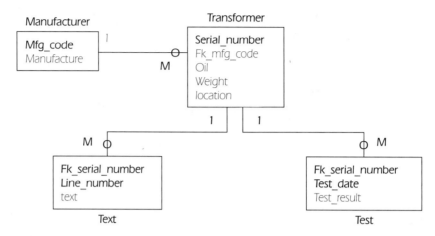

Figure 1.10 *Typical table relationship diagram of a transformer database*

ships to each of the tables in the original relationship should be created. This depiction follows.

Figure 1.10 depicts a typical table relationship diagram.

Employee Database Table Relationship Diagram

The database that will be used in the book examples and exercises represents or models an employee. The entity relationship diagram in Figure 1.6 represents this database. The data schema diagram in Figure 1.8 also represents this database. Figure 1.11 is a table relationship diagram of this database, and it too represents this database. These diagrams give you three valuable tools to help you understand the database and write your SQL. The following is a description of the tables within the employee database:

Department   This table is a descriptive table containing a department code value and the full name of the department. The department_code column is the primary key to the table. It is the base or parent table of the Employee table. A department must exist before an employee record can exist.

Employee   This table contains the unique information about an employee. The payroll number is the primary key. It is a related or child table of the Department table. The

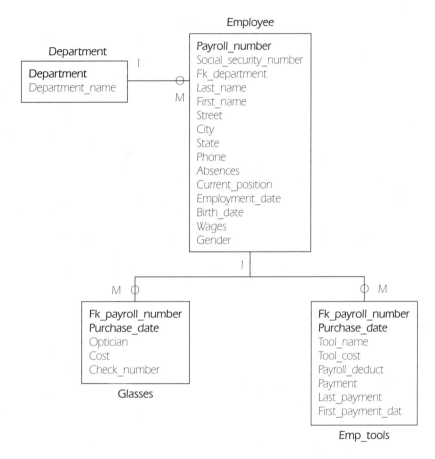

Figure 1.11 *Employee practice database table relationship diagram*

fk_department field is a foreign key that relates an employee record to a specific department record. This table is the base table for both the Emp_tools and Glasses table. Before a record can be placed in either of these related tables, an employee record must exist.

Emp_tools   This table contains the repeating information about employee tool purchases. The table has a composite or concatenated key. This consists of the fk_payroll_number and purchase_date columns. This means that an employee can make only one tool purchase per day. The fk_payroll_number column is a foreign key that relates the table to the Employee table.

Glasses   This table contains the repeating information about employee eyeglasses purchases. The table has a composite or concatenated key. This consists of the fk_payroll_number and purchase_date columns. This means that an employee can make only one eyeglasses purchase per day. The fk_payroll_number column is a foreign key that relates the table to the Employee table.

I would like to note that the Glasses and Emp_tools tables are using a date column as part of the key. This is done for simplicity's sake in the practice database. In real life, dates are not the best type of column to have in a primary key. They are difficult to work with, and the one-record-per-day rule may not work in a business environment. Figure 1.11 depicts the table relationship diagram for the described employee database.

What's Next?

The next chapter begins the discussion of Oracle's structured query language. The chapter deals with the part of the language that is used to create the database objects.

The chapter opens with a discussion of SQL*Plus and the SQL editor. SQL*Plus is Oracle's workhorse product for talking with the database. You will see how to log on to SQL*Plus and how to execute commands to the Oracle database. The chapter will then discuss the various database objects, how to create and maintain the objects, and how to use Oracle's constraints to ensure database integrity. The commands used to maintain the database are part of the Data Definition Language that Oracle uses.

The last part of the chapter covers Oracle's Data Control Language (DCL). This language is also a subset of SQL and is used to grant object and system privileges. Upon completion of this chapter, the reader will be able to create a tablespace, user account, database objects, and grant privileges. The reader will also be introduced to Oracle's data dictionary. Completion of this chapter will give the reader a sound understanding of the inner workings of the Oracle database.

■ PRACTICE

The utility for which I work uses circuit breakers to interrupt the energy that flows through a circuit. They are large pieces of equipment that reside in a substation. As practice, you are to design a circuit breaker database. Within this database, a manufacturer can have many different models. My company can have many circuit breakers for a particular model. A circuit breaker can be tested multiple times. In addition, it is common to document text about the circuit breaker. The following are the attributes that have been identified from the data flow diagram:

Manufacturer	Manufacturer_name	Model
Gallons_of_oil	Weight	Serial_number
Location	Amps	Kva_rating
Text_line_number	Text	Test_date
Test_result		

Create an entity relationship diagram that documents this database. Then create a data schema diagram or table relationship diagram for the database.

2

Building the Database with the Data Definition Language

SQL*Plus is Oracle's product for interfacing with the database and is used to create the database objects, grant privileges, populate and modify the tables, and retrieve data from the tables. All of these functions require you to submit commands to the Oracle database manager.

SQL*Plus is the baseline tool for submitting these commands. By *baseline,* I mean that there are a number of GUI tools available on the market, including some excellent tools from Oracle; however, SQL*Plus is the only tool that *always* comes with the database. Regardless of your information technology tool architectures, SQL*Plus will be available for you to interface with the Oracle database. SQL*Plus will also look and feel the same regardless of the platform, whether it is Windows NT, Windows 2000, UNIX, or Linux.

In this chapter you will see how to perform the following tasks:

- Log on to SQL*Plus
- Enter SQL commands
- Use the SQL*Plus command editor
- Save the commands to an external file
- Create various database objects using the **Data Definition Language (DDL)**

You will need to understand the first four topics for continuance in this book. The last topic is the bulk of this chapter's content and may be skipped at this time. Many books include DDL topics after the reader understands how to retrieve information from the database using the SELECT command.

I include this topic here because creating the database objects is the activity that occurs after designing the database (Chapter 1). You may find it more convenient to move to Chapter 4 (and subsequent chapters) before reading the DDL portion of this chapter and Chapter 3. You can return to these topics later.

Logging on to SQL*Plus

SQL*Plus is launched by selecting the SQL*Plus option from the Windows program palette, displayed in Figure 2.1.

If you have installed Oracle and you do not see an option on the menu palette, you may have to locate the SQL*Plus executable. This executable has different names, and it can be located in different directories. It is sometimes located in an "orant\bin\" or "\orawin95\bin" directory. The filename will begin with *PLUS* followed by a version number. The Windows version will end with a *W*. The MS-DOS command-line version does not have a *W*.

Launching SQL*Plus or trying to connect to an Oracle database causes the Oracle Log On dialog box to be displayed, as shown in Figure 2.2. The dialog box is a prompt for the following information:

- User Name   The Oracle user account ID assigned to the user.
- Password   The password for the user account.
- Host   The character string that describes the location of the database. This value is also called a *connect string*. It is used when you are connected to a network and the Oracle installation you are trying to access is not on the machine on which you are interacting with Oracle. Installations that are located on a server and are accessible over a network are called *remote* and will require a

Figure 2.1 *The SQL*Plus tool and the Windows tool palette*

value in this variable. Installations that are located on your computer are called *local.* A value is generally not needed for local installations.

Press the OK button to connect to the Oracle database and display the SQL prompt. The prompt indicates that SQL*Plus is requesting a command. The SQL prompt is displayed in Listing 2.1.

Listing 2.1 *SQL Prompt*

```
SQL*Plus: Release 9.0.1.0.1 - Production on Tue Apr 16 19:29:00 2002

(c) Copyright 2001 Oracle Corporation. All rights reserved.

Connected to:
Oracle9i Release 9.0.1.1.1 - Production
JServer Release 9.0.1.1.1 - Production

SQL>
```

the SQL prompt

Entering a Command

Database commands are entered at the SQL prompt. There is a large variety of commands that can be entered. The SELECT command (or statement) is used to retrieve data from the database. Other commands can be entered to create or maintain the database objects, to add records to the database, or to grant

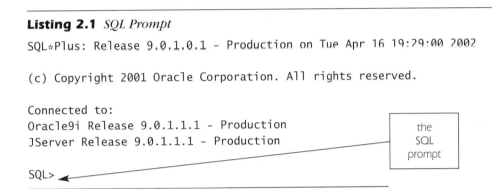

Figure 2.2 *The Oracle database Log On dialog box*

privileges. Entered commands are terminated and executed by a semicolon.
Listing 2.2 displays a SELECT command and the results of its execution.

Listing 2.2 *Basic SQL*Plus Command*

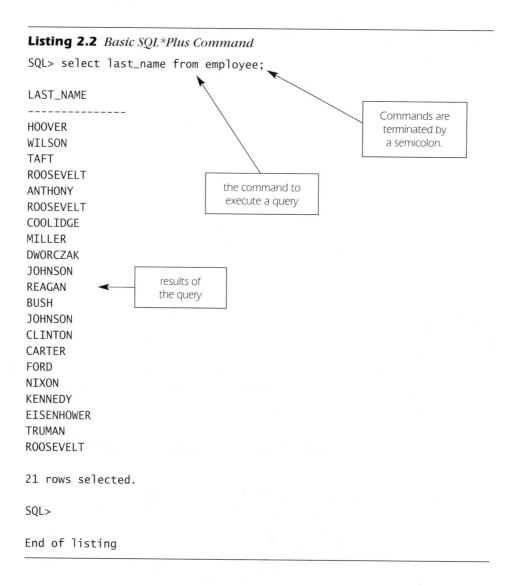

```
SQL> select last_name from employee;

LAST_NAME
---------------
HOOVER
WILSON
TAFT
ROOSEVELT
ANTHONY
ROOSEVELT
COOLIDGE
MILLER
DWORCZAK
JOHNSON
REAGAN
BUSH
JOHNSON
CLINTON
CARTER
FORD
NIXON
KENNEDY
EISENHOWER
TRUMAN
ROOSEVELT

21 rows selected.

SQL>

End of listing
```

Commands are terminated by a semicolon.

the command to execute a query

results of the query

After a command has been entered, the command remains in the memory
buffer. The command LIST (or the letter *l*) will display the last command sent to
Oracle. The command can be executed again by simply typing the word *Run*.
Additional commands can be executed by entering them at the SQL prompt.

SQL*Plus will execute each command as it is entered into the editor. SQL*Plus recognizes that the command is complete when the semicolon is encountered. Some commands are long and cannot be placed on one line. You can press ENTER at any time to get a new line. A number prefaces the new line, rather than the SQL prompt. You may continue entering the command. SQL*Plus will continue placing new lines until it encounters a semicolon. Listing 2.3 displays a command entered on multiple lines.

Listing 2.3 *SQL Command Entered on Multiple Lines*

```
SQL> select last_name, first_name
  2   from employee
  3   order by last_name;
```

line numbers

```
LAST_NAME        FIRST_NAME
---------------  ---------------
ANTHONY          SUSANNE
BUSH             GEORGE
CARTER           JIMMY
CLINTON          WILLIAM
COOLIDGE         CALVIN
DWORCZAK         ALICE
EISENHOWER       DWIGHT
FORD             GERALD
HOOVER           HERBERT
JOHNSON          LYNDON
JOHNSON          ANDREW
KENNEDY          JOHN
MILLER           KEVIN
NIXON            RICHARD
REAGAN           RONALD
ROOSEVELT        THEODORE
ROOSEVELT        ELEANOR
ROOSEVELT        FRANKLIN
TAFT             WILLIAM
TRUMAN           HAROLD
WILSON           WOODROW

21 rows selected.

SQL>
```

End of listing

Using the SQL*Plus Editor

Commands that have been entered into the memory buffer can be modified. SQL*Plus has a series of commands that allow the user to modify buffered commands. This feature is particularly useful when you have entered incorrect commands. Table 2.1 lists the various editing commands.

Table 2.1 *SQL Plus Editor Commands*

Command	Description	Example
l	Displays the contents of the buffer.	L
l*n*	Displays the target line (n), which will become the current line.	l 4
Linenumber *text*	Entering a line number followed by text will cause the indicated line to be replaced with the new text.	2 from department
c/*old*/*new*	Changes the first occurrence of the *old* text characters to *new* text characters for the current line. (A line is made current by listing the line.)	c/slect/select
a *text* append *text*	Appends the text to the end of the current line.	a from employee append from employee
del *linenumber*	Deletes the indicated line. The current line will be deleted if the line number is not included.	Del del 2
i	Allows the user to begin inserting text after the current line.	I
/ or run	Executes the current buffer command.	/ run
save *filename*	Saves the current command to a file.	save c:\test.sql
get *filename*	Loads the contents of a file into the memory buffer.	get c:\test.sql
start *filename* or @*filename*	Loads the contents of a file into the memory buffer and executes the commands.	start c:\test.sql @c:\test.sql
edit *filename*	Launches an external editor, such as Notepad. If a filename is specified, the editor will display the target file. If the name is not specified, the current contents of the memory buffer will be placed into the editor.	Edit c:\test.sql Edit

As your commands become complex, the most effective way to execute the commands in SQL*Plus is to write them in an external editor and execute the commands using the START or @ commands. You will find that it is very easy to make spelling or syntax errors when creating a command. I prefer using a freeware software package called EditPad as my external editor, rather than using Notepad. This product can be downloaded from the Web.

The following steps can be followed if you want to use an external editor:

1. Type your command into the external editor.

2. Save the file.

3. Run the command script using the RUN or @ keywords.

If an error occurs when the script is executed, open the existing file, modify the script, and repeat steps 2 and 3.

The EDIT command can be used to place the most recent command into the designated external editor. You may then use the previous steps to save and execute the edited script. Entering the SAVE command followed by a filename will cause the command to be saved within the designated file. If you do not put the file path along with the name, Oracle will store the file in the same directory as the SQL*Plus executable. This often confuses novice users who expect the file to be saved in the root directory.

Menu Commands

SQL*Plus has a menu bar that can be used to select various commands. This saves the user from having to type them at the SQL*Prompt. Figure 2.3 illustrates the menu bar. The File menu options are displayed in the figure. The following are the various options and descriptions:

File Menu Options

Open	Launches an Open File dialog box. This option is used to locate and bring files into SQL*Plus.
Save	Opens a submenu palette with various options that can be used to save the current buffer command to a file.
Save As	Opens the Save As dialog box. The option is used to save the contents of the current buffer command to a file.

Spool	Opens a submenu that allows you to turn spooling on and off. Spooling consists of sending SQL*Plus output to a file.
Run	Executes the current buffer command.
Cancel	Clears the buffer of the current command and displays the SQL prompt.
Exit	Closes the SQL*Plus session.

Edit Menu Options

Copy	Copies the highlighted text to the Clipboard.
Paste	Pastes the contents of the Clipboard into SQL*Plus.
Clear	Clears the current buffer command and the display within the SQL*Plus window.
Editor	Opens a submenu palette with two options. The first option is Invoke Editor. Selecting this option will cause the designated external editor to open with the current buffer command displayed. The second option is Define Editor, which will open the Define Editor dialog box. This dialog box can be used modify the text editor you want to use when the Invoke Editor option is selected.

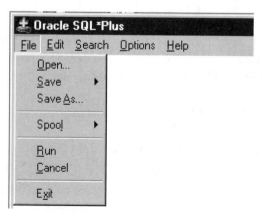

Figure 2.3 *SQL*Plus menu bar with the File menu open*

Search Menu Options

Find	Launches the Find dialog box, which is used to enter search text.
Find Next	Searches for the next instance of the specified text in the current buffer command.

Option Menu Selections

Environment	Launches the Environment dialog box, which contains a variety of options for modifying the SQL*Plus environment. These options will be discussed in Chapter 11.

Database Objects That Store Data

The Oracle database has a variety of important objects. These objects do many things. They are used to hold data, to locate data items efficiently, to combine data, and to make the database user-friendly. The remainder of the chapter will describe the various database objects that are used to store and locate data. A database administrator (DBA), rather than the data administrator, generally performs most of the tasks and commands that are discussed in this section. On rare occasions, a DA may perform some of the tasks, depending on the shop. However, whether you perform the database tasks, it is very important for the successful data administrator or business analyst to understand the basic mechanics and objects in the database. This knowledge will allow you to interact intelligently with the DBA and to make suggestions that will enhance the efficiency and performance of your databases.

The Desk Analogy

A database is comparable to a desk. Desks are comprised of drawers used to store materials. The drawers have dividers used to separate the materials. Within the dividers are sets of index cards. Each card contains attribute values about an entity. The card also contains an attribute value that differentiates it from every other card in the set.

In a database, the drawers that define the maximum allowable space are called **tablespaces**. Tablespaces are not actually physical objects but rather devices for limiting the amount of space, just as a drawer limits physical space. Tablespaces contain settings that specify the maximum size of the database. Unlike drawers that cannot change, when the tablespace limit is reached, additional tablespaces can be created or the tablespace enlarged.

In a drawer, dividers that can be moved or adjusted to increase the size of the area available for records exist. Tablespaces consist of one or more files. The files are the actual physical devices that store the database. To increase the size of the tablespace, an additional file can be added to the tablespace, or an existing file can be enlarged.

The set of index cards within the drawer can be compared to a table. Each index card is a record in a set of records. Tables also consist of a set of records about a certain entity. Both sets of index cards and tables contain information about entity instances. These pieces of information about the entity instance arc called **fields**, **columns**, or items.

One of the pieces of information on the index card or in a table record is used to differentiate the record from all other records in the set. This piece of information is called a primary key. This attribute is used when thumbing through a set of records or searching the records in a table.

The next sections will describe each of these objects in more detail. If you want to practice any of the commands using Personal Oracle, the Oracle master user account is *system,* and the password is *manager.* This ID will have sufficient privileges to perform all the discussed functions.

Tablespaces

Oracle9i has several types of tablespaces:

1.	Data tablespaces	Contains data and the objects that control the data (e.g., indexes, synonyms).
2.	System tablespaces	Contains information Oracle needs to control itself.
3.	Temporary tablespaces	Contains temporary information. For example, the space is used if Oracle needs temporary disk space for sorting a large set of rows.

4. Tool tablespaces   Contains space required for Oracle tools.

5. Rollback tablespaces   Contains information such as uncommitted database changes and enables Oracle's internal mechanisms for read consistency.

6. User tablespaces   Default tablespace assigned to the user.

Creating a Tablespace

The first task needed to establish a database is to create a data tablespace. To create a tablespace, the developer must have DBA authority (one of the privileges discussed in the next chapter). The **CREATE** command is used to create all of the database objects, and the tablespace is no exception. There are several components to the CREATE TABLESPACE command:

- DATAFILE   Contains the name of the file that the tablespace uses.

- AUTOEXTEND clause   Enables or disables the automatic extension of the tablespace. *OFF* disables this feature. *ON* enables the feature. The *NEXT* keyword specifies the amount of disk space to allocate when an extension occurs. *UNLIMITED* sets no limit. The *MAXSIZE* keyword specifies the maximum amount of space to allocate.

- SIZE   Determines the maximum size of the file used for the tablespace. Two setting symbols are used: K and M. Each increment of K increases the file or tablespace size by 1,024 bytes. Each increment of M increases the file or tablespace size by 1,048,576 bytes.

- INITIAL extent   The amount of disk space initially set aside for the tablespace. An extent is a portion of disk space that is reserved for the tablespace. This disk space is unavailable to any other application until it is released.

- NEXT extent   The amount of additional disk space that is reserved for the tablespace each time the existing extents are filled.

- MINEXTENTS

  This option enables the developer to set aside additional extents at the time of creation.

- MAXEXTENTS

  This option sets a limit to the number of extents a tablespace can use.

- Pct Increase

  This option is a growth factor for extents. For example, if it is set at 25, Oracle will add 25 percent to each additional extent.

Listing 2.4 illustrates a CREATE TABLESPACE command. The command creates a tablespace called realistic_employees. The first data file that the tablespace uses is called real.tab. The statement creates a tablespace with a maximum size of 4 M, or 4,194,304 bytes. The default storage parameters will cause the tablespace initially to reserve 25 K, or 25,600 bytes. The next extent will be an additional 25 K. The minimum number of extents is 10, and the maximum will be 50.

Listing 2.4 *Creating a Tablespace*

```
SQL> create tablespace realistic_employees datafile 'real.tab' size 4 m
  2   default storage (initial 25 k next 25 k
  3   minextents 10 maxextents 50)
  4   autoextend on next 50k maxsize 100k;

Tablespace created.

SQL>

End Listing
```

After the tablespace has been created, additional files can be added to the tablespace. The command used to modify the database objects is ALTER. The ALTER TABLESPACE command is used to change tablespace parameters. Some of these parameters are as follows:

ADD DATAFILE

This option is used to add a file to the tablespace. The option uses the same format as used in the

CREATE command ('*filename*' [size K or M] [reuse]). The REUSE keyword, when used in conjunction with the SIZE keyword, causes Oracle to create the file if it does not exist, and to modify the file if it does exist. If the SIZE keyword is not used, Oracle will destroy the contents of any existing file with the name and will replace it with the new file. Specifying the SIZE option alone causes the file to be created if it doesn't exist, and to launch an error message if it already exists.

RENAME DATAFILE	This option is used to change the name of an existing file. The keyword does not actually change the name of the file but associates a new name with the file. The syntax of this command is "rename datafile *filename* to *filename*."
RESIZE	This option can be used to change the size of an existing file. The syntax of the options is "alter database realistic_employees 'real.tab' resize 6m."
AUTOEXTEND	Changes the size of the files as needed. It does this in increments of NEXT size to the maximum of MAXSIZ.

Listing 2.5 contains an example of an ALTER TABLESPACE command that uses the SIZE option to add another file of 8 M to the tablespace. This creates a total tablespace size of 12 M.

Listing 2.5 *Using the ALTER TABLESPACE Command to Increase the Size of the Tablespace by Adding a File*

```
SQL> alter tablespace realistic_employees
  2  add datafile 'real1.tab' size 8 m;

Tablespace altered.

SQL>

End listing
```

To eliminate a tablespace from the database, the **DROP** command can be used. A tablespace cannot be dropped with this command if the tablespace contains data. To drop a tablespace containing data, employ the Including Contents option. Listing 2.6 illustrates a command that deletes the database created using Listing 2.3.

Listing 2.6 *Eliminating the realistic_employee Tablespace*

```
SQL> drop tablespace realistic_employees;

Tablespace dropped.

SQL>

End listing
```

Creating and Modifying Tables

After a tablespace has been established, the objects that will hold the data can be created. One of these objects is a table. Creating tables is one of the database tasks that someone other than a DBA can sometimes perform, especially in a test environment. Tables are created using the CREATE TABLE command, which has a number of components and options:

- Table name

  Determines the table's name. The name must start with an alpha character. The name may contain letters, numbers, and underscores. It must be in one continuous string of not more than 30 characters.

- Column names

  Names of the columns (entity attributes) contained in the table. This component has the same naming restrictions as the table name. The entire set of column definitions *must* be enclosed by parentheses.

- Column data type

  The column definition contains the data type, scale (length), and preci-

	sion of each column. Valid data types are listed in Table 2.2.
▪ Constraints (optional setting)	Constraints are options that are used to maintain the integrity to the database. These will be discussed later in this chapter.
▪ Tablespace (optional setting)	This setting determines the tablespace in which to place the table. If this setting is omitted, the table will be created in the default tablespace assigned to the user who executes the CREATE TABLE command. It is normal practice to assign a default tablespace to a user account when it is created. This tablespace is the default tablespace for the user. If the user has not been assigned a tablespace and this option is omitted from the CREATE TABLE command, the system tablespace will be used. Using the system tablespace for data tables is highly discouraged.
▪ Partitions (optional setting)	The table data can be divided into numerous partitions. These can be within one or more tablespaces. The specifications to partition a table are placed in the CREATE TABLE command.

Syntax rules for the CREATE TABLE command are as follows:

- Parentheses must enclose the entire table specification. The CREATE TABLE keywords and the name of the table are not included in the parentheses.
- A comma completes each column definition.
- Each column name must be unique to the table.
- Oracle reserved words cannot be used as column names.
- A semicolon ends the command.

Table 2.2 *Common Oracle Data Types*

Data Type	Description
CHAR(*n*)	Defines an alphanumeric column of length (*n*). The maximum size is 255 characters. The default size is 1.
DATE	Defines a date format. The column can contain dates from January 1, 4712 B.C. to December 31, 4712 A.D.
DECIMAL	Same as the NUMBER data type. It does not accept size or decimal digits as an argument.
FLOAT	Same as the NUMBER data type.
INTEGER	Same as the NUMBER data type. Values will be whole numbers. Columns defined with this format will not accept decimal digits.
INTEGER(*n*)	Specifies an INTEGER data type of the length *n*.
LONG	Defines a character data type up to 65,535 characters. Only one LONG column may be defined per table. This type of column may not be used in subqueries, functions, expressions, WHERE clauses, or indexes.
LONG RAW	The same as LONG, except it contains raw binary data.
LONG VARCHAR	The same data type as LONG.
MISLABEL	4-byte representation of a secure operating system label.
NUMBER	Defines a numeric data type with space for 40 digits, space for a sign, and a decimal point. The numbers may be expressed in two manners. The first is with numbers from 0 to 9, the signs + and −, and a decimal point. The second manner is in scientific notation (1.951E4 as 19510).
NUMBER(*n*)	Defines a NUMBER column that contains the number of digits equal to the value in *n*. The maximum number of digits is 105.
NUMBER(*n*, *d*)	Defines a NUMBER column that contains an overall size equal to *n* and contains the number of decimal positions specified by *d*. A format specification of NUMBER(3,2) cannot contain a number greater than 9.99.
NUMBER(*)	The same data type as NUMBER.
SMALLINT	The same data type as NUMBER.

Table 2.2 *Common Oracle Data Types (continued)*

Data Type	Description
RAW(*n*)	Defines a column that contains raw binary data with a length specified to the value *n*.
RAW MISLABEL	Defines a column as a binary format for a secure operating system label.
VARCHAR2(*n*)	Defines a variable length character string having a maximum length of the value specified by *n*.
CLOB, BLOB, BFILE	Successors to LONG and LONG RAW.

Listing 2.7 illustrates a command that creates a table called Consultants. Since the TABLESPACE option was not used in the CREATE statement, the table will be created in the default database assigned to the user.

Listing 2.7 *Creating the Consultant Table*

```
SQL> create table consultant
  2    (employee_id      number(5,0),
  3     first_name       varchar2(15),
  4     last_name        varchar2(25),
  5     specialty        varchar2(30));

Table created.

SQL>

End listing
```

Table 2.2 contains valid data types that can be used in a table definition.

Partitioning

Oracle allows the developer to partition the table data. This means that the data can reside in one or more tablespaces. This has some advantages, especially for large databases with a lot of activity. Here's why:

- Reduces downtime for scheduled maintenance
- Reduces downtime caused by data failures
- Decreases I/O
- Can increase performance of some queries by limiting the amount of data that is read
- Increases performance by the reduction of contention for disk arms

To partition a table, the developer must tell Oracle the number of partitions and in which partition to place the data. This is done through a PARTITION clause at the end of the CREATE TABLE command. Partitioning is based on data values within a table column. A common partition value is a date such as a transaction date.

Listing 2.8 illustrates a CREATE TABLE command containing a PARTITION option. The command places the data into four different tablespaces based on the value of the Employee_id column. The option consists of a series of mutually exclusive statements containing a value. All records with a value less than or equal to the value and greater than the value in the previous line will be placed in the named tablespace. The last statement contains the keyword *maxvalue* to indicate that this tablespace is the last partition.

Listing 2.8 *Creating the Consultant Table with a PARTITION Option*

```
SQL> create table consultant
  2    (employee_id       number,
  3     first_name        varchar2(15),
  4     last_name         varchar2(25),
  5     specialty         varchar2(30))
partition by range (employee_id)
   (partition t1 value less than (250) tablespace realistic_employee1,
    partition t2 value less than (500) tablespace realistic_employee2,
    partition t3 value less than (750) tablespace realistic_employee3,
    partition t4 value less than (maxvalue) tablespace
realistic_employee4);

Table created.

SQL>

End listing
```

Copying a Table

The CREATE TABLE and SELECT (discussed in detail in Chapter 4) commands can be used together to copy all or part of the contents of a table into a new table. A SELECT statement is a command that retrieves records from the Oracle database. The SELECT statement replaces the column specification in the CREATE TABLE command. When Oracle encounters the SELECT statement, it will create a table containing the columns identified in the SELECT statement. In addition, each of the records that the SELECT command retrieves will be placed in the new table. Listing 2.9 illustrates a CREATE/SELECT command that copies the Consultant table into a new table.

Listing 2.9 *Using the CREATE/SELECT command to Copy a Table*

```
SQL> create table consultant_copy
  2  as select * from consultant;

Table created.

SQL>

End Listing
```

This technique only creates a new table and populates the table with data. It does not duplicate the indexes and integrity constraints that were placed on the original table. These must be created independently of the command. The data in the new table also does not stay in sync with the original tables.

Altering the Table

The **ALTER** command is used to change table specifications after the table has been created. The following are options that can be used:

1. ADD   This option is used to add new columns or constraints to the table. (Constraints will be discussed in a later section of this chapter.)

2. MODIFY   This option is used to modify an existing specification.

3. DISABLE   Deactivates a constraint placed on the table.

4. ENABLE   Reactivates a constraint that has been disabled.

5. DROP   Permanently removes a constraint from the table.

6. SET UNUSED   Marks one or more columns as unused so that the column can be dropped from the table when system resources are more readily available. Marking the column as unused does not physically remove the column from the table. However, the marked column is treated as if it were removed from the table. You may even add another column with the same name to the table.

7. DROP COLUMN   Removes the target column from the table. The column may or may not contain values. The column and values cannot be recovered.

When changing a column specification, columns that contain data may not be changed from character to number or be reduced in size. They may only be increased in size.

Listing 2.10 illustrates two ALTER TABLE commands. The first command adds a new column to the Consultant table. The second command changes the size of the last_name column.

Listing 2.10 *Altering the Consultant Table*

```
SQL> alter table consultant add birth_date date;
Table altered.
SQL>
SQL> alter table consultant modify first_name varchar2(20);
Table altered.
SQL>

End listing
```

The name of the table can be changed using the RENAME TABLE command. The following is a template of the command:

Rename *old_table_name* to *new_table_name;*

Dropping Tables

Tables and other Oracle objects are removed from the database by the DROP command. Listing 2.11 illustrates the command that was used to drop the table created in Listing 2.9.

Listing 2.11 *Using the DROP Command to Remove a Table from the Database*

```
SQL> drop table consultant_copy;

Table dropped.

SQL>

End listing
```

Indexes

Indexes are database objects that reference table records. An index contains the values for a target column(s) and the Rowid that identifies the location of the record. Database indexes are similar in purpose to book indexes. A book takes a great deal of time to read. If the reader wanted to locate information about a specific topic, the entire book must be read. An index helps the reader more readily locate the topics. Book indexes are ordered (usually in alphanumeric order) and contain references to a page. Database indexes are similar in that they are ordered and reference a record in a table.

Indexes have two very important functions:

1. They are used to locate records efficiently. It is the single most important database object to increase record-retrieval performance.

2. They are used to ensure that a value in a record is unique to the table. Primary-key columns are always indexed columns.

Indexes decrease record-retrieval time because they reduce the amount of disk the RDBMS must read in order to identify the needed records. If a table does not contain an associated index, the RDBMS must read each record in the table in order to determine the records that satisfy the query.

Indexes are based on one or more of a table's columns. The values from these columns are placed in the index along with a rowid to the table record that corresponds to the index values. A rowid is similar to a pointer. It is

Oracle's reference to the physical location of the record in the database. All records in an Oracle database have a unique rowid value. The rowid is the quickest path to a record.

Oracle has a variety of index types. One of the most common is the B-Tree index, which is organized like the branches of a tree. Each of the branches is part of the path to a specific record. By having layers of branches, it is possible for Oracle to locate desired records quickly. Branches reduce the data that Oracle must wade through to locate the records. Chapter 12 further discusses the B-Tree and other types of indexes.

Unique indexes can ensure the uniqueness of a column's value. Whenever a record is placed into a table or a record is modified, indexed column values are compared to the values in their associated index. If the value exists, the transaction is halted. Indexes are powerful tools to ensure the integrity of primary keys.

Indexes require some overhead. Each time an indexed column is modified, the corresponding index must also be updated. This requires Oracle to perform some work. For this reason, indexes should be placed on only primary-key columns, foreign-key columns, other columns that must contain unique values, and those columns that are often used for searches and sorting.

The CREATE INDEX command is used to create an index. The command references the table's name and the name of the indexed column(s). The index column is placed in parentheses. Multiple columns can be contained in the index. These are called concatenated indexes. Commas separate the column names. Listing 2.12 illustrates a command that creates an index on the Consultant table.

Listing 2.12 *Creating a Nonunique Index on the Employee_id Column of the Consultant Table*

```
SQL> create index emp_ind on consultant (employee_id);

Index created.

SQL>

End listing
```

To create a unique index, place the UNIQUE keyword before the INDEX keyword. Indexes are removed from the database using the DROP INDEX command. The UNIQUE INDEX option and the DROP INDEX command are illustrated in Listing 2.13.

Listing 2.13 *Creating and Dropping a Unique Index on the Employee_id Column of the Consultant Table*

```
SQL> create unique index emp_ind on consultant (employee_id);

Index created.

SQL> drop index emp_ind;

Index dropped.

SQL>

End Listing
```

A later section of this chapter will discuss constraints. One of the constraints is the UNIQUE constraint. It ensures that the values in a column are unique. The constraint essentially performs the same function as the Unique Index option, but it is preferable to use the constraint. If the constraint is used, the analyst can identify this constraint in the User_constraints Data Dictionary view. Data Dictionary views are used to identify database objects (and they are covered in Chapter 3). If UNIQUE INDEX is used, it will not appear in this view.

Maintaining the Integrity of the Database

Oracle has included some tools to protect the database. These tools are called constraints. They perform a number of important functions that maintain the integrity of the database. Some of these functions are as follows:

- Ensure the uniqueness of the primary key.
- Ensure that child records in related tables have a parent record.
- Delete child records when the parent record is deleted.
- Ensure that columns always contain a value.
- Ensure that a column contains a value within a specific range.
- Ensure that a default value is placed in a column.

Constraints perform functions similar to programming edits. The difference is that Oracle enforces these edits, instead of a program. It is always better to have Oracle enforce integrity. Errors can occur in application logic. Constraints will ensure that errors will be captured even if the code has holes. These constraints are a part of a table's definition. They can be placed in the CREATE TABLE command or added later using the ALTER TABLE command. This section will describe the various database constraints.

The CHECK Constraint

The CHECK constraint is used to ensure that a value within a column falls within specified parameters. The PARAMETERS statement is similar to the WHERE clause of a SELECT statement. The CHECK constraint uses the same operators. A common operator to use is the IN operator. When it is used, Oracle will compare the new value to the set of values specified in the parameter array. If the value is not in the array of values, Oracle will not let the transaction occur. Listing 2.14 illustrates a CREATE TABLE command using the CHECK constraint. The constraint ensures that the Gender column always contains a value of M or F.

Listing 2.14 *Using a CHECK Constraint with a Table Definition*

```
SQL> drop table consultant;

Table dropped.

SQL> create table consultant
  2  (employee_id        number,
  3   first_name         varchar2(15),
  4   last_name          varchar2(25),
  5   specialty          varchar2(30),
  6   gender             char(1)
  7   constraint gender_validation check (gender in ('M', 'F')));

Table created.

SQL>

End listing
```

In Listing 2.14, the CHECK constraint was named (i.e., gender_validation). It is optional to name constraints. If a constraint is not named, Oracle will create its own name for the constraint. It is good practice to name CHECK constraints. Tables can be imported and exported between Oracle installations. When this happens, it is possible to double the number of constraints. Naming the constraint when it is added will help the DBA determine which constraints have been duplicated. To name a constraint, place the keyword CONSTRAINT followed by the constraint definition as part of a column or table definition.

The DEFAULT Option

The DEFAULT option is used to place a value into a column when a value has not been passed. It does not prevent the passing of a null value. It simply populates the column when no value is passed. Listing 2.15 illustrates this option. In this example, the DEFAULT option is used to ensure that the Salary column is populated with a value of 0 when it is not supplied a value.

Listing 2.15 *Using a DEFAULT Option*

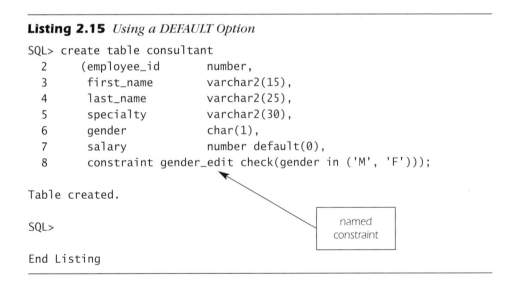

```
SQL> create table consultant
  2      (employee_id       number,
  3       first_name        varchar2(15),
  4       last_name         varchar2(25),
  5       specialty         varchar2(30),
  6       gender            char(1),
  7       salary            number default(0),
  8       constraint gender_edit check(gender in ('M', 'F')));

Table created.

SQL>

End Listing
```

named constraint

The NOT NULL Constraint

The NOT NULL constraint is used to ensure that the constrained column always contains a value. This constraint is always placed on the table's primary-key column(s). It is also placed on table columns that usually contain a value. Columns such as Name, Social Security Number, and Department are examples of columns that should always contain a value.

To place the NOT NULL constraint on a column, place the keywords NOT NULL after the column's data type definition. Listing 2.16 illustrates the definition of this constraint.

Listing 2.16 *Defining a NOT NULL Constraint*

```
SQL> create table consultant
  2    (employee_id        number not null,
  3     first_name         varchar2(15),
  4     last_name          varchar2(25),
  5     specialty          varchar2(30));

Table created.

SQL>
```

End Listing

The UNIQUE Constraint

The UNIQUE constraint ensures that the value in the constrained column is unique to the table. It does this by creating a unique index on the column. Some tables contain columns that must contain unique values even though the column is not a primary key. In these cases, the UNIQUE constraint is a good tool to ensure this database characteristic. An example is the Social Security Number column of an employee record that uses the Payroll Number column as a primary key. Listing 2.17 illustrates the definition of a UNIQUE constraint.

Listing 2.17 *Defining UNIQUE NOT NULL Constraints*

```
SQL> create table consultant
  2    (employee_id        number not null
  3       constraint unique_employee_id unique,
  4     first_name         varchar2(15),
  5     last_name          varchar2(25),
  6     specialty          varchar2(30));
```

named constraint

```
Table created.

SQL>
```

End Listing

The PRIMARY KEY Constraint

A Primary Key constraint is used to maintain the integrity of the primary-key column(s). This constraint makes the values in a column not null and unique. Definition of this constraint causes an implicit unique index and an implicit NOT NULL constraint to be placed on the column(s). This constraint can be defined as part of the column definition or as a table definition. If the constraint is to be placed on multiple columns (as in a concatenated key), the constraint must be defined as part of the table definition.

To define a PRIMARY KEY constraint as part of a column definition, place the keywords PRIMARY KEY after the column's data type definition. Listing 2.18 illustrates the definition of this constraint as part of a column definition.

Listing 2.18 *Defining a PRIMARY KEY Constraint as Part of a Column Definition*

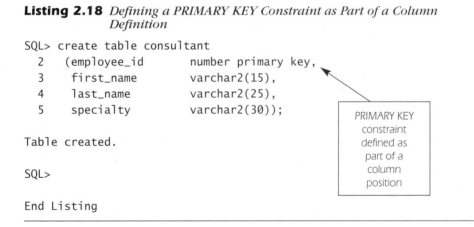

```
SQL> create table consultant
  2    (employee_id       number primary key,
  3     first_name        varchar2(15),
  4     last_name         varchar2(25),
  5     specialty         varchar2(30));

Table created.

SQL>

End Listing
```

PRIMARY KEY constraint defined as part of a column position

A constraint can also be defined on its own. This is called a table definition constraint, and the definition is placed in the CREATE TABLE Command after the last column definition. A comma is placed after the last column definition. The primary-key definition begins with the keywords PRIMARY KEY. The names of the constrained column(s) follow. They are enclosed by parentheses. Listing 2.19 illustrates a PRIMARY KEY constraint defined as part of the table definition.

Listing 2.19 *Defining a PRIMARY KEY Constraint as Part of a Table Definition*

```
SQL> create table consultant
  2    (employee_id        number,
  3     first_name         varchar2(15),
  4     last_name          varchar2(25),
  5     specialty          varchar2(30),
  6     primary key (employee_id));

Table created.

SQL>

End Listing
```

PRIMARY KEY constraint defined as part of the table definition

The FOREIGN KEY Constraint

The FOREIGN KEY constraint is a powerful tool to ensure that tables do not contain orphan records, which are child-table records that do not have a matching record in the parent table. The constraint causes Oracle to check the value in the constrained column against the values in the associated parent column. If the value does not exist, Oracle will stop the transaction. The constraint also contains an option that will cause the child record to be deleted along with the parent record. This is the ON DELETE CASCADE option. When this option is not specified, the FOREIGN KEY constraint forces the user to delete child records before the parent record can be deleted. This constraint should be placed on all foreign keys within the database.

The FOREIGN KEY constraint can be placed on a column as part of a column's definition in a CREATE TABLE command. Place the keyword REFERENCES and the name of the table containing the parent record after the column definition. The name of the column is not needed in the definition. If the column is missing, Oracle will assume that the primary-key column of the named table contains the validation values. The constraint cannot be defined unless the parent table contains a primary-key constrained column. Listing 2.20 illustrates this constraint defined as part of a column definition.

Listing 2.20 *Defining a FOREIGN KEY Constraint as Part of a Column Definition*

```
SQL> create table consultant_projects
  2    (employee_id            number references consultant,
```

```
  3   project_name           varchar(20),
  4   est_completion_date        date);

Table created.

End Listing
```

The FOREIGN KEY constraint can also be defined as part of the table definition. This definition begins with the keywords FOREIGN KEY followed by the name of the constrained column(s). Listing 2.21 illustrates the definition of this constraint as part of a table definition. The sample definition also includes the ON DELETE CASCADE option.

Listing 2.21 *Defining a FOREIGN KEY Constraint as Part of a Table Definition*

```
SQL> create table consultant_projects
  2   (employee_id            number,
  3   project_name           varchar(20),
  4   est_completion_date        date,
  5   foreign key (employee_id)
  6   references consultant (employee_id) on delete cascade,
  7   primary key (employee_id, project_name));

Table created.

SQL>

End Listing
```

Modifying Constraints

Constraints may also be placed on the table after the table has been created. They may also be removed, disabled, and enabled. This is done through the use of the ALTER TABLE command discussed earlier in this chapter. This command has a variety of options that can be used with constraints:

- ADD   Adds the constraint to the table.
- MODIFY   Adds a constraint to an existing column.
- DROP   Removes the constraint from the table. The constraint definition is removed from the data dictionary.

- DISABLE   Allows incoming data, regardless of whether they conforms to the constraint. The constraint definition remains in the data dictionary.
- ENABLE   Ensures that all incoming and existing data conform to the constraint.
- VALIDATE   Ensures that existing data conform to the constraint.
- NOVALIDATE   Allows some of the existing data not to conform to the constraint.

Listing 2.22 illustrates the use of these commands.

Listing 2.22 *Using the ALTER Command to Modify Constraints*

```
SQL> alter table consultant_projects
  2     add primary key (employee_id, project_name);

Table altered.

SQL> alter table consultant_projects
  2     modify project_name varchar2(20) not null;

Table altered.

SQL> alter table consultant_projects
  2     disable primary key;

Table altered.

SQL> alter table consultant_projects
  2     enable primary key;

Table altered.

SQL> alter table consultant_projects
  2     drop primary key;

Table altered.

End listing
```

When to Use Constraints

In general, it is best to use constraints whenever possible. Constraints act as a last defense. However, there are sometimes differing opinions of when to use constraints or when not to use constraints. In some cases, it depends on your philosophy. The following are some thoughts and issues concerning constraints and when to use them:

- PRIMARY KEY constraints should always be used.

- A FOREIGN KEY constraint should be used on all foreign-key columns.

- An exception to the previous rule are foreign keys that reference a table that you have no control over or cases where the parent record could be in multiple tables. I developed a system in which a piece of equipment was assigned to either an employee or a department. A proprietary human resources system and another table that contained custom names supplied the values for the foreign key. A view that unioned the two tables was used to pick out the values from the tables. I could not use the FOREIGN KEY constraint because the DBA would not allow a constraint to be placed on the Human Resources table and because the FOREIGN KEY constraint could not be placed on a view.

- I prefer to use the ON DELETE CASCADE option with the FOREIGN KEY constraint. However, I have found that some DBAs do not like this option because a user may unwittingly delete scores of child records. They think it is better to make a user deliberately delete all of the child records before deleting the parent record. I do not like this because it takes a great deal of work for the user to delete these records. Eventually, the user will have a programmer write a program that performs the same function as the option.

- The NOT NULL constraint should always be used on columns that must contain a value.

- The NOT NULL constraint does not need to be placed on primary-key columns. The PRIMARY KEY constraint will ensure that the columns always contain a value.

- I like to use the CHECK constraint when a column contains non-changing values. Sex is a good example. There are only two values, and they are not likely to change. When a column's valid values can change frequently, I generally do not use the constraint. I handle the integrity programmatically. It is too difficult to get a DBA to make the change to the database.

- The UNIQUE constraint should be used on nonprimary-key columns that must be unique.

Synonyms and Other Nice Things

Oracle has a number of database features that are used to make the database easier to use. These objects allow the developer to create user-friendly names for existing objects. They also allow the developer to create links to remote databases. This section will discuss these tools.

Synonyms

A **synonym** is another name for a database object. They are very useful when the database has a complex name for an object. For example, tables with extremely long names, such as *T_and_d_cable_terminal_poles,* can be difficult and tedious to type and use. A synonym can be used to create an alias for the table name. A possible alias might be a simpler name such as *CTPS.* The developer can then use either *T_and_d_cable_terminal_poles* or *CTPS* when referencing the table.

Synonyms are more commonly used to mask complex schema names. Tables are commonly located in remote databases. Having to qualify the table names (and table columns) with the schema ID and the connect ID can be tedious. For example, I commonly use a table that is fully qualified as *Tdeqp_d_appl.transformer@bd01.* I have had my DBA create a synonyms, called *Transformer,* for this object. This greatly simplifies my SQL when I use this table.

Synonyms can be public or private. By default, synonyms are created for the user who executes the command. A public synonym is one that is available for any user who can access the object. To create a public synonym, place the keyword PUBLIC in the definition, which means "all users." A syntax template for the command is as follows:

Create *[public]* synonym *synonym name* for *database object name*;

To remove a synonym from a database, use the DROP SYNONYM command. Be sure to add the PUBLIC keyword to the statement if it is a public synonym.

Listing 2.23 illustrates the CREATE SYNONYM and DROP SYNONYM commands. The listing will create a public synonym called EMPS for the Employee table. The synonym will then be dropped.

Listing 2.23 *Creating and Dropping a Public Synonym for the Employee Table*

```
SQL> create public synonym emps for employee;

Synonym created.

SQL> drop public synonym emps;

Synonym dropped.

SQL>

End Listing
```

Database links

A **database link** is an object definition that is stored within the database. It furnishes Oracle the user account, password, and the connect string of a remote database. A connect string is a set of characters that identifies the remote database. Databases are sometimes located on multiple servers or on servers other than the one you use to access Oracle. In order to access the remote database, a user account, password, and connect string must be furnished to the remote database. It can be a nuisance to enter continually the information needed to access the remote database.

The database link can alleviate this problem. It furnishes Oracle with the user account, password, and connect ID. After the database link is created, it is placed after the target table name. It is preceded by the at sign (@) (e.g., employee@server1). Oracle will use the link name to locate the server and access the database table. The user will not have to enter the user account and password. This makes the location of the database transparent to the user.

To make the database link available to all users, add the PUBLIC keyword to the definition. To remove a database link, use the DROP DATABASE LINK command. A syntax template of a **CREATE DATABASE LINK** command follows:

Create *[public]* database link *linkname*
Connect to *userid* identified by *password*
Using '*connect string*';

Listing 2.24 illustrates the creation and use of a database link.

Listing 2.24 *Creating a Database Link*

```
Create database link student
Connect to ostu1 identified by pirates
Using 'LEWIS';

Select last_name, first_name
From employee@student;

End Listing
```

Sequences

Sequences are used to generate a new sequential number. This is a useful tool for generating payroll numbers, work-order numbers, or artificial primary keys. Sequences are useful when the developer needs an identifying number that has never been used.

A sequence is, in reality, a single-row, single-column record that contains the last value generated. The developer can obtain this value by requesting a CURRVAL value from the sequence. The developer can generate another number by requesting a NEXTVAL value from the sequence.

To obtain either of these values, qualify the CURRVAL or NEXTVAL keywords with the name of the sequence. The CREATE SEQUENCE command is used to create the sequence. The command has two settings:

1. INCREMENT   This setting is a numeric value that determines the amount to increment each number that the sequence gives.

2. START WITH   This setting is a numeric value that sets the beginning number that the sequence uses.

Listing 2.25 illustrates the command to create a sequence, and its subsequent use in an **INSERT** statement (covered in Chapter 3). The sequence will be used to generate employee payroll numbers. The first number generated will be 200.

Listing 2.25 *Creating and Using a Sequence*

```
SQL> Create sequence payroll_number_sequence
  2  Increment by 1 start with 200;

Sequence created.

SQL>
SQL> Insert into employee (payroll_number, last_name, first_name)
  2  Values (payroll_number_sequence.nextval, 'QUAYLE', 'DAN');

1 row created.

SQL>

End listing
```

Database Triggers

A **database trigger** is a block of **PL/SQL** code stored within the database. PL/SQL is Oracle's proprietary programming language, and it will be discussed in Chapters 14, 15, and 16. Database triggers are fired by a database transaction. They are valuable tools when the developer wants additional work done whenever certain database transactions occur. Here are two examples of the use of database triggers:

- To recalculate and update a value in a summary table each time a record is added to a table containing detail records
- To populate the Payroll Number column with a new sequential number (using a sequence) prior to inserting a new employee into a table

The nice feature about database triggers is that Oracle will see that the PL/SQL code is executed. This ensures that the code will always be performed. It is always better to have Oracle cause an action to occur, rather than to rely on a programmer's application.

There is a variety of events that can fire a database trigger:

- Inserting or adding a record into a table
- Updating a record in a table
- Deleting a record in a table
- Starting the database
- Shutting down the database
- A user logging on to a session
- The occurrence of a database error
- Executing a CREATE, ALTER, or DROP statement on a schema object

Triggers normally fire once for each record transaction. Triggers have two other options that determine timing. They may be fired before or after the transaction. The following is a template for the CREATE TRIGGER command:

> **Create trigger** *[user account]triggername*
> **(before | after)**
> **(delete | insert | update [of** *column, column***]**
> **on** *[user account]* **table name**
> optional   **[referencing (old as** *old name***) | (new as** *new name***)]**
> optional   **[for each row]**
> optional   **[when** *condition***]**
>   *PL/SQL code block*

Here are some of the other available options:

- Specifying the OF keyword and a table column name after the UPDATE option will cause the trigger to be fired only when the named column(s) is updated.
- The FOR EACH ROW option will cause the trigger to be fired for each row that the operation affects.
- The OLD and NEW options enable the developer to change the name of the qualifier used with trigger table names.
- Table columns qualified with OLD contain the column value before the transaction occurs.

- Table columns qualified with NEW contain the column value after the transaction occurs.

- The WHEN keyword can be used to create a condition that must be true for the trigger to be fired.

You can disable triggers by using the ALTER TRIGGER and ALTER TABLE commands. Triggers can be removed from the database by using the DROP TRIGGER command. Listing 2.26 illustrates the command to create a database trigger that generates a payroll number using a sequence. The trigger places this value in the Payroll_number column during an INSERT transaction on the Employee table.

Listing 2.26 *Creating a Database Trigger*

```
SQL> Create or replace trigger payroll_number_generator
  2  Before insert on employee
  3  Referencing new as new
  4  For each row
  4  Begin
  5  Select payroll_number_sequence.nextval
  7         into :new.payroll_number from dual;
  7  End;
  8  /

Trigger created.

SQL>

End Listing
```

In the above trigger, *Dual* is the name of a psuedotable. The SELECT statement in the trigger does not reference actual table columns. The Dual table allows a SELECT statement to be used to populate a variable without having to reference an actual table.

Oracle Object-Oriented Features

The Oracle database changed from a relational database to an object-relational database with the Oracle8i release. I believe that industry primarily uses Oracle in the relational paradigm and will continue to do so for a long time. However, you may encounter some databases that use Oracle's object technology, so it is worth your time to review the basics.

Object technology can potentially eliminate database complexity and increase performance. In the previous chapter, you saw that databases could be very complex. The attributes are contained in multiple tables. It can be extremely difficult to write SQL that retrieves the desired attributes. Even experienced data administrators have difficulty producing the information. If the attributes can be associated to one object rather than to a series of independent tables, the SQL complexity can be reduced. The database user would simply pick out the desired attributes and not have to worry about identifying the names of the tables and how to link (join) the tables.

This is what Oracle's object technology produces. The database objects know how all of the attributes are linked. The linkage is part of the object definition. Thus the SQL needed to extract information is as simple as identifying the object and picking out the attributes.

A second reason for using objects is a possible increase in performance. Oracle's object technology is based on rowids. A rowid identifies the location of a record in the database. Sets of attributes and tables that would normally be in related but independent tables can be embedded directly into a table. This causes related attribute records to be associated to the parent record by rowid rather than by a primary key. The parent record knows the rowid of child records; therefore, Oracle can access these records without having to use the traditional methods (i.e., joining tables). This can increase performance by eliminating the processing that occurs when matching records from independent tables.

Oracle's object technology uses special tables called user-defined data types, or abstract data types (ADTs). An ADT is a set of related fields that do not have a foreign key. They are embedded into a record within a table. ADTs can be considered objects. The same ADT can be used in many different entities. This reuse of components is an important feature of object-oriented theory. This section will discuss how to create and use ADTs and other Oracle object-oriented database components.

User-Defined Data Types

ADTs are user-defined data types that allow the database designer to employ object-oriented techniques in database design. There are two categories of ADTs: object types and collection types. Object types enable a database designer to use the same database components for different entities. This reusability is an important component of object-oriented design, called inheritance. Collection types allow the developer to embed repeating sets of attributes into a table, forming an object.

Object Types

Object types are a set of related attributes similar to a record. The object type is a database definition of a series of attributes somewhat like a record. For example, the attributes house number, street, city, state, and zip code can form an object type called Address. After definition, the Address object type can be embedded into a table.

In reality, there are many entities that have the same addressing attributes. This same object type can be embedded into an Employee, Customer, or Vendor table. Object types allow the database designer to develop once and reuse often.

Figure 2.4 illustrates this relationship. The figure contains two tables and an object type. The tables contain attributes about two entities: Employee and Customer. Each of the tables contains attributes unique to the entity, but

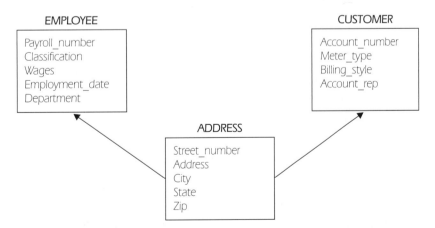

Figure 2.4 *Address object type used in the Employee and Customer tables*

the entities also contain common attributes. Rather than defining these attributes as fields in each of the tables, an object type called Address is created to hold these attributes. The records in the Employee and Customer tables can then use the same object type to define the address attributes.

Listing 2.27 illustrates the commands to create the database structure illustrated in Figure 2.4. The first command creates the object type. The object type is then used as a data type in the Employee and Customer table definitions.

Listing 2.27 *Creating an Object Type and Tables That Use the Object Type*

```
Create type Address as object
    (street_number          varchar2(10),
     street                 varchar2(30),
     city                   varchar2(20),
     state                  char(2),
     zip                    char(7));

Create table employee
    (payroll_number         number,
     classification         varchar2(25),
     wages                  number(7,2),
     employment_date        date,
     department             char(3)
     address_t              address);

Create table customer
    (account_number         number,
     meter_type             varchar2(15),
     billing_style          char(2),
     account_rep            varchar2(20),
     address_t              address);

End listing
```

same ADT

Collection Types

Collection types are objects that contain multiple sets of values. There are two kinds of collection types: varrays and object-type tables.

Varrays

Varrays are a numbered list of values similar to an array of values. Varrays can be included as a type within a table. When used, they violate the first normal form of the normalization process used during relational database design. This form requires repeating columns to be placed in their own tables. This is acceptable because varrays are an object component, and object database design is different from relational database design. The purpose of placing this array into a table is to enhance data acquisition and reduce the number of tables.

To illustrate this concept, consider this example. A local utility has a customer database. This database consists of two tables: Customer and Customer Readings. The utility keeps a maximum of 24 months of electricity readings for each customer. This information is used to determine load and average billing. The readings are repeating; therefore, the first normal form requires them to be in their own table. The purpose of this form step is to reduce the size of the database.

Placing readings in their own table may affect performance and will increase database complexity. In order to calculate customer loads, the developer must join the two tables. These are large tables; therefore, it may require extensive processing. It also requires the user to identify the tables and the primary/foreign keys. If a varray were added to the Customer table, these problems would be eliminated. The varray could be used to hold the readings, and the user would no longer have to join tables.

As I said in Chapter 1, one of the reasons for performing the first normal form is to minimize the database size. Defining the maximum number of repeating instances in the table definition will cause a lot of wasted space. Depending on the data type of the fields, each record in the table will use the same amount of space—whether all of the repeating fields are populated, or just one of them is populated.

Varrays avoid the problems caused by including repeating columns in a table. The varray has characteristics similar to the VARCHAR2 data definition: If a defined element does not contain a value, it is filled with nulls. This means that the unpopulated elements do add to the size of a database.

Listing 2.28 illustrates a command to create a varray that can contain 24 readings. The listing also includes the table definition command that uses the varray.

Listing 2.28 *Defining and Using a Varray with a Table*

```
Create type readings_v as varray(24) as number;

Create table customer
    (account_number         number,
     meter_type             varchar2(15),
     billing_style          char(2),
     account_rep            varchar2(20),
     readings               readings_v);

End listing
```

Object Tables

Object-type or nested tables are tables that are part of a parent record or that can be referenced from a parent record. Rowids are used to identify the location of the embedded records. There are two ways that object tables differ from varrays:

1. An object table record can contain more than one element or field per row.

2. The number of records in an object table does not have to be defined in advance. Records can be continually added to the object table.

Object tables allow the developer to avoid the problem associated with having repeating rows in a table. The table does not have to be redefined when additional records are added. The reason is that object tables act in a way similar to a segment in a hierarchical database. A rowid is created from the parent record to the associated records in the object table. This means that an unlimited number of object-type records can be added for one parent record.

The customer database can again be used to illustrate object tables. The Customer table has a varray used to record readings. It is often beneficial to record the reading dates. A varray can contain only one value; therefore, the varray will not work. If the varray is replaced with an object table, the Customer table can contain repeating sets of reading dates and reading fields. This would satisfy the requirement of recording the reading date with its associated reading. This structure violates the first normal form but would likely enhance the data-retrieval performance.

Listing 2.29 illustrates the command to create an object table within the Customer table. The first command establishes a type for the reading elements. The second command creates an object-type table of the type readings_o. The object table is then used in the Customer table definition.

Listing 2.29 *Defining a Nested Object Table*

```
Create type readings_o as object
   (reading_date        date,
    reading                 number);

Create type readings_table as table of readings_o;

Create table customer
   (account_number        number,
    meter_type            varchar2(15),
    billing_style         char(2),
    account_rep           varchar2(20),
    readings              readings_table);

End listing
```

TOAD

This chapter introduced you to SQL*Plus and various database objects. SQL*Plus is a tool that always comes with the Oracle database. This book will use this tool for all of its examples. However, there are third-party tools that may help you write SQL and view the results more effectively. One of these tools is TOAD, which Quest software sells. A large number of my coworkers prefer this tool to SQL*Plus. I still prefer to use SQL*Plus because I am old school. Quest allows individuals to download the product as a trial and as freeware. You may want to download a copy. All of the SQL concepts discussed in the book are also applicable with that tool. The difference between the two is solely the interface. The following is their most recent link:

www.quest.com/solutions/download.asp

What's Next?

The next chapter will introduce you to the Data Control Language (DCL), Data Manipulation Language (DML), and the data dictionary. The DCL is a set of commands used to grant privileges that enable a user to perform specific database tasks. The DML is used to populate the database. It contains commands to add, modify, and delete records. Finally, the data dictionary is a set of virtual tables that describe the various objects in the database.

■ PRACTICE

1. Log on to SQL*Plus.

2. Enter and execute the following command in SQL*Plus:

select fk_department, last_name from employee;

3. Enter and execute the following command in SQL*Plus (enter the command on multiple lines):

select fk_department, last_name
from employee;
order by fk_department, last_name;

4. List the command entered in question 3.

5. List the first line of the current command.

6. Change last_name to first_name.

7. Save the current command to a file.

8. Execute the file.

9. Create the tables that were designed in Chapter 1.

10. Drop the tables that you created in exercise 9.

11. Re-create the tables created in Chapter 1, with the following constraints:

Each table should have PRIMARY KEY constraints.

Child tables should have FOREIGN KEY constraints.

Ensure that the Test Result column cannot contain a value greater than 50 and less than 100.

Ensure that the Manufacturer Name column always contains a value.

Ensure that the Transformer Weight column has a value of 0 or more.

12. Create, use, and drop a synonym for the Emp_tools table.

13. Create a database trigger that ensures that the last_name, first_name, and state columns are uppercase during an INSERT database transaction. Drop the database trigger.

The Data Control and Data Manipulation Languages and the Data Dictionary

The main topics of this chapter are the Data Control Language (**DCL**), the Data Manipulation Language (**DML**), and Oracle's **data dictionary**. DCL is used to grant the privileges needed to use Oracle. Without privileges, the user cannot even log on to an Oracle session. DML is used to maintain the data within the database. The language has commands for adding, modifying, and deleting records. The data dictionary is a series of tables/views that contain information about the database objects and how the objects are related to each other.

Creating User Accounts

Before the database can be used, a user account must be created and be granted **privileges**. Examples of privileges are the ability to establish an Oracle session, the ability to create database objects (e.g., tables, synonyms), or the ability to modify data that another user account owns. User accounts are also used to denote the owner of a database object.

When Oracle is first installed, two default accounts are created: SYS and SYSTEM. If you have just installed Oracle, you will be interested in the SYSTEM account, the default ID for which is *manager*. This is an account that has the privileges to create other user accounts and to create many of the needed database objects. This account also has the ability to **grant** and **revoke** privileges from any other account and can be used to control all activities on the Oracle installation.

User accounts consist of two components:

1. Username   The name of the account

2. Password   The password associated with the user account

A third component is the **connect string** or **host ID**, which represents the server that the user account exists on. Oracle installations (and databases) often exist on many different servers. The host ID tells Oracle on which server or Oracle installation the desired user account exists.

User accounts are established by the CREATE USER command. They are removed using the DROP USER command. If the user account owns existing database objects, the DROP USER command must be followed by the CASCADE keyword. A number of specifications can be set when establishing a user account:

- The password for the Oracle session can be supplied by the user or by the operating system security. The second parameter in the CREATE USER command determines how security will be handled. The more common method is to have the user supply the password. To have Oracle request the password from the user, place the keyword BY, followed by the password, after the IDENTIFIED keyword. To have the password supplied by the system, place the keyword EXTERNALLY after the IDENTIFIED keyword. (See the syntax template that follows.)

- A default tablespace specification can be established. All database objects created under the user account will be placed in this tablespace by default unless another tablespace is specified in the CREATE TABLE command.

- The user account can be assigned a specific temporary tablespace. If this specification is omitted, Oracle will use the default Oracle SYSTEM tablespace, which is not recommended.

- The user account can be assigned a specific amount of space within the designated tablespace. The QUOTA keyword is used for this specification. This option prevents the user's objects from using more than the allotted amount of tablespace.

A **profile** exists for all Oracle user accounts. Profiles consist of limits on the use of database resources. They affect database settings such as CPU per session, connect time, idle time, and passwords.

The following is a command template for the CREATE USER command:

	Create user *username*
	Identified [by *password* **│ externally]**
Optional	**default tablespace** *tablespace name*
Optional	**temporary tablespace** *tablespace name*
Optional	**quota (***value* **[K│M] │ unlimited) on** *tablespace name*
Optional	**profile** *setting, setting*

Listing 3.1 illustrates a typical command used to create a user account. It is good practice always to specify a default database for the user. If this is not done, the SYSTEM tablespace will become the default tablespace. This tablespace should not be used for user data.

Listing 3.1 *Creating and Dropping a User Account*

```
SQL> create user stu5 identified by huskers
  2     default tablespace electrical_equipment
  3       quota 2m on electrical_equipment;

User created.

SQL> drop user stu5 cascade;

User dropped.

End listing
```

Data Control Language (DCL)

DCL is the language that enables or disables a user's ability to perform tasks within Oracle. A user account without privileges has no functionality. The user cannot even log on to Oracle. This requires a privilege called CREATE SESSION. There are two types of privileges:

1. System privileges　　Allow a user to perform DDL commands (e.g., CREATE TABLE, DROP INDEX)

2. Object privileges　　Allow a user to issue DML commands (e.g., INSERT, UPDATE)

A command template for the granting of privileges is as follows:

Grant *privilege, privilege, privilege* [on *object name*]
To *user account*;

Listing 3.2 illustrates a typical GRANT command. Several of the command privileges allow the user to log on to the database, create tables, and modify the tables. Table 3.1 can be used to obtain descriptions of the remainder of the privileges.

Listing 3.2 *Granting Privileges*

```
SQL> grant create session, alter session, create table,
  2    drop table, create view, drop view,
  3    create synonym, drop synonym, create index,
  4    drop index, create public synonym, drop public synonym,
  5    create sequence,drop sequence to stu6;

Grant succeeded

SQL>

End listing
```

Roles

There is a large number of privileges that may be given to a user account. Assigning privileges is often a job for the data administrator. It can be tedious to grant the numerous privileges to each user. In many cases, a specific class of users has the same privileges. To streamline the process of granting privileges, Oracle allows the developer to grant privileges to a **role** and to grant the role to specific users.

If the group of users requires a new privilege, the privilege can be granted to the existing role. Each user account granted the role will automatically receive the new privilege. Revoking a privilege from the role will cause the entire class of users to lose the privilege also. This reduces the time needed to maintain privileges and ensures that classes of users have the same privileges.

To create a role, use the CREATE ROLE command. Roles can be removed from the database by using the DROP ROLE command. Listing 3.3 illustrates the use of roles. The first statement creates the role. The second command grants privileges to the role. The third command grants the role to a user account. The last command removes the role from the database.

Listing 3.3 *Creating a Role, Granting the Role, and Dropping the Role*

```
SQL> create role student;

Role created.

SQL> grant create session, create table to student;

Grant succeeded.

SQL> grant student to stu6;

Grant succeeded.

SQL> drop role student;

Role dropped.

SQL>

End listing
```

A role is implicitly granted to the user account that creates the role. If this account is used to create many roles, at some point you may not be able to connect to Oracle because you have exceeded the maximum number of roles that can be granted to a user account.

Revoking Privileges

Privileges can be removed from a user. This is done by using the **REVOKE** command. It is possible to revoke multiple privileges from one or more users with a single command. Place a comma after each of the privileges and after each of the user account names. Listing 3.4 illustrates the REVOKE command. The command removes the object privilege CREATE TABLE from user account Cliff.

Listing 3.4 *Revoking a Privilege*

```
SQL> revoke create table from cliff;

Revoke succeeded.

SQL>

End listing
```

Privileges

Table 3.1 lists the various **system privileges** that are available.

Table 3.1 *Database Privileges*

Privilege	Description
ALTER ANY **CLUSTER**	Allows the grantee to modify a cluster on any user account
ALTER ANY INDEX	Allows the grantee to modify an index on any user account
ALTER ANY PROCEDURE	Allows the grantee to modify a procedure on any user account
ALTER ANY ROLE	Allows the grantee to modify a role on any user account
ALTER ANY SEQUENCE	Allows the grantee to modify a sequence on any user account
ALTER ANY **SNAPSHOT**	Allows the grantee to modify a snapshot on any user account
ALTER ANY TABLE	Allows the grantee to modify a table on any user account
ALTER ANY TRIGGER	Allows the grantee to modify a trigger on any user account
ALTER DATABASE	Allows the grantee to modify the user's database
ALTER PROFILE	Allows the grantee to modify the user's profile
ALTER RESOURCE COST	Allows the grantee to modify session costs

Table 3.1 *(continued)*

Privilege	Description
ALTER ROLLBACK SEGMENT	Allows the grantee to modify a rollback segment
ALTER SESSION	Allows the grantee to modify a session
ALTER SYSTEM	Allows the grantee to modify a system
ALTER TABLESPACE	Allows the grantee to modify a tablespace
ALTER USER	Allows the grantee to modify a user account
ANALYZE ANY	Allows the grantee to analyze
AUDIT ANY	Allows the grantee to audit
AUDIT SYSTEM	Allows the grantee to audit the system
BACKUP ANY TABLE	Allows the grantee to export objects from any user account
BECOME USER	Allows the grantee to import objects from any user account.
COMMENT ANY TABLE	Allows the grantee to comment on a table on any user account
CREATE ANY CLUSTER	Allows the grantee to create a cluster on any user account
CREATE ANY INDEX	Allows the grantee to create an index on any user account
CREATE ANY PROCEDURE	Allows the grantee to create a procedure on any user account
CREATE ANY SEQUENCE	Allows the grantee to create a sequence on any user account
CREATE ANY SNAPSHOT	Allows the grantee to create a snapshot on any user account
CREATE ANY SYNONYM	Allows the grantee to create a synonym on any user account
CREATE ANY TABLE	Allows the grantee to create a table on any user account
CREATE ANY TRIGGER	Allows the grantee to create a trigger on any user account

Table 3.1 *Database Privileges (continued)*

Privilege	Description
CREATE ANY VIEW	Allows the grantee to create a view on any user account
CREATE CLUSTER	Allows the grantee to create a cluster on a specific user account
CREATE DATABASE LINK	Allows the grantee to create a database link on a specific user account
CREATE PROCEDURE	Allows the grantee to create a procedure on a specific user account
CREATE PROFILE	Allows the grantee to create a profile on a specific user account
CREATE PUBLIC DATABASE LINK	Allows the grantee to create a database link that will be available to all user accounts
CREATE PUBLIC SYNONYM	Allows the grantee to create a synonym that will be available to all user accounts
CREATE ROLE	Allows the grantee to create a role
CREATE ROLLBACK SEGMENT	Allows the grantee to create a rollback segment
CREATE SEQUENCE	Allows the grantee to create a sequence on a specific user account
CREATE SESSION	Allows the grantee to create a session on a user account
CREATE SNAPSHOT	Allows the grantee to create a snapshot on a specific user account
CREATE SYNONYM	Allows the grantee to create a synonym on a specific user account
CREATE TABLE	Allows the grantee to create a table on a specific user account
CREATE TABLESPACE	Allows the grantee to create a tablespace
CREATE TRIGGER	Allows the grantee to create a trigger on a user account
CREATE USER	Allows the grantee to establish a user account

Table 3.1 *(continued)*

Privilege	Description
CREATE VIEW	Allows the grantee to create a view on a user account
DELETE ANY TABLE	Allows the grantee to drop a table from any user account
DROP ANY CLUSTER	Allows the grantee to drop a cluster on any user account
DROP ANY INDEX	Allows the grantee to drop an index on any user account
DROP ANY PROCEDURE	Allows the grantee to drop a procedure on any user account
DROP ANY ROLE	Allows the grantee to drop a role on any user account
DROP ANY SEQUENCE	Allows the grantee to drop a sequence on any user account
DROP ANY SNAPSHOT	Allows the grantee to drop a snapshot on any user account
DROP ANY SYNONYM	Allows the grantee to drop a synonym on any user account
DROP ANY TABLE	Allows the grantee to drop a table on any user account
DROP ANY TRIGGER	Allows the grantee to drop a trigger on any user account
DROP ANY VIEW	Allows the grantee to drop a view on any user account
DROP PROFILE	Allows the grantee to drop a profile
DROP PUBLIC DATABASE LINK	Allows the grantee to drop a public database link
DROP PUBLIC SYNONYM	Allows the grantee to drop a public synonym
DROP ROLLBACK SEGMENT	Allows the grantee to drop a rollback segment
DROP TABLESPACE	Allows the grantee to drop a tablespace

Table 3.1 *Database Privileges (continued)*

Privilege	Description
DROP USER	Allows the grantee to drop a user account
EXECUTE ANY PROCEDURE	Allows the grantee to run a procedure from any user account
FORCE ANY TRANSACTION	Allows the grantee to force a commit or rollback for a pending transaction
FORCE TRANSACTION	Allows the grantee to force a commit or rollback on a user account
GRANT ANY PRIVILEGE	Allows the grantee to grant a database privilege
GRANT ANY ROLE	Allows the grantee to grant a role to any user account
INSERT ANY TABLE	Allows the grantee to insert records into a table on any user account
LOCK ANY TABLE	Allows the grantee to lock or prevent update of any table
MANAGE TABLESPACE	Allows the grantee to manage any table
READUP	Allows the grantee to query data with a higher access class than the current session normally allows
RESTRICTED SESSION	Allows the grantee to log on during the restricted access mode by SQL*DBA
SELECT ANY SEQUENCE	Allows the grantee to use a sequence on any user account
SELECT ANY TABLE	Allows the grantee to select records from a table on any user account
UNLIMITED TABLESPACE	Allows the grantee to surpass the assigned limits
WRITEDOWN	Allows the grantee to create, alter, drop, insert, update, or delete database objects with access ratings lower than the current session
WRITEUP	Allows the grantee to create, alter, drop, insert, update, or delete database objects with access ratings higher than the current session

Granting Access to Your Tables and Database Objects

Tables created on a user account cannot be accessed by other user accounts unless the owner of the table grants the privileges. The owner of a table is the user account that was used to create the table. There are seven **object privileges** that the owner of a table can assign to other user accounts:

- INSERT   Allows the grantee to add records to the table
- DELETE   Allows the grantee to delete records from the table
- UPDATE   Allows the grantee to modify records within the table
- SELECT   Allows the grantee to retrieve or view records within the table
- REFERENCES Allows the grantee to use the object as the parent key to any FOREIGN KEY constraints that the grantee creates. (The presence of a foreign key can affect the data manipulation of the object.)
- ALTER   Allows the grantee to modify the object
- EXECUTE   Allows the grantee to execute a PL/SQL object

The GRANT command is used to assign object privileges. It has three components:

- The privilege(s) granted
- The name of the table
- The name of the user account receiving the privilege

The REVOKE command is used to rescind object privileges. The following template illustrates the GRANT and REVOKE command:

Grant/Revoke *privilege, privilege* on *tablename*
to *user account, user account*;

Object privileges can be extended to specific user accounts. The privileges may also be extended to everyone. Placing the PUBLIC keyword in the user account section will extend the privilege to anyone who logs on to the Oracle installation.

Users can also be extended the privilege to use views, synonyms, and other database objects by the granting of the SELECT privilege. The same GRANT and REVOKE template is used to extend this privilege on these types of objects. In the case of stored procedures, the EXECUTE privilege is used to authorize another user to execute the procedure.

Data Manipulation Language (DML)

Oracle's DML commands are used to add, update, delete, and save values in the database. Five commands are used:

- INSERT   Adds records to a table
- UPDATE   Changes values in a record
- DELETE   Removes records from a table
- ROLLBACK   Restores the database to the condition before the changes were made
- COMMIT   Permanently saves the changes

Using the INSERT Command

The **INSERT** command is used to add records to the database, and it contains three clauses:

- The TABLE clause. This is the first clause. The target table name follows the INSERT INTO keywords.
- The COLUMNS clause. This is the second clause. It follows the name of the target table. This clause identifies the table columns that will be populated.
- The VALUES clause. This is the final clause and is initiated by the keyword VALUES. This clause identifies the values that will be added to the corresponding table column.

The following is a model of the command construct:

Insert into *tablename (column1, column2, ...)*
Values *(value1, value1, ...);*

Listing 3.5 illustrates the INSERT command. The example adds a new employee to the Employee table.

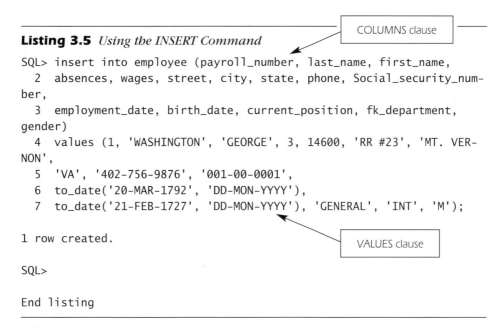

Listing 3.5 *Using the INSERT Command*

COLUMNS clause

```
SQL> insert into employee (payroll_number, last_name, first_name,
  2  absences, wages, street, city, state, phone, Social_security_num-
ber,
  3  employment_date, birth_date, current_position, fk_department,
gender)
  4  values (1, 'WASHINGTON', 'GEORGE', 3, 14600, 'RR #23', 'MT. VER-
NON',
  5  'VA', '402-756-9876', '001-00-0001',
  6  to_date('20-MAR-1792', 'DD-MON-YYYY'),
  7  to_date('21-FEB-1727', 'DD-MON-YYYY'), 'GENERAL', 'INT', 'M');

1 row created.
```

VALUES clause

```
SQL>
```

End listing

The INSERT statement in Listing 3.5 contains two date columns: employment_date and birth_date. The TO_DATE function (see Chapter 7) is used on the incoming values for these columns. A function is a code block that performs an action. The TO_DATE function converts an alphanumeric value into a data value. It is being used here because the incoming date is not in the current century. Oracle places the current century into a date value by default. Date values not in the current century or date values not in the default Oracle format (dd-mon-rr) require the use of the TO_DATE function. The second parameter in the function is a date picture. It represents the format of the incoming value. The employee was born and employed in the eighteenth century; therefore, the value could not be entered in the default format. The TO_DATE function changes the incoming value into a date.

The following rules apply to the INSERT statement:

- The COLUMNS clause does not have to contain all of the record's columns.
- The COLUMNS clause must contain all of the record's required or NOT NULL constrained columns.

- The COLUMNS clause may be left out completely. If this is done, a value must be supplied in the VALUES list for each of the table's columns. The order of the values must match the order of the columns as displayed by the data dictionary.

- Prior to Oracle9i, a single statement cannot add records to multiple tables.

- A record cannot be inserted into a view if the record represents more than one table, contains grouped records, or uses set operators—unless the record is key-preserved or an INSTEAD OF trigger has been defined for the view.

Inserting Records from Another Table

The INSERT command can be used to add records that exist in a table into another table. A **subselect** can be placed in the INSERT statement's VALUES clause in the place of a set of values. A subselect is a SELECT statement that is embedded in another command. The subselect causes Oracle to compile a run-time set of records for insertion into the table. The INSERT statement reads the records that the SELECT statement supplies and adds them to the target table.

Listing 3.6 illustrates an INSERT statement that adds a record to the Sectab table for each record in the Employee table. The statement is used to create default security records for each employee. The default password consists of the first two characters of the Last_name and First_name columns. An Oracle function called SUBSTR is used to extract the characters from the Last_name and First_name columns. The function extracts two characters beginning at position 1 from each column. These character sets are combined using the concatenation operator (||).

Listing 3.6 *Using the INSERT Command with a Subselect*

```
SQL> insert into sectab (payroll_number, security_option)
  2  select payroll_number, substr(last_name,
  3         1,2)||substr(first_name,1,2)
  4  from employee;

21 rows created.

SQL>

End listing
```

DML or SQL statements cannot reference individual elements of a varray. You must pass an entire array of values in order to populate a varray. Listing 3.7 illustrates an INSERT statement that populates the Readings varray in the Customer table.

Listing 3.7 *Inserting Values into the Readings Varray*

```
Insert into customer (account_number, meter_type, billing_style,
   account_rep, Readings)
Values (1024567, 'Maloney', 'MO', 'Crane', (12345, 13456, 14568,
   15679, 16980, 17798, null, null, null, null, null, null, null,
null,
   null, null, null, null, null, null, null, null, null, null));

End listing
```

Using the UPDATE Command

The **UPDATE** statement is used to modify the values in a table record. The statement has three clauses:

- TABLE   This is the first clause in the statement. It contains the UPDATE keyword and the name of the table to be modified.

- SET   This is the second clause. It contains a series of assignments. A comma separates each assignment. The first argument in the assignment is the column to be updated. The second is the update value. The arguments are separated by the equal sign.

- WHERE   This optional clause is used to identify the records that will be modified. If this clause is omitted, all records in the table will be modified.

The construct of the statement is as follows:

Update *tablename*
Set *column1* = *value1*, *column2* = *value2*, ...
Where *arguments*;

Listing 3.8 contains an UPDATE statement that modifies the Wages column in the Employee table. Each employee in the WEL department is given an 8-percent raise.

Listing 3.8 *Updating the Wages Column with an UPDATE Statement*

```
SQL> update employee
  2   set wages = wages * 1.08
  3   where fk_department = 'WEL';

6 rows updated.

SQL>

End Listing
```

Deleting Records

The **DELETE** statement is used to remove records from a table, and it contains three clauses:

- DELETE   The statement starts with the DELETE keyword.
- FROM   This clause begins with the FROM keyword and the name of the table.
- WHERE   The optional final clause that is used to limit deleted records. If this clause is omitted, all of the table's records will be deleted.

Listing 3.9 illustrates a DELETE statement that removes the employees in the POL department from the Employee table.

Listing 3.9 *Deleting Records from the Employee Table*

```
SQL> delete from employee
  2   where fk_department = 'POL';

8 rows deleted.

SQL>

End Listing
```

The COMMIT and ROLLBACK Commands

Changes to tables require two steps:

1. Issuance of an INSERT, UPDATE, or DELETE statement

2. Confirming the change with the **COMMIT** command

When DML commands are issued, Oracle changes the tables and saves a copy of the record before the changes were made. The changes will appear to have taken place to the user. If the user queries the database, the changes can be seen. However, anyone else who queries the database will not see the changes. The data modifications are not visible to users accessing the tables, nor are they made permanent until a COMMIT command is issued. This feature allows the developer to undo any changes. The changes can be reverted by using the **ROLLBACK** command. This command restores the database to the condition at the time of the last COMMIT command.

An implied commit is issued if the developer normally logs off from the database or if a DDL command is issued. This will cause the changes to be stored permanently. If the session is interrupted before the commit has occurred, the changes will not occur. The database will be restored to the last commit point.

It is possible to roll back changes incrementally. The SAVEPOINT command allows the user to discard sets of changed records without discarding all of the changed records. For example, assume that you have executed a series of record modifications. You are not sure that you have changed the records properly, and you want to view the records before committing them. Several SAVEPOINT commands can be issued. You may then roll back the changes to any of the designated savepoints. Rollbacks to a savepoint will restore records that were modified after the SAVEPOINT command was issued. Here's a template of the two commands:

Savepoint *save_point_name;*
Rollback *save_point_name;*

The TRUNCATE Command

When records are deleted from the database by using the DELETE command, each of the records is recorded in the redo log. This can take a considerable amount of time if there is a large number of deletions. It also can cause problems by filling up the rollback tablespace that Oracle uses. This problem can be avoided by using the TRUNCATE command.

This command deletes the entire contents of the specified table without saving the records. The deleted records cannot be restored because they were not moved to the rollback tablespace. The construct of this command is as follows:

Truncate table *tablename;*

Oracle's Data Dictionary

After the object is created and stored in the database, the developer may have a need to identify objects or to determine attributes concerning the object. Fortunately, Oracle has an extensive data dictionary that can be used to identify the objects. This section will introduce you to this dictionary.

The SYS user (the master user account) owns the actual data dictionary tables. The tables contain all of the information that Oracle needs to manage the Oracle installation. The tables are not generally accessed because they are hard to use. Oracle has created a number of views, or virtual tables, that make the data dictionary tables more understandable. Examples of information stored in these views are table names and attributes, indexes, PL/SQL code blocks, privileges, and table constraints.

The data dictionary views have four categories of information. Each category represents a level of information. Each view begins with one of the prefixes. The prefixes and level of information are as follows:

1. USER_   Displays information that pertains to the current user account

2. ALL_   Displays information that pertains to the current user account and to the objects that can be accessed by the current user account

3. DBA_   Displays information that pertains to all objects on the Oracle installation (These views are restricted only to users who have been assigned the DBA role.)

4. V$ Displays information that pertains to database performance and locking

There are over three hundred data dictionary views, most of which will not be of particular interest to you. The views contain information on a variety of topics. One of the views is called Dictionary, which lists the available data dictionary views. The view contains two columns: Table_name and Comments. Table_name identifies the view, and Comments contains a description of the view. A SELECT statement against the view can be used to display its contents. Listing 3.10 illustrates a SELECT statement that displays the contents of the Dictionary view. The listing shows only a partial list, due to the number of views.

Listing 3.10 *SELECT Statement That Displays the Contents of the Dictionary View*

```
SQL> select table_name, substr(comments,1,70)comments from dictionary;

TABLE_NAME                          COMMENTS
----------------------------------  ---------------------------------------
ALL_ALL_TABLES                      Description of all object and rela-
                                    tional tables accessible to the user
ALL_ARGUMENTS                       Arguments in object accessible to the
                                    user
ALL_CATALOG                         All tables, views, synonyms, and
                                    sequences accessible to the user
ALL_CLUSTERS                        Description of clusters accessible to
                                    the user
ALL_CLUSTER_HASH_EXPRESSIONS        Hash functions for all accessible
                                    clusters
ALL_COLL_TYPES                      Description of named collection types
                                    accessible to the user
ALL_COL_COMMENTS                    Comments on columns of accessible
                                    tables and views
ALL_COL_PRIVS                       Grants on columns for which the user
                                    is the grantor, grantee, or owner
ALL_COL_PRIVS_MADE                  Grants on columns for which the user
                                    is owner or grantor
ALL_COL_PRIVS_RECD                  Grants on columns for which the user,
                                    PUBLIC, or enabled role is the gr
ALL_CONSTRAINTS                     Constraint definitions on accessible
                                    tables
ALL_CONS_COLUMNS                    Information about accessible columns in
                                    constraint definitions
```

```
ALL_CONTEXT                         Description of all active context
                                    namespaces under the current session
ALL_DB_LINKS                        Database links accessible to the user
ALL_DEF_AUDIT_OPTS                  Auditing options for newly created
                                    objects
```

End Listing

The following sections illustrate samples of some of the more commonly used views and SELECT statements that can be used to see their contents.

The User_objects and All_objects Views

The User_objects view contains information about the objects that the current user owns. This view can be used to identify your objects, including clusters, database links, functions, indexes, packages, package bodies, procedures, sequences, synonyms, tables, triggers, views, and Oracle9i objects. This table also has a public synonym of OBJ, meaning OBJ can be used in place of User_objects.

The All_objects view is similar to the User_objects view except that it also shows the objects not owned but available to the current user. Listing 3.11 illustrates a DESCRIBE command of the User_objects view. The DESCRIBE (or DESC) command displays the columns of a target view.

Listing 3.11 *The User_objects View Columns*

```
SQL> desc user_objects
 Name                             Null?    Type
 -------------------------------- -------- ----
 OBJECT_NAME                               VARCHAR2(128)
 OBJECT_ID                                 NUMBER
 OBJECT_TYPE                               VARCHAR2(13)
 CREATED                                   DATE
 LAST_DDL_TIME                             DATE
 TIMESTAMP                                 VARCHAR2(75)
 STATUS                                    VARCHAR2(7)

SQL>
```

End Listing

To create a listing of your objects, simply use the User_objects view in a query. Listing 3.12 illustrates the results of such a query. The SUBSTR function was used on the Object_name column to increase the readability of the list.

Listing 3.12 *The Results of a Query on the User_objects Table*

```
SQL> select substr(object_name, 1, 25), object_type from user_objects;
SUBSTR(OBJECT_NAME,1,25)  OBJECT_TYPE

------------------------- -------------
ANSWER3                   PROCEDURE
ANSWER31                  PROCEDURE
ANSWER3A                  PROCEDURE
DEPARTMENT                TABLE
EMPLOYEE                  TABLE
GLASSES                   TABLE
LIST_EMPLOYEES            PROCEDURE
SECTAB                    TABLE
SYS_C0061525              INDEX
SYS_C0061527              INDEX
SYS_C0061529              INDEX
SYS_C0061532              INDEX
SYS_C0061535              INDEX
TOOLS                     TABLE
WGE_MAINT                 TABLE
new wages                 VIEW
total glass               VIEW

17 rows selected.

SQL>

End listing
```

Reviewing PL/SQL Code Blocks with User_source

A data administrator can review the PL/SQL code block of a stored procedure using the User_source view. PL/SQL is covered in Chapters 14, 15, and 16. It is Oracle's proprietary programming language. Stored procedures are PL/SQL code that resides in the database primarily as a function or procedure. The User_source view can be used to display the source code for procedures, functions, packages, and package bodies. The User_triggers view can be used to display the PL/SQL for database triggers. Listing 3.13 illustrates the columns contained in the User_source view.

Listing 3.13 *The User_source View Columns*

```
SQL> desc user_source

 Name                            Null?    Type
 ------------------------------- -------- ----
 NAME                            NOT NULL VARCHAR2(30)
 TYPE                                     VARCHAR2(12)
 LINE                            NOT NULL NUMBER
 TEXT                                     VARCHAR2(2000)

SQL>
```

End listing

The text column contains the actual code block statements. To view the actual contents of the object, execute a query against the User_source view. Listing 3.14 illustrates a query that displays a PL/SQL code block.

Listing 3.14 *A Query Displaying a User_source Code Block*

```
SQL> select line, substr(ltrim(text, ' '),1,70) from user_source
  2* where name = 'ANSWER3A'

      LINE SUBSTR(LTRIM(TEXT,''),1,70)
--------- ----------------------------------------------------------
        1 procedure answer3a
        2 (dept in varchar2, beg_date in date, end_date in date,
        3 lname out employee.last_name%type)
        4 is
        5 begin
        6 select min(last_name) into lname
        7 from employee
        8 where birth_date = (select min(birth_date)
        9 from employee
       10 where fk_department = dept
```

```
        11 and birth_date between beg_date and end_date);
        12 end;

12 rows selected.

SQL>

End listing
```

What's Next?

The next chapter will introduce you to the SELECT command, which is used to produce information by querying the Oracle database. The chapter will also cover the SELECT statement's SELECT, WHERE, and ORDER BY clauses. The SELECT clause is used to identify the attributes from the database. The WHERE clause is used to identify the records that will produce the attributes. The ORDER BY clause causes the SELECT command to return the attributes in a particular order.

▪ PRACTICE

1. Add a new employee to the database. The employee's attributes are as follows:

Last Name	Quayle
First Name	Dan
Payroll Number	50
Department	Int
Social Sec. #	312-33-9089
Gender	Male
Position	Chief Executive
Wages	$50,000
Birth Date	March 9, 1942
Employment Date	January 20, 2001
Phone	712-345-9876
State	Indiana
Street	1234 Western
City	Indianapolis

2. Each of the employees in the WEL department has purchased a pair of safety glasses. The glasses were purchased on May 7, 2001, from Pearl Optical. The cost was $78. Add a record into the Glasses table for each of the employees.

3. Update the wages for the employees. Each employee has received a 3-percent raise. The employees in the WEL also received a $900 bonus.

4. Delete the records you added to the Glasses table.

5. Restore the database to the point before the changes were made.

4

Retrieving Database Records Using SQL: The Select, Where, and Order By Clauses

This chapter starts a discussion of the SELECT command, which is the most commonly used SQL command. It is used to retrieve records and attributes from the database, and it has many powerful tools that allow you to format the retrieved data into meaningful information. This command will be the most important tool you will have in order to provide your users with the information that they request.

The SELECT command (or statement) contains six clauses, the first three of which will be discussed in this chapter. Subsequent chapters will continue the discussion of the SELECT command clauses and other powerful tools called **functions** that you can use with the SELECT command. Before I discuss the SELECT command, I will illustrate in the next section several tools that can be used to identify column and table names.

Identifying Table and Column Names

SQL*Plus has two tools for finding out the names of the database tables and the names of the columns in the tables:

- SELECT TNAME FROM TAB; This SELECT statement will list the table and view names for which you have access.
- DESC (*table name*) or Describe (*table name*) Either version of the command displays the names, data types, and NOT NULL constraints of the columns contained in the table or view.

Identifying table and column names are two of the common tasks you will perform when using a database. If you don't have a table relationship diagram, these tools will be very useful to you.

Listing 4.1 illustrates the use of the former command.

Listing 4.1 *Displays Table Names*

```
SQL> select tname from tab;

TNAME
------------------------------

DEPARTMENT
EMPLOYEE
EMP_TOOLS
GLASSES

4 rows selected.

SQL>

End Listing
```

Listing 4.2 illustrates the **DESCRIBE** or (DESC) command used to identify the table's column names. This command will also display the column's data type, length, and precision and indicates whether the column must always contain a value (NOT NULL constraint).

Listing 4.2 *Using the DESCRIBE Command to Identify the Employee Table's Columns*

```
SQL> desc employee
 Name                            Null?    Type
 ------------------------------- -------- ----
 PAYROLL_NUMBER                  NOT NULL NUMBER(4)
 LAST_NAME                                VARCHAR2(15)
 FIRST_NAME                               VARCHAR2(15)
 ABSENCES                                 NUMBER(2)
 WAGES                                    NUMBER(8,2)
```

```
        STREET                          VARCHAR2(20)
        CITY                            VARCHAR2(15)
        STATE                           CHAR(2)
        PHONE                           CHAR(13)
        SOCIAL_SECURITY_NUMBER          CHAR(11)
        EMPLOYMENT_DATE                 DATE
        BIRTH_DATE                      DATE
        CURRENT_POSITION                VARCHAR2(15)
        FK_DEPARTMENT                   VARCHAR2(4)
        GENDER                          CHAR(1)

     SQL>

     End Listing
```

Making a Simple Database Query

In Chapter 1, we saw that an entity's attributes are contained in a set of related tables. Each table contains records (or instances) about the entity. Each record is composed of related sets of attributes about the entity. In order to produce information about the entity, the attribute values must be retrieved from the database tables in which they reside. This is done using an SQL command called a SELECT statement, which is a powerful tool for extracting attributes from a database and producing information.

SELECT statements contain six clauses:

- SELECT　　Identifies the attributes retrieved from the database
- FROM　　Identifies the table(s) that contains the attributes
- WHERE　　Contains conditions used to identify the retrieved records
- GROUP BY　Groups set of records based on a common value(s)
- HAVING　　Limits retrieved records based on group values
- ORDER BY　Determines the display order of the retrieved records

The first two clauses are the only ones that are required. A simple query consists of these two clauses.

Components of a Simple SELECT

The SELECT clause contains the following:

- Name of the attributes that you want to retrieve from the database. The attributes are called **columns, fields,** or **items.**
- **Expressions.** These are text or computed values that will be displayed on each of the retrieved records.

The FROM clause contains the name of the table(s) that supplies the columns used in the SELECT statement. The simple SELECT does not contain a WHERE clause; therefore, all of the records in the tables identified in the FROM clause will be retrieved.

Examples of Simple SELECT Statements

The first example retrieves the first and last names of the employees within the employee database. This query is displayed in Listing 4.3. Notice the following:

- The names of the columns are First_name and Last_name.
- The column names are placed in the SELECT clause.
- The name of the table is Employee.
- Table names are placed in the FROM clause.
- Commas separate the column and table names.

Listing 4.3 *A Simple SELECT That Displays the First_name and Last_name Attributes in the Employee Table*

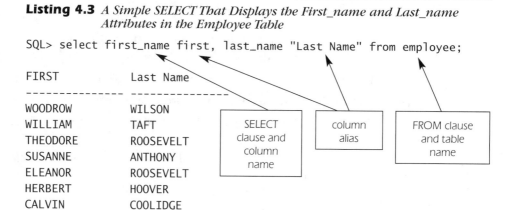

```
SQL> select first_name first, last_name "Last Name" from employee;

FIRST            Last Name
---------------  ---------------
WOODROW          WILSON
WILLIAM          TAFT
THEODORE         ROOSEVELT
SUSANNE          ANTHONY
ELEANOR          ROOSEVELT
HERBERT          HOOVER
CALVIN           COOLIDGE
```

```
KEVIN        MILLER
ALICE        DWORCZAK
LYNDON       JOHNSON
RONALD       REAGAN
GEORGE       BUSH
ANDREW       JOHNSON
WILLIAM      CLINTON
JIMMY        CARTER
GERALD       FORD
RICHARD      NIXON
JOHN         KENNEDY
DWIGHT       EISENHOWER
HAROLD       TRUMAN
FRANKLIN     ROOSEVELT

21 rows selected.

SQL>

End listing
```

The SELECT statement in Listing 4.3 causes Oracle to list the specified column values for each of the employees until the last record in the table is reached. SQL*Plus then displays the number of records retrieved, followed by the SQL prompt. Each of the fields is displayed in its own tabular column. In the next example, the First_name and Last_name columns will be combined with a **text literal** (a set of characters or character string) to make a single, more easily readable value.

When Oracle displays the results of the SELECT statement, by default the column names and values used in the expression determine what is displayed in the heading. Oracle will place as many of the expression characters in the heading as possible. Many times the expression is useless as a heading. It is possible to change the heading values using a **column alias**. Listing 4.3 illustrates the use of a column alias. The first_name expression was changed to FIRST, and the last_name expression was changed to Last Name.

The following are some rules for the use of column aliases:

- The column alias is placed as the last word(s) in the expression. It precedes the comma or the FROM keyword.

- A column alias can consist of one complete word such as *first*. The word does not have to be enclosed by double quotation marks. When a single word is used, the name will be capitalized.

- If you would like the heading to be multiple words or mixed case, you must enclose the characters in double quotation marks.

Creating Character Values in the SELECT Clause

In the previous example, the SELECT clause contained two column names. A comma delineates these column names. Column names and other values delineated by the comma are called expressions. An expression can be a column name, a combination of columns, or a text literal. A comma is used to complete SELECT clause expressions; however, the last expression is completed by the FROM keyword and not by a comma. The FROM keyword indicates that the SELECT clause is completed and that the FROM clause is beginning.

Table columns, text literals, and numbers can be combined to create a computed value or expression. Values are combined using the **concatenation operator** (||). To illustrate, Listing 4.4 uses the concatenation operator to combine the Last_name and First_name columns. These two fields are combined with the text literal ", " to produce a new value. Listing 4.4 also illustrates the use of the concatenation operator to combine two numbers. The SELECT statement concatenates 12 and 34 to make a new number: 1234.

Following are some key points to remember in combining columns and using expressions:

- A text literal is enclosed by single quotation marks (' ').

- A text literal can be treated the same as a column.

- The concatenation operator can be used with alphanumeric and numeric data types.

- When combining values using the concatenation operator, do not separate the column names and text literal by a comma.

Listing 4.4 *Using the Concatenation Operator to Derive an Expression*

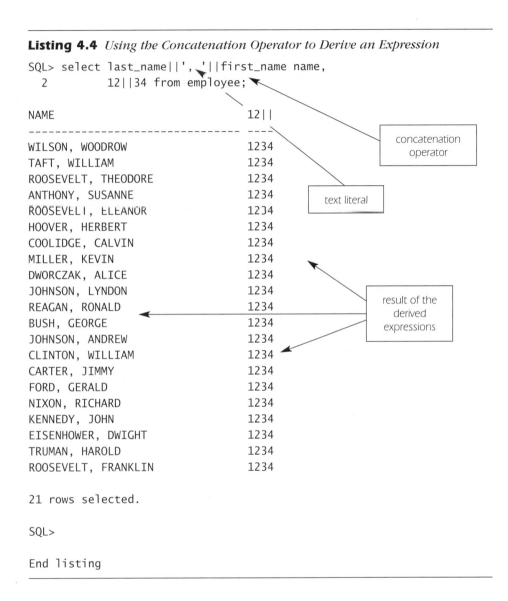

```
SQL> select last_name||', '||first_name name,
  2         12||34 from employee;

NAME                                     12||
---------------------------------------  ----
WILSON, WOODROW                          1234
TAFT, WILLIAM                            1234
ROOSEVELT, THEODORE                      1234
ANTHONY, SUSANNE                         1234
ROOSEVELT, ELEANOR                       1234
HOOVER, HERBERT                          1234
COOLIDGE, CALVIN                         1234
MILLER, KEVIN                            1234
DWORCZAK, ALICE                          1234
JOHNSON, LYNDON                          1234
REAGAN, RONALD                           1234
BUSH, GEORGE                             1234
JOHNSON, ANDREW                          1234
CLINTON, WILLIAM                         1234
CARTER, JIMMY                            1234
FORD, GERALD                             1234
NIXON, RICHARD                           1234
KENNEDY, JOHN                            1234
EISENHOWER, DWIGHT                       1234
TRUMAN, HAROLD                           1234
ROOSEVELT, FRANKLIN                      1234

21 rows selected.

SQL>

End listing
```

concatenation operator

text literal

result of the derived expressions

Computing Numeric Values in the SELECT Clause

You can also use the SELECT clause to compute numeric values. Listing 4.5 illustrates how to calculate a numeric value. The query calculates the future wages and the annual increase in wages for each employee if a 7-percent raise were given. In Listing 4.5 the plus, minus, and multiplication operators are used in the expressions. They are used to perform the needed calculations.

Listing 4.5 *Using Arithmetic Operators in a SELECT Clause to Compute a Value*

```
SQL> select last_name ||', '||first_name, wages,
  2  wages * .07, wages + wages * .07
  3  from employee;
```

LAST_NAME||','||FIRST_NAME	WAGES	WAGES*.07	WAGES+WAGES*.07
HOOVER, HERBERT	10000	700	10700
WILSON, WOODROW	9000	630	9630
TAFT, WILLIAM	8500	595	9095
ROOSEVELT, THEODORE	8000	560	8560
ANTHONY, SUSANNE	7000	490	7490
ROOSEVELT, ELEANOR			
COOLIDGE, CALVIN	9500	665	10165
MILLER, KEVIN	9500	665	10165
DWORCZAK, ALICE	9800	686	10486
JOHNSON, LYNDON	12000	840	12840
REAGAN, RONALD	13500	945	14445
BUSH, GEORGE	14000	980	14980
JOHNSON, ANDREW	7500	525	8025
CLINTON, WILLIAM	15000	1050	16050
CARTER, JIMMY	13000	910	13910
FORD, GERALD	13000	910	13910
NIXON, RICHARD	12500	875	13375
KENNEDY, JOHN	11500	805	12305
EISENHOWER, DWIGHT			
TRUMAN, HAROLD	11000	770	11770
ROOSEVELT, FRANKLIN	10400	728	11128

```
21 rows selected.

SQL>

End listing
```

The following symbols can be used as operators:

- − Subtraction operator
- * Multiplication operator
- / Division operator
- + Addition operator

The SELECT statement did not perform any calculations for *Eisenhower*, or for *Eleanor Roosevelt*, because the Wages values for these records are blank. An unknown or blank value is called **null**. When a null is included in a calculation, the result is null (unknown). This problem can be overcome by using the NVL function, which will be discussed in Chapter 7.

Limiting the Database Records Retrieved

A simple query retrieves all of the records in the table(s). Most queries require the developer to identify conditions that limit the records retrieved by the SELECT statement. These conditions are placed in the WHERE clause. Listing 4.6 illustrates a query of the Employee table that retrieves only the employee records for the Welfare department.

Listing 4.6 *Using the WHERE Clause to Select Welfare Department Employees*

```
SQL> select fk_department, last_name, first_name
  2  from employee
  3  where fk_department = 'WEL';

FK_D LAST_NAME        FIRST_NAME
---- ---------------- ----------------
WEL  HOOVER           HERBERT
WEL  TAFT             WILLIAM
WEL  ANTHONY          SUSANNE
WEL  ROOSEVELT        ELEANOR
WEL  REAGAN           RONALD
WEL  CARTER           JIMMY

6 rows selected.

SQL>

End listing
```

Tips

- All major conditions in the WHERE clause must evaluate to true for the record to be retrieved. Multiple conditions separated by the OR keyword (discussed in a later section of this chapter) are considered subconditions of a major condition. One of the subconditions must be true for the set of two subconditions to be true.

- Alphanumeric arguments such as WEL must be enclosed by single quotation marks.

- Numeric arguments such as the number 10 are not enclosed by single quotation marks.

- Any values used as arguments are case-sensitive. This means that a value of *WEL* is not equivalent to *wel.* Column names, table names, or Oracle keywords are not case-sensitive.

- Blank arguments are null.

- WHERE clause columns do not have to be contained in the SELECT clause.

Evaluation Operators Used in the WHERE Clause

SQL has a variety of operators that can be used in the WHERE clause. The operators are used to evaluate the potential record's column values against a specified argument value. If the evaluation is true, the record is selected for display. The evaluation operators are as follows:

- =   *Equal sign.* The arguments on both sides of the operator must be equivalent.

- >   *Greater Than.* The argument on the left side of the operator must be larger than the argument on the right side.

- >=   *Greater Than or Equal To.* The argument on the left side of the operator must be larger than or equivalent to the argument on the right side.

- <   *Less Than.* The argument on the left side of the operator must be smaller than the argument on the right side.

- <=   *Less Than or Equal To.* The argument on the left side of the operator must be smaller than or equivalent to the argument on the right side.

- IN   The argument on the left side of the operator exists within an array of values specified on the right side of the operator.

- BETWEEN The argument on the left side of the operator is within the range of the two values specified on the right side of the operator.

- LIKE   The argument on the left side of the operator has characteristics similar to the argument on the right side of the operator.

- IS NULL   This is the operator and value that are used when evaluating for a missing or null value.

The NOT keyword and the exclamation point (!) are used to reverse the meaning of the conditional evaluation. The NOT keyword is used with the alphanumeric operators such as IN or BETWEEN. The exclamation point is used with the graphic symbols (e.g., = or >). The NOT keyword and the exclamation point precede the operator (e.g., NOT IN, !>).

Using the Equal (=) and IS Operators

The Equal operator compares a table column value with another argument. In order for the condition to be true, the values must be equal. However, this operator cannot be used if the argument is null. In that case, the operator IS should be used in place of the equal sign. Listing 4.7 displays a query using the Equal and IS operators. In this example, the Last_name column is compared to the alphanumeric value JOHNSON. Oracle retrieved two employee records that matched the condition. The IS operator is used with the NULL argument, which evaluates the Wages column for records that have a null value. This will cause the query to return two additional records.

Listing 4.7 *Using the Equal and IS Operators in a SELECT Statement*

```
SQL> select fk_department, last_name, first_name, wages
  2  from employee
  3  where last_name = 'JOHNSON'
  4     or wages is null;

FK_D LAST_NAME        FIRST_NAME        WAGES
---- ---------------- ---------------- ---------
WEL  ROOSEVELT        ELEANOR
POL  JOHNSON          LYNDON            12000
POL  JOHNSON          ANDREW             7500
INT  EISENHOWER       DWIGHT

SQL>

End Listing
```

Using the Greater Than (>) and Less Than (<) Operators

The Greater Than operator compares the column value with another argument. If the argument on the left side of the operator is greater than the argument on the right side, the condition is true. The Less Than condition is true if the right-hand argument is larger than the left-hand argument. Listing 4.8 displays a query using both of these operators. The query retrieves employee records where the last name is greater than *CARTER* and is less than *NIXON*.

Listing 4.8 *Using the Greater Than and Less Than Operators in a SELECT Statement*

```
SQL> select last_name, first_name
  2   from employee
  3   where last_name > 'CARTER'
  4    and last_name < 'NIXON';

LAST_NAME        FIRST_NAME
---------------  ---------------
HOOVER           HERBERT
COOLIDGE         CALVIN
MILLER           KEVIN
DWORCZAK         ALICE
JOHNSON          LYNDON
JOHNSON          ANDREW
CLINTON          WILLIAM
FORD             GERALD
KENNEDY          JOHN
EISENHOWER       DWIGHT

10 rows selected.

SQL>

End Listing
```

When evaluating alphanumeric data-type arguments, the following rules apply:

- Uppercase characters have a greater value than lowercase characters. *A* is greater than *a*.

- All alpha characters have a greater value than numeric characters. *9* is less than *a*.
- Values are evaluated one position at a time. If the characters in the first position are the same, the evaluation moves to the second position. This procedure continues until an unequal position occurs.

Using the IN Operator

The IN operator is used to evaluate a column value against a set of values. This operator is really a shorthand tool to eliminate a series of conditional statements separated by the OR keyword. Listing 4.9 illustrates the use of this operator. The query retrieves employees who are in the WEL or INT departments.

Listing 4.9 *Using the IN Operator in a SELECT Statement*

```
SQL> select fk_department, last_name, first_name
  2  from employee
  3  where fk_department in ('WEL', 'INT');

FK_D LAST_NAME        FIRST_NAME
---- ---------------- ----------------
WEL  HOOVER           HERBERT
WEL  TAFT             WILLIAM
INT  ROOSEVELT        THEODORE
WEL  ANTHONY          SUSANNE
WEL  ROOSEVELT        ELEANOR
INT  COOLIDGE         CALVIN
INT  MILLER           KEVIN
WEL  REAGAN           RONALD
INT  BUSH             GEORGE
WEL  CARTER           JIMMY
INT  FORD             GERALD
INT  EISENHOWER       DWIGHT
INT  TRUMAN           HAROLD

13 rows selected.

SQL>

End Listing
```

When using the IN operator, follow these rules:

- Enclose the value array in parentheses.
- Enclose alphanumeric values in single quotation marks.

The IN operator is especially useful with subqueries, which is a SELECT statement that replaces the argument list in a condition.

ANY, SOME, or ALL Keywords

The ANY, SOME, and ALL keywords can be used in conjunction with any of the comparison operators. They are used in a manner similar to the IN operator. They allow the comparison to occur against a set of values. This tool is especially effective when using a subquery to produce the set of values. The following list describes combinations of the comparison operators and keywords:

Comparison	Meaning
Payroll_number > any(2, 6, 34, 12)	The payroll number value must be greater than any of the values in the array. In this example, the values must be greater than 2.
Payroll_number < some(2, 6, 34, 12)	The payroll number value must be less than any of the values in the array. In this case, the values must be less than 34.
Payroll_number = all(2, 6, 34, 12)	The payroll number value must equal all of the values in the array. This is an impossible condition; therefore, no records will be selected using this condition.

Listing 4.10 illustrates the SOME keyword.

Listing 4.10 *Using the SOME Keyword to Identify Payroll Numbers Greater Than Any Value in a Set*

```
SQL> select payroll_number from employee
  2  where payroll_number > some (2, 23, 14, 19);

PAYROLL_NUMBER
--------------
            20
            21
            22
            23
            24
            25
            26
            27
            28
            29
            30
            31
            32
            33
            34
            35
            36
            37
            45
            46
            19

21 rows selected.

SQL>

End list
```

Using the BETWEEN Operator

The BETWEEN operator compares the column value with two arguments. If the column value is within the range of the arguments, the condition is true. If the column value equals either the high- or low-range value, the condition is also true. The condition is false if the value falls outside this range. This operator can be used with numeric or alphanumeric values. Listing 4.11 illustrates this command.

The operator consists of two keywords. The first is the keyword BETWEEN, and the second is the keyword AND. The AND keyword separates the high- and low-range values. Be sure to put the lower value to the left of the AND keyword.

Listing 4.11 *Using the BETWEEN Operator in a SELECT Statement*

```
SQL> select last_name, first_name, wages
  2   from employee
  3   where wages between 10000 and 15000;

LAST_NAME         FIRST_NAME          WAGES
---------------   ---------------   ---------
HOOVER            HERBERT              10000
JOHNSON           LYNDON               12000
REAGAN            RONALD               13500
BUSH              GEORGE               14000
CLINTON           WILLIAM              15000
CARTER            JIMMY                13000
FORD              GERALD               13000
NIXON             RICHARD              12500
KENNEDY           JOHN                 11500
TRUMAN            HAROLD               11000
ROOSEVELT         FRANKLIN             10400

11 rows selected.

SQL>

End Listing
```

Using the LIKE Operator

The LIKE operator is a powerful tool that is used to compare character patterns. The argument contains one or more characters, along with some special symbols. If the column value contains this pattern, the condition is true. This operator is extremely useful when the analyst does not know the exact spelling of the value. For instance, *PALINSKI* is often spelled with an *A* or an *O*. The LIKE operator allows the developer to retrieve values that contain the character pattern *P LINSKI*. This will cause records to be retrieved regardless of the spelling.

Two special character symbols are used with the LIKE operator. They are called **wildcard characters** because they represent any character in a comparison.

- % The percent sign causes Oracle to omit any column value characters between the value to the right and the left of the character during the evaluation.

- _ The underscore causes Oracle to omit any column value in the same column as the character during the evaluation.

Listing 4.12 illustrates a SELECT statement that uses the LIKE operator. In this example, employees who have a last name that begins with a *J* and ends with an *N* will be retrieved. The percent sign is used to tell Oracle to omit the characters between the *J* and *N* during the evaluation.

Listing 4.12 *Using the LIKE Operator with the % Wildcard Character*

```
SQL> select last_name, first_name
  2  from employee
  3  where last_name like 'J%N';

LAST_NAME        FIRST_NAME
---------------  ---------------
JOHNSON          LYNDON
JOHNSON          ANDREW

SQL>

End Listing
```

You may use as many percent signs as needed. In Listing 4.13, you can see an example of a query that uses several symbols. The query retrieves employees who have a last name that begins with an *R* and has an *E* somewhere in the remainder of their name.

Listing 4.13 *Using Multiple Wildcard Characters in an Argument*

```
SQL> select last_name, first_name
  2  from employee
  3  where last_name like 'R%E%';

LAST_NAME         FIRST_NAME
---------------   ---------------
ROOSEVELT         THEODORE
ROOSEVELT         ELEANOR
REAGAN            RONALD
ROOSEVELT         FRANKLIN

SQL>
```

End Listing

The second symbol used with the LIKE operator is the underscore, which is a positional wildcard or marker. It is used to depict the location of a character in the argument. Listing 4.14 illustrates a query that uses both wildcard characters to retrieve employees who have the letter *O* in the second position of their last name.

Listing 4.14 *Using the _ Positional and % Wildcard Characters with the LIKE Operator*

```
SQL> select last_name, first_name
  2  from employee
  3  where last_name like '_O%';

LAST_NAME         FIRST_NAME
---------------   ---------------
HOOVER            HERBERT
ROOSEVELT         THEODORE
ROOSEVELT         ELEANOR
COOLIDGE          CALVIN
JOHNSON           LYNDON
JOHNSON           ANDREW
FORD              GERALD
ROOSEVELT         FRANKLIN
```

```
8 rows selected.

SQL>

End Listing
```

In a rare case, you may want to search on the underscore or the percent sign rather than use them as wildcard characters. When this happens, you can define an escape character, which is a character that can be placed into the string argument and tells Oracle to use the next occurrence of a wildcard character as a literal. To designate an escape character, place the keyword ESCAPE followed by the character after the string argument.

Listing 4.15 illustrates this option. This listing contains the same basic SELECT statement as seen in Listing 4.14. The difference is the definition and use of an escape character. The keyword option ESCAPE was added after the string argument. It defines the backslash (\) as the escape character. The escape character was then added to the string argument. It preceded the underscore positional marker. The effect was to disable the positional marker, which causes Oracle to search for values that started with an underscore. The net result was that no records were selected.

Listing 4.15 *Using an Escape Character to Disable a Positional Marker*

```
SQL> select last_name, first_name
  2  from employee
  3  where last_name like '\_0%' escape '\' ;

no rows selected

SQL>

End listing
```

Care should be used with the LIKE operator. Oracle will not use an index to locate records if a wildcard character is placed in the first position of the argument. This will seriously degrade the performance of the statement.

Using AND or OR to Document Multiple Conditions

The majority of queries require more than one condition in the WHERE clause. The conditions are linked through the use of the AND and OR keywords.

- *AND* is used when both the condition that precedes the keyword and the condition that follows it must be true.

- *OR* is used when either the condition that precedes the keyword or the condition that follows it is true.

Listing 4.16 displays a query that has multiple conditions. The evaluation is true if the employee's last name contains a T and the employee is female. In this example, both conditions are separated by the keyword AND, which means both conditions must be true for the record to be selected.

Listing 4.16 *Using the AND Keyword to Join Multiple Conditions in a SELECT Statement*

```
SQL> select last_name, first_name
  2  from employee
  3  where last_name like '%T%'
  4  and gender = 'F';

LAST_NAME        FIRST_NAME
---------------  ---------------
ANTHONY          SUSANNE
ROOSEVELT        ELEANOR

SQL>

End Listing
```

Notice the difference in the query displayed in Listing 4.17. In this example, the AND keyword is changed to the OR keyword; therefore, the record will be selected if either of the two conditions is true. The results of the query include employees with a *T* in the Last_name column and employees who are female.

Listing 4.17 *Using the OR Keyword to Combine Multiple Conditions in a SELECT Statement*

```
SQL> select last_name, first_name
  2  from employee
  3  where last_name like '%T%'
  4  or gender = 'F';

LAST_NAME        FIRST_NAME
---------------  ---------------
TAFT             WILLIAM
ROOSEVELT        THEODORE
ANTHONY          SUSANNE
ROOSEVELT        ELEANOR
DWORCZAK         ALICE
CLINTON          WILLIAM
CARTER           JIMMY
TRUMAN           HAROLD
ROOSEVELT        FRANKLIN

9 rows selected.

SQL>

End Listing
```

Mixing AND and OR in the WHERE Clause

The AND and OR keywords can be used in the WHERE clause at the same time. However, problems can occur because Oracle may combine conditions in a manner that is different from what you may expect. Oracle combines conditions that are separated by the AND keyword first and by the OR keyword next. This can lead to incorrect results if the developer does not expect this order of precedence.

Fortunately, Oracle allows the developer to group conditions by using parentheses. Listing 4.18 illustrates a query that contains three comparisons. Two of the comparisons are grouped together by using parentheses. These are subconditions, and either of the conditions must be true for the main condition to be true. While either of the subconditions can be true, both of the main conditions must be true for the record to be selected.

Listing 4.18 *Using the AND and OR Keywords in the Same WHERE Clause*

```
SQL> select fk_department, last_name, first_name
  2  from employee
  3  where last_name like '%C%'
  4  and (fk_department = 'INT'
  5      or fk_department = 'WEL');

FK_D LAST_NAME       FIRST_NAME
---- --------------- ---------------
INT  COOLIDGE        CALVIN
WEL  CARTER          JIMMY

SQL>

End listing
```

The parentheses are used to form the proper logic of the WHERE clause. This query is saying to select the following:

1. Employees who have a letter *C* in their last name
   AND
2. Employees who are employed in either the WEL department or the INT department

Removing the parentheses from the query changes the logic of the conditions. This is illustrated in Listing 4.19. The conditions in the WHERE clause will default to the order of precedence. The conditions that the AND keyword separates are combined first. The conditions that the OR keyword separates are combined next. The query now selects the following:

1. Employees who are in the INT department and have the letter *A* in their last name
   AND
2. All employees in the WEL department

Listing 4.19 shows the results of the parentheses removal. Compare the results to Listing 4.18.

Listing 4.19 *The Results of Removing Parentheses from the Listing 4.18
              Example*

```
SQL> select fk_department, last_name, first_name
  2  from employee
  3  where last_name like '%C%'
  4  and fk_department = 'INT'
  5   or fk_department = 'WEL';

FK_D LAST_NAME        FIRST_NAME
---- ---------------  ----------------
WEL  TAFT             WILLIAM
WEL  ANTHONY          SUSANNE
WEL  ROOSEVELT        ELEANOR
WEL  HOOVER           HERBERT
INT  COOLIDGE         CALVIN
WEL  REAGAN           RONALD
WEL  CARTER           JIMMY

7 rows selected.

SQL>

End listing
```

Ordering Records

The ORDER BY clause is used to change the order records that the SELECT
statement displays. This clause tells Oracle which columns determine the
record order. Column or expression names placed after the ORDER BY keywords determine the order. A comma is used to separate the names.

This clause is always the last clause in the SELECT statement because the
ordering is performed on the selected records after they are placed in memory. The other clauses tell Oracle what to retrieve from the database. After the
values are retrieved, the ordering occurs.

Listing 4.20 illustrates a SELECT statement that contains an ORDER BY
clause. The clause orders the employees in the POL department by last name.

Listing 4.20 *Ordering the Retrieved Records by the Last_name Expression*

```
SQL> select last_name, first_name
  2  from employee
  3  where fk_department = 'POL'
  4  order by last_name;

LAST_NAME        FIRST_NAME
---------------  ---------------
CLINTON          WILLIAM
DWORCZAK         ALICE
JOHNSON          LYNDON
JOHNSON          ANDREW
KENNEDY          JOHN
NIXON            RICHARD
ROOSEVELT        FRANKLIN
WILSON           WOODROW

8 rows selected.

SQL>

End Listing
```

Ascending/Descending Order

The records in Listing 4.20 were ordered in ascending order. The lowest value precedes the higher values. This is the default style of ordering. The records can also be displayed in descending order. Placing the keyword DESC after the column will cause Oracle to sort the data in descending order. Listing 4.21 illustrates the use of the DESC keyword to order the selected employees in descending order by last name.

Listing 4.21 *Ordering the Records in Descending Order by Using the DESC Keyword*

```
SQL> select last_name, first_name
  2  from employee
  3  where fk_department = 'POL'
  4  order by last_name desc;
```

```
LAST_NAME        FIRST_NAME
---------------  ---------------
WILSON           WOODROW
ROOSEVELT        FRANKLIN
NIXON            RICHARD
KENNEDY          JOHN
JOHNSON          LYNDON
JOHNSON          ANDREW
DWORCZAK         ALICE
CLINTON          WILLIAM

8 rows selected.

SQL>

End listing
```

Records can be ordered by using multiple expressions. However, be sure to separate each expression with a comma. The first column listed in the ORDER BY clause determines the primary sort. Each additional column sorts records within the primary sorts. Each expression can be independently ordered ascending or descending by placing the ASC and DESC keywords in the expression. Listing 4.22 illustrates a SELECT command that has multiple order columns. The primary sort is last_name. The records are further sorted by first name.

Listing 4.22 *Ordering the Records by the Last_name and First_name Expressions*

```
SQL> select last_name, first_name
  2  from employee
  3  where fk_department = 'POL'
  4  order by last_name, first_name desc;
```

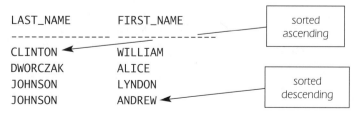

```
LAST_NAME        FIRST_NAME
---------------  ---------------
CLINTON          WILLIAM
DWORCZAK         ALICE
JOHNSON          LYNDON
JOHNSON          ANDREW
```

```
KENNEDY        JOHN
NIXON          RICHARD
ROOSEVELT      FRANKLIN
WILSON         WOODROW

8 rows selected.

SQL>

End Listing
```

Using Expression Numbers as the Names of Sort Columns

Expression numbers may be used in the ORDER BY clause. This is extremely useful. An expression that contains a function uses the name of the function in its name. For instance, an expression summarizing a Wages column will have the name *sum(wages)*. The name of the expression becomes sum(wages). The use of column numbers can reduce the amount of typing in the ORDER BY clause.

Listing 4.23 *Using an Expression Number in the ORDER BY Clause to Sort Records by the Sum of Tool Cost*

```
SQL> select last_name, first_name, sum(tool_cost)
  2  from employee, emp_tools
  3  where payroll_number = fk_payroll_number
  4  group by last_name, first_name
  5  order by 3 desc;
```

LAST_NAME	FIRST_NAME	SUM(TOOL_COST)
EISENHOWER	DWIGHT	375
ROOSEVELT	THEODORE	324
WILSON	WOODROW	116.95
ANTHONY	SUSANNE	88.85
ROOSEVELT	ELEANOR	61.95
BUSH	GEORGE	46.2
COOLIDGE	CALVIN	35
REAGAN	RONALD	28.7
HOOVER	HERBERT	24
TAFT	WILLIAM	23

```
ROOSEVELT       FRANKLIN                    20
NIXON           RICHARD                   18.5
JOHNSON         ANDREW                    16.7
FORD            GERALD                      12

14 rows selected.

SQL>

End Listing
```

Printing the Results of Your Query

The results of your query are permanently captured by using the SPOOL command. This command causes SQL*Plus to begin writing all screen output to an external file. SQL*Plus will continue to output to the file until the SPOOL OFF command is issued. The external file that the SPOOL command created can then be printed using any Windows software, such as Notepad, Word, or WordPerfect. If you would like to stop the spooling process and print the output, use the SPOOL OUT command.

The command can be entered as a line command, selected from the File/Spool menu option, or it can be placed inside the query file. The following is the syntax of the command:

Spool *filename*
Spool c:/test.txt

Chapter 11 has a more complete discussion of spooling and its various command options.

When you output or spool the results of your SELECT statement to a file, Oracle spools it to the file exactly as you see it on the screen. As the amount of expressions in your SELECT clause increase, the more width your results will take. At the hundredth character, Oracle will wrap each row to the following line. You can see this on the screen, and it will appear the same in the output file. Another feature you will see is a heading for each column, which will be repeated every 24 lines. These two settings are called LINESIZE and PAGESIZE; they do not make for very readable results on the screen or in a printed document.

Fortunately, Oracle has a variety of settings that affect the SQL*Plus environment. These settings are discussed in the "Set Commands" section of Chapter 11. The LINESIZE and PAGESIZE settings, discussed in the previous paragraph, can be used to control the height and width of your output. You use a LINESIZE setting of 132 and a PAGESIZE setting of 45 for landscape output. Portrait output can be achieved using a LINESIZE of 80 and a PAGESIZE of 60. When you change the LINESIZE setting to a value greater than the default, you will not be able to see all of the SELECT statement's output on the screen, unless you scroll using the scroll panes.

What's Next?

The next chapter will continue the discussion of the SELECT statement. The chapter will discuss the FROM, GROUP BY, and HAVING clauses. The FROM clause is used to identify the tables that will supply the values. You will learn how to join records from multiple tables to make a virtual record. You will also learn how to make or compute group values with the GROUP BY clause and how to limit these values with the HAVING clause.

▪ PRACTICE

(You may use the table relationship diagram in Figure 1.11 with these questions.)

1. Identify the tables to which you have access.
2. Identify the name of the columns in the Employee table.
3. Retrieve the employee department, last name, first name, and current position.
4. Retrieve the same columns as those in question 3, but combine the Last Name and First Name columns. Preface each name with *Mr.*
5. Compute the future wages for each employee if he or she receives a 6-percent raise, a bonus of $2,300, and a deduction of $250 for charity.
6. Retrieve all of the employees in the database, and display their first and last names. Order the employees by department.

7. Retrieve all of the employees in the database, and display their first and last names. Order the employees by descending department. Within the department, list the employees in ascending alphabetical order.

8. Determine the weekly wages for each employee in the database. Order the employees by department and weekly wage.

9. Retrieve records for employees who are named John.

10. Retrieve records for employees who do not have a value in their wages column.

11. Retrieve records for employees who live in IA, OH, or TX. (Do this in two different methods.)

12. Retrieve records for employees who were employed after "01-JAN-1950" and before "01-JAN-1979." (Write this query in two different manners.)

13. Retrieve records for employees who do not live in IA, OH, or TX.

14. Retrieve records for male employees who have wages greater than or equal to $10,000 and who were born after "01-JAN-1920."

15. Retrieve records for male employees, employees with wages greater than or equal to $10,000, and employees born after "01-JAN-1920."

16. Retrieve records for male employees with wages greater than or equal to $10,000, or for employees born after "01-JAN-20."

Retrieving Records Using SQL: The FROM, GROUP BY, and HAVING Clauses

This chapter will discuss the remaining three SELECT statement clauses: FROM, GROUP BY, and HAVING. The FROM clause is used to identify the location of the data within the database. The GROUP BY clause determines how Oracle will group or aggregate common sets of records. Finally, the HAVING clause is used to eliminate grouped records.

The FROM Clause

The FROM clause is the second mandatory SELECT statement clause. It is used to identify the database objects that store the attributes that satisfy the statement. These attributes can exist in any of the statement's various clauses. This clause is the second clause of the statement and begins with the keyword FROM. The clause follows the last expression in the SELECT clause and can contain the names of tables or views or another SELECT statement. In the examples seen thus far, the FROM clauses have contained only one table name. In the following section, you will see additional FROM clause functionality and options.

Retrieving Records from Multiple Tables

The true power of a relational database is its ability to combine records from different tables into a new virtual record. This virtual record exists for only the life of the query. The process of combining records from multiple tables is called **joining**. Records are joined or matched through the use of common columns. These columns are usually the primary- and foreign-key columns in the joined tables.

Figure 5.1 represents a join or matching of the Department and Employee tables. The Department table contains a record for each department. This table is called a base table because a record must exist in this table before a related record in the Employee table can be created. The Employee table contains a record for each employee. This table is the related table. One of the columns in the Employee table is the employee's department code. The Department and Employee tables have a common column; therefore, they can be related or joined. Records in the Employee table can be combined with the records in the Department table by matching records that have the same value in the Department/Fk_department columns. This will create a new virtual record similar to the one depicted in Figure 5.1.

How to Combine or Join Tables

Two steps are required to join tables:

1. Place the names of the tables in the FROM clause. The table names must be separated by commas.

2. Add a condition to the WHERE clause, describing how the tables are related.

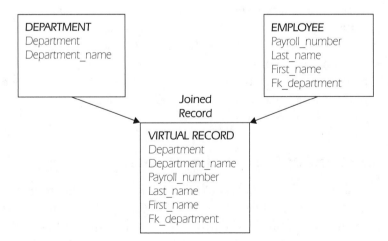

Figure 5.1 *Representation of a join between the Department and Employee tables*

Listing 5.1 illustrates a query that combines the Department and Employee tables. The query retrieves the employees from the WEL department. Rather than displaying the employee's department number, a join to the Department table is performed in order to display the full name of the employee's department.

Listing 5.1 *A SELECT Statement Joining the Department and Employee Tables*

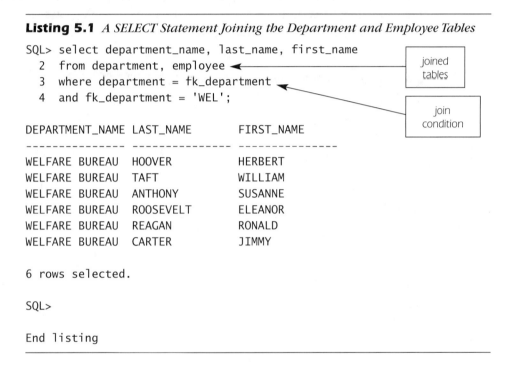

```
SQL> select department_name, last_name, first_name
  2   from department, employee
  3   where department = fk_department
  4   and fk_department = 'WEL';


DEPARTMENT_NAME  LAST_NAME        FIRST_NAME
---------------  ---------------  ---------------
WELFARE BUREAU   HOOVER           HERBERT
WELFARE BUREAU   TAFT             WILLIAM
WELFARE BUREAU   ANTHONY          SUSANNE
WELFARE BUREAU   ROOSEVELT        ELEANOR
WELFARE BUREAU   REAGAN           RONALD
WELFARE BUREAU   CARTER           JIMMY

6 rows selected.

SQL>

End listing
```

joined tables

join condition

What to Do with Join Columns with the Same Name

Sometimes the join columns of the tables have the same name. This causes a problem with Oracle. It does not know the table to which the columns pertain. When this occurs, Oracle will terminate the query with an error message.

The problem is overcome by **qualifying** the columns, which tells Oracle which table the column exists. There are two methods of qualifying a column:

1. Precede the column name with the name of the table. The two names should be separated by a period.

Employee.last_name

2. Creating a **table alias** and using this value as the name of the table.

Emp.last_name

The advantage of the second method is that it allows the developer to use a shorter custom name for the table. Table aliases are created by placing the new name immediately after the name of the table in the FROM clause. Listing 5.2 illustrates a query using table aliases.

Listing 5.2 *Using Table Aliases to Qualify Columns*

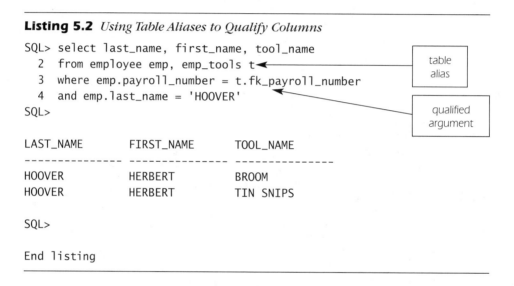

```
SQL> select last_name, first_name, tool_name
  2  from employee emp, emp_tools t
  3  where emp.payroll_number = t.fk_payroll_number
  4  and emp.last_name = 'HOOVER'
SQL>


LAST_NAME         FIRST_NAME        TOOL_NAME
---------------   ---------------   ---------------
HOOVER            HERBERT           BROOM
HOOVER            HERBERT           TIN SNIPS

SQL>

End listing
```

table alias

qualified argument

Tables that are located in remote Oracle installations may also need to be qualified. This qualification will consist of the Oracle ID that owns the data and the connect string that identifies the server. The following is a template for this type of qualification:

Owner_id.table_name@connect_string

Join Types

The previous join examples illustrated a join type called an **equijoin**. This type of join occurs when the joined tables have common and equal values. There are some situations when an equijoin is not appropriate, and there are several other join types available for those cases. The following are the join types with a short description:

- equijoin   Each of the joined tables has common columns and common values.

- nonequijoin   The joined tables do not have common columns and values.

- outer join   The joined tables have common columns, but the records in the joined tables may or may not have common values.

- self join   The table is joined to itself. This occurs when a table contains a column that is a foreign key to its primary key.

- cartesian join Each record in the first table is joined to each record in the second table.

Joining Tables When the Value Exists in Only One Table: The Outer Join

Equijoins combine records when common values are found in a record from each of the joined tables. This means that the join condition describing how the tables are related is true. If a record is encountered in one of the tables that does not have a matching value in the other table, the join condition is false, and the record will be discarded even though it may satisfy the remainder of the selection criteria. For example, if the Department table contained a department that did not have an employee, the record would not be selected in a query joining the Department and Employee tables.

This is a problem with relational databases, which are populated from the top down. The base or parent table often has a record before the related or child tables have records. In our database, the department must exist before the employee can be assigned to the department. This is the root of the problem. You can have records in a parent table that does not have records in the related table. Yet, you want to select these records along with the others.

Fortunately, Oracle allows you to overcome the problem through the use of an **outer join**, which allows records to be selected from one table even though a matching value does not exist in the joined table. The values for the columns that would be supplied by the missing record will be null.

The next two listings illustrate the use and nonuse of outer joins. The query in Listing 5.3 displays a list of the departments and their employees. An equijoin is performed in order to obtain the actual names of the departments. This query retrieves only records that have matching values in each of the tables.

Listing 5.3 *Joining the Department and Employee Tables without an Outer Join*

```
SQL> select department_name, last_name, first_name
  2  from department, employee
  3  where department = fk_department
  4  order by department_name;

DEPARTMENT_NAME LAST_NAME        FIRST_NAME
--------------- ---------------- ----------------
INTERIOR DESIGN ROOSEVELT        THEODORE
INTERIOR DESIGN COOLIDGE         CALVIN
INTERIOR DESIGN MILLER           KEVIN
INTERIOR DESIGN BUSH             GEORGE
INTERIOR DESIGN FORD             GERALD
INTERIOR DESIGN TRUMAN           HAROLD
INTERIOR DESIGN EISENHOWER       DWIGHT
POLITICAL SCIEN WILSON           WOODROW
POLITICAL SCIEN DWORCZAK         ALICE
POLITICAL SCIEN JOHNSON          LYNDON
POLITICAL SCIEN CLINTON          WILLIAM
POLITICAL SCIEN ROOSEVELT        FRANKLIN
POLITICAL SCIEN KENNEDY          JOHN
POLITICAL SCIEN NIXON            RICHARD
POLITICAL SCIEN JOHNSON          ANDREW
WELFARE BUREAU  HOOVER           HERBERT
WELFARE BUREAU  ROOSEVELT        ELEANOR
WELFARE BUREAU  ANTHONY          SUSANNE
WELFARE BUREAU  CARTER           JIMMY
WELFARE BUREAU  REAGAN           RONALD
WELFARE BUREAU  TAFT             WILLIAM

21 rows selected.

SQL>

End listing
```

To perform an outer join, place a plus sign (+) enclosed by parentheses after the name of the WHERE clause join-condition argument for the table that has the missing record.

Listing 5.4 illustrates an outer join. It shows how the results of the previous query change when an outer join is added. In the query illustrated in

Listing 5.3, the Fk_department column does not have a value for each value column for the department column. The Fk_department column resides in the Employee table. The Department table has two departments that do not have employees. In order to display these departments on the listing, the statement uses an outer join.

The outer join is performed by placing the plus sign after the Fk_department column name in the WHERE clause. Notice that the listing has now been expanded. The Census and Treasury departments have been added to the list. These departments do not have any employees, and the values to be supplied by the Employee table are null.

Listing 5.4 *Joining the Employee and Department Tables by Using an Outer Join*

```
SQL> select department_name, last_name, first_name
  2   from department, employee
  3   where department = fk_department(+)          ┌─────────────┐
  4   order by department_name;                    │  outer join │
                                                   └─────────────┘

DEPARTMENT_NAME LAST_NAME        FIRST_NAME        ┌──────────────┐
--------------- ---------------  ---------------   │ department   │
                                                   │ record with  │
CENSUS DEPT ◄───────────────────────────────────  │ no matching  │
INTERIOR DESIGN ROOSEVELT        THEODORE          │ employee     │
INTERIOR DESIGN COOLIDGE         CALVIN            │ record       │
INTERIOR DESIGN MILLER           KEVIN             └──────────────┘
INTERIOR DESIGN BUSH             GEORGE
INTERIOR DESIGN FORD             GERALD
INTERIOR DESIGN TRUMAN           HAROLD
INTERIOR DESIGN EISENHOWER       DWIGHT
POLITICAL SCIEN WILSON           WOODROW
POLITICAL SCIEN DWORCZAK         ALICE
POLITICAL SCIEN JOHNSON          LYNDON
POLITICAL SCIEN CLINTON          WILLIAM
POLITICAL SCIEN ROOSEVELT        FRANKLIN
POLITICAL SCIEN KENNEDY          JOHN
POLITICAL SCIEN NIXON            RICHARD
POLITICAL SCIEN JOHNSON          ANDREW
TRESURY DEPAR
WELFARE BUREAU  HOOVER           HERBERT
WELFARE BUREAU  ROOSEVELT        ELEANOR
WELFARE BUREAU  ANTHONY          SUSANNE
WELFARE BUREAU  CARTER           JIMMY
```

```
DEPARTMENT_NAME LAST_NAME        FIRST_NAME
--------------- ---------------  ---------------
WELFARE BUREAU  REAGAN           RONALD
WELFARE BUREAU  TAFT             WILLIAM

23 rows selected.

SQL>

End listing
```

Nonequijoins

In rare occasions, it is necessary to join records from two tables that do not have common columns and values. In these cases, the **nonequijoin** may be appropriate. A nonequijoin is one in which an operator other than the equal sign is used. Listing 5.5 portrays a Select statement using the practice database table called Tax_rates. To illustrate, our practice database has a table called Tax_rates, which contains the tax rate for the various tax brackets. Each record in the table contains a bottom wage, a top wage, and a corresponding tax rate. To determine the tax rate for each employee, the wages value from the Employee table must be compared to the bottom-wage and top-wage values. If the employee's wages are between the two values, the corresponding tax rate should be used. A nonequijoin using the BETWEEN operator is a perfect tool to produce the desired results.

Listing 5.5 *Using a Nonequijoin to Compute Employee Taxes*

```
SQL> select last_name, wages, tax_rate, wages*tax_rate taxes
  2  from employee, tax_rates
  3  where wages between bottom_wage and top_wage
  4  order by tax_rate;
```

nonequijoin condition

```
LAST_NAME            WAGES  TAX_RATE     TAXES
---------------  ---------  ---------  ---------
TAFT                  8500         .1        850
ROOSEVELT             8000         .1        800
ANTHONY               7000         .1        700
JOHNSON               7500         .1        750
WILSON                9000        .11        990
HOOVER               10000        .11       1100
COOLIDGE              9500        .11       1045
```

```
MILLER              9500        .11     1045
DWORCZAK            9800        .11     1078
ROOSEVELT          10400        .11     1144
TRUMAN             11000        .11     1210
KENNEDY            11500        .11     1265
JOHNSON            12000        .12     1440
REAGAN             13500        .12     1620
CARTER             13000        .12     1560
NIXON              12500        .12     1500
FORD               13000        .12     1560
BUSH               14000        .12     1680
CLINTON            15000        .13     1950

19 rows selected.

SQL>

End Listing
```

Self Joins

A **self join** occurs when a table is joined to itself. This type of join is useful when a table has a unary relationship to itself. An example of this type of relationship is an Employee table that contains a column for the employee's supervisor. The value that identifies the supervisor is the supervisor's payroll number. Payroll number is the primary key of the Employee table; therefore, there is a relationship between the Payroll Number column and the Supervisor column.

When you join a table to itself, you are listing the same table multiple times in the FROM clause. This will require you to create a table alias for the second and subsequent instances of the table. You must also qualify the columns used in the query.

Our practice database does not have a unary relationship; therefore, I will have to create another example to illustrate the self-join query. Assume that you want to produce a report that displays each employee and the employee who was hired previous to the employee. The employee payroll numbers are numeric. Adding a value of 1 to a record will allow the query to determine the previous record because most of the payroll numbers are sequential. This query is illustrated in Listing 5.6. Notice that table aliases were created and the columns qualified.

Listing 5.6 *Using a Self Join to Determine the Previously Hired Employee*

```
`SQL> select emp.payroll_number, emp.last_name,
  2         prev.payroll_number, prev.last_name "Previous hire"
  3  from employee emp, employee prev
  4  where emp.payroll_number = prev.payroll_number(+) + 1
  5  order by emp.payroll_number;


PAYROLL_NUMBER LAST_NAME        PAYROLL_NUMBER Previous hire
-------------- ---------------- -------------- ----------------
            19 ROOSEVELT
            20 ANTHONY                      19 ROOSEVELT
            21 JOHNSON                      20 ANTHONY
            22 ROOSEVELT                    21 JOHNSON
            23 TAFT                         22 ROOSEVELT
            24 WILSON                       23 TAFT
            25 COOLIDGE                     24 WILSON
            26 HOOVER                       25 COOLIDGE
            27 ROOSEVELT                    26 HOOVER
            28 TRUMAN                       27 ROOSEVELT
            29 EISENHOWER                   28 TRUMAN
            30 KENNEDY                      29 EISENHOWER
            31 JOHNSON                      30 KENNEDY
            32 NIXON                        31 JOHNSON
            33 FORD                         32 NIXON
            34 CARTER                       33 FORD
            35 REAGAN                       34 CARTER
            36 BUSH                         35 REAGAN
            37 CLINTON                      36 BUSH
            45 DWORCZAK
            46 MILLER                       45 DWORCZAK

21 rows selected.

SQL>

End Listing
```

The employees in the Employee table do not have sequential payroll numbers. For this reason, several of the listed employees do not have a previous hired employee. The LAG/LEAD functions discussed in Chapter 9 can eliminate this problem. In fact, these functions can sometimes eliminate the need for a self join.

Cartesian Joins

A **Cartesian join** occurs when the condition that joins the tables is omit-ted. There is no specified condition; therefore, Oracle will join each record in the first table to every record in the second. This generally creates worth-less information. It also causes Oracle to create and process a large amount of data.

The Department table in our practice database contains 5 records. The Employee table contains 21 records. Properly joining these two tables will result in 21 virtual records. Listing 5.7 illustrates a SELECT statement that joins these tables. This query does not have a join condition. This will cause a Cartesian join. This query returned 105 records (5 * 21).

Listing 5.7 *Counting the Records Returned from a Cartesian Join of the Department and Employee Tables*

```
SQL> select count(*) from department, employee;

 COUNT(*)
---------
      105

SQL>

End listing
```

This should illustrate the tremendous amount of processing that Oracle must do to compute the results of a Cartesian join. In addition to the extra memory and processing that occurs, the information produced is usually worthless. It is very common for a user to forget join conditions in a query. Most databases are large, and the Cartesian product that the error produces may take a great deal of time to process and, in fact, may never return the results (your DBA will kill the query). This brings up an important check that you should do before executing a SELECT statement:

> **Tip** *Always check your WHERE clause before executing a SELECT state-ment that joins tables. You should have one less join condition than the number of tables listed in the FROM clause.*

Computing Group Values

The SELECT command can be used to compute values for groups of records. These values consist of sums, averages, counts, maximum values, minimum values, standard deviations, and variances. Groups are based on common values in a column(s).

In order to understand groups, we can begin by looking at Table 5.1. It holds tool purchase records. The Employee column contains several records with the same value.

Table 5.2 displays the virtual records that would be created by grouping the records displayed in Table 5.1. The grouping is based on common values in the Employee column. When records are grouped, one virtual record is created for each distinct group value.

Table 5.2 also displays the group values that are computed for each group. They consist of the sum of the purchases and the number of purchases for each employee.

Table 5.1 *Tool Purchase Records*

EMPLOYEE	TOOL COST
B	30
A	15
A	20
C	5
A	17
C	23
A	7

Table 5.2 *Tool Purchases Grouped by Employee*

EMPLOYEE	TOOL COST SUM	RECORD COUNT
B	30	1
A	59	4
C	28	2

Group Functions

Oracle provides a number of functions that can be performed on a group:

- AVG   Computes the average value for the group
- COUNT   Tabulates the number of record instances in a group
- MAX   Determines the maximum value in the group
- MIN   Determines the minimum value in the group
- STDDEV   Computes the standard deviation for the group
- SUM   Computes the sum of the groups values
- VARIANCE   Computes the variance of the group

Counting the Group's Record Instances

The COUNT function is used to compute the number of records containing a not null value in the target column from the specified group. Listing 5.8 illustrates the use of this function. It is used to compute the number of records in the Employee table that have a not null value in the Last_name column. The count column is placed in parentheses following the COUNT function.

Listing 5.8 *Counting the Number of Values in the Last_name Column*

```
SQL> select count(last_name) from employee;

COUNT(LAST_NAME)
----------------
              21

SQL>

End listing
```

Records that have a null value in the count column are not counted. If you would like to count the number of records in a group without worrying whether a column is null, substitute an asterisk (*) for the name of the column. The asterisk is a symbol that means "all values in the selected virtual record."

The DISTINCT keyword can be used with the COUNT function. This keyword discards duplicate records from the target group. When the duplicates are discarded, the results are the number of individual values. Listing 5.9 illustrates the DISTINCT keyword by executing the same SELECT statement as Listing 5.8. The only difference is the addition of the DISTINCT keyword and the Last_name column, which will cause the duplicate Roosevelt and Johnson records to be discarded. Notice the difference.

Listing 5.9 *Counting the Distinct or Unique Last_name Values*

```
SQL> select count(distinct last_name) from employee;

COUNT(DISTINCTLAST_NAME)
------------------------
                      18

SQL>

End listing
```

Summing the Values in a Group

Group values can be added or summed by using the SUM function. Listing 5.10 illustrates the use of this function to determine the cost of all employee tool purchases. The syntax of this function is the keyword SUM followed by the name of the column to be summed in parentheses.

Listing 5.10 *Computing the Total Cost of Tool Purchases by Using the SUM Group Function*

```
SQL> select sum(tool_cost) from emp_tools;

SUM(TOOL_COST)
--------------
       1190.85

SQL>

End Listing
```

Averaging the Values in a Group

The AVG group function illustrated in Listing 5.11 is used to compute the average value of a group.

Listing 5.11 *Computing the Average Tool Cost by Using the AVG Group Function*

```
SQL> select avg(tool_cost) from emp_tools;

AVG(TOOL_COST)
--------------
        35.025

SQL>

End listing
```

If your data contain null values, you can possibly calculate erroneous values with the AVG function. Zero values cause the denominator to increase, while leaving the numerator unchanged. However, null values are removed from the evaluation set; therefore, the denominator will not be incremented as it would be if the null value were zero. The denominator is smaller than it would be if the value contained a zero; therefore, the average will be larger. When using the AVG function, be sure your result set does not contain null values. The NVL function can be used to populate a null value (see Listing 5.14).

Determining the Minimum Value

The MIN function is used to determine a group's smallest value. This function can be used on numeric and alphanumeric values. Listing 5.12 illustrates the use of the MIN function to determine the employee with the smallest value name.

Listing 5.12 *Determining the Employee Last Name with the Smallest Value by Using the MIN Function*

```
SQL> select min(last_name) from employee;

MIN(LAST_NAME)
--------------
```

```
ANTHONY

SQL>

End listing
```

Determining the Maximum Value

The MAX function is used to determine the largest value in a group. This function can be used for numeric and alphanumeric values. Listing 5.13 illustrates the use of this command to determine the employee last name with the greatest value.

Listing 5.13 *Determining the Employee Last Name with the Largest Value by Using the MAX Function*

```
SQL> select max(last_name) from employee;

MAX(LAST_NAME)
--------------
WILSON

SQL>

End listing
```

Using the Group Functions on Smaller Groups

The queries that we have illustrated thus far in this section have employed the group functions against the entire table. In each of the queries, the group consisted of the entire table's records. Oracle also allows you to combine a table's records into smaller groups. The GROUP BY clause of the SELECT statement is used to identify the grouping columns, which are the columns whose distinct set of values identifies a group. In table 5.1, distinct values of the Employee column formed the different groups. In Table 5.2, you can see that three groups were identified.

The following are important rules concerning the GROUP BY clause:

- It can contain multiple columns and expressions.
- Commas separate the column names.
- It must contain all of the columns listed in the SELECT clause that a group function is not using.

Listing 5.14 illustrates a query that uses the GROUP BY clause. The query determines the number of tool purchases and the total and average tool costs per employee. In this query, the group consists of records that have the same value in the employee Last_name and First_name columns.

Listing 5.14 *Computing the Number of Tool Purchases, the Total Tool Purchase Cost, and the Average Tool Cost Per Employee*

```
SQL> select last_name, first_name,
  2    count(tool_cost) count, sum(tool_cost) sum,
  3    avg(nvl(tool_cost,0)) avg
  3  from employee, emp_tools
  4  where payroll_number = fk_payroll_number(+)
  5  group by last_name, first_name;
```

LAST_NAME	FIRST_NAME	COUNT	SUM	AVG
ANTHONY	SUSANNE	3	88.85	29.616667
BUSH	GEORGE	3	46.2	15.4
CARTER	JIMMY	0		0
CLINTON	WILLIAM	0		0
COOLIDGE	CALVIN	2	35	17.5
DWORCZAK	ALICE	0		0
EISENHOWER	DWIGHT	3	375	125
FORD	GERALD	3	12	4
HOOVER	HERBERT	2	24	12
JOHNSON	ANDREW	2	16.7	8.35
JOHNSON	LYNDON	0		0
KENNEDY	JOHN	0		0
MILLER	KEVIN	0		0
NIXON	RICHARD	2	18.5	9.25
REAGAN	RONALD	3	28.7	9.5666667
ROOSEVELT	ELEANOR	3	61.95	20.65
ROOSEVELT	FRANKLIN	2	20	10
ROOSEVELT	THEODORE	2	324	162

```
TAFT            WILLIAM         1              23                  23
TRUMAN          HAROLD          0                                   0
WILSON          WOODROW         3            116.95          38.983333

21 rows selected.

SQL>

End listing
```

The NVL function was used with the AVG function. It is used to substitute a zero value for all null tool cost values used with the function. This function was needed in order to calculate the correct average tool cost. Several of the employees did not have tool purchases. A value of zero was computed for the average tool cost for each of these employees. A null value was computed for some of the sums of the tool costs because the NVL function was not used with the SUM function.

Limiting Selected Records by Using a Group Function

The last SELECT statement clause to be discussed is the HAVING clause. This clause is similar to the WHERE clause in that it determines whether the record is eligible for selection. The clause contains arguments used to evaluate records. Multiple conditions can be placed in the HAVING clause. The AND and OR keywords can also be used within the clause to develop complex logic.

The difference between the HAVING clause and the WHERE clause is that one of the arguments in a HAVING clause condition must be a group function. The HAVING clause is used only when a grouped value is computed by the SELECT statement. This requires a group function to exist in the SELECT clause. Listing 5.15 illustrates this clause.

Listing 5.15 *Using the HAVING Clause to Select Employees Who Have Total Tool Purchases Greater Than $100*

```
SQL> select last_name, first_name, sum(tool_cost)
  2  from employee, emp_tools
```

```
3  where payroll_number = fk_payroll_number
4  group by last_name, first_name
5  having sum(tool_cost) > 100;
```

```
LAST_NAME          FIRST_NAME        SUM(TOOL_COST)
---------------    ---------------   --------------
EISENHOWER         DWIGHT                       375
ROOSEVELT          THEODORE                     324
WILSON             WOODROW                   116.95


SQL >

End Listing
```

What's Next?

The next chapter begins the discussion of functions. A function is an Oracle object that returns a value. Oracle has a large variety of functions. The next chapter covers the character functions, which can be used to determine the length of a value, to change the characters to uppercase, or to extract a set of characters from a target value.

▪ PRACTICE

1. From the database select the employees who have purchased glasses. Display the last name, first name, eyeglasses purchase date, and optician.

2. From the database select the employees who have purchased glasses and the employees who have not purchased glasses. Display the last name, first name, eyeglasses purchase date, and optician.

3. From the database select the employees who have purchased glasses. Display the department name, last name, first name, eyeglasses purchase date, and optician.

4. Reperform question 3. Be sure to qualify each of the columns this time.

5. Determine the minimum wages paid to an employee.

6. Determine the maximum wages paid to an employee.

7. Determine the employee's street that has the largest and smallest value.

8. Determine the number of employees in each department. Be sure to include the departments that do not have employees.

9. Determine the total eyeglasses cost per department.

10. Determine the number of eyeglasses purchases, the total cost of purchases, and the average cost of the eyeglasses per employee. Be sure to include the employees who have not purchased any eyeglasses.

Creating New Values with Character Functions

Oracle has included a number of functions that are used to modify alphanumeric data types. These are the character types VARCHAR and CHAR. The functions may be used as expressions in the SELECT clause or as arguments in the WHERE clause. We have seen one of these functions in a previous chapter: The concatenation operator (| |) was used to combine several column values and a text literal into a new combined value. This chapter will cover other character functions that are available to perform specialized manipulation of character data.

Character Functions

Table 6.1 lists and briefly describes the various character functions.

The INITCAP Function

The INITCAP function is used to modify character values. This function capitalizes the first letter of each set of characters in a character string. The characters following the capitalized character are made lowercase. To illustrate this, Listing 6.1 contains a query that uses this function to capitalize the first letter of two text literals contained in SELECT clause expressions. The initial value of the expression literal is all capital letters. The function modifies this value so that the first character is capitalized, and the remainder are converted to lowercase. The second expression is initially all lowercase characters. The

Table 6.1 *Character Functions*

Function	Format	Description
||	'*string*'||'*string*'	Combines two *strings*
ASCII	ASCII('*string*')	Returns the ASCII value of the first character of the *string*
CHR	CHR(*integer*)	Returns the character-equivalent ASCII value of the specified integer
INITCAP	INITCAP('*string*')	Changes the first letter of the *string* to upper-case (The remaining letters are made lowercase.)
INSTR	INSTR('*string*', set [, Start[, occurrence]])	Determines the beginning location of a set of characters in a *string* that match a specified character set
LENGTH	LENGTH('*string*')	Returns the length of the *string*
LOWER	LOWER('*string*')	Converts the entire *string* to lowercase
LPAD	LPAD('*string*', *length*, [',*set*'])	Changes the target *string* into a string with a specific length by adding a specified set of characters to the left of the string
LTRIM	LTRIM('*string*' [',*set*'])	Trims characters from the left side of a *string* (The characters are trimmed if they match any character in the specified character set.)
REPLACE	REPLACE('*string*','*search string*','*replacement string*')	Exchanges a set of characters with a replacement set of characters
RPAD	RPAD('*string*', *length*, [',*set*'])	Changes the target *string* into a string with a specific *length* by adding a specified set of characters to the right of the *string*
RTRIM	RTRIM('*string*' [',*set*'])	Trims characters from the right side of a *string* (The characters are trimmed if they match any character in the specified character set.)
SOUNDEX	SOUNDEX('*string*')	Converts a *string* to a code value and is used to compare strings that might have small differences in spelling but sound alike (or have the same SOUNDEX value)
SUBSTR	SUBSTR('*string*', *start*, *count*)	Extracts a piece of a *string* beginning at the *start* position in the specified *string* (The number of characters to extract is determined by the *count* parameter.)

Table 6.1 *(continued)*

Function	Format	Description
TO_CHAR	TO_CHAR(*'number'*)	Changes a noncharacter value into a character value
TRANSLATE	TRANSLATE('string', if, then)	Changes a *string*, character-by-character, based on a positional matching of characters in the IF *string* with characters in the THEN *string*
TRIM	TRIM(*option* from *'string'*)	Removes a specified character from the beginning, end, or both the beginning and end of a string of characters
UPPER	UPPER(*'string'*)	Converts the entire string to uppercase

INITCAP function is again used to capitalize the first character, and the remainder are left lowercase.

Listing 6.1 *Using the INITCAP Function to Capitalize the First Letter of a String*

```
SQL> select initcap('WILLIAM CLINTON'), initcap('william clinton')
  2  from dual;

INITCAP('WILLIA INITCAP('WILLIA
--------------- ---------------
William Clinton William Clinton

SQL>

End listing
```

The **DUAL** keyword in the FROM clause takes the place of a data table name. It is a pseudotable in Oracle, which is a real table that has one value and is used when you want to execute a SELECT statement but do not want to use a data table name. It can be used at any time in the FROM clause of the SELECT statement.

The INSTR Function

The INSTR function returns a numeric value that represents the position of a specified set of characters residing within a string. The function contains two parameters: The first is the string, and the second is the target set of characters.

Listing 6.2 illustrates a query that uses this function to determine the position of the character set *OOS* in values contained in the Last_name column. If the target string does not contain the character set, the function returns a value of 0.

Listing 6.2 *Using the INSTR Function to Determine the Position of* OOS *in a Character String*

```
SQL> select last_name, instr(last_name, 'OOS')
  2  from employee
  3  where fk_department = 'POL';


LAST_NAME          INSTR(LAST_NAME,'OOS')
---------------    ----------------------
WILSON                                  0
DWORCZAK                                0
JOHNSON                                 0
JOHNSON                                 0
CLINTON                                 0
NIXON                                   0
KENNEDY                                 0
ROOSEVELT                               2

8 rows selected.
SQL>
```

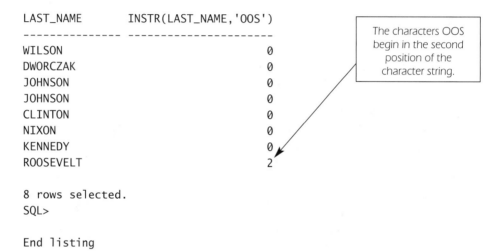

The characters OOS begin in the second position of the character string.

End listing

The LENGTH Function

The LENGTH function returns the number of positions that are within a character string and that are occupied by an actual value. This function is of value only if the target string is VARCHAR. CHAR data types have all positions occupied by default and have the values returned by the function that will always be the same length as the length specified in the column definition within the database. For instance, the string *JOHN* is contained in a VARCHAR table column that is defined with a maximum length of 10. The value actually occupies 4 positions. The LENGTH function will return a value of 4 when used to evaluate the string. If the value *JOHN* is contained in a CHAR table column with a length of 10, the function will return a value of 10. Listing 6.3 uses this function to determine the length of values in the Last_name column.

Listing 6.3 *Using the LENGTH Function to Calculate the Number of Positions in Last_name Values*

```
SQL> select last_name, length(last_name)
  2  from employee
  3  where fk_department = 'POL';

LAST_NAME       LENGTH(LAST_NAME)
--------------- -----------------
WILSON                          6
DWORCZAK                        8
JOHNSON                         7
JOHNSON                         7
CLINTON                         7
NIXON                           5
KENNEDY                         7
ROOSEVELT                       9

8 rows selected.

SQL>

End Listing
```

The LOWER Function

The LOWER function is the second of three case-changing functions. This function makes each character in a string lowercase. Listing 6.4 illustrates the use of this command to change the Last_name values to lowercase.

Listing 6.4 *Using the LOWER Function to Change Last_name Values to Lowercase*

```
SQL> select lower('George'), lower('BUSH'), lower('Jr')
  2  from dual;

LOWER( LOWE LO
------ ---- --
george bush jr

SQL>
End listing
```

The LPAD Function

The LPAD function is used to pad the left side of a character string. The function makes each of the target strings the same overall length by placing the specified character to the left of the original value. The function contains three parameters: The first is the name of the string, the second is the new length of the string, and the third is the character(s) used to pad the string. In Listing 6.5, the Last_name values are changed to a length of 25. In addition, an asterisk is placed in each unoccupied position to the left of the value.

Listing 6.5 *Using the LPAD Function to Pad the Left Side of the Last_name Values*

```
SQL> select lpad(last_name, 25, '*')
  2  from employee
  3  where fk_department = 'POL';


LPAD(LAST_NAME,25,'*')
-------------------------
*******************WILSON
*****************DWORCZAK
******************JOHNSON
******************JOHNSON
******************CLINTON
********************NIXON
*******************KENNEDY
****************ROOSEVELT

8 rows selected.

SQL>

End Listing
```

The LTRIM Function

The LTRIM function is used to remove characters from the left side of a character string, and it does so until it encounters a target-string character that does not exist in the target set of characters. As an example, the query in Listing 6.6 uses the function to remove characters from the Last_name values.

The target character set is *RON*. One of the values returned by the query is *ROOSEVELT.* The function removed the first three characters because they resided in the target character set. In another row, the *N* is removed from the *NIXON* value because the first character is in the target character set. The remainder of the values is unchanged because the first character of the strings is not contained in the set.

Listing 6.6 *Using the LTRIM Function to Trim the Characters* R, O, *and* N *from the Left Side of the Last_name Values*

```
SQL> select last_name, ltrim(last_name, 'RON')
  2  from employee
  3  where fk_department = 'POL';

LAST_NAME        LTRIM(LAST_NAME
---------------  ---------------
WILSON           WILSON
DWORCZAK         DWORCZAK
JOHNSON          JOHNSON
JOHNSON          JOHNSON
CLINTON          CLINTON
NIXON            IXON
KENNEDY          KENNEDY
ROOSEVELT        SEVELT

8 rows selected.

SQL>

End listing
```

The REPLACE Function

The REPLACE function is used to exchange a character string with another character string. The function has three parameters:

1. The target character string

2. The search character string

3. The replacement character string

Listing 6.7 illustrates the REPLACE function, used to replace the characters *OO* with the characters *AA*.

Listing 6.7 *Using the REPLACE Function to Exchange Characters*

```
SQL> select replace(last_name, 'OO', 'AA')
  2  from employee
  3  where last_name like 'ROOS%';

REPLACE(LAST_NAME,'OO','AA')
----------------------------
RAASEVELT
RAASEVELT
RAASEVELT

SQL>

End listing
```

The RPAD Function

The RPAD function is used to make a character string a specified length. It does this by padding the right side of the target value with a specified target character. Listing 6.8 illustrates a query that uses the RPAD function to change the length of the Last_name values to 25. The function also places an asterisk in all unfilled positions to the right of the value.

Listing 6.8 *Using the RPAD Function to Place Asterisks to the Right of the Last_name Values*

```
SQL> select rpad(last_name, 25, '*')
  2  from employee
  3  where fk_department = 'POL';

RPAD(LAST_NAME,25,'*')
------------------------
WILSON*******************
DWORCZAK*****************
JOHNSON******************
JOHNSON******************
CLINTON******************
```

```
NIXON********************
KENNEDY******************
ROOSEVELT****************

8 rows selected.

SQL>

End listing
```

The RTRIM Function

The RTRIM function is used to trim characters from the right side of a value. This function evaluates string characters from right to left. It removes the characters if they match a character in the target set. Removal is stopped when a character that does not exist in the target list of characters is encountered. Listing 6.9 illustrates a query that uses the RTRIM function to remove the characters *O*, *N*, and *L* from the right side of the Last_name values.

Listing 6.9 *Using the RTRIM Function to Remove ONL Characters from the Right Side of the Last_name Values*

```
SQL> select last_name, rtrim(last_name, 'ONL')
  2  from employee
  3  where fk_department = 'POL';

LAST_NAME        RTRIM(LAST_NAME
---------------  ---------------
WILSON           WILS
DWORCZAK         DWORCZAK
JOHNSON          JOHNS
JOHNSON          JOHNS
CLINTON          CLINT
NIXON            NIX
KENNEDY          KENNEDY
ROOSEVELT        ROOSEVELT

8 rows selected.

SQL>

End Listing
```

The SOUNDEX Function

The SOUNDEX function is used to evaluate the sound of a value. This function returns a numeric value based on an algorithm. Like-sounding values will have the same SOUNDEX value even if they are not spelled the same. For example, the values *SUN* and *SON* have the same SOUNDEX value. This function is normally used in the WHERE clause to create arguments based on the SOUNDEX value rather than on the actual value. To be effective, both arguments in the condition must employ the function. Listing 6.10 illustrates a query that uses this function to retrieve employee records that have a Last_name value that sounds like *JOHNSEN*.

Listing 6.10 *Using the SOUNDEX Function to Retrieve Records That Have a Last_name Value Sounding like JOHNSEN*

```
SQL> select last_name, soundex(last_name), soundex('JOHNSEN')
  2  from employee
  3  where soundex(last_name) = soundex('JOHNSEN');

LAST_NAME       SOUN SOUN
--------------- ---- ----
JOHNSON         J525 J525
JOHNSON         J525 J525

SQL>

End listing
```

The following describe how the SOUNDEX algorithm encodes a word:

1. The first character of the string is retained as the first character of the SOUNDEX code.

2. The following letters are discarded from the string: *a, e, i, o, u, h, w,* and *y*.

3. If consonants having the same code number appear consecutively, the number will be coded once (e.g., *J244* becomes *J24*).

4. The following is a list of consonants and codes:
b, p, f, v   1

c, s, k, g, j, q, x, z	2
d, t	3
l	4
m, n	5

5. The resulting code is then modified so that it becomes exactly four characters. If it is less than four characters, zeros are added to the end. If it is more than four characters, the code is truncated.

After analyzing the first step in the algorithm, you might deduce that the SOUNDEX function does not identify values that sound the same but start with different letters. For example, the values *Karl* and *Carl* will have different values. The SOUNDEX function can be effective, but it is not infallible.

The SUBSTR Function

The SUBSTR function is a commonly used function that extracts a set of characters from a string. The extraction is started at a specified position. The function has three parameters:

- String name
- Extraction start position
- Number of characters to extract

Listing 6.11 illustrates an example of this function. It is used to extract three characters from the Last_name values. The extraction begins at the third position. If the third parameter is omitted, Oracle returns all characters to the end of the string.

Listing 6.11 *Using the SUBSTR Function to Extract Characters from the Last_name Values*

```
SQL> select last_name, substr(last_name, 3,3)
  2  from employee
  3  where fk_department = 'POL';

LAST_NAME       SUB
--------------- ---
WILSON          LSO
```

```
DWORCZAK          ORC
JOHNSON           HNS
JOHNSON           HNS
CLINTON           INT
NIXON             XON
KENNEDY           NNE
ROOSEVELT         OSE

8 rows selected.

SQL>

End Listing
```

The TO_CHAR Function

The TO_CHAR function is used to convert a value to a character string. A common use of this function is to convert a date into a different format or date picture. This will be discussed in the next chapter.

The TRANSLATE Function

The TRANSLATE function is used to change characters within a string to a new value. The function examines each character in the target string and changes characters to a different value if it matches a specified character. Listing 6.12 illustrates a query that changes an *O* character to an *A* character in the Last_name values.

Listing 6.12 *Using the TRANSLATE Function to Change the Letter* O *to* A

```
SQL> select last_name, translate(last_name, 'O', 'A')
  2  from employee
  3  where fk_department = 'POL';

LAST_NAME         TRANSLATE(LAST_
---------------   ---------------
WILSON            WILSAN
DWORCZAK          DWARCZAK
JOHNSON           JAHNSAN
```

```
JOHNSON      JAHNSAN
CLINTON      CLINTAN
NIXON        NIXAN
KENNEDY      KENNEDY
ROOSEVELT    RAASEVELT

8 rows selected.

SQL>

End listing
```

The TRIM Function

The TRIM function is similar to the RTRIM and LTRIM functions. The difference is that the function can trim characters from the right end, left end, and both ends of the target character string. The function has three options:

LEADING	Trims characters from the beginning of the target string
TRAILING	Trims characters from the end of the target string
BOTH	Trims characters from both ends of the target string

A syntax template for the function is listed in Table 6.1. An option identification keyword precedes the TRIM character within the function parameter. The TRIM character is followed by the FROM keyword. The target string follows the FROM keyword. If a TRIM character is not specified, white-space characters will be removed.

Listing 6.13 illustrates the function. The first expression in the SELECT statement uses the TRIM function to remove the character *R* from the beginning of the character string. The second expression uses the function to remove the character *N* from the end of the string. The final expression removes the *R* characters from both ends of the string.

Listing 6.13 *Using the TRIM Function to Remove Characters*

```
SQL> select trim(leading 'R' from last_name) "Leading Option",
  2         trim(trailing 'N' from last_name) "Trailing Option",
```

```
  3           trim(both 'R' from last_name) "Both Option"
  4   from employee
  5   where last_name like 'R%'
  6      or last_name like '%N';
```

```
Leading Option  Trailing Option Both Option
--------------- --------------- ---------------
WILSON          WILSO           WILSON
OOSEVELT        ROOSEVELT       OOSEVELT
OOSEVELT        ROOSEVELT       OOSEVELT
JOHNSON         JOHNSO          JOHNSON
EAGAN           REAGA           EAGAN
JOHNSON         JOHNSO          JOHNSON
CLINTON         CLINTO          CLINTON
NIXON           NIXO            NIXON
TRUMAN          TRUMA           TRUMAN
OOSEVELT        ROOSEVELT       OOSEVELT

10 rows selected.

SQL>

End listing
```

The UPPER Function

The UPPER function is used to change the case of the characters in a string. It changes them to uppercase. This is a useful function because the Oracle database is case-sensitive. If you are not sure of the case of values in a column, you can use the UPPER function on both sides of a WHERE clause condition to ensure that both values are the same case. Listing 6.14 illustrates a query that uses this function to change a text literal to uppercase.

Listing 6.14 *Using the UPPER Function to Change Character Strings to Uppercase*

```
SQL> select upper('WiLLiam'), upper('clinton')
  2   from dual;
```

```
UPPER(' UPPER('
------- -------
WILLIAM CLINTON

SQL>

End listing
```

The DECODE Function

The DECODE function is used to change a retrieved value into another value. This function is normally used in the SELECT clause and is part of an expression. The function parameters are as follows:

> **DECODE(*Expression, Value, Replacement Value,***
> ***Value, Replacement Value,***
> ***Catch-All Replacement Value*)**

The first parameter is the column retrieved from the database. This is followed by a series of dual parameters. Each set of parameters is a possible column value and its replacement value. The last parameter is a catchall value that is used when a column value that does not match values in the list of previous values is encountered.

Listing 6.15 illustrates this function. The function is used to change the Fk_department value into the full department name. The catchall value for the function is *UNKNOWN,* which is the value that will be returned if the retrieved value does not exist in the DECODE list.

Listing 6.15 *Using the DECODE Function to Change the Value of the Fk_department Column*

```
SQL> select fk_department,
  2  decode(fk_department, 'POL', 'POLITICAL SCIENCE',
  3         'WEL', 'WELFARE','UNKNOWN'), last_name, first_name
  4  from employee
  5  ;

FK_D DECODE(FK_DEPARTM LAST_NAME       FIRST_NAME
---- ----------------- --------------- ---------------
WEL  WELFARE           HOOVER          HERBERT
POL  POLITICAL SCIENCE WILSON          WOODROW
```

```
WEL   WELFARE            TAFT          WILLIAM
INT   UNKNOWN            ROOSEVELT     THEODORE
WEL   WELFARE            ANTHONY       SUSANNE
WEL   WELFARE            ROOSEVELT     ELEANOR
INT   UNKNOWN            COOLIDGE      CALVIN
INT   UNKNOWN            MILLER        KEVIN
POL   POLITICAL SCIENCE  DWORCZAK      ALICE
POL   POLITICAL SCIENCE  JOHNSON       LYNDON
WEL   WELFARE            REAGAN        RONALD
INT   UNKNOWN            BUSH          GEORGE
POL   POLITICAL SCIENCE  JOHNSON       ANDREW
POL   POLITICAL SCIENCE  CLINTON       WILLIAM
WEL   WELFARE            CARTER        JIMMY
INT   UNKNOWN            FORD          GERALD
POL   POLITICAL SCIENCE  NIXON         RICHARD
POL   POLITICAL SCIENCE  KENNEDY       JOHN
INT   UNKNOWN            EISENHOWER    DWIGHT
INT   UNKNOWN            TRUMAN        HAROLD
POL   POLITICAL SCIENCE  ROOSEVELT     FRANKLIN

21 rows selected.

SQL>

End Listing
```

Another use of the DECODE function is to create a special sorting order. The normal sort orders are ascending and descending. If you were able to change the value used for sorting, it would be possible to arrange values in different orders. In Listing 6.16, each of the Fk_department values is given a specific numeric value which allows the displayed values to be sorted in a special manner.

Listing 6.16 *Using the DECODE Function to Change the Sorting of the Returned Records*

```
SQL> select department, department_name
  2  from department
  3  order by decode(department, 'POL', 5, 'TRF', 1,
  4                              'WEL', 2, 'CEN', 3, 4  'INT', 4);
```

```
DEPA DEPARTMENT_NAME
---- ---------------
TRF  TRESURY DEPAR
WEL  WELFARE BUREAU
CEN  CENSUS DEPT
INT  INTERIOR DESIGN
POL  POLITICAL SCIEN

SQL>

End listing
```

Oracle is planning to drop the DECODE function in future releases and to replace the function with the CASE statement, discussed in the next section.

Case Expressions

Case expressions are an Oracle tool similar in nature to the DECODE statement. CASE statements offer the business analyst added flexibility and logical power, and they are easier to read than the DECODE statement. A CASE statement is a good tool for breaking data into classes or buckets. A syntax template of the statement follows:

Case when *condition1* **then** *expression1*
    When *condition2* **then** *expression2*
        [Else] *expression2a*
End

Listing 6.17 illustrates the use of a CASE statement to create a histogram-type report. The report counts the number of employees who have wages within specific classes. The classes consist of $5,000 increments. A SUM group function is created for each class. A CASE statement is then placed inside the group function. If the employee Wages value meets the criteria in the WHEN clause, a value of 1 is added to the summary. If it does not, a value of 0 is added to the summary.

Listing 6.17 *Using the CASE Statement to Compute a Histogram Displaying the Number of Employees in a Wages Class*

```
SQL> select sum(case when nvl(wages,0) between 0 and 5000
  2                      then 1 else 0 end) as "0 to 5000",
  3         sum(case when nvl(wages,0) between 5001 and 10000
  2                      then 1 else 0 end) as "5001 to 10000",
  3         sum(case when nvl(wages,0) between 10001 and 15000
  4                      then 1 else 0 end) as "10001 to 15000",
  5         sum(case when nvl(wages,0) between 15001 and 20000
  6                      then 1 else 0 end) as "15001 to 20000"
  5  from employee;

0 to 5000 5001 to 10000 10001 to 15000 15001 to 20000
--------- ------------- -------------- --------------
        2             9             10              0

SQL>
```

End Listing

Listing 6.18 depicts another query that determines the number of tools per Tool Cost class. The output of this query consists of consecutive rows. A row is created for each Tool Cost class. The row contains a class description and a count of the tools in the class. The CASE statement is used in two places within the query. The first is in the SELECT clause. The CASE statement evaluates each Tool Cost value and assigns a class description to the record. The CASE statement is also used in the GROUP BY clause. The statement performs the same basic function as it did in the SELECT clause. It translates the Tool Cost values into class descriptions. These unique descriptions are then used to identify the classes for the COUNT function.

Listing 6.18 *Using CASE Statements in the SELECT and WHERE Clauses to Count the Number of Tool Purchases Per Tool Cost Class*

```
SQL> select (case when tool_cost >= 0 and tool_cost <= 10
  2                    then '0 to 10'
  3              when tool_cost > 10 and tool_cost <= 20
  4                    then '10.01 to 20'
  5              when tool_cost > 20 and tool_cost <= 30
```

```
6                       then '20.01 to 30'
7                 when tool_cost > 30 then 'Above 30' end)
8                 "Tool Costs", count(*) as amount
9  from emp_tools
10 group by (case when tool_cost >= 0
11                and tool_cost <= 10 then '0 to 10'
12           when tool_cost > 10 and tool_cost <= 20
13                   then '10.01 to 20'
14           when tool_cost > 20 and tool_cost <= 30
15                   then '20.01 to 30'
16           when tool_cost > 30 then 'Above 30' end);
```

```
Tool Costs      AMOUNT
----------- ---------
0 to 10             15
10.01 to 20          7
20.01 to 30          3
Above 30             9

SQL>

End Listing
```

Using Functions in the WHERE Clause

It is important to understand one of the effects of using a function as an argument in a WHERE clause. In a WHERE clause condition, one of the arguments is a table column. Indexes are often placed on table columns used for selection criteria. This helps Oracle identify the records more efficiently. If the query uses a function on a table column argument, it is essentially changing its format. This means that Oracle cannot use the table column's index.

For example, if you store data in a table column in uppercase, the values placed in an associated index are also uppercase. If the table column is used in the WHERE clause in conjunction with a function such as INITCAP, the computed arguments will not match the indexed values. Oracle will not be able to use the index and will be forced to perform a full table scan.

You need to be aware that a function used in the WHERE clause can dramatically reduce the response of the query. If it is necessary to use one, you may have to consider having a function-based index created. This type of index is discussed in Chapter 12.

What's Next?

The next chapter continues the discussion of functions. The chapter will cover numeric and date functions, as well as date pictures. We will also discuss the TO_CHAR function, which is used to reformat dates, and we will identify the various date formats.

PRACTICE

1. Select the department names and employee names from the database. The department name should be lowercase, the last name should be uppercase, and only the first character of the first name should be capitalized.

2. Select the department names and employee last names. The department name should be 20 characters, and the names should be preceded by the number sign (#). The last names should be 25 characters, and the minus sign (–) should follow the value.

3. Concatenate the first and last names of the employees. Determine the length of the new values.

4. Extract two characters from the employee's first name. The extraction should begin at the second position.

Creating New Values with Numeric and Date Functions

Oracle has a variety of numeric functions that can be used in the SELECT statement. These functions are used to populate null-value columns, to compute values such as sine or cosine, or simply to round values. Table 7.1 contains a listing of the various numeric functions.

The MOD and TO_NUMBER Functions

The MOD function is used to determine the modulus or remainder of a division operation. I have used it to calculate finish dates in scheduling applications. I divide the task hours by 40. Any remainder indicates that the task will be completed in less than a week. I use the MOD function to help me determine the portion (e.g., hours or days) of the week that the task will consume. I can then compute the finish date of the task. The function can be used in any other calculation in which the remainder is of value. Listing 7.1 illustrates a query that uses the function to determine whether a year is divisible by 4. This is a simple but not entirely accurate way to determine whether a year is a leap year.

The query uses several nested functions. The innermost function is TO_CHAR, which is used to change the employee's birth date into a character field. The SUBSTR function is then used to extract the year from the character string. The TO_NUMBER function is then used to convert the character year to a numeric field for use in the MOD function. Finally, the MOD function is used to divide the numeric year by 4. If the remainder is equal to 0, the employee was likely born during a leap year.

Table 7.1 *Numeric Functions*

Function	Syntax	Description
+	*Value1 + value2*	Addition
−	*Value2 – value6*	Subtraction
*	*Value3 * value4*	Multiplication
/	Value1 / value2	Division
ABS	ABS(*value*)	Absolute value
CEIL	CEIL(*value*)	Determines the smallest integer greater than or equal to the *value*
COS	COS(*value*)	Cosine of the *value*
COSH	COSH(*value*)	Hyperbolic cosine of the *value*
EXP	EXP(*value*)	*E* raised to the *value*th power
FLOOR	FLOOR(*value*)	Largest integer less than or equal to the *value*
LN	LN(*value*)	Natural (base e) logarithm of the *value*
LOG	LOG(*base, value*)	Base *base* logarithm of the *value*
MOD	MOD(*value, divisor*)	Determines the remainder
NULLIF	NULLIF(*expression1, expression2*)	Compares the two expressions (If they are equal, it returns a null value. If they are not equal, it returns *expression1*.)
NVL	NVL(*column name, substitute value*)	Substitutes a new *value* for a null value
NVL2	NVl2(*column name, not null substitute value, null substitute value*)	Substitutes a new value for both null values and not null
POWER	POWER(*value, exponent*)	*Value* raised to an exponent
ROUND	ROUND(*value, precision*)	Rounds a *value* to the specified *precision*
SIGN	SIGN(*value*)	Displays a −1 if the *value* is negative, and a +1 if the *value* is positive
SIN	SIN(*value*)	Sine of the *value*
SINH	SINH(*value*)	Hyperbolic sine of the *value*

Table 7.1 *(continued)*

Function	Syntax	Description
SQRT	SQRT(*value*)	Square root of the *value*
TAN	TAN(*value*)	Tangent of the *value*
TANH	TANH(*value*)	Hyperbolic tangent of the *value*
TO_NUMBER	TO_NUMBER(*value*)	Changes the *value* to a numeric format value
TRUNC	TRUNC(*value*, *precision*)	Truncates the *value* to the specified *precision*

Listing 7.1 *Using the MOD Function to Determine Employees Born in a Leap Year*

```
SQL> select last_name, birth_date,
  2  mod(to_number(substr(birth_date, 8, 2)), 4)
  3  from employee
  4  where fk_department = 'POL';

LAST_NAME       BIRTH_DAT MOD(TO_NUMBER(SUBSTR(BIRTH_DATE,8,2)),4)
--------------- --------- ----------------------------------------
WILSON          28-DEC-56                                        0
DWORCZAK        23-MAR-55                                        3
JOHNSON         27-AUG-08                                        0
JOHNSON         29-DEC-08                                        0
CLINTON         03-APR-40                                        0
NIXON           27-AUG-08                                        0
KENNEDY         29-MAY-17                                        1
ROOSEVELT       30-JAN-82                                        2

8 rows selected.

SQL>

End listing
```

born in a leap year

Using the NVL and the NVL2 Functions

The NVL function is used to replace a null value with another value. It can be used with numeric and non-numeric data type values. It is an extremely important function if the AVG group function is used in the query. The AVG function will calculate incorrect averages if the target set of values contains nulls because null values do not equal 0 and will not be included in the divisor as a 0 value would. The divisor of a set of values that has values of 0 will be larger than a comparable set that contains nulls instead of 0s.

The NVL function can be used to overcome this problem. This function can replace null values with a value of 0 (or any other value), which will cause the divisor to increase and correct averages to be computed. Listing 7.2 illustrates a query that uses the NVL function to place a value of 0 in the Wages column when the value is null.

Listing 7.2 *Using the NVL Function to Populate Null Values with 0*

```
SQL> select last_name, wages, nvl(wages,0)
  2  from employee
  3  where fk_department = 'INT';


LAST_NAME            WAGES NVL(WAGES,0)
--------------- --------- ------------
ROOSEVELT             8000         8000
COOLIDGE              9500         9500
MILLER                9500         9500
BUSH                 14000        14000
FORD                 13000        13000
EISENHOWER                            0
TRUMAN               11000        11000

7 rows selected.

SQL>

End listing
```

null value replaced by 0

The NVL2 function is similar to the NVL function except that it operates on null and not null values. This function replaces null values with one value and not null values with another. The function contains three parameters: the target column, a value that replaces not null values in the target column, and a value that replaces null values in the target column.

Listing 7.3 illustrates this function. The function is used to increment any selected not null Wages value by 4 percent. The function also changes any null value to 0.

Listing 7.3 *Using the NVL2 Function to Modify Null and Not Null Values*

```
SQL> select last_name, wages, nvl2(wages, wages*1.04, 0)
  2  from employee
  3  where last_name like 'R%';

LAST_NAME            WAGES NVL2(WAGES,WAGES*1.04,0)
--------------- --------- ------------------------
ROOSEVELT            8000                     8320
ROOSEVELT                                        0
REAGAN           16538.08                17199.603
ROOSEVELT           10400                    10816

SQL>

End Listing
```

The ROUND Function

The ROUND function is used to round a numeric value to a specified precision. If the value is less than 5, the function rounds down. If the value is greater than or equal to 5, the function rounds the value up. The function contains two parameters: The first is the value or column name, and the second is the precision. Listing 7.4 illustrates a query that rounds a calculated value. The first function has a precision setting of 2, which causes the value to be rounded to hundredths. The second function has a setting of –2, which causes the precision to be set at hundreds.

Listing 7.4 *Using the ROUND Function to Round to the Nearest Hundredth and Hundred*

```
SQL> select last_name, wages/3,
  2          round(wages/2,2), round(wages/3,-2)
  3  from employee
  4  where fk_department = 'INT';
```

```
LAST_NAME          WAGES/3 ROUND(WAGES/2,2) ROUND(WAGES/3,-2)
--------------- --------- ---------------- ------------------
ROOSEVELT        2666.6667             4000               2700
COOLIDGE         3166.6667             4750               3200
MILLER           3166.6667             4750               3200
BUSH             4666.6667             7000               4700
FORD             4333.3333             6500               4300
EISENHOWER
TRUMAN           3666.6667             5500               3700

7 rows selected.

SQL>

End listing
```

The TRUNC Function

The TRUNC function is used to truncate or trim values to a specified precision. The function contains two parameters: the target column or value and the specified precision. Specifying a precision of 2 will cause the value to be truncated following the hundredths. A precision of –2 will cause the value to be truncated following the hundred. Listing 7.5 illustrates a query that uses the TRUNC function. Compare the results of this query to the values in Listing 7.4.

Listing 7.5 *Using the TRUNC Function*

```
SQL> select last_name, wages/3, trunc(wages/3,2), trunc(wages/3,-2)
  2  from employee
  3  where fk_department='INT'
  4  group by last_name, wages;

LAST_NAME          WAGES/3 TRUNC(WAGES/3,2) TRUNC(WAGES/3,-2)
--------------- --------- ---------------- ------------------
BUSH             4666.6667          4666.66               4600
COOLIDGE         3166.6667          3166.66               3100
EISENHOWER
FORD             4333.3333          4333.33               4300
MILLER           3166.6667          3166.66               3100
```

```
ROOSEVELT          2666.6667          2666.66          2600
TRUMAN             3666.6667          3666.66          3600

7 rows selected.

SQL>

End listing
```

Dates and Date Functions

Oracle has a number of functions that are used with date columns. Dates are a specially formatted table column. Within the database table, dates are stored as a numeric value. However, the date is displayed in a character format. This allows the developer to calculate dates and still present the date in a readable fashion. Dates can be used in addition and subtraction operations. A value can be added to a date, and another date will be presented. Two dates can be subtracted with a numeric value as the result. Date values have the following components:

- Day of the month
- Month
- Year (including the century)
- Hour of the day
- Minutes of the hour
- Seconds of the minute

The hour, minute, and second values are stored as the decimal portion of the date value. The default date format of an Oracle date is military (08-APR-51). The century is not shown by default. However, Oracle does store the century in the database. By default, Oracle will set the century component if it is not specified at the time the date is modified.

Oracle uses a special calculation when populating the century by default. If the two-digit-year value is between 50 and 99, Oracle will consider the twentieth century the default (e.g., 1950–1999). If the two-digit-year value is between 00 and 49, Oracle will consider the twenty-first century the default (e.g., 2000–2049). The characters *DD-MON-RR* are used to denote the characteristics of the default date. This set of characters is called a date picture. The *DD* characters represent the day of the month. The *MON* characters represent the month in the format of *APR.* The *RR* characters represent a two-digit year and tell Oracle to use the discussed formula for determining the default century. This format is the default. If the *YY* characters are used, the default century will always be the current century. Table 7.2 further discusses the date picture characters.

To display more than the default date picture components, the TO_CHAR function must be used. This function changes the default date picture. The date picture is also used to tell Oracle the format of any nondefault-inputted dates. This function is discussed in the next section. You might also notice that the dates in our practice database range from the 1800s to the 2000s. If you do not put a century component in the arguments for your WHERE clauses, Oracle will place a 20 as the century by default. This may be the cause of some unexpected results.

Date Pictures

Date pictures determine the format in which Oracle displays dates or expects inputted dates to be formatted. The default format can be changed to a wide variety of types. Table 7.2 lists various date picture components.

Changing the Date Picture

The TO_CHAR function is used to modify the date picture. The function has two parameters: the column name (or target value) and the date picture. The date picture is enclosed by single quotation marks and contains the desired date picture components from Table 7.2. Text literals may also be added to the date picture. The text literal is enclosed by double quotation marks within the date picture parameter. The text will be displayed within the date picture, along with the other date picture components.

Listing 7.6 illustrates the TO_CHAR function and date pictures. The second expression uses the YYYY date picture component to change the date picture to display the century. The third expression contains a text literal, along with the YYYY date component. The day and month are not listed because the date picture did not contain those components.

Table 7.2 *Date Picture Components*

Picture Component	Meaning
AM or PM	Displays the meridian indicator.
A.M. or P.M.	Displays the meridian indicator with periods.
am or pm	Displays the meridian indicator in lowercase.
BC or AD	Displays BC or AD.
B.C. or A.D.	Displays B.C. or A.D.
Bc or Ad	Displays Bc or Ad.
b.c. or a.d.	Displays b.c. or a.d.
CC or SCC	Displays the century.
D	Displays the numeric day of the week.
DD	Displays the numeric date of the month (April 8 = 8).
DDD	Displays the numeric date of the year (April 8 = 98).
DY	Displays the date as a three-letter expression (MON). The entire value is uppercase.
DAY	Displays the day of the week fully spelled out (SATURDAY) in uppercase.
Day	Same as DAY, except only the initial character is uppercase (Saturday).
day	Same as DAY, except the value is lowercase (saturday).
Dy	Same as DAY, except only the first letter is uppercase.
dy	Same as DAY, except all of the letters are lowercase.
HH	Displays the hour of the day.
HH12	Same as HH.
HH24	Displays the hours of the day in military format.
J	Displays the date as a Julian date (1998098).
MI	Displays the minute of the hour.
MM	Displays the numeric month (04).
MON	Displays the abbreviated three-letter month in uppercase (APR).

Table 7.2 *Date Picture Components (continued)*

Picture Component	Meaning
Mon	Same as MON, except only the first letter of the value is capitalized (Apr).
mon	Same as MON, except the letters are lowercase (apr).
MONTH	Displays the month fully spelled out in uppercase (APRIL).
Month	Same as MONTH, except only the first letter is capitalized.
month	Same as MONTH, except the letters are lowercase.
P.M.	Displays P.M.
Q	Displays the quarter.
RM	Displays the Roman numeral month.
RR	Displays the last two digits of the year. When this picture component is used, inputted dates will default the century to the current century for year values between 00 and 49. The previous century will be the default for year values between 50 and 99.
SS	Displays the second of the minute.
SSSS	Displays the seconds since midnight. The number is always between 0 and 86,399.
SYYYY	Displays a signed year (1600 B.C. = −1600).
W	Displays the number of the week of the month.
WW	Displays the number of the week of the year.
Y	Displays the last digit of the year (8).
YY	Displays the last two digits of the year (98). When this picture component is used, inputted dates default to the current century.
YYY	Displays the last three digits of the year (998).
YYYY	Displays the four-digit year (2001).
YEAR	Displays the year fully spelled out (TWO THOUSAND ONE).
Year	Same as YEAR, except the first letter of the word is capitalized.
year	Same as YEAR, except the letters are lowercase.

Listing 7.6 *Changing Date Pictures with the TO_CHAR Function*

```
SQL> select birth_date, to_char(birth_date, 'DD-MON-YYYY'),
  2  to_char(birth_date, '"The Year of Our Lord "YYYY')
  3  from employee
  4  where fk_department = 'POL';


BIRTH_DAT TO_CHAR(BIR TO_CHAR(BIRTH_DATE,'"THEY
--------- ----------- --------------------------
28-DEC-56 28-DEC-1856 The Year of Our Lord 1856
23 MAR 55 23-MAR-1955 The Year of Our Lord 1955
27-AUG-08 27-AUG-1908 The Year of Our Lord 1908
29-DEC-08 29-DEC-1908 The Year of Our Lord 1908
03-APR-40 03-APR-1940 The Year of Our Lord 1940
27-AUG-08 27-AUG-1908 The Year of Our Lord 1908
29-MAY-17 29-MAY-1917 The Year of Our Lord 1917
30-JAN-82 30-JAN-1882 The Year of Our Lord 1882

8 rows selected.

SQL>

End Listing
```

date picture components

Date Functions

Oracle has a number of functions that are used with dates. You have already seen the TO_CHAR function used to change the format of the date. Other functions exist to compute dates or to determine the months between dates. Table 7.3 lists the date functions.

The ADD_MONTHS Function

The ADD_MONTHS function is used to compute a new date based on a specified number of months. The function enables you to determine a more accurate date than simply adding a number of days to the target date. Errors can occur in date arithmetic if the computed date occurs in a year that is different from the target date. This function is better than straight arithmetic because it is not affected by leap years.

Table 7.3 *Date Functions*

Function Name	Syntax	Description
ADD_MONTHS	ADD_MONTHS(*date, number of months*)	Adds the specified *number of months* to the *date*
GREATEST	GREATEST(*date1, date2....*)	Determines the largest date in a series of dates
LAST_DAY	LAST_DAY(*date1*)	Determines the last date of the month
MONTHS_BETWEEN	MONTHS_BETWEEN(*date1, date2*)	Determines the number of months between two dates
NEXT_DAY	NEXT_DAY(*date, 'day'*)	Determines the *date* of the next specified *day* of the week
TO_CHAR	TO_CHAR(*date, 'format'*)	Changes the format of the date
TO_DATE	TO_DATE(*string, 'format'*)	Reads a string formatted in the specified manner, and changes the data type to DATE

Listing 7.7 illustrates a query that calculates two dates. The first date expression computes a date that is 365 days later. The second date expression computes a value that is 12 months later than the target date. The former calculation is not one year away, due to the occurrence of a leap day.

Listing 7.7 *Computing Dates by Using the ADD_MONTHS Function*

```
SQL> select employment_date, employment_date+365,
  2  add_months(employment_date, 12)
  3  from employee
  4  where last_name = 'BUSH';

EMPLOYMEN EMPLOYMEN ADD_MONTH
--------- --------- ---------
05-JAN-88 04-JAN-89 05-JAN-89

SQL>

End listing
```

The LAST_DAY Function

The LAST_DAY function is used to determine the last day of the month for the specified date. If you also change the date picture to *day*, you can determine the day of the week. Listing 7.8 illustrates a query that determines the last date and day of the month.

Listing 7.8 *Using LAST_DAY Function to Determine the Last Day of the Month*

```
SQL> select birth_date, last_day(birth_date),
  2  to_char(last_day(birth_date), 'DAY')
  3  from employee
  4  where last_name = 'WILSON';

BIRTH_DAT LAST_DAY( TO_CHAR(L
--------- --------- ---------
28-DEC-56 31-DEC-56 WEDNESDAY

SQL>

End listing
```

The MONTHS_BETWEEN Function

The MONTHS_BETWEEN function is used to determine the number of months between two dates. The query in Listing 7.9 uses this function to determine the age when an employee was hired. The function is also used in the WHERE clause to select employees who were over 60 when they were hired. When using this function, a positive number will be generated if the more recent date is placed in the first function parameter. A negative number will be generated if this is reversed.

Listing 7.9 *Using the MONTHS_BETWEEN Function to Determine the Age at Employment of Employees Who Were Older Than 60 When Hired*

```
SQL> select last_name, months_between(employment_date, birth_date)/12
  2  from employee
  3  where months_between(employment_date, birth_date) > 720;
```

```
LAST_NAME        MONTHS_BETWEEN(EMPLOYMENT_DATE,BIRTH_DATE)/12
---------------  --------------------------------------------
BUSH                                                76.913978
CARTER                                              62.989247
FORD                                                60.362903
NIXON                                               60.301075
EISENHOWER                                          62.432796
TRUMAN                                              60.935484

6 rows selected.

SQL>

End listing
```

The NEXT_DAY Function

The NEXT_DAY function is used to determine the next day of the week following the specified date. The function contains two parameters: The first is the target date, and the second is the day of the week for which the function is to compute the date. Listing 7.10 contains a query that is used to compute the date of the Saturday following the employee's twenty-first birthday. The query also uses a nested ADD_MONTHS function to determine the date of the employee's twenty-first birthday. This value is then used by the NEXT_DAY function to determine the following Saturday.

Listing 7.10 *Using NEXT_DAY to Determine the Saturday Following the Employee's Twenty-First Birthday*

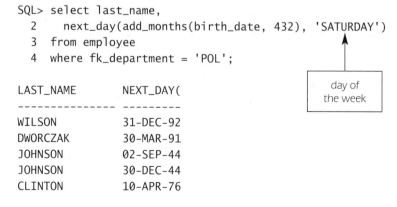

```
SQL> select last_name,
  2    next_day(add_months(birth_date, 432), 'SATURDAY')
  3  from employee
  4  where fk_department = 'POL';

LAST_NAME        NEXT_DAY(
---------------  ---------
WILSON           31-DEC-92
DWORCZAK         30-MAR-91
JOHNSON          02-SEP-44
JOHNSON          30-DEC-44
CLINTON          10-APR-76
```

day of
the week

```
NIXON          02-SEP-44
KENNEDY        30-MAY-53
ROOSEVELT      02-FEB-18

8 rows selected.

SQL>

End Listing
```

The ROUND and TRUNC Date Functions

The ROUND and TRUNC functions can also be used with dates. This is understandable because dates are numbers. Rounding is based on the middle of the target date unit. Examples of target date units are century, year, month, or week. If the date is July 1 and you want to round based on the year date unit, Oracle will return January 1 of the next year. If the TRUNC function is used with the same year date unit, Oracle will return January 1 of the same year. The functions will round to the beginning or end of the specified date unit.

The ROUND and TRUNC functions have two parameters: The first is the target date, and the second is the date unit that determines the rounding. The second parameter is actually a date format model that represents the date unit. The default date model is DD. This model will cause Oracle to round/truncate to the beginning or end of the specified date. Table 7.4 lists the various date format models.

Listing 7.11 depicts the use of the TRUNC and ROUND date functions. A SELECT statement that truncated and rounded several dates using different date format models was executed.

Listing 7.11 *Using the TRUNC and ROUND Date Functions with a Variety of Format Models*

```
SQL> select to_char(round(to_date('01-Aug-2001'), 'YY'),
  2         'DD-MON-YYYY') rnd_yr,
  3         to_char(trunc(to_date('01-Aug-2001'), 'YY'),
  4         'DD-MON-YYYY') trc_yr,
  5         to_char(round(to_date('16-Aug-2001'), 'MONTH'),
  6         'DD-MON-YYYY') rnd_mo,
  7         to_char(trunc(to_date('16-Aug-2001'), 'MONTH'),
  8         'DD-MON-YYYY') trc_mo,
```

```
 9          to_char(round(to_date('17-Aug-2001'), 'WW'),
10          'DD-MON-YYYY') rnd_wk,
11          to_char(trunc(to_date('17-Aug-2001'), 'WW'),
12          'DD-MON-YYYY') trc_wk
13   from dual;


RND_YR       TRC_YR       RND_MO       TRC_MO       RND_WK       TRC_WK
-----------  -----------  -----------  -----------  -----------  ----------
-
01-JAN-2002 01-JAN-2001 01-SEP-2001 01-AUG-2001 20-AUG-2001 13-AUG-
2001


SQL>

End Listing
```

The TO_DATE Function

The TO_DATE function is used to convert a string value into a date. This function is necessary when you want to use a value in a SELECT, UPDATE, or INSERT statement. Date values contain alphanumeric characters, but they are really a numeric value. In order to place a value into the column or to write an expression to use as a comparison argument against a date, you often must first enter the value as a string and then convert the value to a date by using the TO_DATE function. Oracle automatically handles dates that are in military format.

The TO_DATE function contains two parameters: The first is the string value or the column name that supplies the string, and the second describes the format of the string value. If the string is in the default date format (e.g., dd-mon-rr or dd-mon-yy), this parameter does not have to be used. Oracle will convert the date automatically. If it is in a different format (e.g., dd-mon-yyyy), this parameter must be used to describe the format.

Listing 7.12 illustrates a query that retrieves records for employees who were hired after January 1, 1981, and before January 1, 1991. The former date string argument is in the default Oracle date format. As a result, the TO_DATE function date picture parameter is not needed. The latter date argument is not in the default format. The TO_DATE function requires a date picture that describes how the string date argument is formatted.

Table 7.4 *ROUND and TRUNC Date Format Model*

Date Unit	Format Models
Century	CC SCC
Year	SYYYY YYYY YEAR SYEAR YYY YY Y
International Standards Organization (ISO) Year	IYYYY IY I
Quarter	Q
Month	MONTH MON MM RM
Same day of the week as the first day of the year	WW
Same day of the week as the first day of the ISO year	IW
Same day of the week as the first day of the month	W
Day	DDD DD J
Starting day of the week	DAY DY D
Hour	HH HH12 HH24
Minute	MI

Listing 7.12 *Using the TO_DATE Function to Convert String Values into Dates*

```
SQL> select last_name, employment_date
  2  from employee
  3  where employment_date > to_date('01-JAN-1981')
  4    and employment_date < to_date('19910101', 'YYYYMMDD');

LAST_NAME        EMPLOYMEN
---------------- ---------
BUSH             05-JAN-88

SQL>

End listing
```

What's Next?

The next chapter covers set operators, which are tools that allow you to combine the results of multiple queries and to add or merge two groups of records into one set. They can also be used to compare two groups of records and then return records that exist in one group as well as records that exist in both groups.

▪ PRACTICE

1. Determine which employees began employment in a year divisible by 3.

2. Compute the average cost of each employee's eyeglasses purchases.

3. Compute the total cost of glasses per department. Round the cost to the nearest $10.

4. Compute the total cost of glasses per department. Truncate the value after the nearest $10.

5. Determine the month including the century, in which the employees turned 21.

6. Determine the date of the first Saturday following the employees' twenty-first birthdays.

7. Identify the employees who were born before 1890.

8. Determine each employee's age when he or she purchased his or her first pair of eyeglasses.

9. On what day of the week did January 1, 2000, fall?

8

Using Set Operators, Subqueries, and Variables

Set operators are keywords that are used to combine records from different record or result sets. SELECT statements produce the record sets that the set operators combine. Set operations and the operators are based on set theory.

Set theory uses special terminology to describe set relationships. This terminology consists of keywords such as UNION, MINUS and INTERSECTION. Figure 8.1 depicts two sets: E and F. The sets overlap each other, creating subsets or combinations. The various sets or combinations of sets are described here:

SET

A   Items from the first set that do not exist in the second set (E – F)

B   Items in the second set that do not exist in the first set (F – E)

C   Items that exist in both sets (F intersection E)

D   Items that exist in A and in B but not in C (E + F – C)

E   Items that exist in the first set (E)

F   Items that exist in the second set (F)

Just as set theory has a mechanism to describe various ways to assemble records from multiple sets, Oracle has keywords that combine sets. These keywords are the set operators UNION, INTERSECT, and MINUS, and they will be described in the following section.

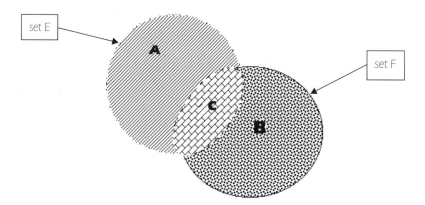

Figure 8.1 *Graphic representation of sets of data*

Set Operator Rules

Set operators are used to combine the records from multiple SELECT statements. The set operator is placed between the two SELECT statements. The operator tells Oracle how the records that each of the SELECT statements retrieves must be merged, compared, or discarded until one virtual table is created. The entire virtual record from each record set is evaluated against each other; therefore, the following rules apply:

1. Each of the SELECT clauses must have the same number of expressions.

2. Each expression in the SELECT clause must have the same data type as the corresponding expression in the other SELECT clauses.

3. Each SELECT statement is part of one overall statement. The minor SELECT statements may have all of the SELECT clauses except the ORDER BY clause, which is placed at the end of the major statement and will sort all of the records in the combined record set.

The UNION and UNION ALL Operators

The UNION operator is used to combine or merge the records that two different queries retrieve. The operator combines the records from the first SELECT statement with those of the second. In Listing 8.1, these records consist of sets A, B, and C (refer to Figure 8.1). This operator will display distinct records from each of the sets. If the retrieved record exists more than once, as it would when the record exists in both sets, the duplicate records are eliminated. Listing 8.1 illustrates a query that displays employees from the POL department who have purchased eyeglasses, purchased tools, or purchased both tools and eyeglasses.

Listing 8.1 *Query Using the UNION Operator*

```
SQL> select last_name, first_name
  2  from employee, emp_tools
  3  where payroll_number = fk_payroll_number
  4    and fk_department = 'POL'
  5  union
  6  select last_name, first_name
  7  from employee, glasses
  8  where payroll_number = fk_payroll_number
  9    and fk_department = 'POL'
 10  order by 1,2;

LAST_NAME        FIRST_NAME
---------------  ---------------
JOHNSON          ANDREW
JOHNSON          LYNDON
NIXON            RICHARD
ROOSEVELT        FRANKLIN
WILSON           WOODROW

SQL>

End Listing
```

You should notice the following about the query in Listing 8.1:

1. The UNION operator is placed between the SELECT statements.

2. The SELECT statements are part of one overall statement, and only one semicolon is needed for the entire statement.

3. The ORDER BY clause is the last clause, and it is at the end of the statement.

4. The ORDER BY clause uses column numbers rather than names.

5. The default column headings are the names of the expressions in the first SELECT clause.

The UNION ALL operator is used when the developer wants to see all of the records from both sets. When this operator is used, the duplicate records are not eliminated. Listing 8.2 illustrates the same query seen in Listing 8.1. The only difference is that the UNION operator is replaced with the UNION ALL operator. This causes the number of selected records to increase because the duplicate records are not discarded.

Listing 8.2 *Query Using the UNION ALL Operator*

```
SQL> select last_name, first_name
  2  from employee, emp_tools
  3  where payroll_number = fk_payroll_number
  4    and fk_department = 'POL'
  5  union all
  6  select last_name, first_name
  7  from employee, glasses
  8  where payroll_number = fk_payroll_number
  9    and fk_department = 'POL'
 10  order by 1,2;


LAST_NAME         FIRST_NAME
---------------   ---------------
JOHNSON           ANDREW
JOHNSON           ANDREW
JOHNSON           ANDREW
JOHNSON           LYNDON
NIXON             RICHARD
NIXON             RICHARD
NIXON             RICHARD
ROOSEVELT         FRANKLIN
ROOSEVELT         FRANKLIN
ROOSEVELT         FRANKLIN
WILSON            WOODROW
WILSON            WOODROW
WILSON            WOODROW
WILSON            WOODROW
```

```
14 rows selected.

SQL>

End Listing
```

The MINUS Operator

The MINUS operator is used to eliminate from the first set any records that exist in the second set. Referring to Figure 8.1, if the first set were E and the second set were F, the resulting set would be A. The MINUS operator allows the developer easily to identify the records that match the requested criteria. Listing 8.3 illustrates a SELECT statement that identifies the employees in the POL department who have purchased tools but have not purchased eyeglasses. The first SELECT statement retrieves the employees from the Emp_tools table. The second SELECT statement retrieves the records from the Glasses table. The MINUS operator causes Oracle to remove from the first-statement result set any records that exist in the result set of the second statement.

Listing 8.3 *SELECT Statement Using the MINUS Set Operator*

```
SQL> select last_name, first_name
  2  from employee, glasses
  3  where payroll_number = fk_payroll_number
  4    and fk_department = 'POL'
  5  minus
  6  select last_name, first_name
  7  from employee, emp_tools
  8  where payroll_number = fk_payroll_number
  9    and fk_department = 'POL';

LAST_NAME       FIRST_NAME
--------------- ---------------
JOHNSON         LYNDON

SQL>

End Listing
```

The INTERSECT Operator

The INTERSECT operator is used to identify the records that exist in both sets. Referring to Figure 8.1, this is set C. This operator compares the two sets of records and eliminates any record that does not exist in both sets. Listing 8.4 illustrates this operator. The query displays employees from the POL department who purchased eyeglasses and tools.

Listing 8.4 *Using the INTERSECT Operator*

```
SQL> select last_name, first_name
  2  from employee, glasses
  3  where payroll_number = fk_payroll_number
  4    and fk_department = 'POL'
  5  intersect
  6  select last_name, first_name
  7  from employee, emp_tools
  8  where payroll_number = fk_payroll_number
  9    and fk_department = 'POL';


LAST_NAME        FIRST_NAME
---------------  ----------------
JOHNSON          ANDREW
NIXON            RICHARD
ROOSEVELT        FRANKLIN
WILSON           WOODROW

SQL>

End listing
```

Subqueries

Subqueries are SELECT statements that retrieve values from the database. The subquery then supplies the values as an argument in a calling SELECT statement. Subqueries that return actual values to the calling SELECT statement are executed before the calling SELECT statement is executed. Correlated subqueries are another type that is executed once for each potential record that the calling SELECT statement retrieves. Correlated subqueries test for existence and return a Boolean value to the calling SELECT statement. If the Boolean is false, the calling SELECT statement discards the record.

Subqueries are also used with DML commands such as INSERT to create a set of records that can be added to a table. We have also seen (in Chapter 2) the use of a subquery in a CREATE TABLE command to copy records into a table when it is created. One of the most common uses of subqueries is to allow the developer to avoid having to write and execute two or more queries to obtain the desired records.

Listing 8.5 is an example of a single-row subquery. The purpose of the Listing 8.5 SELECT statement is to identify the most recently hired employee(s). In order to identify the name of the most recent hiree, you must first find out the most recent hiring date. A single-row subquery is used in the WHERE clause to determine the most recent employment date in the Employee table. This outer SELECT statement uses this value to determine the employee with this employment date. This is the employee who was most recently hired.

Listing 8.5 *Using a Single-Row Subquery*

```
SQL> select last_name, first_name
  2  from employee
  3  where employment_date = (select max(employment_date)
  4                                from employee);

LAST_NAME       FIRST_NAME
--------------- ---------------
MILLER          KEVIN

SQL>

End Listing
```

Single-row subqueries, such as the one illustrated in Listing 8.5, must return only one value. Table 8.1 contains the evaluation operators that can be used with a single-row subquery.

Following are some rules concerning subqueries:

- The subquery must be enclosed in parentheses.
- Place subqueries on the right side of the evaluation operator.

- ORDER BY clauses should not be included as part of the subquery.
- Use single-row operators with single-row subqueries.
- Use multiple-row operators with multiple-row subqueries.

Multiple-Row Subqueries

Multiple-row subqueries return more than one row. These types of subqueries require an operator that can be used to evaluate multiple values. Table 8.2 contains the operators that can be used in multiple-row subqueries.

The IN operator is used with multiple-row subqueries because it evaluates an array of values. Using this operator allows the analyst to create an array of values that can be used as arguments in the WHERE clause. Listing 8.6 illustrates this concept. The query produces a list of employees who are in

Table 8.1 *Single-Row Subquery Evaluation Operators*

Operator	Description
=	equal to
>	greater than
>=	greater than or equal to
<	less than
<=	less than or equal to
<>	not equal to

Table 8.2 *Multiple-Row Evaluation Operators*

Operator	Description
IN	Argument is equal to any of the values that the subquery returns for this condition to be true.
ANY	Compares the argument to each value that the subquery returns. Condition is true if any member of the set meets the condition. The keyword SOME can be used as a synonym.
ALL	Compares the argument to every value that the subquery returns. Condition is true if all members of the set meet the condition.

the same department as *ROOSEVELT.* There are three employees named *ROO-SEVELT* in the database, which will cause the subquery to retrieve three department values from the Employee table. This array of department values will be evaluated by using the IN operator to determine the employees in these departments.

Listing 8.6 *Using the IN Operator with a Subquery*

```
SQL> select fk_department, last_name, first_name
  2  from employee
  3  where fk_department in (select fk_department from employee
  4                          where last_name = 'ROOSEVELT');

FK_D LAST_NAME        FIRST_NAME
---- ---------------  ---------------
INT  ROOSEVELT        THEODORE
INT  COOLIDGE         CALVIN
INT  MILLER           KEVIN
INT  BUSH             GEORGE
INT  FORD             GERALD
INT  EISENHOWER       DWIGHT
INT  TRUMAN           HAROLD
POL  WILSON           WOODROW
POL  DWORCZAK         ALICE
POL  JOHNSON          LYNDON
POL  JOHNSON          ANDREW
POL  CLINTON          WILLIAM
POL  NIXON            RICHARD
POL  KENNEDY          JOHN
POL  ROOSEVELT        FRANKLIN
WEL  TAFT             WILLIAM
WEL  ANTHONY          SUSANNE
WEL  ROOSEVELT        ELEANOR
WEL  HOOVER           HERBERT
WEL  REAGAN           RONALD
WEL  CARTER           JIMMY

21 rows selected.

SQL>

End listing
```

The ANY and ALL operators are used in conjunction with the single-row operators listed in Table 8.1. This differentiates them from the IN operator. The IN operator looks for equality. The ANY and ALL operators are really looking for inequalities, such as greater than or less than. Listing 8.7 illustrates the use of the ANY operator. The multiple-row subquery produces an array of Wages values for employees in the INT department. The outer query then uses the ANY and Greater Than operators to evaluate the value array against the Wages values in the Employee table. The result is a list of employees who have wages greater than any other employee in the INT department.

Listing 8.7 *Using the ANY Operator*

```
SQL> select last_name, first_name, wages
  2  from employee
  3  where wages > any (select wages
  4                     from employee
  5                     where fk_department = 'INT');

LAST_NAME           FIRST_NAME           WAGES
----------------    ----------------    ---------

WILSON              WOODROW               9000
TAFT                WILLIAM               8500
HOOVER              HERBERT              10000
COOLIDGE            CALVIN                9500
MILLER              KEVIN                 9500
DWORCZAK            ALICE                 9800
JOHNSON             LYNDON               12000
REAGAN              RONALD               13500
BUSH                GEORGE               14000
CLINTON             WILLIAM              15000
CARTER              JIMMY                13000
FORD                GERALD               13000
NIXON               RICHARD              12500
KENNEDY             JOHN                 11500
TRUMAN              HAROLD               11000
ROOSEVELT           FRANKLIN             10400

16 rows selected.

SQL>

End listing
```

In Listing 8.8, the ANY operator is replaced with the ALL operator. This will cause the query to return employees who have wages greater than all employees in the INT department. Notice the differences in the results between the two queries.

Listing 8.8 *Using the ANY Operator*

```
SQL> select last_name, first_name, wages
  2  from employee
  3  where wages > all (select wages
  4                     from employee
  5                     where fk_department = 'INT');

no rows selected

SQL>

End listing
```

The query did not return any values. Does this mean that the INT department has the employee with the highest wages? Actually, the POL department has the employee with the highest wages. The reason no records were retrieved was because one of the employees in the INT department had a null value in the Wages columns. Null values can cause problems.

Oracle cannot compare a value against a null because it is unknown. The selected record must be greater than all values that the subquery returns. No record has a higher value than an unknown. Therefore, no record could be selected. In Listing 8.9, the NVL function is used to populate the null values that the subquery returns. This query produces the expected results.

Listing 8.9 *Using the ANY Operator and the NVL Function*

```
SQL> select last_name, first_name, wages
  2  from employee
  3  where wages > all (select nvl(wages,0)
  4                     from employee
  5                     where fk_department = 'INT');
```

```
LAST_NAME        FIRST_NAME          WAGES
---------------  ----------------  ---------
CLINTON          WILLIAM               15000

SQL>

End listing
```

Multiple-Column Queries

The examples that we have seen thus far have used single columns as evaluation arguments. The Wages column was used as an argument against a Wages value that the subquery returned. In some cases, you may want to use multiple columns as evaluation arguments.

For example, assume that you want to identify any employee who has purchased the same eyeglasses as Calvin Coolidge. This requires you to know two items of information: the cost of the eyeglasses and the name of the optician. Listing 8.10 illustrates a subquery that returns the eyeglasses cost and the optician name for each of Calvin Coolidge's eyeglasses purchases. These values are then compared to arguments from the outer query.

Listing 8.10 *Using Multiple-Column Arguments*

```
SQL> select last_name, first_name, optician, cost
  2  from employee, glasses
  3  where payroll_number = fk_payroll_number
  4    and (optician, cost) = (select optician, cost
  5                            from glasses
  6                            where fk_payroll_number = 25);

LAST_NAME        FIRST_NAME        OPTICIAN                   COST
---------------  ----------------  --------------------    ---------
CARTER           JIMMY             Greenberg Optical            175
COOLIDGE         CALVIN            Greenberg Optical            175

SQL>

End Listing
```

In order to perform this type of condition, multiple columns must be listed as one argument. The set of columns must be enclosed by parentheses, and commas must separate the columns.

Correlated Subqueries

The subqueries that we have seen thus far were always executed prior to the execution of the main SELECT statement. This type of subquery returns values to be used as arguments in the main SELECT statement.

Another type of subquery is one that is executed once for each record that the main SELECT statement retrieves. This type of subselect is called a **correlated subquery**. It uses a value that the main SELECT statement supplies in its WHERE clause. The correlated subquery returns only a Boolean value. If the SELECT statement in the subquery can return one or more records, a Boolean value of true is returned. If the SELECT statement cannot return one or more records, a Boolean value of false is returned.

Correlated subqueries are used as the right-positioned argument in a WHERE clause condition. A common use of a correlated subquery is to test for existence by using the EXISTS and NOT EXISTS operators. However, other operators can also be used. The key to the correlated subquery is that it has a WHERE clause argument that references a value from the outer statement. This argument is used to synchronize or correlate the queries.

Listing 8.11 illustrates the use correlated subqueries. The listing contains two SELECT statements whose result sets are combined by using the UNION ALL set operator. Each of the SELECT statements has a correlated subquery as an argument. The first query uses the EXISTS operator to test whether the retrieved employee has purchased tools. If the correlated subquery returns a value of true, the record that the main SELECT statement retrieves is accepted. If the correlated subquery returns a value of false, the record that the main SELECT statement retrieves is rejected. The second query uses the NOT EXISTS operator to test whether the retrieved employee has not purchased tools.

Listing 8.11 *Using the EXISTS and NOT EXISTS Operators*

```
SQL> select 'Employee Has Purchased Tools', last_name, first_name
  2  from employee
  3  where exists (select * from emp_tools
  4                where fk_payroll_number = employee.payroll_number)
  5  union all
  6  select 'Employee Has Not Purchased Tools', last_name, first_name
  7  from employee
  8  where not exists (select * from emp_tools
  9  where fk_payroll_number =
 10  employee.payroll_number);
```

Argument value is supplied from the outer query.

```
'EMPLOYEEHASPURCHASEDTOOLS'              LAST_NAME         FIRST_NAME
-----------------------------------     ----------------  ----------------
Employee Has Purchased Tools            WILSON            WOODROW
Employee Has Purchased Tools            TAFT              WILLIAM
Employee Has Purchased Tools            ROOSEVELT         THEODORE
Employee Has Purchased Tools            ANTHONY           SUSANNE
Employee Has Purchased Tools            ROOSEVELT         ELEANOR
Employee Has Purchased Tools            HOOVER            HERBERT
Employee Has Purchased Tools            COOLIDGE          CALVIN
Employee Has Purchased Tools            MILLER            KEVIN
Employee Has Purchased Tools            REAGAN            RONALD
Employee Has Purchased Tools            BUSH              GEORGE
Employee Has Purchased Tools            JOHNSON           ANDREW
Employee Has Purchased Tools            FORD              GERALD
Employee Has Purchased Tools            NIXON             RICHARD
Employee Has Purchased Tools            EISENHOWER        DWIGHT
Employee Has Purchased Tools            ROOSEVELT         FRANKLIN
Employee Has Not Purchased Tools DWORCZAK                 ALICE
Employee Has Not Purchased Tools JOHNSON                  LYNDON
Employee Has Not Purchased Tools CLINTON                  WILLIAM
Employee Has Not Purchased Tools CARTER                   JIMMY
Employee Has Not Purchased Tools KENNEDY                  JOHN
Employee Has Not Purchased Tools TRUMAN                   HAROLD

21 rows selected.

SQL>

End Listing
```

Correlated subqueries always reference a column from the main SELECT statement in their WHERE clause. In the case of Listing 8.11, the variable was the Payroll_number column. This column does not exist in the Emp_tools table used in the correlated subquery. If the tables used in the correlated subquery have the same column name as one of the columns used in the main SELECT statement, you must qualify the referenced column in the subquery. The qualification can consist of the table name or an alias.

A correlated subquery executes every time a record is identified for the main SELECT, which could cause performance problems. It is best to use these types of subqueries if your main SELECT statement returns only a small number of records.

Variables

Values used in the various SELECT statements that we have seen thus far in this book were fixed, which means that the value was placed in the SELECT statement at the time it was written. It cannot be changed unless the SELECT statement is modified. In some cases, it may be advantageous to be able to enter a value into the SELECT statement at runtime. For example, if an argument used in a SELECT statement can be specified at runtime, it would be possible to obtain different results using the same SELECT statement. A report that displays a list of employee tool purchases can display the tools for different employees if the target employee's payroll number can be added at runtime. Fortunately, Oracle provides a tool called a **substitution variable**, which enables the developer to create a SELECT statement that prompts the user for a value. Oracle also has functionality that allows the developer to create and populate variables that exist throughout the Oracle session. Uses of the substitution variable might consist of dynamically changing report headers and footers, passing values from one SELECT statement to another, or obtaining input values from a file rather than from a person. This section will discuss these variables and the commands used to create custom prompts. I would like to note that the custom prompt is solely an SQL*Plus concept.

Using the Single-Ampersand Substitution Variable

The single ampersand (&) substitution variable causes Oracle to stop and prompt the user for a value before executing the command. This is a very good tool when the developer wants to use the same query to retrieve different sets of data. The single-ampersand variable is generally used in the WHERE or HAVING clauses but could be used anywhere within the statement.

An argument can be turned into a single-ampersand variable by placing an ampersand before the argument. Listing 8.12 illustrates a query that produces a list of employees for the inputted department value (POL). This query allows the user to specify the department argument.

Listing 8.12 *Using a Single-Ampersand Variable*

```
SQL> select fk_department, last_name, first_name
  2  from employee
  3  where fk_department = '&fk_department';
Enter value for fk_department: POL
```

```
old   3: where fk_department = '&fk_department'
new   3: where fk_department = 'POL'

FK_D LAST_NAME        FIRST_NAME
---- ---------------- ----------------
POL  WILSON           WOODROW
POL  DWORCZAK         ALICE
POL  JOHNSON          LYNDON
POL  JOHNSON          ANDREW
POL  CLINTON          WILLIAM
POL  NIXON            RICHARD
POL  KENNEDY          JOHN
POL  ROOSEVELT        FRANKLIN

8 rows selected.

SQL>

End listing
```

The single-ampersand variable used in the SELECT statement was placed within single quotation marks. The value that the single-ampersand variable supplies will be placed within the single quotation marks and is treated as a character value. If the single-ampersand variable had not been enclosed, Oracle would treat the inputted value as a column name, table name, or number, unless the value were inputted with single quotation marks. This sometimes causes a problem. The user does not know whether to enclose the inputted values with single quotation marks. Be sure to warn your users of this.

In Listing 8.12, there are two lines that begin with *old* and *new*. These two lines display the SELECT statement line that contains the single-ampersand variable. The *old* line is the original statement value. The *new* line is the statement value after the substitution has occurred. These lines can be suppressed by issuing the following environmental variable command: SET VERIFY OFF. Environmental variables are settings that affect the SQL*Plus session. They are covered more fully in Chapter 11.

The single-ampersand variable does not have to be used for only the entry of argument values. It literally substitutes the entered value in the place of the single-ampersand variable. Listing 8.13 illustrates the use of the substitution variable to input column names, table names, and even an entire WHERE clause condition.

Listing 8.13 *Using the Single-Ampersand Characters*

```
SQL> select &col1, &col2, &col3
  2   from &table_name
  3   where &condition;
Enter value for col1: last_name
Enter value for col2: first_name
Enter value for col3: wages
old   1: select &col1, &col2, &col3
new   1: select last_name, first_name, wages
Enter value for table_name: employee
old   2: from &table_name
new   2: from employee
Enter value for condition: fk_department = 'POL'
old   3: where &condition
new   3: where fk_department = 'POL'


LAST_NAME          FIRST_NAME          WAGES
---------------    ---------------   ---------
WILSON             WOODROW              9000
DWORCZAK           ALICE                9800
JOHNSON            LYNDON              12000
JOHNSON            ANDREW               7500
CLINTON            WILLIAM             15000
NIXON              RICHARD             12500
KENNEDY            JOHN                11500
ROOSEVELT          FRANKLIN            10400

8 rows selected.

SQL>
```

End listing

Using the Double-Ampersand Variable

In the previous examples in this section, each of the variables had a name that was unique to the statement. If you have single-ampersand variables with the same name, Oracle will still prompt you to enter values for each of the variables (unless a permanent variable is created). This can inconvenience a user when the same value must be used several times in a SELECT statement. Users may not understand why they must enter the same value several times.

This problem is solved by the double-ampersand variable, which will cause Oracle to prompt the user for a value and will create a permanent (to the current session) variable. The permanent variable will use the name that the double-ampersand variable supplies. Subsequent single-ampersand variables using the variable name will use the double-ampersand variable value rather than prompt the user for a value.

Listing 8.14 illustrates this concept. The listing contains two SELECT statements whose results will be combined by the UNION set operator. The first SELECT statement returns employee tool purchases, and the second SELECT statement returns employee eyeglasses purchases. Both statements contain ampersand variables that are used as arguments. The purpose of the arguments is to return records for one employee. In this example, a double-ampersand variable was used to create a variable. A single-ampersand variable was used in the second SELECT statement. As the example indicates, the user was not prompted for this value.

Listing 8.14 *Using the Double-Ampersand Variable to Create a Variable*

```
SQL> select fk_department, last_name, first_name, tool_name
  2  from employee, emp_tools
  3  where payroll_number = fk_payroll_number
  4    and fk_department = &&department_code         User is prompted
  5  union                                           for this value.
  6  select fk_department, last_name, first_name, optician
  7  from employee, glasses
  8  where payroll_number = fk_payroll_number
  9    and fk_department = &department_code;          User is not
Enter value for department_code: 'POL'               prompted for
old   4:    and fk_department = &&department_code     this value.
new   4:    and fk_department = 'POL'
old   9:    and fk_department = &department_code
new   9:    and fk_department = 'POL'


FK_D LAST_NAME           FIRST_NAME       TOOL_NAME
---- ------------------- ---------------- --------------------
POL  JOHNSON             ANDREW           Fountain Pen
POL  JOHNSON             ANDREW           Greenberg Optical
POL  JOHNSON             ANDREW           Shovel
POL  JOHNSON             LYNDON           Peralman Optical
POL  NIXON               RICHARD          Downtown Optical
```

```
POL  NIXON        RICHARD      Hacksaw
POL  NIXON        RICHARD      Pliers
POL  ROOSEVELT    FRANKLIN     CIGARETTE HOLDER
POL  ROOSEVELT    FRANKLIN     HYDE PARK OPTICAL
POL  ROOSEVELT    FRANKLIN     STAPLER
POL  WILSON       WOODROW      DUSTPAN
POL  WILSON       WOODROW      STERLING OPTICAL
POL  WILSON       WOODROW      VACUUM
POL  WILSON       WOODROW      VISE GRIPS

14 rows selected.

SQL>

End listing
```

If the Listing 8.14 SELECT statement were run a second time, the user would not be prompted for a value. The reason is that a double-ampersand variable will not prompt a user for a value if the variable already exists. To remove the variable from memory, use the UNDEFINE command, discussed in the next section.

Defining User Variables

Oracle has additional commands that allow you to define a variable that will reside in memory until it is discarded or until the session is closed. Table 8.3 lists the various commands, along with a description

Table 8.3 *Variable Definition Commands*

Command	Description
DEFINE *variable_name = value*	Creates a user variable with a data type of CHAR and assigns a value to the variable
DEFINE *variable_name*	Displays the variable, its datatype, and its value
DEFINE	Displays all existing variables, including their values and data type
ACCEPT *variable_name*	Sets up a variable that displays a custom prompt when it is called

The DEFINE command can be used to create a user variable. You must assign a value to the variable when it is created. If you do not, Oracle will assume that you want to view information about the variable and will then attempt to display variable values. If the variable cannot be found, an error message will be issued. Listing 8.15 illustrates the following DEFINE command uses:

- Using the command on a variable that does not exist
- Using the command to create and populate a variable
- Using the command to view the variable attribute information
- Using the variable in a SELECT statement
- Using the command to view all variables

Listing 8.15 *Using the DEFINE Command*

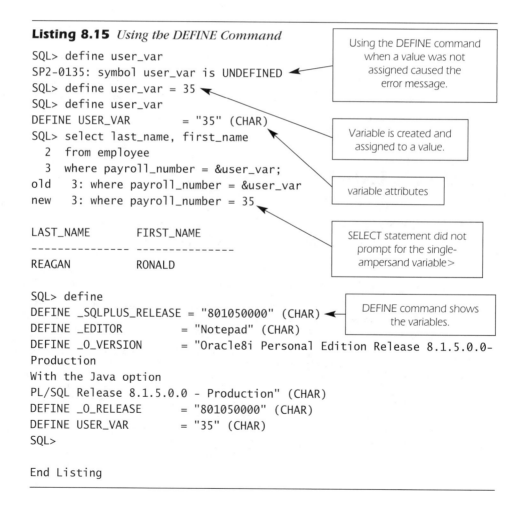

```
SQL> define user_var
SP2-0135: symbol user_var is UNDEFINED
SQL> define user_var = 35
SQL> define user_var
DEFINE USER_VAR         = "35" (CHAR)
SQL> select last_name, first_name
  2  from employee
  3  where payroll_number = &user_var;
old    3: where payroll_number = &user_var
new    3: where payroll_number = 35

LAST_NAME        FIRST_NAME
---------------  ---------------
REAGAN           RONALD

SQL> define
DEFINE _SQLPLUS_RELEASE = "801050000" (CHAR)
DEFINE _EDITOR          = "Notepad" (CHAR)
DEFINE _O_VERSION       = "Oracle8i Personal Edition Release 8.1.5.0.0-
Production
With the Java option
PL/SQL Release 8.1.5.0.0 - Production" (CHAR)
DEFINE _O_RELEASE       = "801050000" (CHAR)
DEFINE USER_VAR         = "35" (CHAR)
SQL>
```

Using the DEFINE command when a value was not assigned caused the error message.

Variable is created and assigned to a value.

variable attributes

SELECT statement did not prompt for the single-ampersand variable>

DEFINE command shows the variables.

End Listing

The UNDEFINE command is used to remove any variable from memory. Exiting the session will also remove the variables. The DEFINE command may also be placed into your user profile (login.sql), which will cause Oracle to create the variables each time you log on.

Chapter 11 discusses SQL*Plus as a report-writing tool. One of the tools discussed is an option called NEW_VALUE, which is used to place a row value into a variable and is then used in the header or footer of a report. This command will be further illustrated in Chapter 11, and it is another option available to you for defining a variable.

The ACCEPT command is used to create a variable and a custom prompt. The command accepts five different parameters:

- VARIABLE NAME   The name of the variable
- DATA TYPE   The variable data type (e.g., CHAR, DATE, NUMBER)
- FORMAT   Oracle determines the format in which the value must be entered. Examples are A10 (alphanumeric) and dates. This parameter setting begins with the keyword FORMAT.
- Prompt   Text that is displayed when the user is prompted for the variable value. This parameter setting begins with the keyword PROMPT.
- HIDE   Suppresses the value that the user enters. This option is useful for passwords.

The following is a template for the ACCEPT command:

Accept *variable_name* [*datatype*] [Format *format*]
[Prompt *text*] [Hide]

Listing 8.16 illustrates the ACCEPT command. The example uses the command to create a variable that is used as an argument in the WHERE clause.

Listing 8.16 *Using the ACCEPT Command*

```
SQL> @ d:\ch08\listings\listing8_16.sql
Enter Payment Amount: 9.95
old   4:    and payment_amount = &payment_amt
new   4:    and payment_amount =        9.95
```

```
LAST_NAME       FIRST_NAME       PAYMENT_AMOUNT
--------------- ---------------- --------------
ANTHONY         SUSANNE                    9.95

SQL> l
  1  select last_name, first_name, payment_amount
  2  from employee, emp_tools
  3  where payroll_number = fk_payroll_number
  4*    and payment_amount = &payment_amt
SQL>

End listing
```

The ACCEPT command works best when it is placed inside a script file and the file is executed, which was done in Listing 8.16. Increasingly you will see that it is impractical to enter commands from the SQL prompt. As variables—as well as formatting options (see Chapter 11)—are added to the queries, script files will become the easiest method of executing SQL in Oracle.

What's Next?

The next chapter will cover analytical tools, which are tools that Oracle added in its 8.1.6 release. They will allow you to perform special computations such as computing totals or cube values.

■ PRACTICE

1. Use the UNION operator to identify the employees who are named JOHN, HAROLD, and WILLIAM.

2. Identify the employees who have purchased tools but not eyeglasses.

3. Identify the employees who were born before and after 1920. For the employees who were born before, use the text literal *Born Before 1920.* For those born after, use *Born After 1920.*

4. Modify your query from question 3 to list only the employees born before 1920 who have purchased tools and those born after 1920 who have purchased eyeglasses.

5. Use a correlated subquery to determine the departments that do not have employees.

6. Create a SELECT statement that can produce a list of tool purchases for an inputted department.

7. Create a SELECT statement that can produce a list of tool purchases and a list of eyeglasses purchases for an inputted department.

8. Use the ACCEPT command to create a custom prompt for the query created in question 7.

9

Analytical Processing with SQL

Oracle has enhanced its ability to develop business intelligence. It has placed a variety of analytical functions in its database. These functions became available with the release of Oracle 8.1.6. The functions allow the business analyst to perform rankings, moving window calculations (i.e., moving averages), and lag/lead analysis. Oracle has also included families of statistic and regression functions in the database. These functions are part of the core SQL processing. Previous to this release, these functions could be obtained only through the use of purchased software. Incorporating these capabilities allows Oracle to enhance scalability, database performance, and simplicity.

Analytic functions are well suited for the data warehouses that are common in the workplace. The purpose of these warehouses is to derive business information. Data warehouses look at data derived from OLTP systems in different ways. One way is to look at the data across different dimensions. For example, a user of our employee data may want to view the data in the following ways:

- Total costs by current position
- Total costs by department
- Total costs by state
- Number of employees by state
- Number of employees by department
- Number of employees by current position

As you can see, there is virtually an unlimited number of ways to look at or analyze the same basic data. Each of these different ways of looking at the data is a dimension. Data warehouses generally have the ability to provide information across different dimensions, which makes them multidimensional databases. You will see that analytic functions like ROLLUP and CUBE are ideally suited for computing values across multidimensions.

ROLLUP

ROLLUP is an extension or option available for the GROUP BY clause. It allows the user to compute subtotals and totals for groups of data. It is highly efficient and adds little overhead to the SELECT statement. A syntax template of the option is as follows:

Group By rollup *(expression1, expression2)*

The ROLLUP keyword will cause a cumulative subtotal row to be created for each of the expressions. When multiple expressions are placed in the parameter list, Oracle will create a grand total for the right-most expression and a subtotal for each of the left-most expressions.

The ROLLUP rows can be identified by null values. The grand-total row will have only the grand-total values. All other row values will be null. If a subtotal is computed, all expressions to the left of the ROLLUP expression will contain nulls. Listing 9.1 illustrates the ROLLUP option. In this query, Wages values are summed for each gender and for each department. The ROLLUP option is used to create a subtotal of female and male wages and a grand total of all wages.

Listing 9.1 *Using the ROLLUP Option to Compute Subtotals and Totals*

```
SQL> select gender, department, sum(wages)
  2  from department, employee
  3  where department = fk_department
  4  group by rollup(gender, department)
  5  order by 1,2;
```

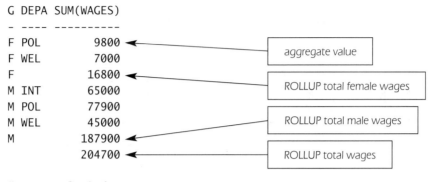

```
G DEPA SUM(WAGES)
- ---- ----------
F POL       9800
F WEL       7000
F          16800
M INT      65000
M POL      77900
M WEL      45000
M         187900
          204700
```

8 rows selected.

End Listing

Partial ROLLUPs can also be computed. If you place GROUP BY expressions outside the ROLLUP option, Oracle will aggregate values based on these expressions. The ROLLUP or subtotals will be based on the expressions within the ROLLUP parameter list. A value will be computed for each unique occurrence of a ROLLUP expression value within the aggregate value. Listing 9.2 depicts this feature.

The example query used in Listing 9.1 was changed. The Department column was moved outside the ROLLUP function. This caused Oracle to compute an aggregate (SUM) value for each department. The gender was left inside the ROLLUP function; therefore, Oracle also computed a rolled-up value for each type of gender for each department. The ROLLUP option no longer computes the total wages for each gender.

Listing 9.2 *Computing a Partial ROLLUP of Wages Per Gender within a Department*

```
SQL> select gender, department, sum(wages)
  2  from department, employee
  3  where department = fk_department
  4  group by rollup(gender), department
  5  order by 2;

G DEPA SUM(WAGES)
- ---- ----------
M INT      65000
```

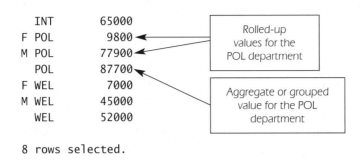

```
     INT          65000
F  POL             9800
M  POL            77900
   POL            87700
F  WEL             7000
M  WEL            45000
   WEL            52000
```

8 rows selected.

End listing

Prior to the development of the ROLLUP function, the only way to compute subtotal values was to use several SELECT statements by using the UNION ALL keyword. Replacing these combined SELECT statements with ROLLUPs substantially reduced the amount of work Oracle had to perform. ROLLUPs are very helpful when the data need to be subtotaled along a hierarchical dimension such as geography or time. It also is useful for the maintenance of summary tables in the data warehouse.

CUBE

The ROLLUPs that we have seen are a small percentage of the numerous possible combinations. For example, the ROLLUP option in Listing 9.1 computed subtotals for gender. Suppose the business analyst wanted to get subtotals for Department while still rolling up the costs of gender per department. This would require the GROUP BY clause to change to the following:

Group by rollup (department, gender)

Suppose the business analyst also wanted to subtotal costs for gender and department. This cannot be done with the ROLLUP option because the SELECT clause can contain only one GROUP BY clause (and only one ROLLUP option). The CUBE option must be used instead.

The CUBE option will compute subtotals for all expressions placed within the parameter list. Listing 9.3 depicts this. The SELECT statement from Listing 9.1

is modified. The ROLLUP option is replaced by the CUBE option, and the SELECT statement will now return subtotals for departments and for gender.

Listing 9.3 *Using the CUBE Option*

```
SQL> select gender, department, sum(wages)
  2  from department, employee
  3  where department = fk_department
  4  group by cube(gender, department)
  5  order by 1,2;

G DEPA SUM(WAGES)
- ---- ----------
F POL        9800
F WEL        7000
F          16800
M INT       65000
M POL       77900
M WEL       45000
M         187900
  INT       65000
  POL       87700
  WEL       52000
          204700

11 rows selected.

End Listing
```

This option should be used with care. It will cause all possible combinations of subtotals to occur, which will place a significant load on the computing environment. The CUBE option can be used in situations that require cross-tabular reports.

In the previous listings, the SUM group function was used. The ROLLUP and CUBE options can be used with the other group functions (i.e., COUNT, AVG, MIN, MAX, STDDEV, and VARIANCE). Finally, just as with the ROLLUP function, partial CUBE operations can be computed. Place outside the parameter list any expressions that you do not want subtotals on.

The GROUPING Function

A problem with the ROLLUP and CUBE options is the difficulty in identifying the rows that are subtotals. One way to identify subtotal rows is to identify the rows that contain null values. Expressions that are subtotaled will have a value in the column that determines the ROLLUP. The other expressions will contain null values. However, if the database contains nulls, this technique will not work because Oracle will also roll up null value records. Oracle developed the GROUPING function to help the identification of ROLLUP records.

GROUPING functions accept only one parameter. The GROUPING function returns a value of 1 if the row is a subtotal row for the target expression. The function will return a value of 0 if the row is not a subtotal row for the target expression. A syntax template follows:

Grouping *(expression)*

Listing 9.4 illustrates the GROUPING function, which was used to identify the rows that are a subtotal (or grand total) of the gender or department.

Listing 9.4 *Using the GROUPING Function*

```
SQL> select gender, department, sum(wages),
  2          grouping(gender) as gdr, grouping(department) as dpt
  3  from department, employee
  4  where department = fk_department
  5  group by rollup(gender, department)
  6  order by 1,2;

G DEPA SUM(WAGES)       GDR        DPT
- ---- ----------- ---------- ---------
F POL        9800          0          0
F WEL        7000          0          0
F          16800          0          1
M INT       65000          0          0
M POL       77900          0          0
M WEL       45000          0          0
M         187900          0          1
          204700          1          1

8 rows selected.

End Listing
```

One excellent use of the GROUPING function is to create descriptions for the aggregated rows. It is possible to populate one of the SELECT statement columns with a text literal when the row has a rolled-up value. The DECODE and CASE functions can be used. The CASE function is discussed later in this chapter. Listing 9.5 illustrates this functionality. The GROUPING and DECODE functions are used to populate the subtotal and grand-total rows. The DECODE function will change the column value to the text literal if the GROUPING function returns a value of 1. Otherwise, the original value will be displayed.

Listing 9.5 *Using the DECODE and GROUPING Functions to Create Descriptive Prompts*

```
SQL> column gdr noprint
SQL> break on gender
SQL> select decode(grouping(gender),1, 'Total Department Wages',
  2            gender) gender,
  3            decode(grouping(department),1,
  4                  decode(grouping(gender),0,'Total Per Gender', ' '),
  5                  department)department,
  6            sum(wages),
  7            grouping(gender) as gdr
  8    from department, employee
  9    where department = fk_department
 10    group by rollup(gender, department)
 11    order by 1,4;

GENDER                  DEPARTMENT       SUM(WAGES)
----------------------  ---------------- ----------
F                       POL                    9800
                        WEL                    7000
                        Total Per Gender      16800
M                       INT                   65000
                        POL                   77900
                        WEL                   45000
                        Total Per Gender     187900
Total Department Wages                        204700

8 rows selected.

SQL>

End listing
```

The GROUPING function has two other uses: It can be used as a filtering argument in the HAVING clause, and it can be used as sort criteria in the ORDER BY clause.

Ranking Functions

Oracle has provided several functions for ranking rows. These functions will calculate rankings, percentiles, and n-tiles of the values. These functions are performed after the SELECT statement assembles the result set and prior to the ordering of the results.

There is an Oracle feature, PARTITIONS, that is used with analytic functions: This feature is totally unrelated to the physical partitioning of data stored within tables, which was discussed in Chapter 2. This partitioning occurs to only the result set of the SELECT statement and is not permanent. The feature allows the user to place into subsets the records that a SELECT statement returns. For example, assume that you would like to determine the top-two wage earners in each department. The PARTITION option can be used to assemble or collate the records by department. The RANK function can then be used to provide the proper rank.

The RANK Function

The RANK function allows the business analyst to compute the rank of a set of values, which is done by comparing all of the values in a set. The following is a syntax template of the function:

> **Rank( ) over (**
> **[partition by *expression, expression*]**
> **order by *expression***
> **[collate clause] [asc | desc]**
> **[nulls first | nulls last]   )**

The following describe these clauses:

- The PARTITION clause is an optional clause that will cause the results to be segregated into subsets. The rank value will be reset each time the partition group changes. If this clause is omitted, the entire group will form the set.

- The ORDER BY clause is mandatory. In order to rank values, the values must be sorted. The ORDER BY clause identifies the expression that will be evaluated for the ranking. This clause is executed after the data is partitioned. Ranks start with a value of 1. The default sort order is ascending. This can be changed to descending with the DESC keyword.

- The NULLS FIRST | NULLS LAST clause determines the position of null values in the ranking. The setting can determine whether the null values appear at the top or the bottom of the ranking.

- If the NULLS FIRST | NULLS LAST clause is omitted, null values will be considered larger than any other value in the list.

Listing 9.6 illustrates the RANK function. It is used to rank the total department wages. The department with the highest wages is ranked 1. The NVL function is used to change null values to 90000. This was done for illustrative purposes only. By making certain that two rows have the same value, I can call attention to the facts that equivalent values will have the same rank and sequential ranks are omitted for all duplicate ranks.

Listing 9.6 *Using the RANK Function*

```
SQL> select department, sum(nvl(wages,90000)),
  2         rank() over (order by sum(nvl(wages,90000)) desc)
  3         as rank_all
  4  from department, employee
  5  where department = fk_department(+)
  6  group by department;

DEPA SUM(NVL(WAGES,90000))  RANK_ALL
---- --------------------- ---------
INT               155000          1
WEL               142000          2
CEN                90000          3
TRF                90000          3
POL                87700          5

End listing
```

> Duplicate values get the same rank.

> #4 rank is missing.

Null values can cause havoc in ranking and ordering. A null value is essentially an unknown value. Normally nulls appear at the end of a value list that is in ascending order. They will appear at the top of a value list that is in descending order. This may not be the ranking order you desire. You may want null values ranked at the top. THE NULLS FIRST | NULLS LAST option can be used to change how the null values are ranked. Table 9.1 describes how the null values will be ranked.

Listing 9.7 illustrates the various options available using the NULLS option. The first use of the option is to rank the nulls as the lowest value in an ascending sort order. The second use is to rank the nulls as the highest value in an ascending sort order. The third use causes the nulls to have the highest values in a descending sort order. The final use causes the nulls to have the lowest value in a descending sort order.

Listing 9.7 *Using the NULLS FIRST | NULLS LAST Option*

```
SQL> select last_name, first_name, wages,
  2    rank() over (order by wages asc nulls first) as ranking_1,
  3    rank() over (order by wages asc nulls last) as ranking_1,
  4    rank() over (order by wages desc nulls first) as ranking_1,
  5    rank() over (order by wages desc nulls last) as ranking_1
  6  from employee;


LAST_NAME        FIRST_NAMEWAGES RANKING_1 RANKING_1 RANKING_1 RANKING_1
---------------  --------- --------- --------- --------- --------- -----
CLINTON          WILLIAM   15000       21        19        3         1
BUSH             GEORGE    14000       20        18        4         2
REAGAN           RONALD    13500       19        17        5         3
CARTER           JIMMY     13000       17        15        6         4
FORD             GERALD    13000       17        15        6         4
NIXON            RICHARD   12500       16        14        8         6
JOHNSON          LYNDON    12000       15        13        9         7
...
TAFT             WILLIAM    8500        6         4       18        16
ROOSEVELT        THEODORE   8000        5         3       19        17
JOHNSON          ANDREW     7500        4         2       20        18
ANTHONY          SUSANNE    7000        3         1       21        19
ROOSEVELT        ELEANOR                1        20        1        20
EISENHOWER       DWIGHT                 1        20        1        20

21 rows selected.

End listing
```

Table 9.1 *NULLS FIRST | NULLS LAST Ranking Descriptions*

	Ascending Sort	**Descending Sort**
NULLS FIRST	Lowest Value/Highest Rank	Highest Value/Highest Rank
NULLS LAST	Highest Value/Lowest Rank	Lowest Value/Lowest Rank

The DENSE_RANK Function

The DENSE_RANK function is similar to the RANK function except for one major difference: It does not skip sequential ranking numbers. In Listing 9.6, two departments had the same total Wages value. The RANK function gave these rows the same rank (3). The rank that would have been used if the fourth row were different (4) was omitted from the ranking scheme. A rank of 5 was given to the first different row. The omitted rank never appeared.

The DENSE_RANK function will ensure that all ranks are used. This function will give duplicate values the same ranking but will use the next sequential rank value for the first nonduplicate value. Listing 9.8 illustrates this function. Unlike Listing 9.6, rank 4 is now used.

Listing 9.8 *Using the DENSE_RANK Function*

```
SQL> select department, sum(nvl(wages, 90000)),
  2          dense_rank() over (order by sum(nvl(wages,90000)) desc)
  3          as rank_dense
  4  from department, employee
  5  where department = fk_department(+)
  6  group by department;

DEPA SUM(NVL(WAGES,90000)) RANK_DENSE
---- --------------------- ----------
INT                 155000          1
WEL                 142000          2
CEN                  90000          3
TRF                  90000          3
POL                  87700          4

SQL>

End listing
```

Rank 4 is used.

Top-N and Bottom-N Queries

The RANK and RANK_DENSE functions can also be used to create Top-N and Bottom-N queries. These types of queries display only a part of the overall ranking. The Top-N query displays a specific number of the highest-ranked values. The Bottom-N query displays a specific number of the lowest-ranked values. To create these types of queries, two steps are required:

1. Create an inline view to develop the data and the rankings.

2. Use the RANK expression in the WHERE clause of the SELECT statement to identify the number of Top and Bottom ranked records.

Listing 9.9 demonstrates a Top-N query. An inline view is used to develop a ranking of employee wages. The NVL function is used to change null values to 0. The ranking expression *emp_wage_rank* is used in the WHERE clause to limit the number of ranks. This query displays the highest-three wage earners.

Listing 9.9 *Top-N Query*

```
SQL> select last_name, first_name, wages, emp_wage_rank
  2  from (select last_name, first_name, wages,
  3         rank() over(order by nvl(wages,0) desc) as emp_wage_rank
  4         from employee)
  5  where emp_wage_rank <= 3;
```

LAST_NAME	FIRST_NAME	WAGES	EMP_WAGE_RANK
CLINTON	WILLIAM	15000	1
BUSH	GEORGE	14000	2
REAGAN	RONALD	13500	3

It is very easy to change the query in Listing 9.9 into a Bottom-N query: Simply change the sort order to ASC (ascending). The bottom-three wage earners will then be displayed.

The PARTITION option is an especially effective tool to use in Top-N and Bottom-N queries. This option allows the business analyst to segment the data and to limit the records for each segment. Examples of uses are result sets that display the top-two selling products among a large set of product groups or, in the case of Listing 9.10, the top-two wage earners in each department. In this example, the data is partitioned by Department_name, each partition is ordered descending, and the top-two ranks are displayed.

Listing 9.10 *Using the PARTITION Option*

```
SQL> select department_name, last_name, first_name, wages,
  2          emp_wage_rank
  3  from (select department_name, last_name, first_name, wages,
  4              rank() over(partition by department_name
  5              order by nvl(wages,0) desc) as emp_wage_rank
  6          from department, employee
  7          where department = fk_department)
  8  where emp_wage_rank <= 2;
```

DEPARTMENT_NAME	LAST_NAME	FIRST_NAME	WAGES	EMP_WAGE_RANK
INTERIOR DESIGN	BUSH	GEORGE	14000	1
INTERIOR DESIGN	FORD	GERALD	13000	2
POLITICAL SCIEN	CLINTON	WILLIAM	15000	1
POLITICAL SCIEN	NIXON	RICHARD	12500	2
WELFARE BUREAU	REAGAN	RONALD	13500	1
WELFARE BUREAU	CARTER	JIMMY	13000	2

```
6 rows selected
```

End listing

The PERCENT_RANK Function

The PERCENT_RANK function computes the percentile of the ranking. The percent rank represents the relative position of the ranking. The ranking is determined by the target value, but the percent rank is not. The percent rank is based on this formula:

(rank of row in its partition – 1) / (number of rows in the partition – 1)

If the partition contains five ranks, the highest-ranked value will be at the 100th (or 1) percent rank. The lowest-ranked value will be at the 0 percent rank. The remainder of the ranked values will be at the 75th, 50th, and 25th percent rank.

Listing 9.11 illustrates the PERCENT_RANK function. The query computes the tool costs for each employee. These costs are then ranked within the respective departments. The PERCENT_RANK function is then used to compute the percent rank of each ranking.

Listing 9.11 *Using the PERCENT_RANK Function*

```
SQL> select department_name, last_name||', '||first_name name,
  2         sum(tool_cost) "Tool Costs",
  3         percent_rank() over
  4         (partition by department_name
  5          order by sum(tool_cost)) percent
  6  from department, employee, emp_tools
  7  where department = fk_department
  8    and payroll_number = fk_payroll_number
  9  group by department_name, last_name, first_name
 10  order by 1, 3 desc;
```

DEPARTMENT_NAME	NAME	Tool Costs	PERCENT
INTERIOR DESIGN	EISENHOWER, DWIGHT	375	1
INTERIOR DESIGN	ROOSEVELT, THEODORE	324	.75
INTERIOR DESIGN	BUSH, GEORGE	46.2	.5
INTERIOR DESIGN	COOLIDGE, CALVIN	35	.25
INTERIOR DESIGN	FORD, GERALD	12	0
POLITICAL SCIEN	WILSON, WOODROW	116.95	1
POLITICAL SCIEN	ROOSEVELT, FRANKLIN	20	.66666667
POLITICAL SCIEN	NIXON, RICHARD	18.5	.33333333
POLITICAL SCIEN	JOHNSON, ANDREW	16.7	0
WELFARE BUREAU	ANTHONY, SUSANNE	88.85	1
WELFARE BUREAU	ROOSEVELT, ELEANOR	61.95	.75
WELFARE BUREAU	REAGAN, RONALD	28.7	.5
WELFARE BUREAU	HOOVER, HERBERT	24	.25
WELFARE BUREAU	TAFT, WILLIAM	23	0

```
14 rows selected.

SQL>

End Listing
```

The CUME_DIST Function

CUME_DIST is similar to the PERCENT_RANK function. It has been called the inverse of percentile. It computes the position of a specified value relative to a set of values. The CUME_DIST function does not compute a 0 percentile as does the PERCENT_RANK. If the partition contains five ranks, the highest-ranked value is at the 100th percentile. The lowest-ranked value has a percent rank of .2. The remaining ranks have values of .8, .6, and .4. The formula used in this calculation is as follows:

Cume_dist(x) =
    Number of values (different from, or equal to, x)
    In the set coming before x in the specified order / size of set

Listing 9.12 is a modification of Listing 9.11. The PERCENT_RANK function was replaced by the CUME_DIST function.

Listing 9.12 *Using the CUME_DIST Function*

```
SQL> select department_name, last_name||', '||first_name name,
  2         sum(tool_cost) "Tool Costs",
  3         cume_dist() over
  4         (partition by department_name
  5          order by sum(tool_cost)) percent
  6  from department, employee, emp_tools
  7  where department = fk_department
  8    and payroll_number = fk_payroll_number
  9  group by department_name, last_name, first_name
 10  order by 1, 3 desc;
```

DEPARTMENT_NAME	NAME	Tool Costs	PERCENT
INTERIOR DESIGN	EISENHOWER, DWIGHT	375	1
INTERIOR DESIGN	ROOSEVELT, THEODORE	324	.8
INTERIOR DESIGN	BUSH, GEORGE	46.2	.6
INTERIOR DESIGN	COOLIDGE, CALVIN	35	.4
INTERIOR DESIGN	FORD, GERALD	12	.2
POLITICAL SCIEN	WILSON, WOODROW	116.95	1
POLITICAL SCIEN	ROOSEVELT, FRANKLIN	20	.75
POLITICAL SCIEN	NIXON, RICHARD	18.5	.5

```
POLITICAL SCIEN JOHNSON, ANDREW                  16.7       .25
WELFARE BUREAU  ANTHONY, SUSANNE                 88.85        1
WELFARE BUREAU  ROOSEVELT, ELEANOR               61.95       .8
WELFARE BUREAU  REAGAN, RONALD                   28.7        .6
WELFARE BUREAU  HOOVER, HERBERT                    24         .4
WELFARE BUREAU  TAFT, WILLIAM                      23         .2

14 rows selected.

SQL>

End Listing
```

The NTILE Function

The NTILE function is used to calculate tertiles, quartiles, and deciles. The function contains a parameter that allows the business analyst to specify the number of segments the distribution will contain. If the value 4 is specified, the values will be placed into one of four quartiles. It may be easier to think of the segments as buckets. The NTILE parameter specifies the number of buckets. The function then places the record into one of the buckets.

Listing 9.13 depicts the NTILE function. The SELECT statement computes the total tool purchases for each employee. The NTILE function is then used to place each of the values into one of four quartiles. The employees with the highest cost of purchases are placed in the first quartile. The employees with no tool purchases are placed in the third and fourth quartiles. The NULLS LAST option was used to force the employees with no tool purchases to the bottom.

Listing 9.13 *Using the NTILE Function to Determine Quartiles*

```
SQL> select last_name||', '||first_name, sum(tool_cost) tool_cost,
  2     NTILE(4) over (order by sum(tool_cost) desc nulls last) quartile
  3   from employee, emp_tools
  4   where payroll_number = fk_payroll_number(+)
  5   group by last_name||', '||first_name;

LAST_NAME||','||FIRST_NAME        TOOL_COST  QUARTILE
--------------------------------  ---------  ---------
EISENHOWER, DWIGHT                     375          1
ROOSEVELT, THEODORE                    324          1
```

WILSON, WOODROW	116.95	1
ANTHONY, SUSANNE	88.85	1
ROOSEVELT, ELEANOR	61.95	1
BUSH, GEORGE	46.2	1
COOLIDGE, CALVIN	35	2
REAGAN, RONALD	28.7	2
HOOVER, HERBERT	24	2
TAFT, WILLIAM	23	2
ROOSEVELT, FRANKLIN	20	2
NIXON, RICHARD	18.5	3
JOHNSON, ANDREW	16.7	3
FORD, GERALD	12	3
CARTER, JIMMY		3
CLINTON, WILLIAM		3
KENNEDY, JOHN		4
TRUMAN, HAROLD		4
MILLER, KEVIN		4
JOHNSON, LYNDON		4
DWORCZAK, ALICE		4

```
21 rows selected.

SQL>

End listing
```

The ROW_NUMBER Function

The ROW_NUMBER function is the last of the ranking functions. It is somewhat similar to the ROWNUM pseudocolumn. It numbers the rows sequentially as they are fetched. The difference is that the PARTITION option can be used, which allows the row numbers to be used repeatedly in the result set.

Listing 9.14 illustrates the function. The ROW_NUMBER function is used to number the employees in each department, and its values return to 1 each time a new department in encountered.

Listing 9.14 *Using the ROW_NUMBER Function*

```
SQL> select department_name, last_name||', '||first_name,
  2        row_number() over
  3          (partition by department_name
```

```
4               order by last_name||', '||first_name nulls last)
5                 "Row Number"
6  from department, employee
7  where department = fk_department(+);
```

```
DEPARTMENT_NAME LAST_NAME||','||FIRST_NAME           Row Number
--------------- -------------------------------- ----------
CENSUS DEPT         ,                                       1
INTERIOR DESIGN BUSH, GEORGE                                1
INTERIOR DESIGN COOLIDGE, CALVIN                            2
INTERIOR DESIGN EISENHOWER, DWIGHT                          3
INTERIOR DESIGN FORD, GERALD                                4
INTERIOR DESIGN MILLER, KEVIN                               5
INTERIOR DESIGN ROOSEVELT, THEODORE                         6
INTERIOR DESIGN TRUMAN, HAROLD                              7
POLITICAL SCIEN CLINTON, WILLIAM                            1
POLITICAL SCIEN DWORCZAK, ALICE                             2
POLITICAL SCIEN JOHNSON, ANDREW                             3
POLITICAL SCIEN JOHNSON, LYNDON                             4
POLITICAL SCIEN KENNEDY, JOHN                               5
POLITICAL SCIEN NIXON, RICHARD                              6
POLITICAL SCIEN ROOSEVELT, FRANKLIN                         7
POLITICAL SCIEN WILSON, WOODROW                             8
TRESURY DEPAR       ,                                       1
WELFARE BUREAU  ANTHONY, SUSANNE                            1
WELFARE BUREAU  CARTER, JIMMY                               2
WELFARE BUREAU  HOOVER, HERBERT                             3
WELFARE BUREAU  REAGAN, RONALD                              4
WELFARE BUREAU  ROOSEVELT, ELEANOR                          5
WELFARE BUREAU  TAFT, WILLIAM                               6

23 rows selected.

SQL>


End Listing
```

Windowing

Oracle has added to its database some functionality that allows you to calculate values based on a window. The window is a period of time. The functions in this class can be used to compute moving, cumulative, and centered aggregates. They include moving averages, moving sums, moving MIN/MAX, cumulative SUM, and LAG/LEAD. These functions create a value that is based on values that precede or follow the record. The windowing functions can be used in the SELECT and ORDER BY clauses.

The following is a syntax template that can be used for the functions:

{Sum | Avg | Max | Min | Count | Stddev | Variance |
    First_value | Last_value} ({*value expression1*> | * })
Over ({partition by <value expression2>[, ...]]
Order by <*value expression3*>[collate clause>] [asc | desc]
    [nulls first | nulls last] [,...]
rows | range {{unbounded preceding | <*value expression4*>
    preceding } | between {unbounded preceding |
    <*value expression4*> preceding }
and {current row | <*value expression4*> following }}

The first clause in the template is used to identify the type of calculation. The bulk of the calculations is self-explanatory. The FIRST_VALUE calculation returns the first value in the window. The LAST_VALUE calculation returns the last value in the window. The following describe the other options:

- OVER — Tells Oracle that the function will operate over a query result set.

- PARTITION BY — Determines how the data will be segregated for analysis.

- ORDER BY — Determines how the data will be sorted within the partition. Options are ASC (default), DESC, NULLS FIRST, or NULLS LAST.

- ROWS | RANGE — These keywords determine the window used for the calculation. The ROWS keyword is used to specify the

	window as a set of rows. RANGE sets the window as a logical offset. This option cannot be used unless the ORDER BY clause is used.
▪ BETWEEN … AND	Determines the starting point and end-point of the window. Omitting the BETWEEN keyword and specifying only one endpoint will cause Oracle to consider the endpoint as the starting point. The current row will then consist of the current row.
▪ UNBOUNDED PRECEDING	Sets the first row of the partition as the window starting point.
▪ UNBOUNDED FOLLOWING	Sets the last row of the partition as the endpoint of the window.
▪ CURRENT ROW	Sets the current row as the starting point or as the endpoint of the window.

The Cumulative Aggregate Function

A cumulative aggregate function is used to create a checkbook-style running balance. The function computes the cumulative balance after the current value is subtracted or added to the aggregate. Listing 9.15 is an example of this function, which is used to develop a cumulative value of the tool purchases. The records are ordered by tool purchase date, which causes the tool purchase balances to be arranged in chronological order. The UNBOUNDED PRECEDING option was used to set the first row returned as the window starting point.

Listing 9.15 *Using the Cumulative Aggregate Function*

```
SQL> select department, last_name, first_name, tool_cost,
  2         sum(tool_cost)
  3         over (order by purchase_date rows unbounded preceding)
           balance
  3  from department, employee, emp_tools
  4  where department = fk_department
```

```
5      and payroll_number = fk_payroll_number;
```

DEPA	LAST_NAME	FIRST_NAME	TOOL_COST	BALANCE
INT	ROOSEVELT	THEODORE	34	34
INT	ROOSEVELT	THEODORE	290	324
WEL	TAFT	WILLIAM	23	347
POL	WILSON	WOODROW	4.95	351.95
POL	WILSON	WOODROW	100	451.95
POL	WILSON	WOODROW	12	463.95
INT	COOLIDGE	CALVIN	25	488.95
INT	COOLIDGE	CALVIN	10	498.95
WEL	HOOVER	HERBERT	8	506.95
WEL	HOOVER	HERBERT	16	522.95
WEL	ROOSEVELT	ELEANOR	55	577.95
POL	ROOSEVELT	FRANKLIN	12	589.95
WEL	ROOSEVELT	ELEANOR	1.95	591.9
POL	ROOSEVELT	FRANKLIN	8	599.9
WEL	ROOSEVELT	ELEANOR	5	604.9
WEL	ANTHONY	SUSANNE	43.95	648.85
WEL	ANTHONY	SUSANNE	34.95	683.8
WEL	ANTHONY	SUSANNE	9.95	693.75
INT	EISENHOWER	DWIGHT	25	718.75
INT	EISENHOWER	DWIGHT	200	918.75
INT	EISENHOWER	DWIGHT	150	1068.75
POL	JOHNSON	ANDREW	5.95	1074.7
POL	JOHNSON	ANDREW	10.75	1085.45
POL	NIXON	RICHARD	12.75	1098.2
POL	NIXON	RICHARD	5.75	1103.95
INT	FORD	GERALD	12	1115.95
INT	FORD	GERALD	0	1115.95
INT	FORD	GERALD	0	1115.95
WEL	REAGAN	RONALD	4	1119.95
WEL	REAGAN	RONALD	7.95	1127.9
WEL	REAGAN	RONALD	16.75	1144.65
INT	BUSH	GEORGE	2.75	1147.4
INT	BUSH	GEORGE	35.95	1183.35
INT	BUSH	GEORGE	7.5	1190.85

```
34 rows selected.

End Listing
```

Moving Averages

The cumulative aggregate function can be used to compute moving averages. A moving average is a calculation based on a number of values. A three-day moving average consists of averaged values from three separate days. The purpose of a moving average is to remove the volatility of the values. Individual values often differ from each other. When an individual value is averaged with neighboring values, the variance is reduced.

Moving averages are computed when several keywords are added to the cumulative aggregate function:

- The RANGE INTERVAL value keywords are needed to identify the number of values to be averaged.

- A time unit value is needed. Common time units consist of the keywords Year, Month, and Day.

- The PRECEDING and/or FOLLOWING keywords must also be included. They indicate which records in the ordered list will be used in the calculation.

The SELECT statement must contain a date/time value. This value is used in the ORDER BY clause of the function to set the proper order of the records.

Listing 9.16 contains a SELECT statement that computes a moving average. The cumulative aggregate function averages tool records for the preceding 20 years. The Purchase_date expression is used to order the records. The RANGE INTERVAL is set to 20 years. This will cause the function to average the current row with any preceding row that has a Purchase_date value within 20 years of the current row.

Listing 9.16 *Computing a 20-Year Moving Average of Tool Purchases*

```
SQL> select department, purchase_date, tool_cost,
  2         avg(tool_cost) over
  3           (partition by department
  4            order by purchase_date
  5            range interval '20' year preceding) balance
  6  from department, employee, emp_tools
  7  where department = fk_department
  8    and payroll_number = fk_payroll_number;
```

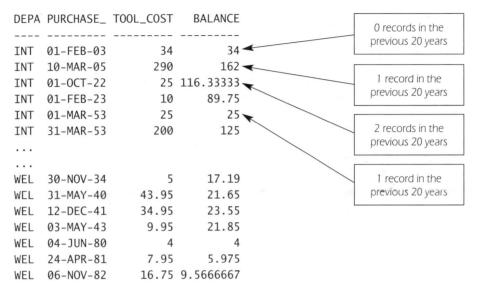

```
DEPA PURCHASE_ TOOL_COST   BALANCE
---- --------- --------- ---------
INT  01-FEB-03        34        34
INT  10-MAR-05       290       162
INT  01-OCT-22        25 116.33333
INT  01-FEB-23        10     89.75
INT  01-MAR-53        25        25
INT  31-MAR-53       200       125
...
...
WEL  30-NOV-34         5     17.19
WEL  31-MAY-40     43.95     21.65
WEL  12-DEC-41     34.95     23.55
WEL  03-MAY-43      9.95     21.85
WEL  04-JUN-80         4         4
WEL  24-APR-81      7.95     5.975
WEL  06-NOV-82     16.75 9.5666667

34 rows selected.

End Listing
```

Changing the PRECEDING keyword to FOLLOWING will cause the function to average records that follow the current record. Some moving-average calculations require records that precede and follow the current value to be averaged. These types of calculations are called centered moving averages. Centered calculations can be developed by using the BETWEEN and AND keywords. Listing 9.17 contains a query that averages records that exist on both sides of the current record. The RANGE statement contains two interval statements: The first allows records from the preceding 20 years to be included in the average, and the second allows records from the following 20 years to be included.

Listing 9.17 *Computing a 40-Year Centered Moving Average*

```
SQL> select department, purchase_date, tool_cost,
  2          avg(tool_cost) over
  3            (partition by department
  4              order by purchase_date
  5            range interval '20' year preceding) balance
```

```
6  from department, employee, emp_tools
7  where department = fk_department
8    and payroll_number = fk_payroll_number;

DEPA PURCHASE_ TOOL_COST   BALANCE
---- --------- --------- ---------
INT  01-FEB-03        34        34
INT  10-MAR-05       290       162
INT  01-OCT-22        25 116.33333
INT  01-FEB-23        10     89.75
INT  01-MAR-53        25        25
INT  31-MAR-53       200       125
INT  31-MAR-53       150       125
...
WEL  12-MAR-29         8      15.5
WEL  31-MAY-29        16 15.666667
WEL  01-MAY-33        55 26.333333
WEL  06-SEP-34      1.95   20.2375
WEL  30-NOV-34         5     17.19
WEL  31-MAY-40     43.95     21.65
WEL  12-DEC-41     34.95     23.55
WEL  03-MAY-43      9.95     21.85
WEL  04-JUN-80         4         4
WEL  24-APR-81      7.95     5.975
WEL  06-NOV-82     16.75 9.5666667

34 rows selected.

SQL>

End listing
```

The RATIO_TO_REPORT Function

The RATIO_TO_REPORT function computes the ratio of the current row's value to the sum of the result set's values. The following is a syntax template of the function:

Ratio_to_report (*<value expression1>*) over
([partition by *<value expression2>* [, . . .]])

The PARTITION BY keywords define subgroups of the data based on an expression. The ratio will then be computed for each of the subgroups. If the keywords are omitted, the function computes ratios based on the sum of the entire record set's values. Listing 9.18 illustrates this function, which is used to compute the ratio of each department's wages compared to the total employee wages.

Listing 9.18 *Using the RATIO_TO_REPORT Function*

```
SQL> select department_name, sum(wages) "Total Wages",
  2         ratio_to_report(sum(wages)) over() as wage_ratio
  3   from department, employee
  4   where department = fk_department
  5   group by department_name;

DEPARTMENT_NAME Total Wages WAGE_RATIO
--------------- ----------- ----------
INTERIOR DESIGN       65000 .31753786
POLITICAL SCIEN       87700 .42843185
WELFARE BUREAU        52000 .25403029

End Listing
```

The LAG and LEAD Functions

The LAG and LEAD functions return the value of a preceding or following row to the current row. These functions are useful for computing the difference between values in different rows. The following is a syntax template of the functions:

Lag (*expression, record offset*)
Lead (*expression, record offset*)

EXPRESSION refers to one of values contained in the SELECT clause. RECORD OFFSET refers to a row. The value identifies the particular row. A value of 1 indicates the previous or following row, depending on the use of LAG/LEAD. A value of 2 indicates the second row that precedes or follows the current row. If this parameter is omitted, it will default to 1. The function can be used with the standard PARTITION BY, ORDER BY, and NULLS FIRST | NULLS LAST options.

Listing 9.19 illustrates the LAG function, which is used to retrieve the value of the previous Wages expression. This value is then subtracted from the current value of Wages. The result is the difference between the Wages value in consecutive rows.

Listing 9.19 *Using the LAG Function*

```
SQL> select last_name, wages,
  2          wages - lag(wages, 1) over (order by employment_date)
  3          as "Wage Differences"
  4   from employee;


LAST_NAME            WAGES Wage Differences
--------------- ---------- ----------------
ROOSEVELT             8000
TAFT                  8500              500
WILSON                9000              500
COOLIDGE              9500              500
HOOVER               10000              500
ROOSEVELT
ROOSEVELT            10400
ANTHONY               7000            -3400
TRUMAN               11000             4000
EISENHOWER
KENNEDY              11500
JOHNSON              12000              500
JOHNSON               7500            -4500
NIXON                12500             5000
FORD                 13000              500
CARTER               13000                0
REAGAN               13500              500
BUSH                 14000              500
CLINTON              15000             1000
DWORCZAK              9800            -5200
MILLER                9500             -300

21 rows selected.

End Listing
```

Listing 9.20 depicts the LEAD function. This query performs the same basic function as the previous query. The difference is that the LEAD function retrieves the following row for the calculation.

Listing 9.20 *Using the LEAD Function*

```
LAST_NAME           WAGES Wage Differences
--------------- --------- -----------------
ROOSEVELT            8000               500
TAFT                 8500               500
WILSON               9000               500
COOLIDGE             9500               500
HOOVER              10000
ROOSEVELT
ROOSEVELT           10400             -3400
ANTHONY              7000              4000
TRUMAN              11000
EISENHOWER
KENNEDY             11500               500
JOHNSON             12000             -4500
JOHNSON              7500              5000
NIXON               12500               500
FORD                13000                 0
CARTER              13000               500
REAGAN              13500               500
BUSH                14000              1000
CLINTON             15000             -5200
DWORCZAK             9800              -300
MILLER               9500

21 rows selected.

End listing
```

Another use of the LEAD and LAG functions is to avoid the use of the self join. Listing 5.6 in Chapter 5 illustrated a SELECT statement that had a self join, the purpose of which was to display the employees hired before a given employee. Listing 9.21 computes similar results using the LAG function. Using the LEAD and LAG functions rather than a self join can offer two important advantages:

1. Enhanced performance. Using the functions allows Oracle to avoid the work of joining records.

2. Reduces the complexity of the statements. Listing 5.6 was substantially more complex. The developer had to perform outer joins and determine how to join the records. Even so, it did not quite display the values correctly because some of the employees in the Employee table did not have sequential payroll numbers. The previous employee was not displayed if the employee did not have the previous sequential payroll number. The SELECT statement in Listing 9.21 avoids this problem.

Listing 9.21 *Using the LAG Function to Determine the Previously Hired Employee and to Avoid Performing a Self Join*

```
SQL> select payroll_number, last_name,
  2         lag(payroll_number, 1) over
  3             (order by payroll_number) prev_payroll_number,
  4         lag(last_name, 1) over (order by payroll_number)
  5         prev_last_name
  4  from employee;

PAYROLL_NUMBER LAST_NAME        PREV_PAYROLL_NUMBER PREV_LAST_NAME
-------------- ---------------  ------------------- ---------------
            19 ROOSEVELT
            20 ANTHONY                           19 ROOSEVELT
            21 JOHNSON                           20 ANTHONY
            22 ROOSEVELT                         21 JOHNSON
            23 TAFT                              22 ROOSEVELT
            24 WILSON                            23 TAFT
            25 COOLIDGE                          24 WILSON
            26 HOOVER                            25 COOLIDGE
            27 ROOSEVELT                         26 HOOVER
            28 TRUMAN                            27 ROOSEVELT
            29 EISENHOWER                        28 TRUMAN
            30 KENNEDY                           29 EISENHOWER
            31 JOHNSON                           30 KENNEDY
            32 NIXON                             31 JOHNSON
            33 FORD                              32 NIXON
            34 CARTER                            33 FORD
            35 REAGAN                            34 CARTER
            36 BUSH                              35 REAGAN
```

```
      37 CLINTON              36 BUSH
      45 DWORCZAK             37 CLINTON
      46 MILLER               45 DWORCZAK


21 rows selected.


SQL>


End listing
```

Statistical Functions

Oracle has added a variety of statistical functions to its database. Statistics such as correlation, covariance, and linear regression can be computed. The functions operate on unordered result sets, and they can be used with the windowing function. Table 9.2 describes the available functions

The use of the various functions is depicted in Listing 9.22. The functions are used to analyze the employee Wages values.

Table 9.2 *Statistical Functions*

Function Name	Description
VAR_POP	Computes the population variance of a number set after discarding all null values
VAR_SAMP	Computes the sample variance of a number set after discarding the null values (This function is similar to the VARIANCE function. The difference occurs when the function takes a single argument. When this occurs, the VARIANCE function returns 0, and the VAR_SAMP function returns a null.)
STDDEV_POP	Computes the standard deviation of the population
STDDEV_SAMP	Computes the standard deviation of the sample
COVAR_POP	Computes the population covariance of a set of number pairs (Oracle will eliminate all pairs that contain a null value.)
COVAR_SAMP	Computes the covariance of the sample set of number pairs (Oracle will eliminate all pairs that contain a null value.)

Listing 9.22 *Using Statistical Functions to Analyze Wages*

```
SQL> select var_pop(wages) var_pop, var_samp(wages) var_samp,
  7            stddev_pop(wages) stddev_pop,
  8            stddev_samp(wages) stddev_samp,
  4            covar_pop(wages, wages * 1.07) covar_pop,
  5            covar_samp(wages, wages * 1.07) covar_samp
  6  from employee;


  VAR_POP   VAR_SAMP STDDEV_POP STDDEV_SAMP COVAR_POP COVAR_SAMP
--------- ---------- ---------- ----------- --------- ----------
5082991.7 5365380.1  2254.5491     2316.329 5438801.1  5740956.7

End listing
```

Oracle also has developed a number of linear regression functions, which are detailed in Table 9.3.

The uses of the various regression functions are depicted in Listing 9.23. This query groups and summarizes tool costs by year within a decade (i.e., 1, 2, 3, etc.). This was done in order to reduce the number of data points.

Listing 9.23 *Using Regression Functions to Analyze Wages*

```
SQL> select regr_count(trunc(substr(purchase_date, 8, 2),-1),
  2                 sum(tool_cost)) regr_count,
  3         regr_avgx(trunc(substr(purchase_date, 8, 2),-1),
  4                 sum(tool_cost)) regr_avgx,
  5         regr_avgy(trunc(substr(purchase_date, 8, 2),-1),
  6                 sum(tool_cost)) regr_avgy,
  4         regr_slope(trunc(substr(purchase_date, 8, 2),-1),
  5                 sum(tool_cost)) regr_slope,
  6         regr_intercept(trunc(substr(purchase_date, 8, 2),-1),
  7                 sum(tool_cost)) regr_intercept,
  8         regr_r2(trunc(substr(purchase_date, 8, 2),-1),
  9                 sum(tool_cost)) regr_r2,
 10         regr_sxx(trunc(substr(purchase_date, 8, 2),-1),
 11                 sum(tool_cost)) regr_sxx,
 12         regr_sxy(trunc(substr(purchase_date, 8, 2),-1),
 13                 sum(tool_cost)) regr_sxy
 17  from emp_tools
 18  group by trunc(substr(purchase_date, 8, 2),-1);
```

```
RG_CNT RG_AVGX RG_AVGY RG_SLP RG_INT   REGR_R2   REGR_SXX  REGR_SXY
------ ------- ------- ------ ------ --------- --------- ---------
     9 132.316      40  -.081 50.771 .15708558 142226.18     -11578

SQL>

End Listing
```

Table 9.3 *Linear Regression Functions*

Function Name	Description
REGR_AVGX	Computes the average of the independent variable of the regression line. This is the average of the second argument after nulls are eliminated.
REGR_AVGY	Computes the average of the dependent variable of the regression line. This is the average of the first argument after nulls are eliminated.
REGR_COUNT	Computes the number of not null number pairs that are used to fit the regression line.
REGR_INTERCEPT	Computes the y-intercept of the regression line.
REGR_R2	Computes the coefficient of determination for the regression line.
REGR_SLOPE	Computes the slope of the regression line. It is fitted to not null pairs.
REGR_SXX	Computes a diagnostic statistic for regression analysis. The following is the formula: REGR_COUNT(e1, e2) * VAR_POP(e2)
REGR_SXY	Computes a diagnostic statistic for regression analysis. The following is the formula: REGR_COUNT(e1, e2) * COVAR_POP(e1,e2)
REGR_SYY	Computes a diagnostic statistic for regression analysis. The following is the formula: REGR_COUNT(e1, e2) * VAR_POP(e1)

What's Next?

The next chapter will cover views and sequences. A view is an important tool for the business analyst. It is a SELECT statement that resides in the database. Views are a very common tool for creating virtual record sets. Sequences are a database tool that returns unique and unused numbers to the calling object. It is a great tool for generating artificial primary keys, payroll numbers, or account numbers.

▦ PRACTICE

1. Determine the cost of tools per classification within gender. Subtotal the costs for each gender.

2. Rank all employees by their total cost of eyeglasses and tool purchases. The employee with the lowest cost should be ranked first.

3. Determine the two employees in each department who had the largest cost of eyeglasses purchases. Include employees who have not purchased eyeglasses.

4. Create a checkbook-style cumulative cost of eyeglasses purchases.

5. Compute the ratio of the total cost of each department's eyeglasses purchases to the cost of all eyeglasses purchases.

6. Determine whether the price of tools per tool is increasing. Use the LAG function to calculate the difference in the costs of each tool.

7. Create a SELECT statement that counts the number of eyeglasses within one of four cost classes: Less than $100, $100 to $125, $126 to $150, and Above $150.

10

Using Database and Materialized Views

Views are virtual tables that are derived at runtime. A view is a specification consisting of a SELECT statement that tells Oracle what records and attributes to retrieve. Views are used as the name of a table in an SQL statement. When an SQL statement calls the view, Oracle executes its SELECT statement and then returns the result set to the calling SELECT statement. A view acts like a table but does not store data. Views return derived data only when they are called.

There are three types of views. The first type consists of a SELECT statement that is embedded in the FROM clause of another SELECT statement. This type of view is called an inline view (or derived table). Like all views, it replaces a physical table in the FROM clause. The inline view is executed at runtime and furnishes its result set to the outer statement. A second type of view is a database view, which performs the same basic function: It retrieves data to a calling object. The main difference is that the inline view resides within another SELECT statement and can be called by only that statement. A database view resides in the database and can be called by many other objects. Another difference between an inline view and a database view is that the database view can be used in a DML statement. The third type of view is a materialized view. This view has some physical properties and consists of data that is moved into the view from other tables.

Views are a very commonly used database object. It is probably the most used object for data administrators (DAs) and business analysts. There are several reasons why views are used so much:

1. A view masks the complexity of retrieving the data. While reading this book, you have probably realized that SQL statements can be very complex. Many statements are beyond the capability of the typical user. DAs often write the SELECT statements and wrap them in a view, which allows the DA to combine data in a manner suitable for a user. Users employing the view see only the final expressions in the SELECT clause. They can treat the view exactly the same as a table. In fact, they usually do not know that they are accessing a view. Users do not have to worry about the FROM, WHERE, and GROUP BY clauses. The complexities are placed in the view by the DA and are hidden from the user.

2. Views enhance the confidentiality of data. A user has access to all of the columns and rows in a table after the user has been granted the SELECT privilege. A view can limit the availability of the table's columns. The view uses a SELECT statement; therefore, the SELECT and WHERE clauses can filter the expressions and records available to the user, which gives the DA a means to hide confidential data.

3. Some information can be produced only through the views. Child data on different branches cannot be joined. The data can be joined only after separate SELECT statements summarize the data to the common parent level. If the SELECT statements are contained in views, the views can be joined, producing the desired information.

DAs use views extensively because they are responsible for providing data access and data content. DAs and business analysts have to write complex queries. Views help them in this task. In addition to making things simpler for users, a smart DA creates reusable views for his or her work. If a complex statement must be written repeatedly, why not place it in a view and do it once? In the following section, you will see how to create and administer views.

Administering Database Views

Database views are database objects just as tables, synonyms, or sequences are database objects. The CREATE VIEW command is used to add the views to the database. The following is a syntax template of the command:

Create [or replace] [force | noforce]
view *viewname* as *select statement*
[with check option [constraint *constraint*]]
[with read only];

Listing 10.1 illustrates the creation and use of a database view. The view is typical of one that might be used to mask the complexity of the query. The query has the following features:

- The Last_name and First_name columns were concatenated into one expression with a column alias of Name.

- Two runtime values are created. The query computes and formats the employees' ages and seniority.

- The query joins the Department and Employee tables.

The name of the view is Employee_data. After creation, the view can be used as a data source in the FROM clause of any SELECT statement.

The SELECT statement in Listing 10.1 demonstrates this. The SELECT statement uses the name of the view as if it were a table. In fact, if you did not know that Employee_data was a view, you would think it was a physical table. It is even possible to issue a DESCRIBE command against the view, as illustrated in the listing. The only way to determine whether a data source is a table or a view is to run a query against the User_objects data dictionary table.

Listing 10.1 *Using a View to Mask the SQL Complexity*

```
SQL> create or replace view employee_data as
  2  select department_name, last_name||', '||first_name name,
  3         wages, birth_date,
  4         trunc(months_between(sysdate, birth_date)/12,0) age,
  5         employment_date,
  6         trunc(months_between(sysdate, birth_date)/12,0)
  7            seniority_yrs
  8  from department, employee
  9  where department = fk_department;

View created.
```

```
SQL> select department_name, name, seniority_yrs
  2  from employee_data
  3  order by seniority_yrs desc;
```

using the view

derived age values

```
DEPARTMENT_NAME NAME                                     SENIORITY_YRS
--------------- ------------------------------------     -------------
POLITICAL SCIEN WILSON, WOODROW                                    144
WELFARE BUREAU  TAFT, WILLIAM                                      143
INTERIOR DESIGN ROOSEVELT, THEODORE                                142
INTERIOR DESIGN COOLIDGE, CALVIN                                   129
WELFARE BUREAU  HOOVER, HERBERT                                    127
POLITICAL SCIEN ROOSEVELT, FRANKLIN                                119
INTERIOR DESIGN TRUMAN, HAROLD                                     117
WELFARE BUREAU  ROOSEVELT, ELEANOR                                 116
INTERIOR DESIGN EISENHOWER, DWIGHT                                 110
POLITICAL SCIEN NIXON, RICHARD                                      93
POLITICAL SCIEN JOHNSON, LYNDON                                     93
POLITICAL SCIEN JOHNSON, ANDREW                                     92
INTERIOR DESIGN BUSH, GEORGE                                        90
INTERIOR DESIGN FORD, GERALD                                        88
WELFARE BUREAU  CARTER, JIMMY                                       88
POLITICAL SCIEN KENNEDY, JOHN                                       84
WELFARE BUREAU  ANTHONY, SUSANNE                                    81
WELFARE BUREAU  REAGAN, RONALD                                     76
POLITICAL SCIEN CLINTON, WILLIAM                                    61
POLITICAL SCIEN DWORCZAK, ALICE                                     46
INTERIOR DESIGN MILLER, KEVIN                                       25

21 rows selected.
```

issuing a DESCRIBE command on the view

```
SQL> desc employee_data
 Name                                             Null?    Type
 ------------------------------------------------ -------- ------
 DEPARTMENT_NAME                                           VARCHAR2(15)
 NAME                                                      VARCHAR2(32)
 WAGES                                                     NUMBER(8,2)
 BIRTH_DATE                                                DATE
 AGE                                                       NUMBER
 EMPLOYMENT_DATE                                           DATE
 SENIORITY_YRS                                             NUMBER

SQL>
```

```
SQL> drop view employee_data;

View dropped.

SQL>

End listing
```

A major part of a data administrator's job is to create views similar to the previous one. These views are then given to users. The GRANT SELECT command is needed for a user to access the view from an ID other than the one that owns the view.

The CREATE VIEW command has several available options, which are detailed in Table 10.1.

Table 10.1 *CREATE VIEW Command Options*

View Option	Description
OR REPLACE	Replaces an existing view with the new one. If this option is missing, Oracle will not allow you to overwrite an existing view. It must first be dropped.
FORCE	Allows the view to be created even if the tables do not exist or if the view references any invalid components.
NOFORCE	Allows the view to be created only if the tables exist and the components are valid. This is the default.
WITH CHECK OPTION	Restricts DML operations to only the rows that are accessible to the view.
WITH READ ONLY	Ensures that no DML operations can be performed using the view.

DML and Views

There are two types of views: simple and complex. Table 10.2 compares the two types of views.

Simple views can be used in DML statements because the records displayed in a simple view relate to one row of a table. Complex-view records are virtual records and do not generally relate to one row of a table. The DELETE command cannot be used against a complex view if the view has any of the following features:

- Contains a group function
- Contains a GROUP BY clause
- Contains the DISTINCT keyword
- Contains the pseudocolumn ROWNUM

A view cannot be updated if the view contains any of the above properties. It also cannot be updated if the view has the following property:

- Contains a column that is defined by expressions. These are columns that are concatenated or modified with functions such as SUBSTR or ADD_MONTHS.

A view cannot be used to add records to the database if the view contains any of the above properties. The view also cannot be used to insert records if the base tables have the following property:

- Contains NOT NULL constrained columns that do not exist in the view

Table 10.2 *View Type Properties*

Property	Simple View	Complex View
Number of Tables	One	One or more
Contains Functions	No	Yes
Grouped Values	No	Yes
DML Allowed	Yes	Not Always

The INSTEAD OF trigger, which will be discussed in a later section of this chapter, can be used to overcome the limitations discussed earlier. This trigger is initiated when a DML command is executed against the view. Rather than the view tables being modified, the trigger will execute the statements within the trigger.

The WITH CHECK OPTION Clause

Placing the WITH CHECK OPTION clause in the view will prevent some DML operations. This is useful for maintaining data integrity. The option will not allow an INSERT or DELETE operation that uses the view to change a value so that the change disables the view's ability to select the record. To illustrate, Listing 10.2 depicts a view that contains the names of the employees for the INT department. The view has the WITH CHECK OPTION clause. Notice the following about the listing:

- Following the creation of the view is an UPDATE command, which unsuccessfully attempts to update the view. The statement failed because it attempted to change the value of the Fk_department column. If the change were successful, the view would no longer be able to retrieve the record. This is the reason the WITH CHECK OPTION clause prevented the modification.

- Following the previous UPDATE statement is another UPDATE statement that uses the view to modify the First_name column. This statement was successful because it had no effect on the view's ability to select the record.

- The last UPDATE statement updates the Fk_department column and uses the name of the table rather than the view name. The modified record is no longer retrieved by the view. This statement was included in the listing to demonstrate that the WITH CHECK OPTION clause does not affect normal DML operations.

Listing 10.2 *Examples of Creating a View with the WITH CHECK OPTION Clause and Executing UPDATE Commands against the View*

```
SQL> create view employee_names as
  2   select fk_department, last_name, first_name
  3   from employee
```

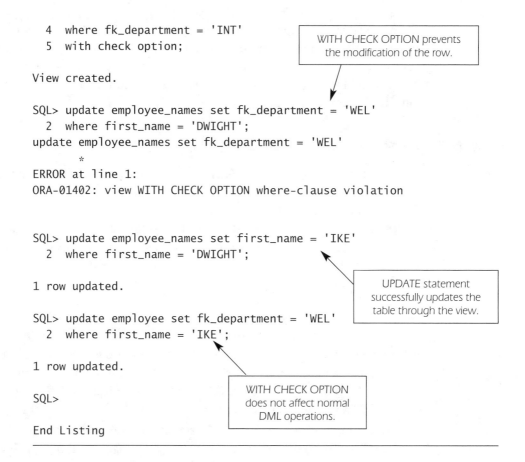

```
    4   where fk_department = 'INT'
    5   with check option;

View created.

SQL> update employee_names set fk_department = 'WEL'
  2   where first_name = 'DWIGHT';
update employee_names set fk_department = 'WEL'
        *
ERROR at line 1:
ORA-01402: view WITH CHECK OPTION where-clause violation


SQL> update employee_names set first_name = 'IKE'
  2   where first_name = 'DWIGHT';

1 row updated.

SQL> update employee set fk_department = 'WEL'
  2   where first_name = 'IKE';

1 row updated.

SQL>

End Listing
```

WITH CHECK OPTION prevents the modification of the row.

UPDATE statement successfully updates the table through the view.

WITH CHECK OPTION does not affect normal DML operations.

The WITH READ ONLY Option

The WITH READ ONLY option prevents any DML operation from occurring. Listing 10.3 contains a CREATE VIEW command that employs the WITH READ ONLY option. Following this command is an UPDATE statement that unsuccessfully attempts to update the view.

Listing 10.3 *Using the WITH READ ONLY Option*

```
SQL> create view employee_names as
  2   select fk_department, last_name, first_name
  3   from employee
  4   where fk_department = 'INT'
  5   with read only;
```

```
View created.

SQL> update employee_names set first_name = 'IKE'
  2  where first_name = 'DWIGHT';
where first_name = 'DWIGHT'
      *
ERROR at line 2:
ORA-01733: virtual column not allowed here


SQL>

End Listing
```

How to Update Records by Using a View That Can't Be Updated

Oracle has developed a tool that allows a developer to update views that are not normally able to be updated. This tool is called an INSTEAD OF trigger, which is similar to the database triggers that were discussed in Chapter 2. This trigger can be used only if the target is a view. It executes the trigger's PL/SQL rather than the DML transaction that launched the trigger.

To illustrate, Listing 10.4 contains a view that derives values. This is a view that computes an employee's eyeglasses and tool purchases as a percentage of the department's total purchases. This is a complex view that is not able to be updated. However, suppose you wanted to use this view in an application used to assign pay increases. The application would assign a 6-percent raise to employees who have purchases less than the departmental average. All other employees would get a 5-percent raise. The view can be used to identify the employees and the raise percent. The INSTEAD OF trigger can be used to update the employee record.

The first task is to create the complex view. Listing 10.4 contains a complex view used to compute employee purchases and the department averages. This view is comprised of a SELECT statement that has three inline views that compute each employee's total cost of tools and glasses, each department's total cost of tools and glasses, and the number of employees in a department. These summary values are then joined to the employee records.

Listing 10.4 *Complex View*

```
SQL> create or replace view wages_difference as
  2   select employee.fk_department, payroll_number, last_name,
  3          first_name, wages,
  4          employee_purchases/(dept_purchases/employee_amt)
  5          percent_of_Department_Avg
  6   from employee,
  7       (select fk_payroll_number, sum(cost) employee_purchases
  8        from (select fk_payroll_number, nvl(tool_cost,0) cost
  9              from emp_tools
 10              union all
 11              select fk_payroll_number, nvl(cost,0)
 12              from glasses)
 13        group by fk_payroll_number) e,
 14       (select fk_department, sum(cost) dept_purchases
 15        from (select fk_department, nvl(tool_cost,0) cost
 16              from employee, emp_tools
 17              where payroll_number = fk_payroll_number(+)
 18              union all
 19              select fk_department, nvl(cost,0)
 20              from employee, glasses
 21              where Payroll_number = fk_payroll_number(+))
 22        group by fk_department) f,
 23       (select fk_department, count(*) employee_amt
 24        from employee
 25        group by fk_department) c
 26   where employee.payroll_number = e.fk_payroll_number(+)
 27     and employee.fk_department = f.fk_department(+)
 28     and employee.fk_department = c.fk_department;

View created.

SQL> Select * from wages_difference order by 1,2;
```

FK_D	PAYROLL_NUMB	LAST_NAME	FIRST_NAME	WAGES	PERCENT_o
INT	22	ROOSEVELT	THEODORE	8000	2.3409784
INT	25	COOLIDGE	CALVIN	9500	.83041464
INT	28	TRUMAN	HAROLD	11000	.4349791
INT	29	EISENHOWER	DWIGHT		1.5421986

```
INT   33          FORD        GERALD         13000   .6208338
INT   36          BUSH        GEORGE         14000  .18269122
INT   46          MILLER      KEVIN           9500  1.0479042
POL   21          JOHNSON     ANDREW          7500  1.6477923
POL   24          WILSON      WOODROW         9000  2.1760472
POL   27          ROOSEVELT   FRANKLIN       10400  1.3512441
POL   30          KENNEDY     JOHN           11500
POL   31          JOHNSON     LYNDON         12000  1.5416879
POL   32          NIXON       RICHARD        12500  1.2832285
POL   37          CLINTON     WILLIAM        15000
POL   45          DWORCZAK    ALICE           9800
WEL   19          ROOSEVELT   ELEANOR               1.5981925
WEL   20          ANTHONY     SUSANNE         7000  .98475442
WEL   23          TAFT        WILLIAM         8500  .79214145
WEL   26          HOOVER      HERBERT        10000  .11316306
WEL   34          CARTER      JIMMY          13000  1.5984283
WEL   35          REAGAN      RONALD         13500  .91332024

21 rows selected.

SQL>

End Listing
```

The Wages_difference view cannot be updated directly; therefore, the developer would have to develop special programming to handle the DML transactions, which is where the INSTEAD OF trigger can be used. A trigger can be placed on the Wages_difference view. When an update occurs to the view, the Employee table (where the Wages column exists) will be updated. Listing 10.5 illustrates such a trigger. Whenever an UPDATE statement is executed against the Wages_difference view, the Wages_update trigger statements will be used in its place. These statements are part of PL/SQL code block and can contain UPDATE, DELETE, and INSERT statements. The statement can even modify tables that are not part of the view. In the case of the Wages_update trigger, the Wages value will be updated with an UPDATE statement.

Listing 10.5 *INSTEAD OF Database Trigger for Updating the Wages Column*

```
create or replace trigger wages_update
instead of update on wages_difference
for each row
begin
  update employee set wages = :new.wages
  where payroll_number = :new.payroll_number;
end;
/
End listing
```

Why Use Views?

Inline views and database views are the only devices that enable some queries to retrieve the proper results. The next several paragraphs describe a typical situation in which a view is the best tool to provide the desired results.

Databases contain many paths through the data. It is very common for multiple branches to exist. Figure 10.1 illustrates this concept. Parent table Employee has two child tables: Glasses and Emp_tools. This results in two different branches beneath the Employee table.

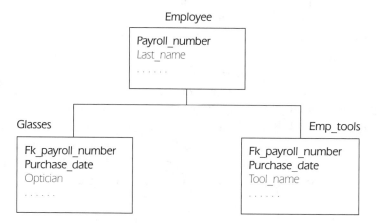

Figure 10.1 *Table relationship drawing depicting different branches*

It is possible to join Employee to Glasses and Employee to Emp_tools. However, you cannot join Employee to Glasses, nor the resulting virtual record to Emp_tools. In addition, Glasses cannot be joined directly to Emp_tools. Even though all three tables have common columns, Payroll_ number and Fk_payroll_number, there is no relationship between Emp_tools and Glasses. The relationship of the tables is through their parent: Employee. Thus Glasses and Emp_tools cannot be directly joined.

The joining of child records is one of the most common errors that people new to Oracle make. The new users see common columns in the child tables and assume that they can be joined. They ignore the missing relationship between the data.

To drive home this concept, I often challenge my students to produce the following query results: *Display the employees' names, wages, sum of their tool purchases, and the sum of their eyeglasses purchases on one row per employee.* If the student is able to accomplish this query, I give him or her an automatic A in the course.

The students know that the SUM group function (discussed in the next section) can be used to calculate the sum of tools and eyeglasses. They also realize that the Employee, Glasses, and Emp_tools tables have common columns: Payroll_number and fk_payroll_number. The first query they write, as well as all of the subsequent queries, generally consists of joins between the detail records of the three tables. Listing 10.6 illustrates a typical student query.

Listing 10.6 *Typical Incorrect Student Query*

```
SQL> select last_name, wages, sum(cost) glasses, sum(tool_cost) tools
  2  from employee, glasses, emp_tools
  3  where payroll_number = glasses.fk_payroll_number(+)
  4    and payroll_number = emp_tools.fk_payroll_number(+)
  5  group by last_name, wages;
```

LAST_NAME	WAGES	GLASSES	TOOLS
ANTHONY	7000	360	88.85
BUSH	14000		46.2
CARTER	13000	339	
CLINTON	15000		
COOLIDGE	9500	350	35

```
DWORCZAK            9800
EISENHOWER                        45        375
FORD                13000        435         12
HOOVER              10000                     24
JOHNSON              7500        330       16.7
JOHNSON             12000        170
KENNEDY             11500
MILLER               9500        330        100
NIXON               12500        246       18.5
REAGAN              13500        495       28.7
ROOSEVELT            8000        536        648
ROOSEVELT           10400        258         20
ROOSEVELT                        831      123.9
TAFT                 8500        145         23
TRUMAN              11000        110
WILSON               9000        369     116.95

21 rows selected.

SQL>

End listing
```

The query in Listing 10.6 was incorrect because it caused Oracle to create records before the summation occurred. Joining the employee records to the glasses records caused one new virtual record to be created for each of the matches between the two tables. The number of employee record values was multiplied to match the number of glasses records. This is all right because we are still on the same branch of the data tree.

The next step that occurs is joining the emp_tools records to the new virtual record. This is where the inaccuracies occur. The number of records and values will multiply due to the matching of payroll numbers. This occurs because of the joining, and it causes the error.

The key to solving the dilemma is to create a virtual record computing the summary values before the join operation. The glasses and emp_tools virtual record for each employee are then joined to the employee record. This can be done only by using a view or an inline view, as they are the tools that compute virtual records for a SELECT statement.

Listing 10.7 illustrates the correct answer. This query uses an inline view to create a virtual record before the joining operation occurs.

Listing 10.7 *Correctly Solving the Student Challenge by Using an Inline View*

```
SQL> select last_name, wages, eyeglass_cost, tool_cost
  2  from employee,
  3        (select fk_payroll_number, sum(cost) eyeglass_cost
  4         from glasses
  5         group by fk_payroll_number) glasses_iv,
  6        (select fk_payroll_number, sum(tool_cost) tool_cost
  7         from emp_tools
  8         group by fk_payroll_number) emp_tools_iv
  9  where payroll_number = glasses_iv.fk_payroll_number(+)
 10    and payroll_number = emp_tools_iv.fk_payroll_number(+),
```

LAST_NAME	WAGES	EYEGLASS_COST	TOOL_COST
ROOSEVELT		277	61.95
ANTHONY	7000	120	88.85
JOHNSON	7500	165	16.7
ROOSEVELT	8000	268	324
TAFT	8500	145	23
WILSON	9000	123	116.95
COOLIDGE	9500	175	35
HOOVER	10000		24
ROOSEVELT	10400	129	20
EISENHOWER		15	375
NIXON	12500	123	18.5
FORD	13000	145	12
REAGAN	13500	165	28.7
BUSH	14000		46.2
MILLER	9500	165	100
CLINTON	15000		
KENNEDY	11500		
DWORCZAK	9800		
TRUMAN	11000	110	
CARTER	13000	339	
JOHNSON	12000	170	

```
21 rows selected.

SQL>
```

End listing

As you can see, an inline view is a SELECT statement embedded in the FROM clause. There are only two requirements for their use:

1. The SELECT statement must be enclosed by parentheses.

2. The inline view must have a name or table alias.

I prefer to use inline views in my SELECT statements, rather than using a view, because a view is a database object. This may mean that a DBA has to create the object. It also clutters the database. When you list your tables, you will also list the views. You may not want to clutter your database with temporary SELECT statements that are used for only one query.

Materialized Views

The two types of views that we have seen thus far, inline view and database view, create a virtual table at runtime. This means the view must execute the SELECT statement at the time it is used. A benefit of this is that the derived records do not have to be stored on the database. The problem with complex views is in the time needed to derive the records. Complex queries (or views) can take minutes or longer to derive the result set.

Oracle has a third type of view that has physical properties: a **materialized view**. Materialized views or snapshots are used to replicate data. This can be at a remote site for query performance or in a local data warehouse. The beauty of materialized views is the available options. Materialized views can be set up to refresh remote data automatically or to move only the changes to the remote data site, which can substantially reduce the amount of data that is transferred.

Data warehouses generally consist of data derived from production OLTP systems. The warehouse tables are copies of the production data or computed summary information. The data copies are placed in the data warehouse located on another server in order to maintain production system performance. Data analysis is performed against the data warehouse rather than the production system. Data warehouses also contain summary data. Data is summarized because it can save substantial analysis time. The problem with the maintenance of data-warehouse data is the processing time to move or summarize data for the data warehouse. Materialized views are a perfect tool for maintaining data warehouses tables because they contain a SELECT statement that can summarize data and they can be set up to move or reconcile the data at special intervals or times.

Databases no longer reside on centralized mainframes or servers. They are located on many servers. The data can exist anywhere in the world. I have a client located in Omaha, Nebraska, who regularly accesses databases in Vicksburg, Mississippi, and Portland, Oregon. The requests for data must be sent over a phone line to these locations, and the data are returned over the same phone lines. This continual transfer of data can decrease performance and increase the usage of the machine. To alleviate this problem, data can be replicated at the Omaha site and be synchronized occasionally, which eliminates the constant data transfer during peak hours. Materialized views are an excellent tool to maintain the replicated data at remote sites, as well as for data warehouses.

The creation of materialized views is a database administration task that the developer, data administrator, or business analyst generally does not perform. However, these personnel are involved in the design of data warehouses or are interested in quick retrieval of data. If your queries do not have the performance you desire, if they affect the performance of a production system, or if you access remote databases, materialized views might be a benefit.

Listing 10.8 is an example of a materialized view that could be used to create summary department information on our practice database. There are far too many command parameters to discuss in this book, but I think several of them are worth exploring:

- Materialized views contain a SELECT statement, which produces the information stored in the view.
- A TABLESPACE parameter can be entered, which identifies where the database will be stored and controls the size of the data stored in the view.
- A START WITH parameter is available (and not shown). It indicates the date Oracle should refresh the view. Oracle will be responsible for this automatic refresh of the data.
- A NEXT parameter is available (and not shown). It is used to determine the dates for subsequent automatic data refreshes.
- A FAST option is available (and not shown). It causes Oracle to update the existing view based on changed values in the original data stores.

- A COMPLETE option (not shown) will cause the entire view to be replaced with new data.

- An ON COMMIT option (not shown) will cause the view to be updated the next time a COMMIT command is issued.

- An ON DEMAND option (not shown) will cause the view to be updated only when it is requested.

Listing 10.8 *Example of a Materialized View for a Summary Table*

```
Create materialized view department_costs
  Pctfree 0 tablespace data_warehouse
  STORAGE (INITIAL 16k NEXT 16k PCTINCREASE 0)
  PARALLEL
  BUILD DEFERRED
  REFRESH COMPLETE
  ENABLE QUERY REWRITE
  AS
  SELECT department, sum(wages) department_wages,
         Department_tool_costs, department_eyeglass_costs
  From department, employee,
       (select fk_department, sum(tool_costs) department_tool_costs
        from employee, emp_tools
        where payroll_number = fk_payroll_number(+)
        group by fk_department) tool_cost,
       (select fk_department, sum(cost) department_eyeglass_costs
        from employee, glasses
        where payroll_number = fk_payroll_number(+)
        group by fk_department) eyeglass_cost
  Where department.department = employee.fk_department(+)
    And department.department = tool_cost.fk_department(+)
    And department.department = eyeglass_cost.fk_department(+)
  Group by department, department_tool_costs,
           Department_eyeglass_costs;


End Listing
```

As indicated, materialized views contain SELECT statements that move data into a table. The analytic functions discussed in Chapter 9 are excellent tools to use with materialized views. Data warehouses often contain summary information for performance reasons. OLTP databases can contain enormous amounts of data. Summarization can reduce the size of the data, thereby reducing the number of records that Oracle must process in order to return the desired results. The analytic functions CUBE and ROLLUP are designed to compute aggregate values of different dimensions efficiently. They can be used to populate the materialized view. Ranking and windowing functions are also good candidates for materialized views. Placing these values into the view will simplify queries of the less technical user, as well as increase performance.

What's Next?

The next chapter will discuss the report-writing features that are available in SQL*Plus. These features are available in all installations of Oracle. They are generally used for formatting query results. It is sometimes easier to create a simple report in SQL*Plus rather than launching a report writer and creating a report. The format options are limited, but people working with Oracle often use them.

▪ PRACTICE

1. A user you support is in need of a mailing list. The names of the employees on the list must be formatted with each employee's title. Precede female-employee names with *Ms*. Precede male-employee names with *Mr*. This type of data does not exist in the database. You have been asked to create a database view that contains this feature.

2. Create a view that displays employee records and wages for the WEL department. Put a check option on the view. Using the view, change the department number to *INT* for employees living in plains. (You should not be able to update the record.)

11

Using SQL*Plus as a Report-Writing Tool

SQL*Plus has limited report-writing capabilities. It was Oracle's original report-writing tool, and it has retained its report-writing capabilities. The technology is reminiscent of the report-writing technology used in the mid-1980s. There are many other tools that can be used to create Oracle reports, but they may not be available to you. If they are not, you can always use the tools explained in this chapter to make reports. Many DBAs and analysts use SQL*Plus to make quick, simple reports. This feature is especially useful for making DBA-type reports such as lists of user accounts, performance statistics, or user objects.

Format commands entered prior to the SELECT statement enable you to format reports. The commands can be entered at the SQL prompt but are more commonly placed in a script file that is loaded into SQL*Plus by using the at sign (@) command. Placing the commands in a script file allows you to reexecute them repeatedly along with the SELECT statement.

Title and Footer Settings

The displayed record listing can be given a title and footer by using the TTITLE and BTITLE commands, which are entered prior to the execution of the SELECT statement. The TTITLE command will cause a text string composed of literal text and variables to appear at the top of each new page of displayed records. The BTITLE command will do the same for the bottom of each page of displayed records. The TTITLE OFF and BTITLE OFF commands are used to remove the settings from memory.

Following the TTITLE and BTITLE keywords, you can enter literal text, variables, and special formatting options. The literal text must be enclosed by single quotation marks. The TTITLE and BTITLE formatting options are listed in Table 11.1.

Format commands reside in memory and will be reused on every SELECT statement until they are removed from memory by using the OFF option or until they are replaced with new commands. This is true for all of the formatting commands discussed in this chapter.

Formatting commands are terminated by the ENTER key. However, the commands can be quite long, often requiring multiple lines. Placing a dash (-) at the end of a line will tell Oracle that the command is carried onto the next line. This will allow you to use multiple lines for a command. Listing 11.1 illustrates a simple query that uses the TTITLE and BTITLE commands.

Table 11.1 *TTITLE and BTITLE Formatting Options*

Option Keyword	Description
CENTER	Places the item following the option in the center of the current title line
COL *n*	Places the text following the option at the specified column (The column number is specified by the *n*.)
LEFT	Places the text following the option on the left side of the current line
RIGHT	Places the text following the option on the right side of the current line
OFF	Clears the specified COLUMN command from memory
SKIP *n*	Causes SQL*Plus to skip the specified number of lines and to print the remainder of the title (The letter *n* represents the number of lines to skip.)
SQL.PNO	Causes the current page number to appear at the designated location in the title
- (dash)	Allows the developer to record title commands on multiple lines

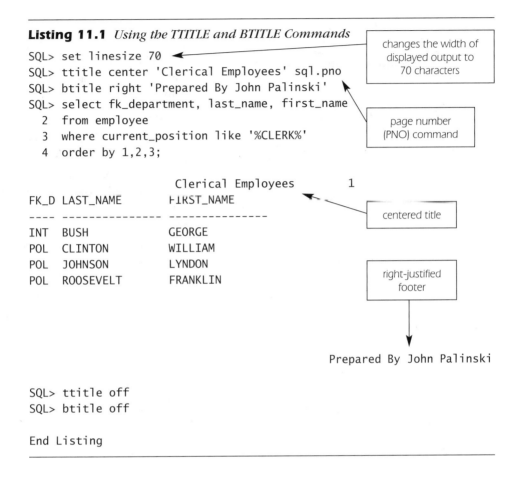

Listing 11.1 *Using the TTITLE and BTITLE Commands*

```
SQL> set linesize 70
SQL> ttitle center 'Clerical Employees' sql.pno
SQL> btitle right 'Prepared By John Palinski'
SQL> select fk_department, last_name, first_name
  2  from employee
  3  where current_position like '%CLERK%'
  4  order by 1,2,3;

                              Clerical Employees         1
FK_D LAST_NAME       FIRST_NAME
---- --------------- ---------------
INT  BUSH            GEORGE
POL  CLINTON         WILLIAM
POL  JOHNSON         LYNDON
POL  ROOSEVELT       FRANKLIN



                                             Prepared By John Palinski


SQL> ttitle off
SQL> btitle off

End Listing
```

changes the width of displayed output to 70 characters

page number (PNO) command

centered title

right-justified footer

Formatting Columns

The next formatting command available to you is the COLUMN command, which can do a variety of tasks. Some of its functionality allows you to define a column heading, word wrap the values, format the data, store a value for use in the title, or stop the printing of a particular column.

Table 11.2 contains the various options available for the command. Many of the keywords can be abbreviated. The abbreviated name is outside the brackets.

Column commands can be entered at the SQL prompt or can be included in a script. The command will remain in memory until it is cleared or until a new command is entered for the column. You may use any combination of

Table 11.2 *COLUMN Command Format Options*

Option Keyword	Example	Description
ALI[AS]	Column state ali st	Gives the target column a different name
CLE[AR]	Column state cle	Eliminates from memory the target column's formatting options
FOR[MAT]	Column wages for $999.99	Formats the data displayed in the column (Format character data by using the letter *A* followed by a numeric value. See Table 3.5 for numeric formats.)
HEA[DING]	Column a hea 'Total Wages' Column a hea 'Total|Wages'	Determines the text to be used in the column's heading (Adding a pipe symbol [|] will cause following text to be displayed on the next line.)
JUS[TIFY]	Column wages jus right	Aligns the displayed data on the right
LIKE	Column wages like a	Sets the format options of the target column the same as another column
NEW[LINE]	Column wages new	Places subsequent displayed row data on the next line
NEW_V[ALUE]	Column last_name new_v name	Creates a temporary variable, places the value of the target column into the variable for each new row, and allows the developer to place row data into a variable for use in the report title
NOPRI[NT]	Column sysdate nopri	Suppresses the display of the target column
NUL[L]	Column wages nul 0	Determines the value to be placed into the target column of a row that contains a null value
OFF	Column a off	Suppresses the column-formatting options of the target column without removing them from memory

Table 11.2 *(continued)*

Option Keyword	Example	Description
OLD_V[ALUE]	Column sysdate old_v current_date	Creates a temporary variable, places the target column value into the variable for each new row, and allows the developer to place row data into the report footer
ON	Column a on	Reactivates the column-formatting options of the target column
TRU[NCATED]	Column street tru	Causes the displayed value to be truncated at the defined width of the target column
WOR[D_WRAPPED]	Column street wor	Causes the data within the column to appear on multiple lines and causes Oracle to avoid placing partial words on a row
WRA[PPED]	Column street wra	Causes the data within the column to appear on multiple lines and causes Oracle to leave partial words on a row

options in one command. As an example, to change the heading of the column Wages to Yearly Wages, to right align the data, and to format the data with a dollar sign, the command is as follows:

Column wages hea 'Yearly Wages' jus right format $99,999.99

The FORMAT option can be used to change the default length of a character column. For example, if you create an expression such as *last_name||',*
'||*first_name*, you might want to change the column width to 35. This can be done using the character format definition of *A35*.

Numbers can be formatted in a variety of ways, which are illustrated in Table 11.3.

To see the current COLUMN format in memory, type *Column column_name*.

Table 11.3 *Numeric Formats*

Format	Example	Result	Description
9999990	Column wages for 999990	10000	The entire count of 9s and 0s determines the overall length of the expression. Ending the format with a 0 will cause zero values to be displayed. Beginning the expression with a 0 will cause the expression to display leading zeros (012456).
9,999,999.99	Column wages for 99,999.99	10,000.00	Commas and decimals can be placed in the format.
$99,999.99	Column wages for $99,999.00	$10,000.00	Dollar signs can be placed within the format.
B99999	Column wages for B99999	10000	Default format. Zero values are suppressed.
99999MI	Column temperature for 999MI	25	Causes the negative sign to be displayed on the right rather than on the left (which is the default).
99999PR	Column net_income for 99999PR	<10000>	Causes negative numbers to be bracketed.
99999EEEE	Column num_of_stars for 99999EEEE	1E+08 (Using a value of 123456789)	Displays the results in scientific notation. You must use four Es.
999V99	Column percent_of_total for 999V99	87 (Using a value of .87)	Multiplies the target number by a factor of 10. The values on the right determine the factor. The values on the left format the result.
Date	Column birth_date for 'DD-MON-YYYY'	'08-APR-2000'	Changes the default date picture of the date.

To illustrate, Listing 11.2 uses COLUMN commands to format a simple report displaying employee wages for the POL department. The commands do the following:

- Printing of the Fk_department column is suppressed. Its value populates a variable called dept. The variable is used in the title.

- The width of the employee name expression is expanded to 35 spaces. The expression is given a new heading that is to be displayed on two lines.

- The Current_position column is given a new heading and a width of 16 spaces.

- The Wages column is formatted with a leading dollar sign and two decimal positions.

- The current date (SYSDATE) is suppressed from printing and is assigned to the DAY variable used in the footer.

Listing 11.2 *SQL*Plus Script Using COLUMN Commands*

```
SQL> set linesize 70
SQL> column fk_department noprint new_val dept
SQL> column name head 'Employee|Name' for a35
SQL> column current_position head 'Classification' for a16
SQL> column wages for $99,999.00
SQL> column sysdate noprint old_val day
SQL> ttitle center 'Employees For Department' skip 1 center dept
SQL> btitle day center sql.pno
SQL> select sysdate, fk_department, last_name||', '||first_name name,
  2    current_position, wages
  3  from employee
  4  where fk_department = 'POL';


                    Employees For Department
                             POL

Employee
Name                                  Classification        WAGES
------------------------------------- ----------------  -----------
WILSON, WOODROW                       MAINT. MAN 3       $9,000.00
DWORCZAK, ALICE                       ADMINISTRATOR      $9,800.00
JOHNSON, LYNDON                       TREASURER CLERK   $12,000.00
```

```
JOHNSON, ANDREW              SALESPERSON 1      $7,500.00
CLINTON, WILLIAM             CLERK 1           $15,000.00
NIXON, RICHARD               TREASURER         $12,500.00
KENNEDY, JOHN                PROGRAMMER 1      $11,500.00
ROOSEVELT, FRANKLIN          CLERK 1           $10,400.00



03-APR-00                              1

8 rows selected.

SQL> clear columns
columns cleared
SQL> ttitle off
SQL>

End listing
```

Breaks

The reports and listings we have seen thus far are called tabular reports, which consist of a series of columns and rows. If the rows have repeating values, the repeating values will be displayed on each row. It is not generally desirable to do this. A much more pleasing and effective technique is to print a column value only when it changes. This reduces the amount of data on your report and helps the reader identify pertinent information. The type of report that prints values only when they change is called a group left report.

To create a group left report, you must group your like data. This means that records with repeating column values must be placed together on the report. This is done by using the ORDER BY clause of the SELECT statement. The BREAK command is the formatting tool that will cause the suppression of duplicate values. The command also has some other uses:

- It can cause the changed record to appear on a new page. This is called a page break.

- It can cause spaces to appear between records when the values change.

- It can identify the end of a group of like records for the computation of a subtotal.

Various BREAK option keywords are listed in Table 11.4.

Placing the ON keyword and another target column after the primary-break specification will create secondary breaks. Each of the break specifications can have its own option. For example, to create a report that prints each department's records at the top of a new page and skips two lines whenever the employee Current_position value changes, use this BREAK command:

Break on fk_department page on current_position skip 2

Be sure to synchronize the ORDER BY clause of the SELECT statement with the columns listed in the BREAK command.

The BREAK command is similar in nature to the other format commands. It is not a part of the SELECT statement. It is generally placed in a script file with other formatting commands. The BREAK command options will remain

Table 11.4 *Break Options*

Option Keyword	Example	Description
REPORT	Break on report	Breaks at the end of the report
ROW	Break on row	Breaks on each row
PAGE	Break on page	Breaks at the end of each physical page of output
SKI[P] lines	Break on fk_department skip 2	Skips the specified number of lines when the value of the target column changes
SKI[P] page	Break on fk_department page	Skips to the next page when the value of the target column changes
NODUP[LICATES]	Break on fk_department nodup	Suppresses the display of duplicate values for the target column (a default option)
DUP[LICATES]	Break on fk_department dup	Overrides the suppression of duplicate values

in memory until cleared or until another BREAK command is issued. The CLEAR BREAKS command can be used to remove the settings from memory.

Listing 11.3 is a partial report that illustrates the use of the BREAK command. This report prints a list of employees for all the departments in our practice database. Each department's employees will be printed on a new page so that the report can be distributed to various department heads. Some of the departments have employees with the same last name. The duplicate name values will be suppressed.

Listing 11.3 *Departmental Employee Report Illustrating the BREAK Command*

```
SQL> set linesize 70
SQL> column fk_department noprint new_val dept
SQL> column last_name head 'Employee|Last Name' for a20
SQL> column first_name head 'Employee|First Name' for a20
SQL> column current_position head 'Classification' for a16
SQL> column wages for $99,999.00
SQL> column sysdate noprint old_val day
SQL> break on fk_department page on last_name
SQL> ttitle center 'Employees For Department' skip 1 center dept
SQL> btitle day center sql.pno
SQL> select sysdate, fk_department, last_name, first_name,
  2      current_position, wages
  3  from employee
  4  order by 2,3;
```

```
                    Employees For Department          secondary break
                            POL                        on last_name
Employee            Employee
Last Name           First Name     Classification           WAGES
------------------- ------------------ ---------------- -----------
CLINTON             WILLIAM        CLERK 1            $15,000.00
DWORCZAK            ALICE          ADMINISTRATOR       $9,800.00
JOHNSON             LYNDON         TREASURER CLERK    $12,000.00
                    ANDREW         SALESPERSON 1       $7,500.00
KENNEDY             JOHN           PROGRAMMER 1       $11,500.00
NIXON               RICHARD        TREASURER          $12,500.00
ROOSEVELT           FRANKLIN       CLERK 1            $10,400.00
WILSON              WOODROW        MAINT. MAN 3        $9,000.00
```

```
04-APR-00                              2
                        Employees For Department
                                WEL
Employee                 Employee
Last Name                First Name        Classification       WAGES
-------------------      -------------------  ----------------  -----------
ANTHONY                  SUSANNE           SALESPERSON 2         $7,000.00
CARTER                   JIMMY             LABORER 3            $13,000.00

End listing
```

new page created
when the
department
changed

Subtotals

The COMPUTE command is often used with the BREAK command and is used to calculate subtotals at breakpoints because summary totals are a very desirable report feature. The COMPUTE command, however, cannot be used without a complimentary BREAK command and is often confused with the group functions. In essence, they compute the same value. The difference is that the COMPUTE command allows the display of the detail (or grouped) records, while the GROUP BY clause used with the function compresses them into a single row.

The COMPUTE command is a format command, and it will reside in memory until cleared with the CLEAR COMPUTES command or until over-written with a new command. The structure of the command is as follows:

Compute *value(s)* label *text* of *target columns* on *break name*

The COMPUTE command can calculate any or all of the values listed in Table 11.5. You may list any number of these within the *value(s)* section of the command. You need to separate the various values with a space, not a comma. The LABEL option can follow any of the listed values. It will change the default label of the value to the specified one. The default value of a label is the value keyword (e.g., AVG, COUNT).

The target column's clause is initiated by the keyword ON. This clause contains report expressions on which a summary calculation is desired.

Table 11.5 *Calculated Values and Keywords*

Keyword	Example	Description
AVG	Compute avg of wages on fk_department	Calculates the average of the target column's group
COUNT	Compute count of last_name on fk_department	Counts the not null occurrences of the target column's group
MAXIMUM	Compute maximum of wages on fk_department	Determines the maximum value of the target column's group
MINIMUM	Compute minimum of wages on fk_department	Determines the minimum value of the target column's group
NUMBER	Compute number of last_name on report	Counts the number of returned rows of the target column's group
STD	Compute std of wages on report	Calculates the standard deviation of the target column
SUM	Compute sum of wages on fk_department	Calculates the sum of the target column's group
VARIANCE	Compute variance of wages on fk_department	Calculates the variance of the target column's group

Names are separated by spaces. The BREAK clause determines when the calculation will occur. You may use the following options:

- *break column*   This is the term used for the name of any expression listed in the BREAK command.
- REPORT   The calculations will occur at the end of the report.
- ROW   The calculations will occur after each selected row.
- PAGE   The calculations will occur at the end of each physical page of data.

Listing 11.4 illustrates the COMPUTE command. The command calculates the sum of wages for each department. This subtotal is calculated at the end of each department's set of records. The default label of the value is SUM. The LABEL option is used to change the calculation name to Total Department Wages. The name of the value is displayed in the column that determines the break. In the case of Listing 11.4, it is the Department_name column. The default length of this field is 15, which is too small for the label value. Thus the Department_name default length was changed to 25 with a COLUMN command.

Listing 11.4 *Using the COMPUTE Command*

```
SQL> set linesize 70
SQL> column department_name hea Department Name for a25
SQL> column last_name head 'Employee|Last Name' for a15
SQL> column first_name head 'Employee|First Name' for a15
SQL> column wages for $99,999.00
SQL> column sysdate noprint old_val day
SQL> break on department_name page on last_name
SQL> compute sum label 'Total Department Wages' of wages on
department_name
SQL> ttitle center 'Departmental Employees And Wages'
SQL> btitle day center sql.pno
SQL> select sysdate, department_name, last_name, first_name,
  2        wages
  3  from employee, department
  4  where fk_department = department
  5  order by 2,3;
```

COMPUTE command

```
                 Departmental Employees And Wages
                          Employee          Employee
Department Name           Last Name         First Name           WAGES
------------------------- ----------------- --------------- -----------
INTERIOR DESIGN           BUSH              GEORGE           $14,000.00
                          COOLIDGE          CALVIN            $9,500.00
                          EISENHOWER        DWIGHT
                          FORD              GERALD           $13,000.00
                          MILLER            KEVIN             $9,500.00
                          ROOSEVELT         THEODORE          $8,000.00
                          TRUMAN            HAROLD           $11,000.00
************************** ***************                   -----------
Total Department Wages                                       $65,000.00
.
.
```

subtotal label

subtotal

```
04-APR-00                                    3
21 rows selected.

SQL> clear columns
columns cleared
SQL> clear breaks
breaks cleared
SQL> ttitle off
SQL> btitle off
SQL> clear computes
computes cleared
SQL>

End listing
```

Sending the Output to the Printer

Sending your output to a printer was first touched on in Chapter 4. The results of a SELECT statement cannot be printed directly from SQL*Plus. Before the results can be sent to the printer, the results must be placed into a file that is stored on the hard drive. Saving the results of the SELECT statement is called **spooling**. Table 11.6 contains the names of the commands used to spool the results. The commands are generally placed in a script immediately before and after the SELECT statement. Doing so will suppress the formatting statements from being saved in the output file.

Table 11.6 *Spooling Commands*

Command	Example	Description
SPOOL *filename*	Spool c:\depart_rep	Sends the output to a file called depart_rep.lst on drive C (All screen output following this command will be sent to the target file.)
SPOOL OFF	Spool off	Suppresses the output of values to the spool file
SPOOL OUT	Spool out	Stops the spooling of the displayed records and sends the contents of the spool file to the printer

You do not have to specify the name of the file after the SPOOL keyword. Oracle will determine its own default name and will put on a default extension (.lst). It will also put this file in the default directory in which SQL*Plus is located, which is generally the \orant\bin directory. If you include the name of the file but do not enter a full file path, Oracle will put the file in the default Oracle directory. Many people new to Oracle have trouble locating the file. Be sure to put the full file path after the SPOOL keyword.

There are two other methods of spooling your results: You may enter the commands at the SQL prompt, or you may use the Spool option on the File menu. Listing 11.5 illustrates the placement of the SPOOL commands.

Listing 11.5 *Placement of SPOOL Commands*

```
set linesize 70
column department_name hea department_name for a25
column last_name head 'Employee|Last Name' for a15
column first_name head 'Employee|First Name' for a15
column wages for $99,999.00
column sysdate noprint old_val day
break on department_name page on last_name
compute sum label 'Total Department Wages' of wages on department_name
compute sum of wages on report
ttitle center 'Departmental Employees And Wages'
btitle day center sql.pno
spool c:\department_rep.lst
select sysdate, department_name, last_name, first_name,
     wages
from employee, department
where fk_department = department
order by 2,3;
spool off
clear columns
clear breaks
ttitle off
btitle off
clear computes

End listing
```

Spooling is turned on prior to the SELECT statement. None of the format statements will be contained in the listing.

Spooling is terminated after the SELECT statement. None of the following statements will be contained in the listing.

SET Commands

You might have noticed the SET LINESIZE 70 command as the first line of most of the script files seen in this chapter. This command is used to tell Oracle to wrap the results to the next line after 70 characters. I used this command in order to get the results formatted for a portrait (8.5-by-11-inch) document. SQL*Plus has a number of environmental variables that can be used to change how SQL*Plus looks and operates. Some of these, like the LINESIZE variable, are used to format results. Table 11.7 describes the majority and most common of the SET command variables. A full list is available on

Table 11.7 *SQL*Plus Environmental Variables*

Name	Description
APPI[INFO]	Enables the registration of command files using the DBMS_APPLICATION_INFO package. Values are ON (default) and OFF.
ARRAY[SIZE]	Determines the number of records Oracle will fetch at one time. The default is 20. The range is between 1 and 5,000.
AUTO[COMMIT]	Determines whether Oracle will commit changes immediately or after a specified number of commands. The default is OFF. Other acceptable values are IMM (immediately), ON, or a specified integer.
AUTO[PRINT]	Determines whether SQL*Plus automatically displays bind variables used in a PL/SQL block. The default is ON. The other value is OFF.
AUTOT[RACE]	Allows you to see the execution path for a query after it has been executed. Acceptable values are ON, OFF, EXP[LAIN], and STAT[ISTICS].
BLOCKTERMINATOR	Determines the symbol used to denote the end of a PL/SQL block.
BUFFER	Sets the specified buffer as the default.
CLOSECUR[SOR]	Determines whether a cursor will close and reopen after each SQL statement. Acceptable values are ON (default) and OFF.
CMDS[EP]	Determines the character used to separate multiple SQL*Plus commands. ON and OFF (default) control whether multiple commands can be entered on a line. A symbol is also an acceptable value.

Table 11.7 *(continued)*

Name	Description
COLSEP	Determines the value to be printed between columns.
COM[PATIBILITY]	Sets the version of Oracle to which you are connected.
CONCAT	Changes the symbol used to concatenate string values. The default is a pipe symbol (|).
COPYCOMMIT	Commits rows on a cycle of *n* batches of rows. Values range from 0 to 5,000.
COPYTYPECHECK	Enables the suppression of data-type checks when using the COPY command.
DCL[SEP]	Sets the symbol used to separate multiple operating-system commands entered in SQL*Plus.
DEF[INE]	Defines the character used to indicate a substitution variable. The default is an ampersand (&). The setting may also be changed to ON or OFF. The latter settings determine whether SQL*Plus will scan for a substitution variable.
DOC[UMENT]	A setting of ON allows the command to work. This command tells SQL*Plus that a block of documentation is beginning. The default is OFF.
ECHO	The ON setting causes the SQL commands to display on the screen as they are executed from a command or script file. The default is OFF.
EDITF[ILE]	Sets the default filename that the EDIT command uses.
EMBEDDED	The ON setting allows a new report within a series of reports to begin anywhere on a page. The OFF setting forces the new report to start at the top of a new page.
ESCAPE	The escape symbol may be changed from the default backslash (\) with this setting. OFF disables this setting.
FEED[BACK]	Determines when the "records selected" value displays. If the amount of records selected is greater than or equal to the specified value, the amount of records that the query selected will be displayed. The default setting is six records. To turn off the display, use the OFF setting. This setting is used when a command file can be run without needing any display or interaction until it is completed. It enables the operating system to avoid sending output to the display.

Table 11.7 *SQL*Plus Environmental Variables (continued)*

Name	Description
FLAGGER	Sets the FIPS level for SQL92. Values are OFF, ENTRY, INTERMED[IATE], and FULL.
FLUSH	Used when an external file is to be executed without any display or interaction. The OFF setting suppresses the operating system from sending output to the display. ON restores output to the user's display. OFF may improve performance.
HEA[DING]	The OFF setting suppresses column headings. The default is ON.
HEADS[EP]	Changes the default heading separator (|) to another symbol. The settings are ON and OFF.
INSTANCE	Replaces the default instance of your session. This command does not cause Oracle to connect to another database.
LIN[ESIZE]	Specifies the length of a line of output. Output longer than this line will wrap to the next line. The default is 80.
LOBOF[FSET]	Sets the beginning position from which CLOB and NCLOB data are retrieved and displayed.
LONG	Determines the maximum width for displaying or copying long values. The value may be set from 1 to 32,767.
LONGC[HUNKSIZE]	Sets the size of the increments in which SQL*Plus retrieves a LONG value. The default is 80.
MARK[UP] HTML	Causes Oracle to output HTML. The arguments OFF and ON determine whether the output is in HTML. A HEADING *text* option allows you to specify a value for the <HEAD> tag. A BODY text option allows you to specify a value for the <BODY> tag. A SPOOL ON and OFF option determines whether SQL*Plus writes tags to the start and end of each file by the normal SPOOL command.
MAXD[ATA]	Determines the maximum total row width that SQL*Plus can process. The default and maximum value vary with the operating system.
NEWP[AGE]	Specifies the number of blank lines to be printed between the bottom of one page and the top title of the next. A value of 0 sends a form feed at the top of each page.
NULL	Enables you to substitute *text* for a null value when they are encountered.

Table 11.7 *(continued)*

Name	Description
NUMF[ORMAT]	Changes the default width for number displays.
NUM[WIDTH]	Changes the default width for number displays. The original default is 10 digits.
PAGES[IZE]	Determines the number of lines per page. The default is 14.
PAU[SE]	The ON setting causes SQL*Plus to wait for you to press ENTER before displaying the next page. The default is ON. The setting may also be used to specify text that will be displayed during a pause.
RECSEP	Defines when a line of characters is printed. The EACH setting will print the characters after each line. The WRAPPED setting prints after the wrapped line. The OFF setting suppresses the printing.
RECSEPCHAR	Sets the character used for the RECSEP setting.
SCAN	Suppresses substitution variables that may be defined in the command file. The settings consist of ON and OFF. This is a command from an earlier version and may be obsolete at some point. The ON option works similarly to the SET DEFINE ON command.
SERVEROUT[PUT]	Allows the display of the output of PL/SQL procedures from the DBMS_OUTPUT package. Values are ON and OFF (the default). Several option settings are also available: WRA[PPED], WOR[D_WRAPPED], TRU[NCATED], and FOR[MAT].
SQLC[ASE]	Converts all text in SQL commands or PL/SQL blocks before it is executed. MIXED, UPPER, or LOWER settings may be used to change the case.
SQL[CONTINUE]	Changes the character(s) used in the editor for the CONTINUE line prompt. The default prompt is greater than (>).
SQLN[UMBER]	When this setting is ON, each line of an SQL command will have a line number. When the setting is OFF, subsequent lines of the command will not have line numbers. The default is ON.
SQLPRE[FIX]	Changes the SQL*Plus prefix character.
SQLP[ROMPT]	Changes the SQL*Plus prompt from the default to a new text string.
SQLT[ERMINATOR]	Changes the symbol that terminates an SQL statement from a semicolon to a new value. The terminator can be turned off with the OFF setting. The ON setting returns it to a semicolon.

Table 11.7 *SQL*Plus Environmental Variables (continued)*

Name	Description
SUF[FIX]	Changes the default filename extension the editor uses. The default is SQL.
TAB	The OFF setting causes SQL to use spaces in formatting columns and text on reports. The default setting is system dependent. The SHOW TAB command displays the setting. The ON setting tells SQL*Plus to use tabs rather than spaces.
TERM[OUT]	Setting this value to OFF suppresses the display of SQL*Plus output to the screen. The default setting of ON causes the output to display.
TI[ME]	A setting of ON causes the current time to display before each prompt command. The default value is OFF.
TIMI[NG]	A setting of ON shows timing statistics for each SQL command run. The default value OFF suppresses this display.
TRIM[OUT]	A value of ON trims blanks at the end of each displayed line rather than displaying them. The SET TAB ON setting must be in effect.
TRIMS[POOL]	The ON setting removes blanks at the end of each spooled line. OFF allows SQL*Plus to include trailing blanks at the end of each spooled line.
TRU[NCATE]	Clips the excess of a column so it will fit in the allowed width. This is a command from an earlier version and may be obsolete at some point. It works similarly to the WRAP command.
UND[ERLINE]	This setting turns the underline OFF and ON.
VER[IFY]	ON causes SQL*Plus to show the old and new values of a variable before executing the SQL in which they have been embedded.
WRAP	Wraps a row to the next line. The default is ON.

the Oracle Web site. The shortcut version of the variable name is contained outside the brackets. These commands can be placed inside a script file or entered on the command line.

If you should want to change an environmental variable for your session, you may enter the SET command at the SQL prompt. A more convenient way is to launch the Environment dialog box, which is done through the Options menu. This dialog box contains a list box that will allow you to scroll through the various variables, and it shows you the default and acceptable settings. The Environment dialog box is illustrated in Figure 11.1.

Listing 11.6 is an example of a script that uses several commonly used SET commands. The commands were placed at the beginning of the script, and one of the settings was returned to the default after the SELECT statement was executed. The commands have the following purposes:

- SET LINESIZE 80   Sets the maximum length of each row to 80
- SET PAGESIZE 60   Sets the length of the page to 60 (This is the normal length for a portrait report.)
- SET TERMOUT OFF   Suppresses the display of output to the screen (This increases the performance of the report because Oracle does not have to display the information on the screen.)
- SET TERMOUT ON   Enables the display of output to the screen

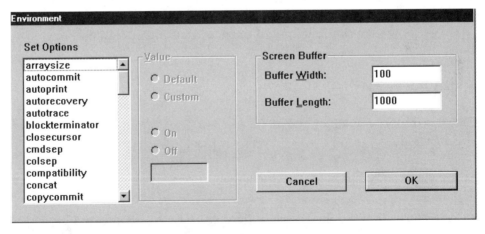

Figure 11.1 *The Environment dialog box*

Listing 11.6 *Using SET Commands*

```
set linesize 80
set pagesize 60
set termout off
spool c:\test.txt
select last_name, first_name, current_position
from employee
order by 1, 2;
spool off
set termout on

End listing
```

What's Next?

The next chapter will discuss techniques and tools that can be used to increase the performance of your SQL statements. The chapter will discuss the various indexes that can be used and will also discuss EXPLAIN, which is used to learn what work an SQL statement must perform. Finally, the chapter will discuss when to use a full table scan rather than an index lookup and how to optimize joins, grouping, and sorting operations.

■ PRACTICE

Create a report for all of the departments. The report should have the following specifications:

- The employees' names, employment date, current position, wages, and tool purchases.
- Tool information should consist of purchase date, tool name, and tool cost.
- The report should be landscape (132 characters wide).
- Compute the total cost of each employee's tool purchases.
- Use a custom label for the total cost subtotal.

- Display the current date in the title.
- Create an appropriate title for the report.
- Each department's records should begin on a new page.
- Display the page number on the lower right of each page.
- Suppress duplicate values.
- Create custom headings for all columns.

What You Can Do If Your SQL Does Not Perform

The purpose of this chapter is to offer some simple techniques that will help make your SQL more efficient and effective. A few weeks after I had taken my first SQL course, I could write statements that produced the results I desired. As the complexity of my queries increased, I began to notice that I was spending a lot of time watching the hourglass cursor blink. I was very happy knowing that I knew how to make the computer work hard. This went on until a colleague took one of my statements, changed parts of the statement, and got it to execute three times faster. I learned then that mastering the SQL language was half the battle. The other part of the battle was to get the SQL to perform efficiently. This reduces overall usage of the machine and, more important, increases the productivity of you and your users.

This chapter will not cover all of the available techniques, as the topic is large enough for a book of its own. In fact, I find Guy Harrison's *Oracle SQL: High Performance Tuning* an especially good book. The problem is that many of the techniques discussed in Harrison's book require a DBA to help. This chapter will focus on the more common things a business analyst or data administrator can perform. Proper use of these techniques will greatly increase the efficiency of your SQL. This chapter will also give you enough of a background in performance tuning to discuss the issues with your DBA.

Some of the topics covered in this chapter are indexes, rule-based and cost-based optimizers, optimizer hints, the EXPLAIN PLAN statement, and optimizing joins and subqueries.

Indexes

Database performance can be greatly affected by the proper use of indexes. They are one of the first objects you should investigate when encountering performance problems. However, you should remember that placing an index on a column may not necessarily provide the desired remedy. In those cases, you will commonly need to explore other performance tools.

Indexes are primarily used for two reasons:

1. To ensure the uniqueness of the indexed column's values

2. To enhance performance

An index is an ordered set of records that correspond to records in a table. The index record consists of a column that relates to a corresponding column in the associated table. Each index record also has a rowid value, which is the location of the desired table record. Knowledge of the rowid allows Oracle to go directly to the record. Figure 12.1 illustrates this concept.

Indexes enhance performance by reducing the amount of data that is read to locate the records. They reduce the amount of work that Oracle must do to order the retrieved records. Assume that you have a table that does not contain an index. In order to find the desired records, Oracle must read each record in the table and then compare each record's values to the arguments specified in the WHERE clause of the SELECT statement. This is called a **full table scan**, and it may be a performance problem. In fact, the purpose of SQL tuning is to avoid performing full table scans of large tables.

A full table scan reads database bytes equal to the length of the record multiplied by the number of records in the table. A small customer database

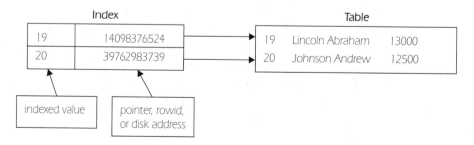

Figure 12.1 *Representation of an index and its corresponding table record*

containing 200,000 records with a record length of 100 bytes will contain 20,000,000 bytes of data. The full table scan will cause Oracle to read the entire 20,000,000 bytes before returning the records. The same number of bytes will need to be read even if one database record is retrieved. Performance can be greatly enhanced if the number of bytes read is reduced. This is what an index achieves.

The index record is considerably smaller than the corresponding record in the table. Returning to the previous example, assume the first 10 bytes of a customer record contain the customer account number. If this field were indexed, the index record length would be 10 bytes plus the length of the record pointer, considerably less than the length of the table's record. Using the index to identify customer records could increase performance by an order of 5 just because of the lower record length. If the entire index were scanned to identify the customer records, a maximum of 4,000,000 bytes would need to be read.

The values in the index are ordered, which provides two additional performance benefits:

1. Special algorithms are available to avoid having to read every record in the index. Oracle can determine if the desired record is greater or lesser in value than the current record.

2. Queries that use the index to identify records that are to be sorted will be in the proper sort order by default.

One of the commonly used indexes is called a B-Tree index, which is arranged similarly to a tree. The index consists of levels of records. Each level points to a record in a lower level. At the lowest level, the index record contains the table record's rowid. This structure allows Oracle to employ algorithms to locate records quickly without having to scan a number of records. This ordering property increases performance by reducing the number of records that have to be read in order to locate the record. Coupling this property with the smaller record size and the elimination of sorting, you can see how beneficial indexes are.

Which Columns Should Be Indexed?

You might be thinking that all columns should be indexed. If so, the business analyst would always be assured maximum performance. Indexing every column might increase query performance but would surely degrade DML performance. Each time an INSERT, UPDATE, or DELETE transaction occurred, the indexes would need to be rebuilt, which could seriously degrade the performance of the system. Another factor is that the retrieval can sometimes be faster if multiple columns are indexed in one index. This is called a multicolumn index. Indexing all combinations of individual columns and multiple columns is totally impractical. The possible combinations are astronomical. It is best to identify the most beneficial columns.

The following are factors to consider in determining the columns to index:

- Selectivity of the column. This property indicates the individuality of column values. If a column has totally unique values such as a primary key, the selectivity is high. If a column has common values such as those for the column gender, the selectivity is low. Indexes can help with highly selective columns.

- Frequency in which the column is used in a WHERE clause. If a column is commonly used in the clause, the more likely it should be indexed.

- Column is used in the WHERE clause, and the number of rows returned is commonly less than 4 percent of the table. This is a strong candidate for an index.

- Columns are used in joins. Joined columns should normally be indexed. Joined columns are normally primary- and foreign-key columns.

Multicolumn Indexes

In some cases, it is better to have multicolumn indexes. Multicolumn indexes are called composite indexes or **concatenated indexes**. An Oracle index can contain up to 32 columns; however, that many columns are not generally used. Multicolumn indexes are beneficial when two or more columns are referenced in the WHERE clause. They can also be beneficial if an additional column is always used in combination with another value. For example, a person's first name is often used with a last name. Placing the first name in the same index as the last name may eliminate the work Oracle has to do when retrieving the first name from the table. Adding multiple columns to the index also increases selectivity, which may increase performance.

The following criteria should be used in determining the leading column in the index:

- The column used most often in the WHERE clause, unless the selectivity is low
- The column used most often as the primary sort column in an ORDER BY clause
- The column with the best selectivity

Index Types

Oracle has a number of index types. We have already discussed the B-Tree index, which is generally used for primary- and foreign-key columns. Depending on the data, other types of indexes may improve performance. Table 12.1 describes the various index types.

Bitmap Indexes

Bitmap indexes are useful when column selectivity or cardinality is poor. When selectivity is very poor, a B-Tree index is not effective because Oracle has to search too many index leafs in order to find the rowid. A normal index stores lists of indexed values and their corresponding rowids. Similar values are repeated along with their corresponding rowids. A bitmap index contains a bitmap for each distinct value, rather than containing a list of rowids.

Table 12.1 *Index Types*

Type	Description
B-Tree	Contains levels and pointers (rowids) to table rows
Bitmap	Contains a bit for each distinct value in the column
Reverse-key	Reduces index hot spots and consists of reversing the digits in the indexed column
Index-organized tables	Stores all table data in a B-Tree index
Descending	Organizes index in descending order
Function-based	Uses a function to create the indexed value (Useful when a function is used with the indexed column in a WHERE clause)

Rowids correspond to bits in the bitmap. A function converts the bit to the rowid, which Oracle then uses to locate the desired record. Bitmap indexes are very small when the number of distinct indexed values are small.

Figure 12.2 illustrates this schema. The figure displays a few sample records and their corresponding index records. The indexed value is Gender. Notice that there are two distinct bit patterns: one for Male and one for Female. Index records with the same bit pattern are stored close to each other in the index table. This, along with the small size of the index, allows Oracle quickly to identify the records that match the searched value.

Bitmap indexing is an excellent tool for data warehouses. Some of the benefits are as follows:

- Smaller space usage as compared to other indexes
- Greater performance for parallel DML and loads
- Performance gains and reduced response time

A B-Tree index can be larger by several magnitudes than the indexed table. This means that a B-Tree index is very expensive in terms of space. Bitmaps are much smaller than the B-Tree index, making them good candidates for data warehouses or decision support systems. Data warehouses often contain enormous amounts of data, and you may not want indexes that are larger than the data warehouse.

A bitmap index is a poor tool for OLTP systems that have large amounts of concurrent transactions. It is a good tool if a column has more than 100 occurrences of the same value. Another feature of a bitmap index is that it includes null values, which most of the other indexes do not include. This feature can give a bitmap index for some types of SQL statements such as ones that use the aggregate function COUNT. The COUNT(*) function will always use a bitmap index.

Employee Record			Bitmap Index Record		
Payroll_number	Name	Gender	Male	Female	Rowid
1	Ron	Male	1	0	AA687
2	Sarah	Female	0	1	BB898
3	Linda	Female	0	1	BB890
4	Pete	Male	1	0	AA999

Figure 12.2 *Employee records and associated bitmap index records*

Reverse-Key Indexes

Some databases have sequence-generated primary keys. As an example, the company I work for gives a sequential number to each customer. The customer number is an eight-position number. The first customer number starts with the value 10,000,000. The value is then incremented by 1 for each subsequent customer. As sequential customer numbers are generated, you will find that most of the inserts and other work will occur on the most recently created index leaf because index records are always stored close to each other, based on the indexed value. As we retrieve records, the work will take place on one leaf at a time because all recent numbers are similar. This is a poor use of the leaf concept.

Performance can be increased if Oracle can access multiple index leafs simultaneously. This is especially true if the Oracle Parallel Server environment is used. Reversing the index values of sequential numbers allows Oracle to spread common valued records across multiple leafs.

For example, if a leaf contained 10,000 records, all customers with numbers between 10,000,000 and 10,010,000 would be stored on one leaf. If the numbers could be reversed, the records would be stored across various segments rather than sequentially. To further illustrate, notice the large gap in values caused by reversing the sequential numbers 10,012,345 and 10,012,346 to 54,321,001 and 64,321,001. Reversing the digits in the values greatly expanded the range between the two. Oracle will see the difference and will place the two sequential records on different leafs. This can have positive performance benefits.

Index-Organized Tables

Index-organized tables are tables that do not have data blocks. All of the data in this type of table is stored in a B-Tree index. This type of table is useful for sets of records that are comprised of key values, intersection tables, and code tables. An example of this type of table is the Department table in the practice database, a descriptive table that contains two columns: the primary-key department code and the full name of the department.

Index-organized tables are effective because they eliminate the need for the table-access step. If the length of the record exceeds 50 bytes, Oracle will be forced to use an overflow segment, which will diminish performance benefits. This type of table is created by using the standard CREATE TABLE command. The only modification to the command is the addition of the keywords

ORGANIZATION INDEX at the end of the command. The following is a syntax template of the command:

> **Create table** *table_name*
> (*field1*   *datatype,*
> *field2*   *datatype)*
> **organization index;**

Function-Based Indexes

Using a function on a COLUMN argument in the WHERE clause of a SELECT statement will cause Oracle to avoid using the index that had been placed on the column because the argument as modified by the function does not match the value in the index. If a function is commonly used on a column, it might be beneficial to have an index value that matches this value. That is what the function-based index does. Rather than the index value being based on the table value, it is based on the value that the function computes. Thus the SELECT statement has a common value in the index to use.

It is necessary to use the cost-based optimizer (discussed in the next section) with this type of index. The following functions are allowed in the function-based index:

- SQL functions
- Arithmetic expression
- PL/SQL functions
- Java functions
- C callouts

Aggregate functions are not allowed.

The standard CREATE INDEX command is used to create function-based indexes. The function is placed in the command referencing the indexed column. The following is a syntax template:

> **Create index** *index_name* **on** *table_name*
> (*function*(**column**));

Optimization

SQL statements are analyzed and optimized before the data is retrieved from the various tables. Optimization occurs during the parsing of the statement. It consists of determining the most efficient method of processing statements. Oracle evaluates the various methods and selects the best method. The best method is then included in the execution plan. Indexes, **hints**, and variations in the syntax of the statement affect the decisions that the optimizer makes. Thus there are a number of things that may be done to change the execution plan and, hopefully, the performance of the statement.

The Rule-Based Optimizer

Oracle has two optimizers, which are the tools that create and evaluate the various extract methods. The optimizer chooses which method to place in the execution plan. The oldest optimizer is the rule-based optimizer, which has been available since release 7 but may not be available in future releases. It determines the best method based on access paths. Database managers must use access paths to locate (and join) the records. Table 12.2 lists the access paths and ranks that this optimizer used.

Even if the rule-based optimizer is not used, it is useful to review the access paths described in Table 12.2. They will give you an idea of the relative work that must be performed when using this technique. The access paths are not dependent on rule-based optimizers. Either of the optimizers can cause one of the access paths to occur.

SQL tuning occurs when a more efficient access path replaces the current path. The most efficient path in the table is the single row by rowid. Each record in an Oracle database has a unique rowid value. You may see this value by adding ROWID to the SELECT clause of any statement. This value describes where the record resides in the database. With the knowledge of this value, Oracle can go directly to that location on the disk and read the record. Conversely, a full table scan is the most time-consuming path. It requires Oracle to read each record in the table in order to identify the requested records. The remaining access paths fall somewhere between those two extremes.

The ranks are generally based on the ability to use indexes, the amount of computational work Oracle must do, and whether the results must be sorted. Selecting a record based on its indexed primary-key value requires a small reading of the index to identify the rowid of the record. This is a very efficient

Table 12.2 *Access Paths and Rule-Based Ranks*

Rank	Access Path
1	Single row by rowid
2	Single row by cluster join
3	Single row by hash cluster key with unique or primary key
4	Single row by unique or primary key
5	Cluster join
6	Hash cluster key
7	Indexed cluster key
8	Composite index
9	Single-column indexes
10	Bounded range scan on indexed columns
11	Unbounded range scan on indexed columns
12	Sort-merge or nested-loops join
13	MAX or MIN of indexed columns
14	ORDER BY on indexed columns
15	Full table scan

path. Table 12.2 is a valuable reference that can be used to check the access paths of your SQL statements. If the table indicates you are using a costly technique, you can identify a cheaper method and then attempt to employ it.

Using nonindexed columns in the WHERE clause will likely trigger a full table scan. Placing an index on these columns will lower the rank and will increase performance. The rule-based optimizer is no longer the default optimizer. Oracle recommends the use of the next one we will discuss: the cost-based optimizer. However, DBAs with whom I often work think that Oracle has not yet fully developed this optimizer. They recommend that the rule-based optimizer be used whenever performance enhancement is needed.

The RULE hint (discussed later in this chapter) can be used to designate rule-based as the optimizer. I have used this technique in many cases to increase performance, and I recommend that you try this technique after you have ensured that the tables are properly indexed.

The Cost-Based Optimizer

This optimizer works differently from the rule-based optimizer. One of the problems with the rule-based optimizer is that it does not take into consideration factors such as the amount of data that the access technique will read. For example, the rule-based optimizer considers a full table scan as the worst access path. This is generally true. However, it may be beneficial to scan small tables rather than read an index and retrieve the record. Scanning a table of 200,000 records is far different from scanning a table of 100 records. The rule-based optimizer cannot distinguish the two, but the cost-based optimizer can.

The cost-based optimizer uses statistics that reside within the data dictionary to compute the costs of the various paths. After parsing the statement, the cost-based optimizer estimates the costs by using the statistics. The execution plan with the smallest cost is selected. The DBA produces the statistics used in this method. For effective use of this optimizer, it is important to have current statistics. If the statistics are not current, a DBA should request to run the DBMS_STATS package or the ANALYZE command.

It is possible to determine when statistics were computed. The User_table data dictionary table contains statistic values. One of these is the Last_analyzed value. Execute a SELECT statement against this table to determine the last time statistics were calculated. This statement is illustrated in Listing 12.1.

Listing 12.1 *Determining the Last Time the Employee Table Was Analyzed*

```
SQL> select last_analyzed from user_tables
  2* where table_name = 'EMPLOYEE'

LAST_ANAL
---------
12-JAN-01

SQL>

End listing
```

The cost-based optimizer has three modes:

FIRST_ROWS   This mode requires the optimizer to use the path that produces the best response time for the retrieval of the first row. This is a good candidate for SQL used in an on-line environment.

ALL_ROWS   This mode requires the optimizer to use the path that produces the best response time for the retrieval of all the rows that the query will return.

CHOOSE   This is the default mode and allows the optimizer to decide the access path.

Setting the Optimizer

The optimizer and optimizer modes can be set in the following ways:

1. Set the OPTIMIZER_MODE parameter in the Init.ora profile file to determine the default session optimizer.

2. Use the ALTER SESSION command to modify the current session's default optimizer.

3. Use a HINT option (discussed in a later section of this chapter) in the statement to modify the optimizer for the particular statement.

To identify the current optimizer, use the following SELECT statement. It will be necessary for your DBA to grant the SELECT ANY TABLE privilege in order to execute this statement.

```
Select name, value
from v$parameter
where name = 'optimizer_mode';
```

Another Word or Two on Access Paths

The full table scan, index scan, and rowid access paths were mentioned and discussed in previous sections. There are a number of additional considerations that may be important to you:

- Index access is efficient when the selectivity is good. It is poor if the selectivity is bad. When selectivity is poor, the amount of data read from the index increases, which results in poorer performance.

- Index access may be inefficient if the selectivity is good but the clustering factor is poor. *Clustering* means that the records are located close to each other on the disk. If they are scattered in many locations, Oracle must spend time moving to different locations. Asking your DBA to reorganize the table may help this situation.

- Index access is inefficient when the table size is small. It may be better to perform a full table scan and place the results into memory.

- The table-access step of an index access may be unnecessary if the selected columns are part of a multicolumn index. For example, Last Name columns in Employee tables often have indexes placed on them because the columns are often used to identify records. After a potential record is identified, a table access must be performed to determine whether the proper record has been located (as in the case of employees with the same last name) or to retrieve additional employee attributes. If a multicolumn index that contained commonly used attributes such as first name or department were used, the table-access steps might be eliminated in many cases, which would increase performance.

Join Operations

When the SQL statement contains a join condition, the optimizer must decide which method to use in order to combine the retrieved records. There are several available methods. Each of the methods is better in a certain situation. Normally Oracle will choose the proper join operation. However, algorithms are not always perfect. It may be necessary to change the selected join type using a hint. The following sections will describe the various join types.

Nested-Loop Join

In a nested-loop join, Oracle identifies target records in one table, called the driving table, and then locates corresponding records in a second table, called the inner table. Oracle generally uses an index to identify records in the driving table and scans the inner table to locate the corresponding records. Looping occurs when the driving table has more than one target record. Oracle returns to the driving table after retrieving records from the inner table. This procedure is repeated until the last record in the driving table is retrieved. Here are some facts about this join:

- Nested-loop joins are good to use when the driving table is small and the inner table has a unique or very selective index.
- It is normally best if the smaller table is the driving table.
- The cost-based optimizer will normally choose the smaller table as the driving table.
- If the tables are large, or if selective indexes are not available, this can be a poor type of join.
- This type of join returns the first records quickly.

Sort-Merge Join

When a sort-merge join occurs, Oracle first sorts the records in the two tables. The records are then merged, based on corresponding values. Here are some facts about this type of join:

- Sort-merge joins can be effective even if no indexes exist or the selectivity of existing indexes is poor.
- This join requires preprocessing. It will not start retrieving rows until the sorting/merging is complete.
- This join is best for overall throughput.

Hash Join

A hash join transforms the inner table into a hash table, which is a table with a computed key that helps Oracle more effectively locate records within the table. The table is then accessed by using values that the driving table supplies. Common records are then joined. Here are some facts about this type of join:

- Hash joins are done in memory.
- Hash joins can be effective when indexes are not available or are not selective.

- Hash joins can be faster than sort-merge joins because only one table has to be sorted: the hash table that will reside in memory.
- Hash joins can be faster than nested-loop joins because the hash table (inner table) resides in memory rather than on disk.
- Hash joins will perform poorly if adequate memory is not available.
- Hash joins can be used with only equijoins.

EXPLAIN PLAN Statement

Oracle has some tools that allow you to see the work Oracle will perform to satisfy the SQL statement. One such tool is an **EXPLAIN PLAN** statement, which contains the results of the EXPLAIN command. The results consist of steps ORACLE must perform to retrieve the data. Executing an EXPLAIN PLAN statement causes Oracle to analyze the target SQL statement and then to place the steps in an Oracle table called PLAN_TABLE.

To tune an SQL statement using the PLAN_TABLE table, perform the following steps:

1. Create the PLAN_TABLE table. This is a one-time task. The results from previous EXPLAIN PLAN commands can be deleted, and the table can be reused. The PLAN_TABLE CREATE statement is contained in the Utlxplan.sql file located in the $oracle_home\rdbms\ admin directory.
2. Execute the EXPLAIN PLAN statement on the target SQL statement.
3. View the results by using a SELECT statement.
4. Analyze the results.
5. Rewrite the target SQL statement.
6. Delete the results from the PLAN_TABLE table.
7. Start again with step 2.

PLAN_TABLE

The PLAN_TABLE table contains a number of columns that hold information that is useful in analyzing the execution plan. These are listed in Table 12.3.

Table 12.3 *PLAN_TABLE Columns and Descriptions*

Column Name	Description
STATEMENT_ID	String value of the optional EXPLAIN PLAN statement STATEMNET_ID parameter. The column can be used for information that identifies the contents.
TIMESTAMP	The date and time the EXPLAIN PLAN statement was executed.
REMARKS	Comments that can be associated with the steps of the plan.
OPERATION	The first table row identifies the type of SQL statement. Subsequent rows identify the perform action (e.g., TABLE ACCESS, INDEX, SORT).
OPTIONS	This field can hold additional information about the type of operation. For instance, a TABLE ACCESS operation may have a value of FULL or BY ROWID. An INDEX ACCESS may be described by UNIQUE SCAN or RANGE SCAN.
OBJECT_NODE	The name of the database link used to access the database objects.
OBJECT_OWNER	User ID of the owner of the database objects that the SQL statement references.
OBJECT_NAME	Name of the referenced database object.
OBJECT_INSTANCE	A value corresponding to the position of the object as it appears in the SQL statement. The positions are numbered from left to right and from outer to inner.
OBJECT_TYPE	A value that provides descriptive information about the object.
SEARCH_COLUMNS	Not used.
ID	A number representing the step in the execution plan.
PARENT_ID	A value that identifies the step that executes on the row that this step produces.
POSITION	The sequence number of execution for steps that have the same PARENT ID.
COST	The cost of the statement.
CARDINALITY	Holds the number of distinct values to be returned. This field helps determine if a full table scan or index should be used.

Table 12.3 *(continued)*

Column Name	Description
BYTES	Holds the number of bytes that the statement returns.
OTHER_TAG	This value is used in parallel query processing. This field is useful in determining how the parallel process is run.
OTHER	Contains information specific to the execution step.
PARTITION_START	Holds the start position of a range of access partitions.
PARTITION_STOP	Stop range for accessed partitions.
PARTITION_ID	The step that computed the range of partitions.

Populating PLAN_TABLE

PLAN_TABLE is populated by the EXPLAIN PLAN statement, which has four components:

- The keywords EXPLAIN PLAN
- An optional SET clause for populating the STATEMENT_ID field
- An optional INTO clause for placing the results in a table other than PLAN_TABLE
- The target SQL statement, preceded by the keyword FOR.

The following is a syntax template of the command:

Explain plan
[set statement_id = *string literal***]**
[into *table name* **]**
for *sql statement*;

Listing 12.2 illustrates the execution of an EXPLAIN PLAN statement. The SELECT statement that is being analyzed is a complex statement that contains two inline views and a total of five joins.

Listing 12.2 *Executing an EXPLAIN PLAN Command and Displaying the Results*

```
SQL> delete from plan_table;

11 rows deleted.

SQL> explain plan for
  2  select last_name, first_name, wages, tool_cost, eyeglass_cost
  3  from employee,
  4      (select fk_payroll_number, sum(tool_cost) tool_cost
  5       from employee, emp_tools
  6       where payroll_number = fk_payroll_number(+)
  7       group by fk_payroll_number) tools,
  8      (select fk_payroll_number, sum(cost) eyeglass_cost
  9       from employee, glasses
 10       where payroll_number = fk_payroll_number(+)
 11       group by fk_payroll_number) glasses
 12  where payroll_number = tools.fk_payroll_number
 13    and payroll_number = glasses.fk_payroll_number;

Explained.
SQL>

End listing
```

Reading the EXPLAIN PLAN Results

The first task needed to display the EXPLAIN PLAN results is to create and execute a SELECT statement. There are a variety of SELECT statements that can retrieve the data, but the one contained in Listing 12.3 is one that I particularly like. It places the various actions at different levels or indents, which creates a child/parent structure. The levels are based on the PARENT_ID and POSITION columns. This is an important property in understanding what is happening.

When reading an EXPLAIN PLAN result, the child activity is always performed first. It also can be performed more than once. If a parent has multiple children, the children actions are performed in the order specified in the POSITION field.

In reviewing Listing 12.3, the first set of actions is to retrieve the records contained in the Glasses view. The first action that occurred was INDEX FAST FULL SCAN SYS_C00809, an index scan of the Employee table. It was not necessary to look at the Employee table because the index had all of the information needed (Payroll_number). The next step was to perform the TABLE ACCESS FULL GLASSES. This action retrieved the records from the Glasses table. The parent action of these actions, HASH JOIN OUTER, was then performed, joining the results of the first two actions. The next step was to execute the next parent action: SORT GROUP BY. Completion of this task resulted in the result set for the view: Glasses.

Oracle then processes the second view. It follows the same pattern as described in the previous paragraph. After the two view actions are completed, two hash joins are performed. The result of all of the activities is the result step. It has a cost of 13.

Listing 12.3 *Viewing the Results of an EXPLAIN PLAN Command*

```
SQL> select lpad(' ',2*(level-1)) || operation ||
  2          ' ' || options || ' '|| object_name ||
  3          ' ' || decode(id, 0, 'Cost = '||position )
  4          "Execution Plan"
  5  from plan_table
  6  start with id = 0
  7  connect by prior id = parent_id;


Execution Plan
--------------------------------------------------------------------
SELECT STATEMENT    Cost = 13
  HASH JOIN
    HASH JOIN
      TABLE ACCESS FULL EMPLOYEE
      VIEW
        SORT GROUP BY
          HASH JOIN OUTER
            INDEX FAST FULL SCAN SYS_C00809
            TABLE ACCESS FULL EMP_TOOLS
    VIEW
      SORT GROUP BY
        HASH JOIN OUTER        ◄——    third action
                                      performed
```

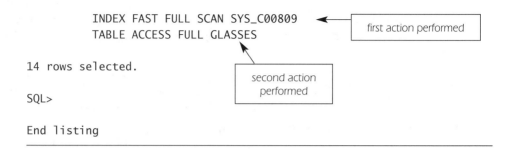

```
        INDEX FAST FULL SCAN SYS_C00809    ◄──    first action performed
        TABLE ACCESS FULL GLASSES

14 rows selected.                        second action
                                          performed
SQL>

End listing
```

It is apparent that a lot of tasks are occurring in the execution plan in Listing 12.3. If some of the tasks are eliminated, there may be less work and possibly better performance. One of the things that can be done is to eliminate one of the join processes. The Listing 12.2 SELECT statement contains two inline views. Each of these views joins two tables. The view result sets are then joined to the Employee table.

It is possible to rewrite the SELECT statement, reducing the number of joins (see Listing 12.4). Rather than creating an inline view for each of the Employee child table (Glasses/Emp_tools) results and then joining the results to the Employee table, why not join one of the child tables to the Employee table in the parent SELECT statement? Doing so would reduce the overall number of join operations. That is exactly what was done in Listing 12.4. The Glasses table was joined to the Employee table in the parent SELECT statement, thereby eliminating one of the inline views and its join operation. An EXPLAIN PLAN command was then executed against this revised query. Listing 12.4 then shows the new execution plan. Notice that the execution plan has fewer steps and a lower cost (11), yet it produces the same results as the SELECT statement.

Listing 12.4 *Executing the EXPLAIN PLAN Statement after Tuning Has Occurred*

```
SQL> delete from plan_table;

14 rows deleted.

SQL> explain plan for
  2   select last_name, first_name, wages, tool_cost,
  3   sum(cost) eyeglass_cost
```

```
 4  from employee,glasses,
 5      (select fk_payroll_number, sum(tool_cost) tool_cost
 6        from employee, emp_tools
 7        where payroll_number = fk_payroll_number(+)
 8        group by fk_payroll_number) tools
 9  where payroll_number = tools.fk_payroll_number
10    and payroll_number = glasses.fk_payroll_number
11  group by last_name, first_name, wages, tool_cost;

Explained.

SQL>
SQL> select lpad(' ',2*(level-1)) || operation ||
 2          ' ' || options || ' '|| object_name ||
 3          ' ' || decode(id, 0, 'Cost = '||position )
 4          "Execution Plan"
 5  from plan_table
 6  start with id = 0
 7  connect by prior id = parent_id;

Execution Plan
-----------------------------------------------------------------------
SELECT STATEMENT    Cost = 11
  SORT GROUP BY
    HASH JOIN
      HASH JOIN
        TABLE ACCESS FULL EMPLOYEE
        VIEW
          SORT GROUP BY
            HASH JOIN OUTER
              INDEX FAST FULL SCAN SYS_C00809
              TABLE ACCESS FULL EMP_TOOLS
      TABLE ACCESS FULL GLASSES

11 rows selected.

SQL>

End listing
```

The tuned query might execute only a marginal difference as compared to the original. In fact, with the small amount of data in the practice database, you will likely not see any difference. However, if larger amounts of data were involved, you would likely see a performance difference. An important point to remember is that SQL statements can be written in different ways. Each of these methods can have different performance properties, and the EXPLAIN PLAN statement will help you understand what is happening.

Oracle has added to Oracle9i two scripts that display the contents of the PLAN TABLE table:

- UTLPLS.SQL   Useful for showing output for serial processing
- UTLXPLP.SQL   Useful for showing output with parallel execution columns

Dynamic Performance Views

Oracle has a number of views that can be used for performance tuning. These views are called dynamic performance tables. A user can get access to these tables after being granted the SELECT ANY TABLE privilege. The table begins with the characters V$. These views should normally be used by DBAs, but one view is of interest to the data administrator: V$SQL_PLAN.

V$SQL_PLAN is an information view. It has the same functionality as the EXPLAIN PLAN command. The difference is that EXPLAIN PLAN depicts a theoretical plan for a statement, whereas V$SQL_PLAN lists the actual plan for a cursor. The two can be different due to differing values of the session parameters. V$SQL_PLAN can be useful for the following:

- Determining the effect of placing an index on a table
- Viewing the current execution plan
- Determining indexes that the optimizer may or may not use
- Locating cursors containing a specific access path

It should be noted that V$SQL_PLAN depicts the plan used by a cursor, not by SQL statements. SQL statements may have multiple cursors, so the results of this view may not identify all tasks in a statement.

Trace

A second tool that is often used for performance tuning is the trace facility, which captures statistics about the amount of data and the amount of time spent on actions. Such statistics include the following:

- CPU time
- Parse, execute, and fetch counts
- Elapsed time
- I/O counts (physical and logical)
- Number of rows accessed
- Misses on the library cache

The trace facility is not the easiest tool to use. The basic problem is that the trace statistics are written to a file on the operating system. The file can be hard to locate because it may be on the server on which the Oracle installation resides. It also can contain a lot of information. Statistics are placed into this table for everything Oracle does once the trace facility is turned on. It is necessary to wade through this information to find the desired statistics. However, this tool can give performance insights that can be gained in no other way.

Running and Viewing the Trace Statistics

The trace facility can be turned on in one of two methods:

1. Change the profile by modifying parameters in the Init.ora file. This will permanently change the parameters. The parameters and changes are as follows:

   Timed_statistics = true
   User_dump_dest = *directory*

2. Change the above parameters temporarily by using the following ALTER SESSION commands:

   Alter session set sql_trace = true;
   Alter session set sql_trace = false;

Oracle has provided a tool for viewing the results of the trace: the TKPROF command. This command is executed from the operating system, not from SQL*Plus, and reads the trace file and then creates a readable output file. The TKPROF command has a number of arguments, which are contained in Table 12.4, that can be entered.

Trace files end with the file extension *.trc*. The files can be found in one of the Oracle home directories. One of the best ways to find the file is to use the Find utility on the Start menu. Search for the file extension *.trc*. If trace has been used before, you may locate several files. It can be difficult to determine which file contains statistics about the current query. I like to delete old

Table 12.4 *TKPROF Command Options*

Argument	Description	
INFILE	Name of the trace file	
OUTFILE	Name of the output file	
EXPLAIN	Creates an execution plan for each SQL statement	
TABLE	Name of the table that will contain the execution plan results	
INSERT	Places an SQL script into the named file for storage of the trace statistics	
PRINT	Determines the number of statements to generate output for	
SORT	Determines the sort order of the SQL statements Options include the following:	
	PRSCNT	Number of times parsed
	PRSCPU	CPU time spent parsing
	PRSELA	Elapsed time spent parsing
	PRSDSK	Number of physical reads from disk during parse
	PRSQRY	Number of consistent mode block reads during parse
	PRSCU	Number of current mode block reads during parse
	PRSMIS	Number of library cache misses during parse
	EXECNT	Number of executes

Table 12.4 *(continued)*

Argument	Description	
	EXECPU	CPU time spent executing
	EXEELA	Elapsed time spent executing
	EXEDSK	Number of physical reads from disk during execute
	EXEQRY	Number of consistent mode block reads during execute
	EXECU	Number of current mode block reads during execute
	EXEROW	Number of rows processed during execute
	EXEMIS	Number of library cache misses during execute
	FCHCNT	Number of fetches
	FCHCPU	CPU time spent fetching
	FCHELA	Elapsed time spent fetching
	FCHDSK	Number of physical reads from disk during fetch
	FCHQRY	Number of consistent mode block reads during fetch
	FCHCU	Number of current mode block reads during fetch
	FCHROW	Number of rows fetched

trace files before running the trace facility; doing so makes it much easier to locate the file.

Trace can be enabled using the two methods previously discussed. I prefer the ALTER SESSION method as it allows me to control exactly what is being traced. After the trace has been performed, it is necessary to view the output. This is done by using the TKPROF facility, executed from an MS-DOS prompt or from the Run utility on the Start menu. The following example is the one I used to create the output files used in later listings. You may use this command after modifying it to your directory structure.

trace file name   output file name

tkprof c:\oracle\admin\orcl\udump\ora33495.trc c:\trace.lst

Listing 12.5 contains an excerpt of the trace file generated for the SELECT statement in Listing 12.2. The displayed statistics were preceded by the SELECT statement and were followed by the EXPLAIN PLAN steps. The SELECT statement was omitted for brevity. You might notice that the number of rows processed precedes the EXPLAIN PLAN steps.

In looking at Listing 12.5, notice that the SQL statement has three steps:

1. PARSE   Translation of the SQL into the execution plan (The optimizer performs this step.)

2. EXECUTE   Modification or rows that occur during INSERT, UPDATE, and DELETE operations

3. FETCH   Retrieval of rows for the SELECT statement

There are seven statistics that the trace command computes, and they are cumulative for a single statement:

1. COUNT   The number of times the particular step was performed

2. CPU   CPU time the computer took in executing the step

3. ELAPSED   Number of seconds it took to execute the step

4. DISK   Number of physical reads of data blocks from disk

5. QUERY   Number of buffers retrieved for consistent reads (This usually happens for SELECT statements.)

6. CURRENT   Number of buffers retrieved in current mode (This usually happens for UPDATE, INSERT, or DELETE statements.)

7. ROWS   Number of rows that the SQL statement processes

Listing 12.5 *Excerpt of the Trace File for the SELECT Statement in Listing 12.2*

```
call      count    cpu     elapsed    disk       query      current     rows
-------   ------  --------  --------  ---------  ---------  ----------   ------
Parse      1       0.00      0.01       0          0          0           0
Execute    1       0.00      0.00       0          0          0           0
Fetch      2       0.00      0.00       0          6         20          13
-------   ------  --------  --------  ---------  ---------  ----------   -----
total      4       0.00      0.01       0          6         20          13
```

```
Misses in library cache during parse: 0
Optimizer goal: CHOOSE
Parsing user id: 24
Rows      Row Source Operation
-------   --------------------------------------------------
    13    HASH JOIN
    15     HASH JOIN
    21      TABLE ACCESS FULL EMPLOYEE
    16      VIEW
    16       SORT GROUP BY
    42        HASH JOIN OUTER
    21         INDEX FAST FULL SCAN (object id 11002)
    36         TABLE ACCESS FULL EMP_TOOLS
    17     VIEW
    17      SORT GROUP BY
    24       HASH JOIN OUTER
    21        INDEX FAST FULL SCAN (object id 11002)
    19        TABLE ACCESS FULL GLASSES
End Listing
```

There is a number of ratios that can be computed from the trace statistics. These are listed in Table 12.5.

Table 12.5 *Performance Ratios Based on Trace Statistics*

Ratio	Description
(Total Query + Total Current) / Total Rows	This gives an indication of the expense of a query. The more blocks that are read relative to the rows returned indicate an expensive query. Ratios above 10 to 20 indicate a need for improvement.
Fetch Rows / Fetch Count	This ratio indicates the level of use the array fetch facility has been used. A ratio close to 1 indicates it has not been used. This may indicate an opportunity for optimization.
Total Disk / (Total Query + Total Current)	This ratio measures the "miss rate" with the data buffer cache. A good benchmark is 10 percent or less.
Parse Count / Execute Count	This ratio should be close to 1. If it is not, the statement may be needlessly reparsed.

In the previous section on EXPLAIN PLAN Statements, the SELECT statement from Listing 12.2 was modified. In the modified listing, the cost of the SQL statement was reduced. Listing 12.6 contains the trace report for the Listing 12.4 SELECT statement. You might notice that the total elapsed time actually increased rather than decreased. The difference is the .1 second that was spent fetching records. This should be an indication of the importance of using the trace facility to tune your SQL, in addition to using the EXPLAIN PLAN statement. All of the tools are necessary to perform the job well.

Listing 12.6 *Excerpt of the Trace File for the SELECT Statement in Listing 12.4*

```
call      count   cpu     elapsed   disk       query       current    rows
-------   ------  ------- --------- ---------  ----------  ----------  -----
Parse     1       0.00    0.01      0          0           0          0
Execute   1       0.00    0.00      0          0           0          0
Fetch     2       0.00    0.01      0          5           16         13
-------   ------  ------- --------- ---------  ----------  ----------  -----
total     4       0.00    0.02      0          5           16         13
Misses in library cache during parse: 0
Optimizer goal: CHOOSE
Parsing user id: 24
Rows      Row Source Operation
-------   ------------------------------------------------------
     13   SORT GROUP BY
     15    HASH JOIN
     15     HASH JOIN
     21      TABLE ACCESS FULL EMPLOYEE
     16      VIEW
     16       SORT GROUP BY
     42        HASH JOIN OUTER
     21         INDEX FAST FULL SCAN (object id 11002)
     36         TABLE ACCESS FULL EMP_TOOLS
     19     TABLE ACCESS FULL GLASSES
End Listing
```

Hints

Oracle allows you to add to the SQL statement some text that can change the access path decisions. This text is called a **hint**. Hints can be used to change the optimizer from rule-based to cost-based, to change the join operation, and even to change the order in which tables are joined. Hints allow the business analyst to help the optimizer make the right decision.

Oracle has spent a lot of time developing the optimizers. In most cases, the optimizer will make the proper decision. However, the optimizer is not as intuitive as a human. In some cases, a human can spot something that the optimizer missed, and that's when a hint comes in handy.

A hint is placed in the SELECT statement after the SELECT keyword. The following is a syntax template:

/*+ hint1 [hint2] */

The plus sign must directly follow the comment deliminator. If it does not, Oracle will ignore the hint. Table 12.6 contains the available hints.

Table 12.6 *Hints*

Hint	Description
ALL_ROWS	Causes the optimizer to choose the cost-based optimizer with the goal of best throughput
AND_EQUAL	Causes the optimizer to merge the result sets of several single-column index scans
BITMAP(*table name index name*)	Uses the named index to retrieve rows
CACHE	Encourages rows retrieved by a full table scan to remain in the buffer cache
CHOOSE	Causes a cost-based optimizer to be used
CLUSTER(*table name*)	Causes the optimizer to choose a cluster scan
DRIVING_SITE(*table name*)	When the data is contained on multiple sites, causes the site at which the specified table is located to be the driving table
FIRST_ROWS	Causes the optimizer to choose the cost-based approach with the goal of best response time for the first record
FULL(*table name*)	Causes the optimizer to choose a full table scan
HASH(*table name*)	Causes the optimizer to use a hash scan

Table 12.6 *Hints (continued)*

Hint	Description
HASH_AJ	Causes an antijoin to occur by using the hash join method
INDEX(*index name*)	Causes the optimizer to use an index scan (Optionally, a specific index can be specified.)
INDEX_ASC	Similar to INDEX, except ensures that the table will be read in ascending order
INDEX_DESC	Similar to INDEX, except ensures that the table will be read in descending order
MERGE_AJ	Causes an antijoin to occur by using the sort-merge method
NOCACHE(*table name*)	Discourages Oracle from keeping rows obtained by a full table scan in the buffer cache
NOPARALLEL	Causes Oracle to avoid using parallel processing (consists of using multiple processors) for the statement
NO_EXPAND(*table name*)	Prevents Oracle from expanding statements containing an OR condition into multiple SQL statements combined by a UNION operation
NO_MERGE	Causes the optimizer to avoid using a sort-merge join for the table in question
ORDERED	Forces the first table specified in the FROM clause to be the driving table for nested loop joins and hash joins
PARALLEL(*table_name, degree of parallelism*)	Tells the optimizer to conduct parallel scans on the target table
PUSH_SUBQ	Causes subqueries to be processed earlier in the execution plan (Normally they are processed last.)
RULE	Causes the rule-based optimizer to be used
STAR	Causes Oracle to consider using the star join methodolgy
USE_CONCAT	Forces the optimizer to change OR conditions into a UNION ALL
USE_HASH	Forces a hash join
USE_MERGE	Forces a sort-merge join
USE_NL	Forces the use of a nested-loop join

Odds and Ends

The previous sections should have given you a basic idea of what processing occurs and how Oracle satisfies the SQL statements. The purpose of this chapter was to introduce you to some basic tools and techniques. This topic is much too large for only one chapter. I would suggest that you purchase a tuning book after you become comfortable with SQL. I recommend Guy Harrison's *SQL Tuning*, which is the book that I keep on my desk when it is necessary to tune SQL.

Before leaving this topic, I would like to present some simple techniques that may help you use SQL:

- The placement of the conditions in the WHERE clause may have an effect. It is preferable to place the limiting conditions prior to the join conditions.

- Modify your session with the SET TIMING ON command. This will cause performance statistics to be displayed after every SQL*Plus command. It will help you determine the most efficient methods.

- Avoid conditions that do not use access paths based on an index. For example, if column x and column y are in the same table, the following conditions shouldn't be used:

  column x > column y

  column x < column y

  column x >= column y

  column x <= column y

- Avoid conditions that cannot use access paths based on an index. Computed arguments based on columns cannot use an index. Null values are not contained in indexes. Thus arguments that evaluate nulls cannot use an index. Here are some examples:

  Column x is null

  Column x is not null

  Column x not in

  Column x != '*expression*'

  Column x like '%*pattern*'

  Column x + 7 => 60

Column x || column y = '*expression*'

Substr(Column x, 1, 3) = '*expression*'

- Index access paths are generally faster than full table scans. This is particularly true if a small set of records is returned. Consider indexing columns used as arguments.

- Use EXISTS instead of the NOT IN operator. NOT IN negates the use of an index.

- Use joins in place of EXISTS.

- Avoid functions on indexed columns.

- Avoid NOT on indexed columns.

- Avoid using modified values as arguments in the WHERE clause.

- Rewrite WHERE clause conditions if possible so that only equijoins are used.

- Use the UNION keyword instead of OR when both conditions have indexes.

- Use the LIKE operator rather than the SUBSTR function.

- Use concatenated indexes rather than multiple indexes.

- Avoid using mixed data types as arguments.

- Keep the size of the tables small.

- Use the PARALLEL query hint.

- Minimize the use of the DISTINCT keyword. It always causes a SORT operation.

- Use the AND keyword rather than the OR keyword if possible.

What's Next?

The next chapter will discuss the use and creation of business objects for business information and analysis. It will also discuss the use of summary tables to increase performance and aid the analysis. The chapter will then describe some of the various business object characteristics. It will conclude with a discussion of OLAP analysis and will identify some of the major tools.

13

Using Business Objects

As a business analyst or data administrator, one of your jobs will be to analyze data and distill business information. Databases have become increasingly complex, especially databases for purchased packages such as Oracle Financials or PeopleSoft. Despite your skill in writing and tuning SQL, it can be very difficult to extract information from these systems. Analysts also find that performance is extremely bad when producing information from these complex databases. The purpose of this chapter is to discuss some techniques and tools that you can employ when creating and analyzing management information systems.

Data Warehouses

A data warehouse consists of a series of tables that hold the data from an OLTP system. Data warehouses' characteristics include the following:

- The data is not current. It may be only minutes older than the production data. It may also be considerably older, as in the case of historical data. Some data warehouses keep data for years. This data are used to compute trends or other types of analysis.
- The data are used to produce business information.

Unless you are a developer, you will be executing your SQL against a data warehouse. DBAs think that executing SQL against a production system for the creation of business information will degrade the performance of the system. Production OLTP systems are used in the day-to-day business of a company. Slowing down performance of these systems is not a good thing. With the low cost of memory and hardware, it is cost-effective to move data to a different server rather than use production databases. DBAs and system administrators will allow only business analysts to access production data, if it is absolutely necessary.

As said earlier, data warehouses consist of copies of production system data. They also contain other specialized tables, which can consist of the following:

- Summary tables. These are tables that contain summarized information. An example would be a table that has a record containing an employee's wages, total cost of tools, and total cost of glasses. Placing these values into a table allows for better performance for the user/business analyst. Oracle can avoid the work of joining and summarizing records. Summary tables may also decrease overall computer use by shifting the major computing to an off period. In addition, summarizing the data once at night rather than multiple times during the day reduces computer usage.

- Historic tables. Enormous amounts of data can be generated by OLTP systems. As the tables increase in size, performance is degraded. In order to maintain performance, records are deleted or purged from systems when they are no longer of use. These records are often placed in the data warehouse. While they may have little benefit for the production system, they can be extremely useful for computing trends and performance.

- Business object tables. These are special tables that contain attributes about a particular business entity. Examples of entities are employees, sales regions, departments, or salesmen. They are a very important analysis tool and will be discussed further in the next section.

Data warehouse tables are often populated by a nightly extract procedure from a production system. The extract can be a replication of the production database or the creation of the special business object tables. These extracts often take place during the evening hours when the daytime strain on production systems is gone. However, the work can be done during business hours. Materialized views are a good tool to use for populating data warehouses. They can be set up to perform the work at a specific time. In addition, they can be configured to move only the modified records from the OLTP system. These two features make materialized views an extremely cost-effective and easy tool to use in order to maintain the data warehouse.

Business Objects

One of the problems with modern databases is that they can be very complex, especially ERP systems. These databases can consist of scores of tables. The systems are very broad in functionality and are designed to work for any type of business. The systems support the day-to-day work of a business. However, they are not designed to provide business information. I use an ERP system at the company for which I work and it is common to join 10–12 tables and write SQL statements of 50–60 lines. Needless to say, it is extremely difficult to write SELECT statements for these types of databases. Small changes in the desired information can require hours for the business analyst to write and test the revised statements. It is a far more effective use of a business analyst's time to identify the desired attributes and place them in a business object.

The electric utility for which I work has an Indus work management system called Passport. All company business units use this package. The company's Power Delivery business unit, Nuclear business area, Corporate business area, and Fossil business area use the same system. This system is used to create work requests, bills of material, purchase orders, material requisitions, and work orders. The system works as well as any other comparable ERP package as an OLTP system. However, deriving any custom business information from the system is a nightmare. The system is based on code tables that allow the system to be customized without modifying the application code. Analysts must understand the codes that each business area uses. They must repeatedly join code tables to parent tables. It is not efficient to write SQL against this database repeatedly. A better use of your time is to create business objects and write your SQL against these objects.

A fellow employee spends the majority of his time developing business objects. After these business objects are tested, the object is given to the end users. The business object generally consists of one table that contains only the relevant attributes and records. Because the interested attributes are in one table, the SQL is much simpler, the table is smaller, and performance is enhanced. Business objects are generally so simple that fairly unsophisticated end users can use OLAP tools to create their business information. Following is a partial list of the business areas that my associate developed. It may give you an idea of the scope of a business object.

- Delivery Active Work Orders
- Delivery Complete Work Orders
- Material Requisition Headers
- Material Requisition Lines
- Delivery Department Summary Costs

There are several steps needed to develop a business object:

1. Identify the object in which you are interested.

2. Identify the attributes that describe the object.

3. Create a table to hold the attributes.

4. Write the SQL to populate the table.

5. Tune the SQL.

6. Schedule the SQL to be run.

The rules of normalization do not apply to business objects. These tables must be designed to produce information quickly. This is in contrast to OLTP systems where the concern is the maintenance of records. Business object tables are used for analysis. It is more effective if you do not have to join tables. Performance will be increased, and the SQL will be much simpler.

To illustrate further the need for a business object that can be analyzed in various ways, assume that a company has an employee database that records the following:

- Employee information such as department, name, address, position, and wages
- Tool purchases
- Eyeglasses purchases

The vice president of manufacturing would like to analyze the company's personnel costs comprised of: wages, eyeglasses purchases, and tool purchases. The vice president initially asks for the personnel costs per department. This query requires three views and a query. Listing 13.1 illustrates the views and SELECT statement. Notice the complexity.

Listing 13.1 *Views and SELECT Statement Computing Departmental Personnel Costs*

```
SQL> Create or replace view dept_wages
  2      as select fk_department, sum(wages) dept_wages
  3          from employee
  4          group by fk_department;

View created.

SQL> Create or replace view dept_tools
  2      as select fk_department, sum(tool_cost) dept_tools
  3          From employee, emp_tools
  4          Where payroll_number = fk_payroll_number(+)
  5          Group by fk_department;

View created.

SQL> Create or replace view dept_glasses
  2      as select fk_department, sum(cost) dept_glasses
  3          From employee, glasses
  4          Where payroll_number = fk_payroll_number(+)
  5          Group by fk_department;

View created.

SQL> Select dept_wages.fk_department,
  2          dept_wages+dept_tools+dept_glasses
  3  From dept_wages, dept_tools, dept_glasses
  4  Where dept_wages.fk_department = dept_tools.fk_department(+)
  5      And dept_wages.fk_department = dept_glasses.fk_department(+);

FK_D DEPT_WAGES+DEPT_TOOLS+DEPT_GLASSES
---- ----------------------------------
INT                         66770.2
POL                        88582.15
WEL                         53272.5

SQL>

End listing
```

After the vice president reviews the results, a request is made to see the personnel cost per current position. The analyst then produces the views and SELECT statement shown in Listing 13.2.

Listing 13.2 *Views and SELECT Statement Computing Costs Per Current Position*

```
SQL> Create or replace view position_wages as
  2  select current_position, sum(wages) position_wages
  3  from employee
  4  group by current_position;

View created.

SQL> Create or replace view position_tools as
  2  select current_position, sum(tool_cost) position_tools
  3  From employee, emp_tools
  4  Where payroll_number = fk_payroll_number(+)
  5  Group by current_position;

View created.

SQL> Create or replace view position_glasses as
  2  select current_position, sum(cost) position_glasses
  3  From employee, glasses
  4  Where payroll_number = fk_payroll_number(+)
  5  Group by current_position;

View created.

SQL> Select position_wages.current_position,
  2         position_wages+position_tools+position_glasses costs
  3  From position_wages, position_tools, position_glasses
  4  Where position_wages.current_position =
  5         position_tools.current_position(+)
  6  And position_tools.current_position =
  7         position_glasses.current_position(+);

CURRENT_POSITIO     COSTS
--------------- ---------
ADMINISTRATOR
CLERK 1             25549
```

```
CLERK 2
CONTROLLER              8592
COUNSELOR 2
GUARD 4
JANITOR                 9710
LABORER 2              13157
LABORER 3
MAINT. MAN 2
MAINT. MAN 3         9239.95
PRESIDENT           13693.7
PROGRAMMER 1
SALESPERSON 1        7681./
SALESPERSON 2       7208.85
SYSTEM ANALYST
TREASURER           12641.5
TREASURER CLERK
VICE PRESIDENT        18433

19 rows selected.

SQL>

End listing
```

The vice president would then like to have the data manipulated into other patterns. It is needless to say the requesting and writing of additional queries can become tedious. For this reason, business objects and tools such as Discoverer9iAS were created. They provide the user-friendly type of analysis that the vice president and other business decision makers need.

A multidimensional table is a great tool to use for analysis. It can quickly provide the answers that the vice president requested in the previous example. When thinking of multidimensional tables, think of cubes, as they are sometimes called. The cube is a set of values, and each of the cube's dimensions represents an analysis attribute.

Figure 13.1 illustrates this concept. The figure represents a cube comprised of a number of minor cubes. Relating the cube to our employee database example, each minor cube represents a total cost variable. The height dimension represents the departments, the width represents the employees, and the depth represents the current positions. OLAP analysis allows the user to combine the various cubes for different results. The cube in Figure 13.1 represents the following:

- The front face of the cube contains all of the values for a specific current position.
- The top face of the cube contains all of the values for a specific department.

Multidimensional databases break the rules of normalization, which is appropriate because they are designed for analysis rather than for transactional processes. In this type of table, the primary key is generally a composite key composed of the key attributes. The following is a CREATE command for a multidimensional or business object table for the employee database.

```
Create table personnel_costs
(fk_department              char(4),
gender                      char(1),
name                        varchar2(20),
current_position            varchar2(20),
actual_employee_tool_cost   number,
```

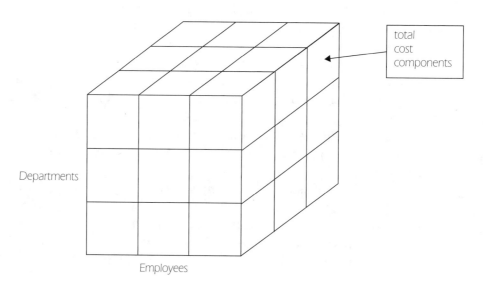

Figure 13.1 *Representation of a multidimensional employee database*

budgeted_employee_tool_cost	**number,**
actual_employee_eyeglass_cost	**number,**
budgeted_employee_eyeglass_cost	**number,**
actual_employee_wages	**number,**
budgeted_employee_wages	**number,**
total_cost	**number);**

In this table, the analysis variables are fk_department, gender, name, and current_position. The name field will be a concatenation of the Last_name and First_name columns. This will enable the business analyst to avoid having to concatenate the values whenever the table is used. The table also contains a Total_cost column. This is a summation of the Tool_cost, Eye_cost, and Wages values, which were calculated in order to avoid having to perform the calculations in the SQL executed against the table. The Tool_cost and Eye_cost values are summary values. They are computed by summing the child record in the Emp_tools and Glasses tables. The SQL that is used to populate this table has some complexity, but the design of the table makes the SQL analysis simple.

The table schema is in reality a star schema, in which the analysis variables surround the values. These schemas will allow you to develop business objects that are easy to analyze and will be very effective for report writing. You can compute a large number of values without having to write complex SQL. Some of these values are as follows:

- Total cost and specific costs per employee
- Total cost and summed costs per classification
- Total cost and summed costs per department
- Total cost and specific costs per department and classification
- Differences between budgeted and actual costs

A small table can have a large number of easily computed values. They will make your work much easier to perform.

Drilling Down and Exceptions

There are two important concepts for developing management information systems: exception reporting, and drilling down. Managers are extremely busy people. They do not want to wade through the detail to find the information they need. Managers are most interested in determining the work that is out of variance. This allows them to act on the trouble. Work that is within variance does not require attention. When a manager identifies the problem, additional information is often needed in order to zero in on the exact problem. Exception reporting and drilling down will allow you to offer these types of reporting to your management.

Exception reporting is based on SQL that is written to identify objects that are outside the norm. Exception information is most often based on summary information. An example of an object is a project that has exceeded budget cost or one that is in danger of missing its completion date. These are the types of objects that a manager is interested in. A summary table is an excellent tool to use when performing exception reporting. It affords a quicker return of the results. In addition, the SQL needed to produce the same results from the production database will likely be complex. Joining and summarizing hundreds of thousands of records is best left to a different process and should be performed only infrequently.

Detail records are accessed after the exception is found. This is the drilling down procedure. The detail records for an exception will be a subset of the total set of detail records. Performance should be quick for the drilling down procedure. The SQL will be extracting only a subset of records, and the primary-key value will be used in the search. Figure 13.2 illustrates a typical schema for a management information systems database.

At the top of the schema is a summary table that contains the actual and budgeted cost of tools, eyeglasses, wages, and total department costs. It is likely that this table and its values would be created in a nightly production run. This table would be of value to a division manager because the division manager is responsible for multiple departments. The exceptions would be identified by the differences between actual and budgeted costs. Any department with costs over the budgeted amount would be an exception and would require investigation.

Investigation requires drilling down to another table. In this case, it's the Personnel_costs table, which is also a calculated table. At each level, the tables contain increasingly larger numbers of records. The division manager, however, is interested in only a subset of the records: the employee records for the department out of variance. The second-level table would also be of value to the department manager, who would be interested in the employee vari-

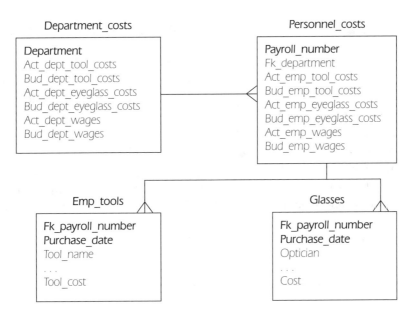

Figure 13.2 *Employee cost management information database*

ances. The exceptions in this table would be the employees who were outside the budgeted amount. After identifying this exception, the division and department managers will likely need more information, which will require drilling down to the Emp_tools and Eyeglasses tables.

The Emp_tools and Eyeglasses tables replicate the production tables. There are no calculations performed on these tables. They contain the maximum number of available records and the highest level of detail. Even though these tables may be large, the managers will need to see only a small subset of records. These records would be the detail records for a specific employee. The search criteria would be the employee's payroll_number value, a primary-key value. Retrieval will be quick.

In summary, a good information system consists of summary, business object, and detail tables. Managers will begin at the top of the table chain and then drill down to select detail records. Complex, long executing SQL should be postponed to off-hours. It is extremely important for managers to be able to retrieve their information quickly because they will not use it if they must wait. The next section will discuss tools that can help.

Oracle Discoverer 4.0: The OLAP Tool of Choice

In the not too distant past, information was furnished to managers by using combinations of paper and online reports. A manager who was interested in drilling down to the detail would need multiple reports. Each level of detail required a separate report. It's needless to say that this was cumbersome for management, and the reports were seldom used.

In the last several years, a new type of tool has emerged, one that is used for online analysis. Several vendors have developed these tools, but Oracle's is the one that I prefer: Discoverer 4.0. An evaluation copy can be downloaded from the Oracle Web site (www.oracle.com). Why is this my tool of choice?

- It's cheaper.
- Oracle includes it with installations of its application packages.
- It requires very little training for both the administrator and the user.
- I have seen users creating their own reports after 1–2 hours of training.

The beauty of Discoverer and the other comparable tools is that the user does not have to be proficient in SQL. The tool dynamically creates the SQL based on the requested information. The tool has a number of other features:

- Drilling down is performed by touching a value.
- Data may be displayed in tabular or cross-table formats.
- Data can be easily graphed.
- Records are easily filtered without having to requery the database.
- Subtotals and totals can be computed by touching a button.

I could go on about the features of this tool, but that would be outside the scope of this book. I mention this tool here because as a business analyst/data administrator, you will be responsible for providing information to your clients. Having a tool such as Discoverer will make you productive, will make your end user productive, and will allow your end user to obtain needed information more effectively than has ever been possible.

Discoverer is based on business areas. A business area is one or more related tables. The tables displayed in Figure 13.2 comprise a business area. The attributes in the business area relate to one object, such as an employee or department. The business analyst uses the SQL to populate the specialty tables. These tables and their relationships are then documented in the Discoverer Administration tool. The business analyst can also document WHERE clause conditions, special calculations, and PL/SQL functions within the business area. Another important task is to document the hierarchy of data, which describes the drilling down path.

It requires a firm grasp of SQL and PL/SQL to be able to create the business area. When it is done, the business area is used in the Discoverer Plus tool to derive information. Users simply click the desired attributes, WHERE clause conditions, and calculated items to make them appear on the screen. I have seen end users develop their own reports within minutes. This greatly alleviates the workload of the business analyst, which is a good thing. It can take a considerable amount of time to design and populate the management information systems tables. It is a far more effective use of your time to design business areas than it is to write reports. Discoverer and other OLAP tools will greatly enhance your ability to provide information to your users.

Figure 13.3 depicts Discoverer Plus. The figure is displaying the Edit Sheet dialog box and the Results pane. The Edit Sheet dialog box has the following interesting features:

- It allows the user to pick out a business area. In the case of the example, the objects in business area Test are displayed.

- The dialog box lists attributes for the Employee business object. This object contains attributes from the main Employee table and its child tables Emp_tools and Glasses. A user can simply select the desired attributes without having to worry about the SQL.

- Discoverer will change the level of summarization depending on the selected attributes. A user can view the total wages per department by selecting the Department and Wages attributes. The wages for each employee within each department can also be displayed by selecting the Last Name attribute. A user can find out needed information by simply selecting attributes.

- Discoverer has a wealth of formatting tools for the selected values.

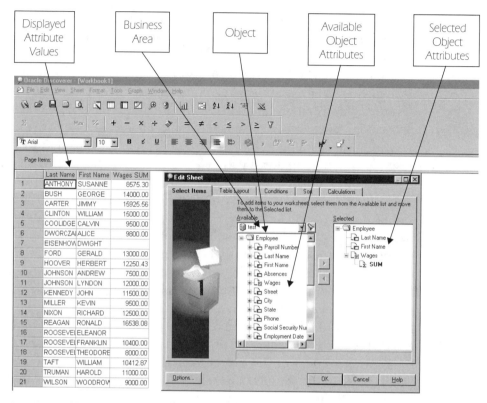

Figure 13.3 *Discoverer Plus workbook*

The simple example shown in Figure 13.3 should illustrate the power of the new OLAP tools. If the data administrator properly sets up the business object, users will be able to develop their own information.

What's Next?

The next chapter will begin the coverage of PL/SQL, which is Oracle's proprietary programming language. It is a powerful extension of the SQL language and will allow you to perform calculations based on programming logic. This language is also used in the Oracle development tools.

The Basics of PL/SQL

PL/SQL (Procedure Language SQL) is Oracle's programming language and is a powerful programming tool. It is comparable to COBOL, Fortran, C, or Java. PL/SQL is used to tell the Oracle database how to process records. It is also used in Oracle's development tools. Just as Visual Basic is the power behind Microsoft's Visual Basic, PL/SQL is the power behind Oracle Forms and Reports. The language is used to define a form's behavior, to perform special calculations in a report, and to process records.

As with COBOL, PL/SQL allows the developer to define local variables, cursors, IF-THEN-ELSE constructs, and several different types of looping procedures. Cursors allow the developer to process records one at a time. The IF-THEN-ELSE constructs allow special logic to be applied. PL/SQL also allows the developer to construct procedures and functions that can be grouped into packages and libraries. This allows the developer to create reusable code.

This wealth of tools makes PL/SQL a formidable development tool. An effective Oracle developer must be able to use this language. It will greatly increase your effectiveness as a business analyst if you have a sound background in PL/SQL.

Writing Your First Program

PL/SQL programs can be written and executed from the SQL prompt in SQL*Plus. Due to the complexity of the programs, this is not the preferable mechanism. It is best to develop the program in an external text editor such as Notepad or in Oracle's Procedure Builder. The program files can then be called from SQL*Plus and be executed.

Our first program will output the message *Hello*. This program is contained in Listing 14.1.

Listing 14.1 *A Simple PL/SQL Code Block That Displays the Word* Hello

```
SQL> set serveroutput on
SQL> begin
  2    dbms_output.put_line ('Hello');
  3  end;
  4  /
Hello

PL/SQL procedure successfully completed.

SQL>

End listing
```

This program consists of a PL/SQL code block that contains a command. The DBMS_OUTPUT.PUT_LINE keywords launch a **procedure** (program) in a **package** (group of programs) that outputs the value in its parameter list. The effect is to output the word *Hello*. Some important features of the program are as follows:

- The executable portion of a PL/SQL code block starts with the keyword BEGIN and is terminated with the keyword END.
- PL/SQL code blocks are comprised of statements. Each statement ends with a semicolon.
- PL/SQL code blocks are followed by a slash (/) in the first position of the following line. This causes the code block statements to be executed.
- The END keyword is the only PL/SQL code block keyword that is followed by a semicolon.

The first line of the program in Listing 14.1 is an SQL*Plus SET command that instructs the server to display messages sent by procedures contained within the DBMS_OUTPUT package, which is generally used for debugging purposes or for instructional purposes. The command changes an environmental variable; therefore, it needs to be entered only once per session. If you are not using the DBMS_OUTPUT package, you do not need to use the command at all.

Executing the PL/SQL Program

PL/SQL code blocks that are contained in an external file are called *anonymous block procedures* and can be executed from the SQL prompt by using the START keyword. The location and name of the file follow the START keyword. This keyword causes SQL*Plus to load, compile, and execute the code block contained in the file. Listing 14.2 illustrates the execution of the code block illustrated in Listing 14.1.

Listing 14.2 *Executing a PL/SQL Program*

```
SQL> start c:\business\oracle~1\plsql1\l1.sql

HELLO

PL/SQL procedure successfully completed

End listing
```

Upon completion of the PL/SQL code block, Oracle will output the message "PL/SQL procedure successfully completed," which means that the program completed execution. If an error occurred, Oracle will issue error messages.

Code Block Components and Block Labels

A PL/SQL code block can consist of several section types and can contain nested code blocks. This section will discuss the various code block sections, nested code blocks, and the GOTO keyword.

Code Block Sections

There are four types of code block sections:

- Header — This is the optional first section of the code block. It is used to identify the type of code block and its name. The code block types are anonymous procedure, named procedure, and function. A header is used for only the latter two types.

- Declaration — This is an optional section of the code block. It contains the name of the local objects that will be used in the code block. These include variables, cursor definitions, and exceptions. This section begins with the keyword DECLARE.

- Executable — This is the only mandatory section. It contains the statements that will be executed, which consist of SQL statements, DML statements, procedures (PL/SQL code blocks), functions (PL/SQL code blocks that return a value), and built-in subprograms. This section starts with the keyword BEGIN.

- Exception — This is an optional section. It is used to handle any errors that occur during the execution of the statements and commands in the executable section. This section begins with the keyword EXCEPTION.

The code block is terminated by the END keyword, which is the only construct keyword that is followed by a semicolon. The only required section is the executable section, which means that the code block must have the BEGIN and END keywords. The code block is executed by the slash (/).

Listing 14.3 illustrates a typical code block for an anonymous procedure. The code block starts with the keyword DECLARE. This section has one local variable defined, which will be used to hold a character value.

The executable section starts with the keyword BEGIN and contains an SQL statement and a command. The SELECT command is used to compute the number of employees in the database, concatenate this value with another string, and assign the value to the variable defined in the declaration section. The next command outputs the value to the screen. The final section is the exception section. It contains a catchall error handler, the statement which is executed when a database error occurs and when an error handler is not available.

Listing 14.3 *Executing a PL/SQL Program*

```
SQL> set serveroutput on;
SQL> declare
  2     local_variable          varchar2(30);
  3   begin
  4     select 'Number of Employees'||to_char(count(last_name),'999')
  5       into local_variable
  6     from employee;
  7     dbms_output.put_line (local_variable);
  8   exception
  9     when others then dbms_output.put_line('ERROR OCCURED');
 10   end;
 11   /
Number of Employees   19

PL/SQL procedure successfully completed.

End Listing
```

Block Labels, Labels, and the GOTO Keyword

A code block can contain labels and block labels. Labels are devices used to mark sections of the code block. The GOTO command can then be used to branch unconditionally from one section of the code block to another. It can even be used to move to previous sections of the code block. There are some rules to remember:

- Labels are defined by placing two less than (<<) signs before the label name and two greater than (>>) signs after the label name.

- The GOTO keyword is used to redirect the focus of the code block. The name of the label is placed after the GOTO keyword.

A block label is similar to a label except that it can be used to qualify the contents of a block. The block label is placed at the beginning of the block. The label is then placed following the END keyword. By placing the label definition and the END label, you can identify the code block and the variables within the labeled block. This can be a useful device when the program contains multiple code blocks.

Listing 14.4 illustrates a block label, a label, and a GOTO command. The code block is labeled *b_label*. The block label is placed after the BEGIN keyword, and the name is also placed after the END keyword. The code block also contains several labels and GOTO commands that are used to redirect the focus of the procedure. The commands are used to change the normal flow of the program. The middle section is performed first, the top section is performed next, and finally the bottom section is performed.

Listing 14.4 *A Block Label, Label, and GOTO Command*

```
SQL> begin <<b_label>>
  2     goto middle;
  3     <<top>>
  4     dbms_output.put_line ('Top Statement');
  5     goto bottom;
  6     <<middle>>
  7     dbms_output.put_line ('Middle Statement');
  8     goto top;
  9     <<bottom>>
 10     dbms_output.put_line ('Bottom Statement');
 11   end b_label;
 12   /
Middle Statement
Top Statement
Bottom Statement

PL/SQL procedure successfully completed.

SQL>

End listing
```

Many PL/SQL experts recommend that you do not use the GOTO command. It is easy to lose control of your applications. This command is illustrated because in rare cases it can simplify your code.

Comments

Comments can be entered into the code block. Two devices are available:

`--` single line comment delimiter	Two dashes placed at the beginning of the line will comment out the entire line.
`/* */` multiline comment delimiters	The first symbol (/*) marks the beginning of a commented area. The second symbol (*/) marks the ending. Multiple statements can be included in the commented section.

Declaring Variables and Assigning Values

The power of PL/SQL is that it allows the developer to read data into the code block and to manipulate it. In order to bring the attributes into the program, you must have variables that will hold the values. Oracle cannot use the values until they are placed into memory, which happens when they are assigned to a variable. Variables are defined in the declaration section of the code block and will be discussed in this section.

Defining Variables

Variables are defined in the declaration section of the program. The syntax is as follows:

Variable_name   **datatype(precision);**

Oracle treats a variable definition similarly to other statements. The definition must end with a semicolon. The definition statement begins with the variable name and contains the data type. These are the mandatory parts of the definition. A value may also be assigned to the variable during the definition statement. The variable may also be constrained.

Character Definitions

Variables that contain alphanumeric values are normally defined VARCHAR2 or CHAR. The former data type is a variable definition, which contains null spaces in each position that a character does not occupy. CHAR definitions contain white space in the unoccupied positions. *White space* and *null spaces* are not the same and are not comparable.

The definition also includes the length. The default length (length when not specified) of a CHAR data type is 1. The maximum length is 32,767. A VARCHAR2 definition requires a length to be specified. The maximum length is 32,767.

The following are examples of definitions:

```
first_name               varchar2(15);
social_security_number   char(11);
```

The PL/SQL maximum length of the CHAR and VARCHAR2 data types is larger than the length allowed in the Oracle database.

Numeric Definitions

Numeric data definitions can include two parameters: precision and scale. Precision defines the overall length of the value. Scale determines the number of digits to the left or right of the decimal point. The range of the scale is −84 to 127.

If a scale is specified, rounding will occur at the end. The following rules apply:

- Positive scale definitions cause rounding to the right of the decimal point.
- Negative scale definitions cause rounding to the left of the decimal point.
- Zero scale definitions cause rounding to the nearest whole number.

The default precision of a number is 38. Below are three examples of numeric definitions. The first defines an integer value with a precision of 3. The value must be a whole number not exceeding 999. The second defines a number with unspecified scale. This value can contain up to three decimal positions and up to three positions to the left. The overall length of the value cannot contain more than three positions. The third statement defines a number with an overall length of 8. This variable will also have two positions to the right of the decimal.

age   integer(3);
gallons   number(3);
salary   number(8,2);

Other Definitions

Several other types of definitions are available:

- Boolean   This variable type is used to record a condition. The value can be true, false, or null.
- Date   This variable type is used to record date values.
- Exception   This variable type is used to define a custom-named exception or error handler.

The following are several sample definitions:

yes   boolean;
e_day   date;
big_error   exception;

Constrained Definitions

Constraints can be placed on the variables defined in the code block. A constraint is a condition that is placed on the variable. Two common constraints are as follows:

- CONSTANT   This constraint will cause Oracle to ensure that the value is not changed after a value is initially assigned to the variable. If a statement tries to change the variable value, an error will occur.
- NOT NULL   This constraint will cause Oracle to ensure that the variable always contains a value. If a statement attempts to assign a null value to the variable, an error will occur.

The following are examples of constrained variable definitions:

pi   constant number(9,8) := 3.14159265;
birth_date   not null date := '08-APR-53';

Aggregate and PL/SQL Record Definitions

An aggregate variable definition is based on a database or PL/SQL object. They consist of one or more variables and are extremely useful. They have two advantages:

1. The developer can automatically define a variable with the same data specifications as a table column or cursor variable, without actually knowing the specifications.

2. The developer can set up an array of variables for a cursor or table record with one statement. The variables will have the same specifications as the table or cursor variables.

The first aggregate definition tool is %TYPE, which allows the developer to define a variable with the same specifications as the indicated table or cursor variable. The syntax of this declaration is as follows:

Variable_name   table_cursor_name.column_name%type;

The %TYPE keyword is preceded by the table/cursor name and column/variable name. A period is used to qualify the column name with the table/cursor name. This definition will cause the defined variable to have the same specifications as the column that precedes the %TYPE. The following is an example of a variable that will have the same specifications as the Last_name column in the Employee table:

lname   employee.last_name%type;

The %ROWTYPE keyword is used to establish an array of variables based on the columns in a cursor or table. This aggregate is called a PL/SQL record. The keyword will create a variable for each column in the identified table/cursor. Each variable in the array will have the same name and specification as its counterpart in the table/cursor. The PL/SQL record name at the beginning of the definition is used as a qualifier for the variable. It lets Oracle know the name of the array that contains the variable. In the definition, %ROWTYPE is preceded by the name of the table/cursor. The syntax of this declaration is as follows:

Array_name   table/cursor_name%rowtype;

The following is an example of an aggregate array definition that creates a variable for each of the columns in the Department table:

Dept_var   department%rowtype;

When using one of the PL/SQL record variables, the name of the aggregate variable qualifies the variable. The following is the name of the variables created by the above definition:

Dept_var.department
Dept_var.department_name

Assigning Values to Variables

A PL/SQL procedure would not be useful unless there were a way to populate the variables with a value. Fortunately, PL/SQL gives us two ways to accomplish such a task:

- := assignment operator   This (a colon followed by an equal sign) assigns the argument on the left of the operator to the argument or variable on the right of the sign.

- INTO   The INTO keyword is used in a SELECT or FETCH statement. When used in a SELECT statement, it assigns the values in the SELECT clause to the variables following the INTO keyword. When used with the FETCH statement, it assigns the cursor values to the variables that follow the INTO keyword.

Listing 14.5 illustrates a PL/SQL code block that performs several types of assignments. This procedure computes the retirement date of the oldest employee. The declaration section defines a variable and an aggregate array. The aggregate array contains a variable for each column in the Employee table. The SELECT statement in the executable section uses the INTO keyword to assign the minimum employee birth date to the birth_date PL/SQL record variable. The next statement uses the assignment operator to assign the computed retirement date to the retirement_date variable.

Listing 14.5 *Assigning Values to Variables*

```
SQL> declare
  2     retirement_date          date;
  3     emp_var                  employee%rowtype;          [PL/SQL record definition]
  4   begin
  5     select min(birth_date)
  6     into emp_var.birth_date  ◄── [assigning values to variables]
  7     from employee;
  8     retirement_date := add_months(emp_var.birth_date, 12*65);
  9     dbms_output.put_line (to_char(retirement_date));
 10   end;
 11   /
29-DEC-73

PL/SQL procedure successfully completed.

SQL>

End Listing
```

When using the INTO keyword in a SELECT clause, be sure that only one record is retrieved. If more than one record is retrieved, an error will occur. The INTO keyword can assign only one record's values into the variables.

Using the INTO Assignment Keyword with PL/SQL Records

In Listing 14.5, the SELECT clause contained only one column, meaning that the INTO clause needed only one variable. If your SELECT clause contained more variables, additional variables must also be included in the INTO clause.

If you have defined a PL/SQL record for the table, you can assign the values from the selected record into the array without having to list each variable. This is done by using the asterisk (*)—meaning *all*—in the SELECT clause and the PL/SQL record name in the INTO clause. Listing 14.6 illustrates this technique. The SELECT clause used in Listing 14.6 was modified with these changes. In addition, a WHERE clause was added so that only one record would be selected.

Listing 14.6 *Assigning Values to Variables*

```
SQL> declare
  2     retirement_date          date;
  3     emp_var                  employee%rowtype;
  4  begin
  5     select *
  6     into emp_var
  7     from employee where last_name = 'ANTHONY';
  8     retirement_date := add_months(emp_var.birth_date, 12*65);
  9     dbms_output.put_line (to_char(retirement_date));
 10  end;
 11  /
15-FEB-85

PL/SQL procedure successfully completed.

SQL>

End listing
```

The IF-THEN-ELSE and ELSIF Structures

To be effective, a code block or procedure needs to have commands that allow the developer to document the logic necessary to determine the behavior. Oracle uses conditional logic statements to form the procedure's behavior. The logic statements come in two forms:

IF-THEN-ELSE structures
ELSIF statements

The IF-THEN-ELSE Structure

The most common conditional logic device is the IF-THEN-ELSE structure. This is a very powerful device that allows developers to create the most intricate logic. The structure contains required keywords (IF-THEN-END IF) and one optional (ELSE) keyword. The basic structure is as follows:

> **If (*conditional expression*) then**
> > *Statements;*
> > > **Else**
> > > *Statements;*
> > > > **End if;**

The structure begins with the keyword IF. This is followed by a set of one or more conditional expressions. The set of expressions must be evaluated as true for the statements following the THEN keyword to be executed.

If the set of conditional expressions is evaluated as false, the commands following the ELSE keyword will be executed. The ELSE keyword is optional. If this part of the structure is omitted and the set of conditional expressions is false, none of the structure's commands will be executed.

Listing 14.7 illustrates a simple IF-THEN-ELSE structure. The procedure first determines the average hiring age for males. It then determines the average hiring age for females. The calculation and assignment are performed by using SELECT/INTO statements. An IF-THEN-ELSE structure follows the SELECT/INTO statements. The values are then evaluated in the conditional expression following the IF keyword. If the average hiring age of males is highest (or the conditional expression is true), the first statement in the structure will be executed. If the average hiring age of females is highest (or the conditional expression is false), the statement following the ELSE keyword will be executed.

Listing 14.7 *An IF-THEN-ELSE Structure Example*

```
SQL> declare
  2     male_avg        number;
  3     female_avg      number;
  4   begin
  5     select avg(months_between(employment_date, birth_date)/12)
  6       into male_avg
  7     from employee
```

```
 8      where gender = 'M';
 9      select avg(months_between(employment_date, birth_date)/12)
10        into female_avg
11      from employee
12      where gender = 'F';
13      if (male_avg > female_avg) then
14        dbms_output.put_line ('Males have the greatest avg hiring
          age');
15        dbms_output.put_line ('With and avg age of
          '||to_char(male_avg));
16      else
17        dbms_output.put_line ('Females have the greatest avg hiring
          age');
18        dbms_output.put_line ('With and avg age of
          '||to_char(female_avg));
19      end if;
20    end;
21    /
Males have the greatest avg hiring age
With an avg age of 55.9176154332700822264389626818469323214l

PL/SQL procedure successfully completed.

SQL>

End Listing
```

Nested IF-THEN-ELSE Structures

IF-THEN-ELSE structures can also be placed with the statements following the IF-THEN keywords, with the statements following the ELSE keyword, or in both sections at the same time. These IF-THEN-ELSE structures are called nested IF statements. They allow the developer to specify subconditions or very detailed logic trails. Nested IF statements can be compared to the branches of a tree. Each nested IF is a new fork of the branch. As the application moves down the branch, additional forks are encountered, and a decision must be made as to which fork to take. Each tip of the branch is a bud or, in the case of an IF-THEN-ELSE structure, a behavior distinct from any other.

Listing 14.8 illustrates a nested IF statement. This procedure is a modification of the procedure in Listing 14.7. The nested IF statements evaluate whether the average age for the particular gender is more than 10 years greater than the average age of the other gender. If this condition is true, a message is displayed indicating such.

Listing 14.8 *An IF-THEN-ELSE Structure with a Nested IF Statement*

```
SQL> declare
  2    male_avg        number;
  3    female_avg      number;
  4  begin
  5    select avg(months_between(employment_date, birth_date)/12)
  6      into male_avg
  7    from employee
  8    where gender = 'M';
  9    select avg(months_between(employment_date, birth_date)/12)
 10      into female_avg
 11    from employee
 12    where gender = 'F';
 13    if (male_avg > female_avg) then
 14     dbms_output.put_line ('Males have the greatest avg hiring
          age');
 15     dbms_output.put_line ('With and avg age of
          '||to_char(male_avg));
 16     if (male_avg > female_avg + 10) then
 17      dbms_output.put_line ('The male average is greater than 10
          years');
 18     end if;
 19    else
 20     dbms_output.put_line ('Females have the greatest avg hiring
          age');
 21     dbms_output.put_line ('With and avg age of
          '||to_char(female_avg));
 22    end if;
 23  end;
 24  /
Males have the greatest avg hiring age
With and avg age of 55.91761543327008222643896268184693232141
The male average is greater than 10 years

PL/SQL procedure successfully completed.

SQL>
```

outer IF condition

inner or nested IF condition

End Listing

The ELSIF/THEN Structure

Decision logic sometimes requires a mutually exclusive set of events to be evaluated. *Mutually exclusive* means that only one event in the set of events can occur. The occurrence of one event excludes the occurrence of any other. This set of events can be modeled in the procedure as a series of IF-THEN structures. For this to work, each of the structures in this construct must have a condition that is unique from any other possible event. This method requires a well-designed set of conditional logic. A better way to set up a series of mutually exclusive events is to use the IF-THEN structure with the ELSIF keyword.

In this construct, the ELSE keyword is replaced with the ELSIF/THEN keywords. These keywords are followed by a conditional expression that must evaluate to true for the statements following it to be executed. If the expression is false, the focus is shifted to the next ELSIF. This repeats until one of the events occurs or until the end of the structure is reached.

The ELSE keyword can also be placed in the structure. It is the last section of the construct and serves as a catchall event. If none of the events occurs, the behavior that the ELSE keyword controls will be executed.

Listing 14.9 illustrates the ELSIF structure. The procedure begins by determining the current month. This value is then used as an argument in a series of mutually exclusive conditions in an IF-THEN-ELSIF structure. If the month value agrees with one of the conditions, a special message will be issued. The structure also has a catchall clause that issues a distinct message.

Listing 14.9 *An IF-THEN-ELSIF Structure*

```
SQL> declare
  2     current_month        char(3);
  3  begin
  4     select to_char(sysdate, 'MON') into current_month from dual;
  5     if current_month = 'JAN' then
  6        dbms_output.put_line ('My daughter Jane was born in
           January');
  7     elsif current_month = 'FEB' then
  8        dbms_output.put_line ('My good friend Ron was born in
           February');
  9     elsif current_month = 'MAR' then
 10        dbms_output.put_line ('My father was born in March');
 11     elsif current_month = 'APR' then
 12        dbms_output.put_line ('I was born in April');
```

```
13    elsif current_month = 'MAY' then
14      dbms_output.put_line ('My son Matt was born in May');
15    elsif current_month = 'OCT' then
16      dbms_output.put_line ('My wife was born in October');
17    else
18      dbms_output.put_line ('I do not have any relatives
19                            born in '||current_month);
20    end if;
21  end;
22  /
I do not have any relatives born in JUN

PL/SQL procedure successfully completed.

SQL>

End Listing
```

Cursors

A **cursor** is a device that is used to retrieve a set of records from a table/view into memory. Cursors allow each of the records to be read into the code block and then to be processed one at a time. A cursor can be compared to a book containing a page mark. Each of the pages is a record in the set of records retrieved when the cursor is executed. The bookmark indicates the current page. When using a cursor, Oracle always knows the current record. As one record is read into the code block, the current record is changed, just as the bookmark is changed as a page is read. Cursors are important tools for the processing of records. They allow the developer to bring records into the code block and to process them by using a complex set of statements. This section will discuss how to declare and execute the cursor and how to assign the record attributes to local variables.

Declaring the Cursor

Cursors are defined in the declaration section of the code block. The definition consists of the keywords CURSOR and IS, the name of the cursor, and the SELECT statement used to retrieve the record set. The following is an example of the cursor definition structure:

Cursor *cusor name* is *select statement*;

Cursor Commands

There are three commands that are used in conjunction with cursors, and I've listed them in Table 14.1.

There are several items to remember about cursor commands:

- The commands end with a semicolon.
- Issuing the OPEN command when the cursor is currently open will cause an error and will terminate the procedure.
- Issuing the CLOSE command when the cursor is not open will cause an error and will terminate the procedure.
- Issuing the FETCH/INTO command when the cursor is not open will cause an error and will terminate the procedure.
- Issuing the FETCH/INTO command after the last record has been fetched will not cause an error. The values from the last record will be reassigned to the local variables.

Listing 14.10 illustrates the use of several cursors in a code block. The first cursor (find_old_b_day) identifies the birth date of the oldest employee. This value is then used with the second cursor (id_employee) to identify the name of this employee. Notice how the cursors are opened, the values are

Table 14.1 *Cursor Commands*

Command	Example	Description
OPEN	Open *cursor_name*;	This command executes the cursor's SELECT statement and places the records into memory. The first record in the set is the current set.
FETCH/INTO	Fetch *cursor_name* into *variables*;	This command assigns the values from the current cursor record to the listed local variables or PL/SQL record. It also makes the next record in the set the current record.
CLOSE	Close *cursor_name*;	This command terminates the cursor and frees the memory that the cursor uses.

assigned to the local variables using the FETCH command, and the cursors are closed.

Listing 14.10 *Using Cursors and Cursor Commands*

```
SQL> declare
  2     oldest_birth_date      date;
  3     lname                  employee.last_name%type;
  4     fname                  employee.first_name%type;
  5     cursor find_old_b_day is select min(birth_date) from employee;
  6     cursor id_employee is select last_name, first_name
  7                           from employee
  8                           where birth_date = oldest_birth_date;
  9   begin
 10     open find_old_b_day;
 11     fetch find_old_b_day into oldest_birth_date;
 12     close find_old_b_day;
 13     open id_employee;
 14     fetch id_employee into lname, fname;
 15     close id_employee;
 16     dbms_output.put_line ('The Oldest Employee Is'
 17                           ||lname||', '||fname);
 18   end;
 19   /
The Oldest Employee Is JOHNSON, ANDREW

PL/SQL procedure successfully completed.

SQL>
```

Value from the old_b_day cursor is used as an agrument here.

cursor commands

End Listing

Using Aggregate Variables with Cursors

In the example in Listing 14.10, local variables were defined for each of the columns that the cursors retrieved. The developer had to declare each of the variables used in order to assign cursor values and to include them in the FETCH statements. There are two potential problems with this method:

1. The developer must document the local variable's size and type. If the size of the cursor variable is larger than the size of the local variable that its value is assigned to, an error will occur, and the procedure will terminate. The procedure will also terminate if the data types are different.

2. If the size of the column is changed, the procedure variables will also need to be changed. Failure to change the procedure may cause the procedure to terminate when run.

These problems can be eliminated through the use of the %ROWTYPE variable definition, which can be used in conjunction with the cursor. The %ROWTYPE definition will cause a PL/SQL record to be created with columns for each cursor column at runtime. Each of these variables will have the correct size and type. The problems described can be avoided by using this technique.

Another benefit of using %rROWTYPE is the reduced number of statements in the procedure. %ROWTYPE creates all of the needed variables with one statement. In addition, the PL/SQL record name can replace the variables used in the FETCH statement, which will reduce the overall length of the FETCH statement. This is important because it is more effective to have smaller, more concise programs.

Listing 14.11 illustrates the use of PL/SQL record variables using the %ROWTYPE definition. This technique produces the same results with more-concise code.

Listing 14.11 *Using %ROWTYPE to Define Cursor Variables*

```
SQL> declare
cursor find_old_b_day is select min(birth_date) day
from employee;
  4    old_date              find_old_b_day%rowtype;
  5    cursor id_employee is select last_name, first_name
  6                          from employee
  7                          where birth_date = old_date.day;
  8    id                    id_employee%rowtype;
  9  begin
 10    open find_old_b_day;
 11    fetch find_old_b_day into old_date;
 12    close find_old_b_day;
 13    open id_employee;
 14    fetch id_employee into id;
 15    close id_employee;
```

PL/SQL records

```
16     dbms_output.put_line ('The Oldest Employee Is '
17                          ||id.last_name||', '||id.first_name);
18   end;
19   /
The Oldest Employee Is JOHNSON, ANDREW

PL/SQL procedure successfully completed.

SQL>

End Listing
```

PL/SQL
record variable

There are several things to remember when using %ROWTYPE:

- The cursor must be defined before the PL/SQL record definition.
- All cursor columns must have a name. When expressions are included, such as in the case of group functions, you must include a column alias.

Cursor Attributes

PL/SQL provides the developer with four cursor attributes, which are listed in Table 14.2.

Table 14.2 *Cursor Attributes*

Name	Description
%FOUND	This attribute is true if the last FETCH statement returned a record. It is false if it did not.
%NOTFOUND	This attribute is true if the last FETCH statement did not return a record. It is false if it did.
%ROWCOUNT	This attribute returns the number of FETCH commands that have been issued for the cursor.
%ISOPEN	This attribute is true if the indicated cursor is currently open. It is false if the cursor is currently closed.

The commands listed in Table 14.2 are used in a condition within the procedure and are used to evaluate the condition of a cursor. Based on this condition, an action will occur. The syntax of the expression is as follows:

Cursor_name%isopen

Cursor attributes are expressions, not statements. This means that they are part of a statement and are not followed by a semicolon. Listing 14.12 illustrates the %ISOPEN cursor attribute, which determines whether a cursor is currently open. The attribute is included in an IF-THEN structure. If the cursor is open, the OPEN command will not be issued. This technique is often used when in the procedure there is a danger of opening a cursor that is currently open or closing a cursor that is not open. Either of these two events will cause an error to occur. Listing 14.12 uses two IF-THEN structures to check the status of the cursor. This will prevent the error from occurring.

Listing 14.12 *Using the %ISOPEN Cursor Attribute to Control Errors*

```
SQL> declare
  2     cursor name is select max(first_name) fname,
  3                     max(last_name) lname
  4                     from employee;
  5     names       name%rowtype;
  6  begin
  7     if not name%isopen then       ←——  %ISOPEN
  8       open name;                         cursor variable
  9     end if;
 10     fetch name into names;
 11     dbms_output.put_line (names.fname||' '||names.lname);
 12     if name%isopen then
 13       close name;
 14     end if;
 15  end;
 16  /
WOODROW WILSON

PL/SQL procedure successfully completed.

SQL>

End listing
```

The %FOUND, %NOTFOUND, and %ROWCOUNT attributes will be illustrated in a later section.

Differences between a Cursor and a SELECT/INTO Statement

A cursor and a SELECT/INTO statement are similar in that they both can be used to retrieve values for local variables. However, there are two shortcomings with the SELECT/INTO statement:

1. It cannot be used to process multiple database records. If the SELECT command retrieves more than one record, an error will occur.

2. If it does not return a record from the database, an error will occur.

A cursor does not have these limitations. Cursors can process multiple records. In addition, failure of the cursor to retrieve a record will not cause an error to occur. Null values will be brought into the procedure variables by the FETCH command. For these two reasons, a cursor is preferable to the SELECT/INTO statement.

Loops

Loops are a construct that causes Oracle to repeat the same set of code. This is an important tool for processing records. A loop can contain numerous statements and logic. These statements can then be applied to each individual record in a set, thereby allowing the developer to use the same statement to modify many records.

There are three types of **looping structures**: LOOP, WHILE, and FOR. The former two structures will be discussed in this section. The FOR looping structure will be discussed in the next section.

Each of the loop structures has three things in common:

1. Each structure contains the LOOP keyword.

2. Each structure ends with the END LOOP keywords.

3. Each structure uses a conditional expression to determine whether to stop the looping.

The LOOP Structure

The LOOP structure is a very simple structure. It begins with the keyword LOOP. The keyword END followed by a semicolon terminates the structure. When Oracle encounters the END LOOP keywords, the focus returns to the LOOP keyword and the structure's statements are reexecuted. The structure also contains a breakout conditional statement (IF-THEN or WHEN), which contains the EXIT command. When the breakout condition is evaluated as true, the focus of the procedure will shift to the first statement following the structure.

The following is a template of the LOOP structure:

Loop
    Statements;
    When *break_out condition* **then exit;**
    Statements;
End loop;

Listing 14.13 illustrates the LOOP structure. This procedure is used to read and display the first six records from the Employee table. The LOOP structure is used to fetch each record and display the values. The cursor commands OPEN and CLOSE are placed outside the loop and cannot be repeated without an error. The procedure also has a counter that is a numeric variable. Each iteration increments the counter. The EXIT WHEN statement evaluates this counter. If the value is equal to 7, the focus of the procedure leaves the loop. The procedure assigns a value to the counter when it is defined. It is necessary to initialize the counter in order to increment the variable. The counter cannot be incremented if it contains a null value.

Listing 14.13 *The LOOP Structure*

```
SQL> declare
  2    counter_variable   number := 1;
  3    cursor a is select last_name from employee;
  4    cur_var            a%rowtype;
  5  begin
  6    open a;
```

```
 7    loop
 8      exit when counter_variable = 7;
 9      fetch a into cur_var;
10      dbms_output.put_line (cur_var.last_name);
11      counter_variable := counter_variable +1;
12    end loop;
13  end;
14  /
```

beginning of loop

breakout statement

end of the LOOP structure

```
COOLIDGE
JOHNSON
REAGAN
BUSH
JOHNSON
CLINTON

PL/SQL procedure successfully completed.
SQL>
```

End listing

The EXIT WHEN statement can be replaced by an IF-THEN construct. Listing 14.14 illustrates such a change. The results of the procedure are the same.

Listing 14.14 *The LOOP Structure Using the IF-THEN Structure to Terminate the Loop*

```
SQL> declare
 2    counter_variable    number := 1;
 3    cursor a is select last_name from employee;
 4    cur_var             a%rowtype;
 5  begin
 6    open a;
 7    loop
 8      if counter_variable = 7 then exit; end if;
 9      fetch a into cur_var;
10      dbms_output.put_line (cur_var.last_name);
11      counter_variable := counter_variable +1;
12    end loop;
13  end;
14  /
```

IF statement used to break out of the loop

```
COOLIDGE
JOHNSON
REAGAN
BUSH
JOHNSON
CLINTON
PL/SQL procedure successfully completed.

SQL>

End listing
```

The WHILE Loop

Another type of looping structure is the WHILE loop. This structure is similar to the simple LOOP except that the breakout condition is located at the top of the LOOP structure rather than within the structure. This structure is used when the developer wants the breakout condition checked before the focus enters the structure. If the breakout condition is false, the focus never enters the looping structure.

The structure begins with the keyword WHILE, followed by the breakout condition. The structure's statements, enclosed by the LOOP and END LOOP keywords, follow the condition. The following is a syntax template of the WHILE looping structure:

> **While *breakout_condition***
> **Loop**
> ***Statements;***
> **End loop;**

Listing 14.15 illustrates the WHILE loop. This example uses the same basic procedure as the two previous listings. The breakout condition statement was eliminated and is now part of the LOOP structure header. The breakout condition is now not part of the LOOP statements; therefore, the logic must be changed. If the condition were left as *counter_variable* = 7, the focus would never enter the structure because the variable was initially set to 1. The evaluation operator must be changed to NOT EQUAL in order for the loop to operate correctly. This condition will then be true when the structure is first encountered, and it will remain true for the first six iterations.

Listing 14.15 *The WHILE Loop Structure*

```
SQL> declare
  2    counter_variable    number := 1;
  3    cursor a is select last_name from employee;
  4    cur_var             a%rowtype;
  5  begin
  6    open a;
  7    while counter_variable != 7          WHILE loop
  8    loop                                 condition
  9      fetch a into cur_var;
 10      dbms_output.put_line (cur_var.last_name);
 11      counter_variable := counter_variable +1;
 12    end loop;
 13  end;
 14  /
COOLIDGE
JOHNSON
REAGAN
BUSH
JOHNSON
CLINTON

PL/SQL procedure successfully completed.

SQL>

End listing
```

Using the %FOUND Cursor Attribute with Loops

The cursor attribute %FOUND is an extremely useful tool to use with loops that contain cursors. Cursor attributes determine whether the last FETCH command returned a fresh record. Loops generally are used to process cursor-retrieved records one at a time; therefore, the cursor attributes are perfect to control the completion of the processing. This technique eliminates the need to use counter variables.

The following is a syntax template of a WHILE loop that uses the %FOUND attribute to control the breakout of the loop. In this structure, the cursor is opened before the focus encounters the keyword LOOP. Two FETCH statements are placed in the structure. The first precedes the WHILE keyword. It is necessary to fetch a record before entering the LOOP structure. If the cursor retrieves a record, the focus will enter the LOOP structure. If is does not, the LOOP structure will be bypassed. The second FETCH command is the last statement and is necessary in order to update the %FOUND attribute before the focus returns to the top of the structure and the value is tested. The CLOSE command is issued after the looping structure.

> **Open** *cursor_name;*
> **Fetch** *cursor_attributes* **into** *local_variables;*
> **While (***cursor_name*%**found)**
> **Loop**
>   **Statements;**
>   **Fetch** *cursor_attributes* **into** *local_variables;*
> **End loop;**
> **Close** *cursor_name;*

Listing 14.16 illustrates a loop using the %FOUND cursor attribute.

Listing 14.16 *A WHILE Loop Using the %FOUND Attribute*

```
SQL> declare
  2     cursor a is select last_name from employee;
  3     cur_var            a%rowtype;
  4  begin
  5     open a;
  6     fetch a into cur_var;          ◄———  A record is
  7     while a%found                        fetched before
  8     loop                                 the loop.
  9        dbms_output.put_line (cur_var.last_name);
 10        fetch a into cur_var;
 11     end loop;
 12  end;
 13  /
COOLIDGE
 .
 .
 .
```

Another FETCH command is used at the end of the loop.

```
ROOSEVELT
ANTHONY
ROOSEVELT

PL/SQL procedure successfully completed.

SQL>

End listing
```

Nested Loops

Loops can contain loops within themselves. Embedded loops are called nested loops. They can be used to provide additional processing for an instance retrieved in the outer loop. To illustrate this usage, Listing 14.17 contains a procedure that retrieves the employees from the Employee table for the WEL department. A nested loop is then used to retrieve each of the employee's tool records. The highest-priced tool is then displayed for each of the employees.

Listing 14.17 *Nested WHILE Loop*

```
SQL> declare
  2    cursor a is select payroll_number, last_name from employee
  3                where fk_department = 'WEL';
  4    a_var        a%rowtype;
  5    cursor b is select tool_name, tool_cost from emp_tools
  6                where fk_payroll_number = a_var.payroll_number;
  7    b_var            b%rowtype;
  8    hi_tool_name     emp_tools.tool_name%type;
  9    hi_tool_cost     emp_tools.tool_cost%type;
 10  begin
 11    open a; fetch a into a_var;
 12    while a%found loop
 13      open b; fetch b into b_var;
 14      while b%found loop                    ┌─────────────┐
                                               │ nested loop │
                                               └─────────────┘
 15        if b_var.tool_cost > hi_tool_cost or b_var.tool_cost is
           null then
 16            hi_tool_name := b_var.tool_name;
 17            hi_tool_cost := b_var.tool_cost;
 18        end if;
```

```
19        fetch b into b_var;
20        end loop;
21        close b;
22        dbms_output.put_line (a_var.last_name||'
          '||b_var.tool_name);
23        hi_tool_name := null;
24        hi_tool_cost := null;
25        fetch a into a_var;
26      end loop;
27      close a;
28    end;
29  /
REAGAN Tool Chest
CARTER Tool Chest
HOOVER TIN SNIPS
TAFT FOUNTAIN PEN
ANTHONY STAPLER
ROOSEVELT PLIERS

PL/SQL procedure successfully completed.

SQL>

End listing
```

Locking Records with the FOR UPDATE Option

When a record is marked for UPDATE or DELETE, Oracle places a lock on the record, which means that another user cannot modify the record before the record is permanently saved (and the lock removed). This is an important database feature for controlling **concurrency**. You would not want another user to modify a record that a second user was currently modifying. The database manager should make the second user wait until the first user has performed the change. This is what a lock performs. Another user cannot modify the locked record until the original user releases the lock with a COMMIT or ROLLBACK command.

Cursors are often used to update a set of records. The main component in a cursor is a SELECT statement used to identify the records. Unfortunately, SELECT statements do not lock the identified records, which means that another user can modify the cursor-retrieved records before the procedure using the cursor can. If another user modifies a cursor-retrieved record, the procedure will terminate when it attempts to modify this record. Oracle will not allow a user to update a record that another user has modified.

In order to avoid this situation, the developer can lock the cursor-retrieved records. The keywords FOR UPDATE following the SELECT statement will cause Oracle to lock each cursor record. Other users will not be able to update these records until the cursor is closed or until a COMMIT or ROLLBACK command is issued.

Listing 14.18 illustrates the syntax of this command. The procedure contains a cursor that retrieves the records from the Employee table for the WEL department. The SELECT statement using the FOR UPDATE keywords causes these records to be locked. The executable section contains a WHILE loop that fetches each record. This procedure does not contain an UPDATE statement. It is not mandatory for any of the records that the cursor locked actually to be updated or deleted.

Listing 14.18 *A Cursor SELECT Statement Using the FOR UPDATE Option*

```
SQL> declare
  2     cursor a is select last_name, first_name from employee
  3                    where fk_department = 'WEL'
  4                    for update;
  5     a_var        a%rowtype;
  6  begin
  7     open a;
  8     fetch a into a_var;
  9     while a%found loop
 10        dbms_output.put_line (a_var.last_name);
 11        fetch a into a_var;
 12     end loop;
 13  end;
 14  /
REAGAN
.
ROOSEVELT
PL/SQL procedure successfully completed.
SQL>
```

> FOR UPDATE keyword that locks the cursor records

End Listing

The FOR UPDATE OF Option

The FOR UPDATE keywords can be followed by the keyword OF and the names of columns. When this keyword is included, the cursor will lock the records only if the SELECT clause in the cursor definition contains the name of one of the columns listed after the OF keyword. Listing 14.19 illustrates this. This procedure is a modified form of the procedure shown in Listing 14.18. The OF keyword and the column name Wages are added to the SELECT statement. The SELECT clause does not contain the Wages column; therefore, the FOR UPDATE option will not cause the records to be locked.

Listing 14.19 *A Cursor with the FOR UPDATE OF Option*

```
SQL> declare
  2    cursor a is select last_name, first_name from employee
  3                where fk_department = 'WEL'
  4                for update of wages;
  5    a_var        a%rowtype;
  6  begin
  7    open a;
  8    fetch a into a_var;
  9    while a%found loop
 10      dbms_output.put_line (a_var.last_name);
 11      fetch a into a_var;
 12    end loop;
 13  end;
 14  /
REAGAN
CARTER
HOOVER
TAFT
ANTHONY
ROOSEVELT

PL/SQL procedure successfully completed.

SQL>

End listing
```

> This FOR UPDATE statement will not lock records because the Wages column is not in the SELECT clause.

I do not see a great use for this option except to identify the columns that the cursor is intended to update later in the procedure. In this case, the columns should be listed after the keyword.

The WHERE CURRENT OF Option

As Oracle is fetching records from a cursor, it always marks the current record. If the developer wants to modify this record, the WHERE CURRENT OF option can be used. Adding these keywords to the end of an UPDATE or DELETE statement will cause Oracle to modify the currently marked cursor record. This has two important benefits:

- Performance
  Oracle always knows the rowid of the current record. When the record is modified, Oracle can go directly to the record without having to locate the record in the table. If the option is missing, the UPDATE and DELETE statements will need a WHERE clause to locate the proper record. This will require some I/O. The WHERE CURRENT OF option can dramatically increase performance of data modification procedures.

- Code Simplification
  The option eliminates the need to create a WHERE clause for the DML commands. This eliminates the need to create local variables, fetch values for the variables, and include them in the WHERE clause. The option will reduce the size of the procedure.

This option can be used with the DML commands only if the FOR UPDATE keywords lock the records. A syntax template of an UPDATE statement is as follows:

> **Update *tablename* set *column_name* = *value***
> **Where current of *cursor_name*;**

Listing 14.20 illustrates this option. Listing 14.18 was modified to include an UPDATE statement with the WHERE CURRENT OF option. This statement updates the Wages value by 3 percent. A second loop was included in the procedure to display the wages after the record was updated.

Listing 14.20 *An UPDATE Statement Using the WHERE CURRENT OF Option*

```
SQL> declare
  2    cursor a is select last_name, first_name, wages from employee
  3                 where fk_department = 'WEL'
  4                 for update;
  5    a_var      a%rowtype;
  6  begin
  7    open a;
  8    fetch a into a_var;
  9    while a%found loop
 10      dbms_output.put_line (a_var.last_name||'
          '||to_char(a_var.wages));
 11      update employee set wages = wages * 1.03
 12        where current of a;
 13      fetch a into a_var;
 14    end loop;
 15    close a;
 16    open a;
 17    fetch a into a_var;
 18    while a%found loop
 19      dbms_output.put_line (a_var.last_name||'
          '||to_char(a_var.wages));
 20      fetch a into a_var;
 21    end loop;
 22    close a;
 23  end;
 24  /
REAGAN 14500
CARTER 14000
HOOVER 10000
TAFT 8500
ANTHONY 7000
ROOSEVELT
REAGAN 14905
CARTER 14390
HOOVER 10300
TAFT 8755
ANTHONY 7210
ROOSEVELT

PL/SQL procedure successfully completed.

SQL>

End Listing
```

> This clause tells Oracle exactly where the record to be updated exists.

FOR Loops

Oracle has another powerful looping structure that we have not seen: the FOR loop. There are a number of variations of this structure, the simplest of which is the numeric FOR loop. The most sophisticated and powerful is the cursor FOR loop. This section will discuss the various versions of this looping structure.

Numeric FOR Loops

The chief characteristic of a numeric FOR loop is that it contains a counting variable. This variable is used to determine when the focus should move from the looping structure to the next statement in the procedure. The structure is similar to the simple LOOP structure, except that the counting variable and the number of iterations are defined in the header of the numeric FOR structure. This makes it easier for the developer to identify the location of the statement that determines the break point of the looping structure.

A syntax template for the structure follows:

> **For *counting_variable***
>   **in *lower_range_number .. highest_range_number***
> **Loop**
>   ***Statements;***
> **End loop;**

The FOR looping structure begins with a header that defines the looping parameters. The first word in the header is the keyword FOR. This is followed by a numeric counting variable that also serves as the qualifier of the structure variables.

The counting range is defined next. The range consists of two numeric values separated by double periods. The values can be variables or numbers. The lower value is listed first, followed by the higher value.

Normally, the counting variable will be initialized with the lower-range value. The variable will then be incremented until the higher value is reached. The focus will then move away from the structure. If the REVERSE keyword is placed before the counting range, the counting variable will be initialized with the higher-range value. The variable will then decrement until the lower-range value is met. The focus will then shift away from the looping structure.

The actual loop begins with the keyword LOOP and is terminated by the keywords END LOOP. The statements within this section do not contain an EXIT command. Reaching the higher- or lower-range limit terminates the loop.

Listing 14.21 illustrates the normal numeric FOR loop. This structure fetches and displays the last name for the first 10 employee records from the Employee table. Each of these records is prefaced by the current value of the counting variable CNT_VAR.

Listing 14.21 *Using the Numeric FOR Loop*

```
SQL> declare
  2     cursor a is select first_name, last_name from employee;
  3     emp_var         a%rowtype;
  4   begin
  5     open a;
  6     for cnt_var in 1..10          ←——  numeric FOR
  7       loop                              loop header
  8         fetch a into emp_var;
  9         dbms_output.put_line(to_char(cnt_var)||'
           '||emp_var.last_name);
 10       end loop;
 11     close a;
 12   end;
 13   /
1 COOLIDGE
2 JOHNSON
3 REAGAN
4 BUSH
5 JOHNSON
6 CLINTON
7 CARTER
8 FORD
9 NIXON
10 KENNEDY

PL/SQL procedure successfully completed.
SQL>
```

End listing

Listing 14.22 illustrates the use of the numeric FOR loop with the REVERSE keyword. This option causes the counting variable to be initialized with the highest-range value. In this example, the lower-range value was also changed to 3. The procedure now fetches and displays 10 employee last names. Notice that the counting variable decrements from 10 to 3 and that the counting variable does not have any effect on which cursor records are displayed.

Listing 14.22 *The Numeric FOR Loop Using the REVERSE Option*

```
SQL> declare
  2    cursor a is select first_name, last_name from employee;
  3    emp_var       a%rowtype;
  4  begin
  5    open a;
  6    for cnt_var in reverse 3..10
  7     loop
  8      fetch a into emp_var;
  9      dbms_output.put_line(to_char(cnt_var)||'
          '||emp_var.last_name);
 10     end loop;
 11    close a;
 12  end;
 13  /
10 COOLIDGE
9 JOHNSON
8 REAGAN
7 BUSH
6 JOHNSON
5 CLINTON
4 CARTER
3 FORD

PL/SQL procedure successfully completed.

SQL>

End listing
```

Same list of last_name values as in Listing 14.21. Only the corresponding counter variables is reserved.

The numeric FOR loop has one main disadvantage: It relies on range values and a counter to terminate the looping procedure. When processing cursor records, the range value likely does not reflect the actual number of records to process. This is an ever-changing value. A better way to process cursor records is to use the cursor FOR loop, discussed in the next section.

The Basic Cursor FOR Loop

The basic cursor FOR loop eliminates the shortcomings of the numeric FOR loop when the latter is used with cursors. The cursor FOR loop is similar to the numeric FOR loop but has four main differences:

1. The high- and low-range values in the header are changed to the name of the cursor. This, in effect, tells Oracle to use an implied %NOTFOUND cursor attribute to denote that the cursor records have been processed.

2. The structure does not have a counting variable. The range values are not needed; therefore, a counting variable is not created or needed.

3. The cursor commands OPEN, FETCH, and CLOSE are not needed. The LOOP structure implicitly issues these commands.

4. The local variables used within the loop do not have to be defined. Oracle will create a PL/SQL record for the cursor's fetched attributes. The name of the cursor FOR loop qualifies these variables.

If the value will be used outside the cursor FOR loop, it must be assigned to a local variable declared outside the LOOP structure.

Listing 14.23 illustrates the basic cursor FOR loop. In this example, the procedure from Listing 14.21 was modified. The PL/SQL record Emp_var was eliminated. The range values were replaced by the name of the cursor (a). This procedure is now terminated after the last cursor record has been fetched. It displays the last names for each of the employees in the Employee table. The %ROWCOUNT cursor attribute is used to number the records because the counting variable does not exist. The cursor commands are also implicitly issued. The records will be selected and fetched until the loop is terminated after the last record is fetched (the %NOTFOUND cursor attribute turns true).

Listing 14.23 *The Basic Cursor FOR Loop*

```
SQL> declare
  2     cursor a is select first_name, last_name from employee;
  3   begin
  4     for cnt_var in a
  5       loop
  6         dbms_output.put_line(to_char(a%rowcount)||'
          '||cnt_var.last_name);
  7       end loop;
  8   end;
  9   /
1 COOLIDGE
.
.
.
19 ROOSEVELT

PL/SQL procedure successfully completed.

End Listing
```

PL/SQL record

cursor name

Defining the Cursor in the Cursor FOR Header

In its most powerful form, the cursor FOR looping structure allows the developer to define the cursor within the structure. The benefit of this is that the cursor SELECT statement is in close proximity to the actual place it is used within the procedure. The developer does not have to search throughout the procedure for the pertinent statement.

Listing 14.24 illustrates this concept. Listing 14.23 was modified. The SELECT statement used in the cursor that was defined in the declare section is now defined as part of the cursor FOR header. In addition, the rows are no longer numbered. A cursor was not defined; therefore, the %ROWCOUNT attribute that was used in Listing 14.23 is not available. A developer-defined counting variable is needed to count fetched rows in a cursor FOR loop.

Listing 14.24 *The Cursor FOR Loop with the Cursor Defined within the Loop*

```
SQL> begin
  2      for cnt_var in (select first_name, last_name from employee)
  3        loop
  4          dbms_output.put_line(cnt_var.last_name);
  5        end loop;
  6   end;
  7   /
COOLIDGE
JOHNSON
.
.
.
ANTHONY
ROOSEVELT

PL/SQL procedure successfully completed.

SQL>

End Listing
```

Nested FOR Loops

FOR loops, including cursor FOR loops, may also be nested. Listing 14.25 illustrates this concept and shows a rework of the nested WHILE loop example from Listing 14.17. This procedure contains two cursor FOR loops. The outer loop retrieves the employees from the WEL department. The payroll number attribute is used in the inner loop to identify each employee's tool records. The highest-priced tool for each employee is retained after the completion of the inner loop. The employee's name and the name of the tool are then displayed. Notice how the employee's payroll number retrieved in the outer loop is used in the WHERE clause of the SELECT statement of the inner loop. A cursor FOR loop is an excellent tool to use when all of a cursor's records will be processed. Notice the compactness of this procedure as compared to the one used in Listing 14.17.

Listing 14.25 *A Nested Cursor FOR Loop*

```
SQL> declare
  2    hi_tool_name        emp_tools.tool_name%type;
  3    hi_tool_cost        emp_tools.tool_cost%type;
  4  begin
  5    for outer_loop in (select payroll_number, last_name from
      employee
  6                             where fk_department = 'WEL')
  7      loop
  8        for inner_loop in (select tool_name, tool_cost from
          emp_tools
  9                             where fk_payroll_number =
                                 outer_loop.payroll_number)
 10        loop
 11        if (inner_loop.tool_cost > hi_tool_cost
 12            or hi_tool_cost is null) then
 13          hi_tool_name := inner_loop.tool_name;
 14          hi_tool_cost := inner_loop.tool_cost;
 15        end if;
 16        end loop;
 17        dbms_output.put_line (outer_loop.last_name||'
          '||hi_tool_name);
 18      hi_tool_name := null;
 19      hi_tool_cost := null;
 20    end loop;
 21  end;
 22  /
REAGAN Tool Chest
CARTER
HOOVER TIN SNIPS
TAFT FOUNTAIN PEN
ANTHONY BRIEFCASE
ROOSEVELT CALCULATOR

PL/SQL procedure successfully completed.

SQL>
```

> outer loop variable used in the inner loop cursor

End listing

What's Next?

In the next chapter, you will learn how to trap errors that occur in your PL/SQL. You will also learn how to create named procedures, which are procedures that exist within the database in a compiled form and consist of named procedures, functions, and packages.

■ PRACTICE

1. Create a program that outputs the message "I am soon to be a PL/SQL expert."

2. Create a PL/SQL procedure that has four sections. Each section should output a statement. Use labels and the GOTO command to output the section messages in the following order:

Section 3

Section 2

Section 1

Section 4

3. Create a PL/SQL procedure that computes the retirement age of the youngest employee. You should also list the employee's name.

4. Modify the program in Question 3 to compute the number of days between today and the employee's retirement date.

5. Identify the number of tool purchases for Harold Truman and George Bush. Output the name of the employee with the greater number of tool purchases.

6. Use a nested IF statement to the Question 5 PL/SQL script. The statement should be used to determine whether Harold Truman and George Bush have a difference of more then two tool purchases.

7. Output which decade of the twentieth century Bill Clinton was born in.

8. Create a PL/SQL procedure that computes and displays the average starting age of the set of employees in the employee database.

9. Create a PL/SQL procedure that computes the hiring age of the first employee whom the WEL department hired.

10. Cause a "cursor already open" error to occur.

11. Fix the error produced in Question 10, using the %ISOPEN cursor attribute.

12. Determine the hiring date for Ronald Reagan and how many tool and eyeglasses purchases he made.

13. Use a simple LOOP to list the first 12 records of the Emp_tools table. Use the WHEN keyword to construct the loop breakout.

14. Modify your procedure in Question 13. Use the IF-THEN structure to construct the loop breakout.

15. Create a procedure that displays the employees in the INT department. Use a WHILE loop.

16. Create a procedure that determines the number of tool purchases and the number of eyeglasses purchases per employee. Use the %ROWCOUNT cursor attribute to number the displayed rows.

17. Re-create Question 15 using the %NOTFOUND cursor attribute.

18. Create a procedure that updates the Absences column in the Employee table. The value should be set to 0. Use the WHERE CURRENT OF option.

19. Create a procedure that displays the five oldest employees. Use a numeric FOR loop in your procedure, and number each record.

20. Modify the procedure you built in Question 19, to number the records in reverse order.

21. Create a procedure to list the employees in the INT and POL departments. Use a cursor FOR loop in this procedure. The procedure should define a cursor.

22. Modify the procedure in Question 21. Define the SELECT statement used in the cursor FOR loop within the cursor FOR structure.

23. Create a procedure that determines the date of the highest-priced tool and the date of the highest-priced eyeglasses purchase for each employee. Use nested cursor FOR loops.

Handling Exceptions and Using Named Procedures

This chapter continues the discussion of PL/SQL. The first chapter section covers the code block exception section, which is used to trap errors. The remainder of the chapter will cover named procedures, which are code blocks that have a name and that reside within the database. The most important of these, from the viewpoint of a data administrator, is a function. Functions return a value to the calling statement, thereby allowing the data administrator to calculate a host of special values such as employee age, employee seniority, or average department costs. Function values can be returned in a SELECT statement. A very effective technique is to add functions to the SELECT statement in a view. The view can then be granted to the end user, who never knows that some of the values are derived. Functions allow the data administrator not to have to calculate continually or format a value that is used in SQL. Functions will allow you to create a calculation or formatted value once and then to use it repeatedly.

Exception Handling

When a problem, error, or abnormal condition occurs in a code block, the focus of the program is shifted to the exception section. Oracle moves through the statements within this section, looking for an **exception handler**—a structure that provides Oracle with directions that should be followed for a particular error. If Oracle cannot find an exception handler, the procedure will be terminated abnormally, and all work that the procedure completed will be rolled back. This section discusses the exception section of the code block and exception handlers.

Predefined SQL Exceptions

Oracle has a large array of exceptions that can occur—many more exceptions than can be considered here. However, Oracle has predefined several exceptions with a name. These are the most common exceptions. The name is a developer-friendly method of identifying the particular error condition. The predefined exceptions are listed and described in Table 15.1. At the end of the description is an SQLCODE number, which is the number that Oracle has assigned to the exception. When an error occurs, this number is assigned to a

Table 15.1 *Predefined PL/SQL Exceptions*

Name	Description
CURSOR_ALREADY_OPEN	Occurs when the code block attempts to open a cursor that is currently open (SQLCODE = –6511)
DUP_VAL_ON_INDEX	Occurs when a DML command violates a unique value constraint on a column (SQLCODE = –1)
INVALID_CURSOR	Occurs when the code block references an undefined cursor (SQLCODE = –1001)
INVALID_NUMBER	Occurs when the code block attempts to assign an incorrect value to a local variable or database column (e.g., assigning of an alphanumeric value to a number or assigning a value that is larger than the variable definition) (SQLCODE = –1722)
LOGIN_DENIED	Occurs when the procedure fails to log on to the database (Entry of an incorrect user ID or password can cause the error) (SQLCODE = –1017)
NO_DATA_FOUND	Occurs when a SELECT statement is executed and no records were retreived (does not apply to cursors) (SQLCODE = +100)
NOT_LOGGED_ON	Occurs when a database command was issued and the application was not connected to the database (SQLCODE = –1012)

Table 15.1 *(continued)*

Name	Description
PROGRAM_ERROR	Occurs when an internal PL/SQL error happens (SQLCODE = -6501)
STORAGE_ERROR	Occurs when memory is used up (SQLCODE = -6500)
TIMEOUT_ON_RESOURCE	Occurs when Oracle stops waiting for a resource to become available, often occurring when another user has locked the table or when the available database threads are used (SQLCODE = -5100)
TOO_MANY_ROWS	Occurs when a SELECT statement that is using the INTO assignment keyword returns more than one row (SQLCODE = -1422)
TRANSACTION_BACKED_OUT	Occurs when part of a database transaction has been rolled back (SQLCODE = -61)
VALUE_ERROR	Occurs when PL/SQL cannot convert character data to numbers and when errors that are related to constraints and truncation happen (SQLCODE = -6502)
ZERO_DIVIDE	Occurs when Oracle attempts to divide a number by 0 (SQLCODE = -1476)
OTHERS	A catchall exception used to handle any undefined or unnamed error condition

variable called SQLCODE. This code is another device used to identify the error and to define a particular error with a name. The SQLCODE variable has a value of 0 when no error conditions have been encountered.

Handling an Exception with a Predefined Exception

Error conditions can be trapped and handled by using the exception section of the code block. This section, the last section of the code block, is initiated by the keyword EXCEPTION. Within the section are one or more WHEN statements, which are the exception handlers. An exception handler statement begins with the keyword WHEN, followed by the name of an exception. The exception name precedes the THEN keyword and the statement(s).

A semicolon terminates the clause. A syntax template of a WHEN statement is as follows:

When *exception_name* then
Statement(s);

When an error condition is encountered, Oracle shifts the focus of the procedure to the exception section and then evaluates the various exception handlers. If Oracle encounters a WHEN statement that has the proper exception name, Oracle will then execute the exception handler statements and will continue executing statements until another WHEN statement or the end of the code block is encountered.

Listing 15.1 illustrates the capture and handling of an error condition. The listing contains two procedures. Both procedures create a "too many rows" error. The SELECT/INTO statement does not contain a WHERE clause, causing more than one record to be retrieved from the database and assigned to variables. This will cause an error because only one value at a time can be assigned to a variable. The first procedure does not contain an error handler. This procedure is included to show you the results of an unhandled error condition. The second procedure traps and handles the error and is a user-friendly technique.

Listing 15.1 *Trapping and Handling a "Too Many Rows" Error*

```
SQL> declare
  2     lname       employee.last_name%type;
  3  begin

  4     select last_name into lname from employee;
  5     dbms_output.put_line (lname);
  6  end;
  7  /
declare
*
ERROR at line 1:
ORA-01422: exact fetch returns more than requested number of rows
ORA-06512: at line 4
```

procedure terminated abnormally

```
SQL> declare
  2     lname        employee.last_name%type;
  3  begin
  4     select last_name into lname from employee;
  5     dbms_output.put_line (lname);
  6  exception
  7    when too_many_rows then
  8          dbms_output.put_line ('Error occured in procedure');
  9  end;
 10  /
Error occured in procedure

PL/SQL procedure successfully completed.

SQL>

End Listing
```

error handled and
the procedure
completed

Defining Error Handlers

In the previous section, the error handler used a predefined name. Oracle has predefined the more common error conditions with a name, as seen in Table 15.1. Many other error conditions exist, and names can be defined for these errors and for the error trapped in the code block.

Exceptions are defined in the DECLARE section of the procedure. The declaration consists of the exception's name followed by the keyword EXCEPTION, which indicates the data type. The exception is then linked to a specific Oracle error code. This requires a second declaration: It begins with the keywords PRAGMA EXCEPTION_INIT, followed by the name of the exception and the Oracle error number. A syntax template of an exception definition is as follows:

> **Exception_name   exception;**
> **Pragma exception_init (exception_name,**
> **   exception_number);**

Listing 15.2 illustrates the naming and use of an exception. The procedure attempts to insert a record in the Employee table. The INSERT statement did not include a payroll number. This table column contains a NOT NULL constraint. On that column the INSERT statement violates the constraint, causing a –1400 Oracle error to occur.

Listing 15.2 *Naming an Exception Handler to Trap a NOT NULL Constraint Exception*

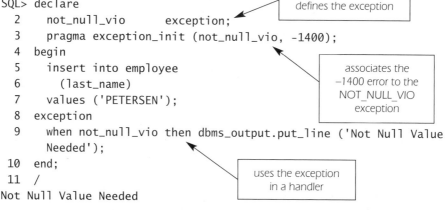

```
SQL> declare
  2    not_null_vio        exception;          ── defines the exception
  3    pragma exception_init (not_null_vio, -1400);
  4  begin                                     ── associates the
  5    insert into employee                       -1400 error to the
  6      (last_name)                              NOT_NULL_VIO
  7    values ('PETERSEN');                       exception
  8  exception
  9    when not_null_vio then dbms_output.put_line ('Not Null Value
       Needed');                               ── uses the exception
 10  end;                                          in a handler
 11  /
Not Null Value Needed

PL/SQL procedure successfully completed.

SQL>
```

End Listing

The OTHERS Exception

The OTHERS exception is a catchall exception that can be used in any code block. It will trap any exception and will ensure that the procedure is not terminated abnormally. This is an important feature. It is virtually impossible to define error handlers for all errors individually. When a code block is included in a form, report, or procedure that the developer does not want to be terminated abnormally, this exception can be invaluable. It is important to note that the OTHERS exception *is always* the last exception handler in the EXCEPTION section.

Listing 15.3 illustrates this exception handler. The procedure used in Listing 15.2 is modified. Rather than defining an exception handler, the OTHERS exception is used to trap the error. The results of the procedures are exactly the same.

Listing 15.3 *Using the OTHERS Exception Handler*

```
SQL> begin
  2     insert into employee
  3       (last_name)
  4     values ('PETERSEN');
  5  exception
  6     when others then dbms_output.put_line ('Not Null Value
       Needed');
  7  end;
  8  /
Not Null Value Needed

PL/SQL procedure successfully completed.

SQL>
```

End Listing

Using SQLCODE and SQLERRM

Developers sometimes want to trap the number of the Oracle error and its associated message and to terminate the code block normally. The OTHERS exception, SQLCODE variable, and the SQLERRM variable allow this to happen. This is a good technique to employ in an Oracle form. The OTHERS exception tells Oracle that an exception handler and statements are to be performed in the event of an error. SQLCODE is a function that returns the numeric Oracle error number. SQLERRM is a character string that contains a description of the error. It is a 250-byte, VARCHAR2 value.

Listing 15.4 illustrates this technique. The procedure used in Listing 15.3 was modified. The SQLCODE and SQLERRM variables were included in output statements in the exception section of the code block. Notice the error number and message that are displayed.

Listing 15.4 *Using SQLCODE and SQLERRM to Display Error Messages*

```
SQL> begin
  2    insert into employee (last_name)
  3    values ('PETERSEN');
  4  exception
  5    when others then dbms_output.put_line (to_char(sqlcode));
  6                     dbms_output.put_line (sqlerrm);
  7  end;
  8  /
-1400
ORA-01400: mandatory (NOT NULL) column is missing or NULL during
insert

PL/SQL procedure successfully completed.

SQL>

End Listing
```

Using the Exception Section for Your Own Processing

The exception section of the code block can be used for purposes other than error handling. A common use is to place developer-defined exceptions in this section. These are the edits that applications commonly have. An example is a procedure that checks the value a user might have entered. If the value is incorrect, the procedure raises an exception. The processing then shifts to the exception section. This is a good technique. It allows the focus of the program to move to the exception section without performing other edit checks.

To use the exception section for developer-defined processing, perform the following steps:

1. Declare an exception in the Declare section of the code block.

2. Place the exception and associated statements in the Exception section.

3. Call the exception with the RAISE command.

Listing 15.5 illustrates this technique. This procedure is similar to an edit that can be performed in an Oracle form. The SELECT statement retrieves the value of the State column for the CLINTON record. If this value is not equal to *NJ*, the edit fails, and the focus shifts to the error handlers in the exception section of the procedure. The RAISE keyword followed by the exception name INCORRECT_STATE causes the focus to change.

Listing 15.5 *Using the Exception Section for Your Own Custom Processing*

```
SQL> declare
  2    incorrect_state         exception;
  3    new_state               employee.state%type;
  4  begin
  5    select &new_state into new_state from dual;
  6    if new_state not in ('NE', 'IA', 'OH') then
  7      raise incorrect_state;    ◄─────────────    forces the focus
  8    end if;                                        to the exception
  9  exception                                        section
 10    when incorrect_state then
 11      dbms_output.put_line ('You entered the wrong state code');
 12      dbms_output.put_line ('Enter NE, IA, or OH');
 13  end;
 14  /
Enter value for new_state:   'ne'
old   5:    select &new_state into new_state from dual;
new   5:    select    'ne' into new_state from dual;
You entered the wrong state code
Enter NE, IA, or OH

PL/SQL procedure successfully completed.

SQL>
```

End Listing

PL/SQL Records and Arrays

PL/SQL also allows the developer to define and use array-type objects within a code block. An array is a predefined series of value holders, cells, or rows of cells that have the same data type(s). A unique number called an *integer identifier* distinguishes the different rows. In PL/SQL the array-type object is called a PL/SQL table. There are some differences between a typical array and a PL/SQL table record:

- Each table row consists of at least two columns: The integer identifier and the corresponding cell(s). Arrays can consist of only one column.
- You do not specify the maximum number of rows in the PL/SQL table when it is defined. Arrays require the maximum rows to be defined.
- There is no limit to the number of rows that can be added to the table (except by memory). Arrays are limited by the original definition.
- The integer identifier value that distinguishes each table row can be arbitrarily set. It does not have to be sequential.
- The %TYPE and %ROWTYPE definitions can be used to define the table.

PL/SQL tables are defined in the declaration section of the code block. Two steps are required:

1. Define a type. A type can be a PL/SQL record or some other type of variable definition, such as an object.
2. Assign the type to a variable that identifies the PL/SQL table.

A syntax example of these two steps follows:

Type *table_type_name* **is table of** *record_type*
             index by binary_integer;
Pl_sql_table_name   *table_type_name*;

Listing 15.6 illustrates a PL/SQL table that will hold calculated values for employees. The procedure will calculate the total cost of tool purchases for each employee. A PL/SQL table (tool_statistics_table) comprised of records based on the cursor will hold the calculated employee values. A counter variable was created in order to populate the integer identifier for each row of the table. After the table was populated, a series of statements output the PL/SQL table values.

Table 15.2 replicates the contents of the PL/SQL table that is created in Listings 15.6 and 15.7. It will help you determine whether the procedure results are correct.

Table 15.2 *Contents of the PL/SQL Table Created in Listings 15.6 and 15.7*

Integer Identifier	Fk_payroll_number	Cost
1	19	61.95
2	20	88.85
3	21	16.7
4	22	324
5	23	23
6	24	116.95
7	25	35
8	26	24
9	27	20
10	29	375
11	32	18.5
12	33	12
13	35	28.7
14	36	46.2

Listing 15.6 *Example of a PL/SQL Table That Holds the Cost of Tools*

```
SQL> declare
  2     cursor a is select fk_payroll_number,
  3                    sum(tool_cost) cost from emp_tools
  4     group by fk_payroll_number;
  5     type tool_statistics_table is table of a%rowtype index by
  6          binary_integer;
  7     tool_statistics      tool_statistics_table;
```

creates the PL/SQL table

defines the type of record in the table

```
 8     counter        number := 1;
 9   begin
10     open a;
11     fetch a into tool_statistics(counter);
12     counter := counter + 1;
13     while a%found loop
14       fetch a into tool_statistics(counter);
15       counter := counter + 1;
16     end loop;
17     close a;
18     dbms_output.put_line ('Array Variable 1');
19     dbms_output.put_line ('Array Variable 3'
20                    ||tool_statistics(3).cost);
21     dbms_output.put_line ('Array Variable 6'
22                    ||tool_statistics(6).cost);
23   end;
24   /
Array Variable 1 61.95
Array Variable 3 16.7
Array Variable 6 116.95

PL/SQL procedure successfully completed.

SQL>

End Listing
```

populates the
PL/SQL table

PL/SQL Table Attributes

Oracle has provided a number of attributes that can be used with a PL/SQL table. These attributes allow you to identify the integer identifier for the next, previous, or last record in the table. They also allow you to count the number of records in the table or to delete a record. Table 15.3 lists the various attributes.

The integer value that identifies a record in the table does not have to be sequential as it was in Listing 15.6. These variables are very useful in identifying and moving a table that does not have sequential values.

To illustrate their use, Listing 15.7 illustrates each of the attributes. Their values are displayed.

Table 15.3 *PL/SQL Table Attributes*

Attribute Name	Returned Value	Description
COUNT	Number	Returns the number of records in the table
DELETE	Not Applicable	Deletes the indicated rows in the table
EXISTS	Boolean	Returns true if the target value exists in the table
FIRST	Binary Integer	Returns the integer value of the first record in the table
LAST	Binary Integer	Returns the integer value of the last record in the table
NEXT	Binary Integer	Returns the integer value of the next record in the table after the specified row
PRIOR	Binary Integer	Returns the integer value of the previous record in the table before the specified row

Listing 15.7 *Illustrating the Use of the COUNT, EXISTS, FIRST, LAST, NEXT, and PRIOR PL/SQL Attributes*

```
SQL> declare
  2    cursor a is select fk_payroll_number, sum(tool_cost) cost
  3    from emp_tools
  4    group by fk_payroll_number;
  5    type tool_statistics_table is table of a%rowtype index
  6         by binary_integer;
  7    tool_statistics     tool_statistics_table;
  8    counter       number := 1;
  9    i     binary_integer;
 10  begin
 11     open a;
 12     fetch a into tool_statistics(counter);
 13     counter := counter + 1;
 14     while a%found loop
 15       fetch a into tool_statistics(counter);
 16       counter := counter + 1;
 17     end loop;
 18     close a;
 19     dbms_output.put_line ('Array Variable 1'
 20                   ||tool_statistics(1).cost);
 21     dbms_output.put_line ('Array Variable 3'
 22                   ||tool_statistics(3).cost);
```

```
23      dbms_output.put_line ('Array Variable 6'
24                  ||tool_statistics(6).cost);
20  -- The Count attribute outputs the
21  -- number of rows in the table
22      dbms_output.put_line ('Total Record Count'
23                  ||tool_statistics.count);          COUNT attribute
23  -- The First attribute outputs the
24  -- integer value of the first record
25      i := tool_statistics.first;               FIRST attribute
26      dbms_output.put_line ('First Employee'
27              ||tool_statistics(i).fk_payroll_number);
28  -- The Last attribute outputs the
29  -- integer value of the last record
30      i := tool_statistics.last;                LAST attribute
31      dbms_output.put_line ('Last Employee'
32              ||tool_statistics(i).fk_payroll_number);
33  -- The Next attribute determines the integer value
34  -- of the record following record 2
35      i := tool_statistics.next(2);             NEXT attribute
36      dbms_output.put_line ('Following Employee 2'
37              ||tool_statistics(i).fk_payroll_number);
38  -- The Prior attribute determine the integer value
39  -- of the record preceding record 2
40      i := tool_statistics.prior(2);            PRIOR attribute
41      dbms_output.put_line ('Preceding Employee 2 '
42              ||tool_statistics(i).fk_payroll_number);
43  -- The Exist attribute determines whether the
44  -- integer identifier exists in the table
45      if tool_statistics.exists(35) then        EXISTS attribute
46          dbms_output.put_line ('Record 35 exists');
47      else
48          dbms_output.put_line ('Record 35 does not exist');
49      end if;
50  end;
51  /
Array Variable 1 61.95
Array Variable 3 16.7
Array Variable 6 116.95
Total Record Count 14
First Employee 19
Last Employee 36
Following Employee 2 21
Preceding Employee 2 19
Record 35 does not exist
```

```
PL/SQL procedure successfully completed.

SQL>

End listing
```

Deleting PL/SQL Table Records

Oracle also allows you to delete the records in the PL/SQL table. You are given three options: You can delete all of the records at one time, a range of records, or one record at a time. The following are syntax templates for each of the options:

- All records   *pl_sql_table.*delete;
- One record   *pl_sql_table.*delete*(i)*;
- Range of records   *pl_sql_table.*delete*(l, u)*;

When deleting a range of values, you must enter two values: the upper- and lower-range values. Listing 15.8 illustrates the use of each of these options. The first option used in the illustration deletes record 7. The second option deletes records 2 through 4. The final option deletes all of the records in the table. Following each deletion, the EXISTS attribute is used to confirm that the record was actually deleted.

Listing 15.8 *Using the Various Delete-Record Options*

```
SQL> declare
  2    cursor a is select fk_payroll_number,
  3                    sum(tool_cost) cost from emp_tools
  4            group by fk_payroll_number;
  5    type tool_statistics_table is
  6      table of a%rowtype index by binary_integer;
  7    tool_statistics      tool_statistics_table;
  8    counter       number := 1;
  9    i    binary_integer;
 10  begin
 11    open a;
 12    fetch a into tool_statistics(counter);
 13    counter := counter + 1;
 14    while a%found loop
```

```
15        fetch a into tool_statistics(counter);
16        counter := counter + 1;
17     end loop;
18     close a;
19     tool_statistics.delete(7);  ◄────  [deletes record 7]
20  -- Checks to see if record 7 is deleted
21     if tool_statistics.exists(7) then
22        dbms_output.put_line ('Record 7 exists');
23     else
24        dbms_output.put_line ('Record 7 does not exist');
25     end if;
26     tool_statistics.delete(2,4);  ◄────  [deletes records 2–4]
27  -- Checks to see if record 3 is deleted
28     if tool_statistics.exists(3) then
29        dbms_output.put_line ('Record 3 exists');
30     else
31        dbms_output.put_line ('Record 3 does not exist');
32     end if;
33     tool_statistics.delete;  ◄────  [deletes all the records]
34  -- Checks to see if record 1 is deleted
35     if tool_statistics.exists(1) then
36        dbms_output.put_line ('Record 1 exists');
37     else
38        dbms_output.put_line ('Record 1 does not exist');
39     end if;
40  end;
41  /
Record 7 does not exist
Record 3 does not exist
Record 1 does not exist

PL/SQL procedure successfully completed.

SQL>

End listing
```

Named Procedures

The code blocks that have been illustrated thus far have been anonymous procedures that may be executed from only an external file. This requires Oracle to search the hard drive for the file, load it into memory, compile the statements, and execute the procedure. Code blocks may also be defined as database objects, meaning that the code block resides within the database in a compiled form; therefore, performance will be greater using these types of procedures.

There are two types of database code blocks: named procedures and functions. The difference between the two is that the named procedure can be executed as a statement of its own, and a function is always used as an argument within a statement. Another difference is that the function always returns a value; the procedure does not have to return a value. This section will discuss the creation and execution of named procedures.

Named procedures and functions are important tools used to create modular code. These objects often contain code and calculations that can be used in many other code blocks, thereby allowing the developer to create and debug code once instead of repeatedly.

Creating or Changing, Executing, and Deleting a Named Procedure

Before another procedure can call a named procedure, the named procedure must be created in the database. In Oracle9i, all database objects are created by using the CREATE keyword, which is placed as the first word in the procedure. After the procedure is stored within the database, the procedure can be called by simply using the procedure name as a statement.

To modify an existing procedure, place the keywords OR REPLACE after the CREATE keyword. These keywords will cause any previous version of the procedure to be erased and replaced by the new version. If you do not use this option and a named procedure with the same name exists in the database, the CREATE statement will terminate without replacing the original procedure.

To execute the procedure from the SQL prompt, the procedure name is preceded by the keyword EXECUTE (or EXEC). This command will launch the procedure. If the procedure is called from another procedure, the EXECUTE keyword is not needed. The procedure name can be used as a statement.

The DROP command is used to erase the named procedure from the database. Listing 15.9 illustrates the creation, execution, and deletion of a named procedure. The procedure contains one statement (named *goodday*) that outputs the words *Good day to you*. The CREATE or REPLACE option is used to create the procedure, which is then executed from the SQL prompt in SQL*Plus. Finally, the procedure is deleted with the DROP PROCEDURE command.

Listing 15.9 *Creating, Executing, and Dropping a Named Procedure*

```
SQL> create or replace procedure goodday is
  2      begin
  3          dbms_output.put_line ('Good Day to You');
  4      end;
  5  /

Procedure created.

SQL> execute goodday;
Good Day to You

PL/SQL procedure successfully completed.

SQL> drop procedure goodday;

Procedure dropped.

SQL>

End listing
```

The Header Section

Named procedures need to have a header section, which is the first section of the code block and contains important information. The procedure illustrated in Listing 15.10 has a simple header. The header can contain other information:

- The type of PL/SQL object (i.e., function or procedure)
- The name of the object
- Parameters (optional for procedures)
- The keyword IS

The following is a syntax template of a header section:

Procedure_function objectname (parameter1, parameter2) is

The following are examples of procedure header sections:

Procedure example1 is
Procedure example2 (lname in employee.last_name) is

Header Parameters

The header section can optionally contain parameters, which are used to input values into the procedure and to obtain values from the procedure. Parameter declarations follow the PL/SQL object name and are enclosed by parentheses. The declaration consists of the formal parameter name, the mode, and the parameter data type. As many parameters as necessary can be included in the declaration. Each declaration must be separated from other declarations by a comma. The following is a syntax template:

(parameter_name1 mode datatype, parameter_name2 mode datatype)

The formal parameter name is the name that is placed in the parameter list during the declaration. These are the names that the procedure will use. The actual parameter names are the names of variables that will supply values to the declared parameters from the calling procedure.

The mode represents the manner in which the procedure will use the parameter. The modes are listed in Table 15.4.

Table 15.4 *Parameter Modes*

Mode	Description
IN	This parameter may be populated only by an external source. The value is a constant in the called procedure and can be used or assigned to only another variable.
OUT	This parameter cannot receive a value from an external source. It may receive or be assigned a value only within the procedure.
In out	This parameter can receive a value from an external source. The procedure may modify the parameter value, and the calling procedure may use the modified value.

The IN mode creates a variable that is similar to a constant. The value may not be changed after initialization at execution time. Several IN mode characteristics are as follows:

- When a mode is not defined, the variable will use the IN mode.
- When the procedure is called, an IN parameter value can be a variable or a text literal.
- The literal can be assigned as a permanent default value at the procedure definition time. Place the keyword DEFAULT after the parameter data type, followed by the default value. If you use the default, do not populate the parameter when calling the procedure.

The OUT mode is used to return a value to the calling procedure. A parameter defined with this mode may not be assigned a value by the calling procedure. This means that when the procedure is invoked, an OUT parameter should contain a variable that will be used in the calling procedure. This variable will be assigned a value. The following are rules concerning OUT parameters:

- The value cannot be assigned to another variable.
- A default value cannot be assigned to the parameter. The value must be assigned within the procedure.
- When the procedure is called, OUT parameters must be a variable. They cannot be a text literal because they will receive a value.

IN OUT parameters can be assigned a value from the calling procedure. The procedure may modify the value, and the parameter value can be passed to the calling procedure. The only restriction concerning IN OUT parameters is this:

- When the procedure is called, the parameter must be a variable.

The data type parameter definition describes the type of variable. Rules concerning the parameter data are as follows:

- The parameter data type can be any of the normal data types, such as VARCHAR2, CHAR, NUMBER, or BOOLEAN.

- The data type definition must be unconstrained, which means that a precision cannot be defined.
- %TYPE and %ROWTYPE can be used in the declaration even if they reference constrained columns.

Inputting Values by Using the IN Parameter Mode

The previous section discussed parameters. The parameter section of the procedure header is used to bring values into and out of the procedure. Listing 15.10 illustrates this technique. The procedure lists the employees of a specific department.

When the procedure is defined, the formal parameter name DEPARTMENT is placed within the parameter section. The parameter mode is set to IN. This declaration tells Oracle that the procedure needs a value from an external source. This parameter or variable is used in the WHERE clause to retrieve the proper records from the database.

When the procedure is executed, a parameter section follows the name of the procedure. The text literal WEL is placed in the parameter and will be assigned to the variable DEPARTMENT, which is used to identify the proper employees. If a value is not placed in the procedure parameter, the default value of POL will be used.

Listing 15.10 *Using an IN Mode Parameter*

formal parameter name with an unconstrained data type

parameter used in the WHERE clause

```
SQL> --This section creates the procedure
SQL> create or replace
  2  procedure list_dept_employees (department in varchar2
  3                                    default 'POL') is
  4  begin
  5  for a in (select * from employee
  6              where fk_department = department)
  7      loop
  8        dbms_output.put_line (a.last_name);
  9      end loop;
 10  end;
 11  /

Procedure created.
```

```
SQL> --This section executes the procedure
SQL> exec list_dept_employees('WEL');          ◄───────     actual parameter
REAGAN                                                            value
CARTER
HOOVER
TAFT
ANTHONY
ROOSEVELT

PL/SQL procedure successfully completed.

SQL> --This section deletes the procedure from the database
SQL> drop procedure list_dept_employees;

Procedure dropped.

SQL>

End Listing
```

Calling a Procedure from a Procedure and Outputting Values by Using the OUT Parameter Mode

The name of a procedure can be used as a calling statement in another procedure. The called procedure can also supply a value to the calling procedure by using the OUT parameter mode.

Listing 15.11 illustrates this concept. The first section of the listing displays the script to create a named procedure to determine the oldest employee in a department. The DEPARTMENT parameter is used to tell the procedure what department to use in determining the oldest employee. The employee first and last name are returned to the calling procedure. The FNAME and LNAME parameters that are defined by using the OUT parameter mode are used to perform this function. These parameters are declared by using the %TYPE attribute.

The second part of the listing illustrates an anonymous procedure that retrieves each of the records in the Employee table. This procedure calls the named procedure and assigns the current value of the department to the DEPARTMENT parameter. The returned values are then used in an output statement in the calling procedure.

The final part of the listing illustrates the results of the procedures. Notice that two of the departments did not have employees. The named procedure did not return values for these departments.

Listing 15.11 *Using an OUT Mode Parameter and a Called Procedure*

```
SQL> -- This is the named procedure that determines the oldest employee
SQL> -- in a department
SQL> create or replace
  2  procedure find_oldest_employee
  3    (department in varchar2,
  4     fname out employee.first_name%type,
  5     lname out employee.last_name%type) is
  6     cursor b is select first_name, last_name from employee
  7                 where birth_date = (select max(birth_date)
  8                                     from employee
  9                                     where fk_department =
                                        department);
 10  begin
 11    open b; fetch b into fname, lname; close b;
 12  end find_oldest_employee;
 13  /

Procedure created.

SQL> -- This is the anonymous procedure that calls the named procedure
SQL> declare
  2     cursor a is select * from department;
  3     a_var          a%rowtype;
  4     last_name      employee.last_name%type;
  5     first_name     employee.first_name%type;
  6  begin
  7    open a;
  8    fetch a into a_var;
  9    while a%found loop
 10      find_oldest_employee (a_var.department, first_name,
 11                            last_name);
 12      dbms_output.put_line (a_var.department||' '||first_name||
 13                            ' '||last_name);
 14      fetch a into a_var;
 15    end loop;
 16    close a;
```

```
17   end;
18   /
POL WILLIAM CLINTON
INT GERALD FORD
WEL RONALD REAGAN
TRF
CEN
PL/SQL procedure successfully completed.

SQL> -- This section deletes the procedure from the database
SQL> drop procedure find_oldest_employee;

Procedure dropped.

SQL>

End listing
```

Defining a Named Procedure within a Procedure

In our previous examples, the named procedures were created as database objects. It is possible to define a named procedure within the declaration section of the code block. When this is done, the procedure acts similarly to a macro. There is one rule that pertains to this technique: The named procedure must be the last object listed in the declaration section.

Listing 15.12 illustrates this technique. This example modifies Listing 15.11. The named procedure FIND_OLDEST_EMPLOYEE is defined within the declaration section. The results of operating the anonymous procedure are exactly the same as the results for Listing 15.11.

Listing 15.12 *Defining a Procedure*

```
SQL> declare
  2    cursor a is select * from department;
  3    a_var        a%rowtype;
  4    last_name    employee.last_name%type;
  5    first_name   employee.first_name%type;
  6    procedure find_oldest_employee
  7      (department in varchar2,
  8       fname out employee.first_name%type,
  9       lname out employee.last_name%type) is
```

```
10        cursor b is select first_name, last_name from employee
11              where birth_date = (select max(birth_date)
12              from employee
13                      where fk_department = department);
14      begin
15        open b; fetch b into fname, lname; close b;
16      end find_oldest_employee;
17   begin
18     open a;
19     fetch a into a_var;
20     while a%found loop
21       find_oldest_employee (a_var.department, first_name,
22                             last_name);
23       dbms_output.put_line (a_var.department||' '||first_name||
24                             ' '||last_name);
25       fetch a into a_var;
26     end loop;
27     close a;
28   end;
29   /
POL WILLIAM CLINTON
INT GERALD FORD
WEL RONALD REAGAN
TRF
CEN

PL/SQL procedure successfully completed.

SQL>

End listing
```

Overloading

Overloading is a technique that allows the developer to have objects with the same name that have different behaviors. PL/SQL allows the developer to define two or more PL/SQL objects (e.g., procedures, functions) with the same name within a procedure. Developers can create another object with the same name by simply changing a parameter definition. The combination of procedure name and parameters determines uniqueness. When Oracle encounters the name of a PL/SQL object, it evaluates the parameters for all objects with the same name. The PL/SQL object with the same defined parameters as the calling statement will be used.

To illustrate overloading, Listing 15.13 contains two procedures with the same name (LIST_EMPLOYEES). The first procedure lists the employees for a given department. The value for the department is input through the parameter section. The second procedure lists the employees in a given department who were hired after a specific date. This is the overloaded procedure. It differs from the original procedure in that it requires two parameters to be input.

Listing 15.13 *An Anonymous Procedure Using an Overloaded Procedure Name*

```
SQL> --This is an anonymous procedure that contains two
SQL> --procedures. Both procedures use the same name.
SQL> --The procedure uses the overloading function.
SQL> declare
  2  -- The first procedure that lists the employees in the
  3  -- specified department
  4    procedure list_employees (department in varchar2)
  5    is
  6    begin
  7      for a in (select last_name, employment_date from employee
  8               where fk_department = department)
  9    loop
 10      dbms_output.put_line (a.last_name||
 11                            ' '||to_char(a.employment_date));
 12    end loop;
 13    end;
 14  -- The overloaded procedure that lists the employees in the
 15  -- specified department hired after a specific date
 16    procedure list_employees
 17    (department in varchar2, hired in date)
 18    is
 19    begin
 20      for a in (select last_name, employment_date from employee
 21               where fk_department = department
 22                 and employment_date > hired)
 23    loop
 25      dbms_output.put_line (a.last_name||
 26                            ' '||to_char(a.employment_date));
 27    end loop;
 28    end;
```

```
29  begin
30    dbms_output.put_line ('Results of the first procedure');
31    list_employees('WEL');
32    dbms_output.put_line ('----');
33    dbms_output.put_line ('Results of the second procedure');
34    list_employees('WEL', '01-JAN-60');
35  end;
36  /
Results of the first procedure
REAGAN 03-MAR-80
CARTER 10-JUL-76
HOOVER 06-APR-28
TAFT 01-JUN-08
ANTHONY 30-MAR-40
ROOSEVELT 20-MAR-32
----
Results of the second procedure
REAGAN 03-MAR-80
CARTER 10-JUL-76

PL/SQL procedure successfully completed.

SQL>

End listing
```

Functions

Functions are another important PL/SQL object. They are similar to procedures except that functions cannot be a statement. They must be the argument on the right side of an assignment or evaluation. In addition, a function must *always* return a value to a calling statement. This section will cover these valuable objects.

As a business analyst, functions can make your life easier by eliminating repeated calculations and formatting. For example, it is common to format multiple name values into one expression, such as *Dworczak, Alice*. It is much easier to create and use a function that performs the formatting, rather than continually having to format the data. Calculations are an even better use of a function. It is somewhat common for different business analysts to code and perform a calculation but get different results. Differences in the calculations (and mistakes) are the causes. Placing the calculation in a function will allow you to test once and to compute the same value every time. When the calculation is sophisticated, placing the calculation into a function will save you a great deal of time because you do not have to recode the calculation continually. Adding functions to your database will also increase the amount of information that is available to your end users. This section will discuss how to create and use functions in your SQL.

Function Structure

The structure of a function is similar to that of a procedure. Functions must have a header. The header begins with the keyword FUNCTION, followed by an optional parameter section. The mandatory keyword RETURN and the return data type follow the parameter section. The return data type describes the type of value that the function will return to the calling statement. The keyword IS terminates the header.

The remainder of the function structure is similar to a standard code block. Declarations are placed after the IS keyword and before the executable section, which starts with the keyword BEGIN. The executable section *must have* a RETURN *variable* statement, which returns the value to the calling assignment statement. The function code block can also contain an exception section.

The following is a template structure of a function:

```
Function function_name
(parameter_name mode data_type, parameter_name mode
      data_type)
return return data_type is
begin
      statements;
      return variable;
exception
      statements;
end;
```

Creating and Using a Function

Listing 15.14 illustrates the creation and use of a simple function. The function is created by using the CREATE command. The OR REPLACE option discussed earlier can also be used. The return data type is VARCHAR2. It must be unconstrained (i.e., does not have a precision).

The function contained in the listing returns the text literal *Have a Good Day* to the calling statement. This listing also contains an anonymous procedure that uses the function to assign the value to a variable. The function is deleted from the database by using the DROP command.

Listing 15.14 *Creating, Using, and Dropping a Function*

```
SQL> -- This script creates the function goodday
SQL> create or replace function goodday
  2     return varchar2
  3  is
  4  begin
  5     return 'Have a Good Day';
  6  end;
  7  /

Function created.

SQL> -- This procedure uses the function goodday
SQL> declare
  2    a        varchar2(30);
  3  begin
  4    a := goodday;
  5    dbms_output.put_line (a);
  6  end;
  7  /
Have a Good Day

PL/SQL procedure successfully completed.

SQL> -- The following command deletes the function from the database
SQL> drop function goodday;

Function dropped.

SQL>

End listing
```

Creating and Using a Function in a SELECT Clause

User-defined functions can also be included in the SELECT clause of a SELECT statement. When the function is stored within the database, it can be used in the same manner as other functions such as SUBSTR or UPPER.

Listing 15.15 illustrates this concept. Employee age is a constantly changing value. A function called AGE is created in Listing 15.15 to compute the employees' current ages. The function requires the calling program or SQL statement to supply the employees' birth date values. The function then determines the employees' ages. The function also uses the TRUNC built-in function to create a formatted age. By creating this function, the developer does not have to keep coding the more complex age calculation.

Following this function, the listing illustrates a SELECT statement that uses the function in an expression. The parameter value of this function is the employee's birth date. The SELECT statement feeds this value to the function for each row that the query retrieves.

Listing 15.15 *Creating and Using a Function in a SELECT Statement*

```
SQL> create or replace function age (birth_date in date)
  2  return number is
  3    age    number;
  4  begin
  5    age := trunc(months_between(sysdate, birth_date)/12, 0);
  6    return age;
  7  end;
  8  /

Function created.

SQL> select last_name, age(birth_date)
  2  from employee
  3  where fk_department = 'WEL';

LAST_NAME        AGE(BIRTH_DATE)
---------------  ---------------
REAGAN                        73
CARTER                        84
HOOVER                       123
TAFT                         140
```

```
ANTHONY                        178
ROOSEVELT                      113

6 rows selected.
SQL>

End Listing
```

Using a Function in an Assignment Statement within a Procedure

Functions are often the right-side argument in an assignment because the purpose of a function is to return a value. Listing 15.16 illustrates a function that is used in an anonymous procedure. The procedure lists the employee in each department who has the greatest seniority. It also contains a cursor that retrieves each of the records from the Department table. For each record retrieved, the function that identifies the employee with the most seniority is called. The function returns the first and last names of the employee. The function also contains an IF-THEN-ELSE structure. If the department does not contain any employees, the function will return a text string rather than an employee name.

Listing 15.16 *A Function Used to Assign a Value to a Variable in an Anonymous Procedure*

```
SQL> -- This script creates the function that determines the employee
SQL> -- with the greatest seniority
SQL> create or replace function highest_seniority
  2    (department in varchar2)
  3    return varchar2
  4  is
  5  cursor a is select * from employee
  6              where employment_date =
  7                    (select min(employment_date)
  8                      from employee
  9                      where fk_department = department);
 10  a_var         a%rowtype;
 11  begin
 12    open a;
 13    fetch a into a_var;
 14    if a%notfound then
```

```
15        return 'No Employees in the Department';
16   else
17        return a_var.last_name||', '||a_var.first_name;
18   end if;
19 end;
20 /

Function created.

SQL> -- This procedure retrieves the various departments and calls
SQL> -- the highest_seniority function
SQL> declare
  2    name      varchar2(50);
  3  begin
  4    for a in (select department from department)
  5    loop
  6      name := highest_seniority(a.department);
  7      dbms_output.put_line (a.department||' '||name);
  8    end loop;
  9  end;
 10  /
POL JOHNSON, ANDREW
INT ROOSEVELT, THEODORE
WEL ANTHONY, SUSANNE
TRF No Employees in the Department
CEN No Employees in the Department

PL/SQL procedure successfully completed.

SQL> -- The following command deletes the function from the database
SQL> drop function highest_seniority;

Function dropped.

SQL>
End listing
```

Packages

Encapsulation is the principle whereby the functions, calculations, extraction routines, and programs are linked with the data. To illustrate, an employee is an entity. Encapsulation would consist of the employee attributes (e.g., name, age, weight, address) and programs or methods (e.g., age calculation, wage calculations, retirement calculation) to be in one class. Oracle9i allows the developer to link these functions, calculations, extraction routines, and programs into a grouping called a package.

Packages offer the developer several important benefits:

- Object-oriented capabilities. The developer can group all PL/SQL components into a logical group. The developer can maintain better control of objects by using these groupings.
- Performance. When an object is called from a package, all of the other objects in the package are also placed in memory. The objects remain in memory throughout the session. Performance is increased because Oracle does not have to locate and load these objects.
- Global data. Objects declared in a package act as global data for other applications that have the privilege to execute the package. You may access the package with one application, modify data within the package, and access the modified data with another application. If an application opens a cursor in a package, it remains open for another application.
- Top-down design. When creating packages, the high-level specifications are prepared first. You can develop the detailed lower-level objects at a later date.

Package Components

Packages can contain cursors, variables, constants, exception names, procedures, and functions. A package consists of two parts: the package specification and the package body.

The package specification is the first part of the package that is created. It has the following features:

- It contains the name of the package objects that other applications can reference. These are called public objects because the objects are not hidden.
- It does not contain the detailed statements for any of the objects.

The package body is created after the package specification. It has the following features:

- It contains the detailed specifications for all defined package objects.
- It contains objects that are not defined in the package specification. These objects are called private objects and can be referenced only by an object within the package.
- The package body does not have to be created. Statements will be executed if the object in the package specification does not find a corresponding object in the package body.

Package Specification Template

The package specification begins with the keyword PACKAGE, followed by the package name. The keyword IS completes the header. The object declarations follow and consist of the following:

- Type of object (e.g., procedure, function, cursor)
- Name of the object
- Parameters (where applicable)
- The keyword RETURN and the return data type (cursors and functions only)
- To complete the specification, use the keyword END followed by the optional name of the package

The following is a template:

Package package_name is
  Object type object_name (parameters) return datatype;
  Object type object_name (parameters) return datatype;
End package_name;

Package Body Specification

The package body header begins with the keywords PACKAGE BODY followed by the package name. The keyword IS terminates the header. The various object definitions follow. The definitions contain the exact same components as the object would if it were defined outside of the package body. The keyword END, followed by the optional package name, terminates the package body. The package body may also contain its own executable section, which is used to initialize variables or to execute statements before the package is initiated.

The following is a template:

```
Package body package_name is
  PL/SQL object definition;
  PL/SQL object definition;
Begin
  Executable statements;
Exception
  Exception handlers;
End;
```

Employee Package Example

The following example illustrates the statements needed to create and use a package of PL/SQL objects that pertain to the employee entity. These objects will consist of the following:

- A cursor that retrieves each of the employees and their attributes from the Employee table
- A function that computes the employees' current ages
- A procedure that lists the number of tool and eyeglasses purchases per employee

The first step is to create the package specification for the employee objects. Listing 15.17 illustrates the CREATE statement that creates the package specification. Like all other objects, the CREATE command is used to place the object into the database. (DROP is used to delete the object.) The specification contains headers for a cursor called LIST_EMPLOYEES, a function called AGE, and a procedure called TOTAL_EMPLOYEE_PURCHASES. Notice that each of the headers contains the required components listed in the previous section.

Listing 15.17 *The Package Specification for the Employee Objects*

```
SQL> create or replace package employee_objects is
  2    cursor list_employees  return employee%rowtype;
  3    function age (birth_date in date) return number;
  4    procedure total_employee_purchase
  5      (payroll_number in number, total_tools out number,
  6        total_glasses out number);
  7  end;
  8  /

Package created.

SQL>

End listing
```

The second step is to create the package body for the employee objects. The package body must have the same name as the package specification. The detailed specifications for the objects are placed in the package body. Listing 15.18 illustrates the package body for the employee objects.

Listing 15.18 *The Package Body for the Employee Objects*

```
SQL> create or replace package body employee_objects is
  2    cursor list_employees  return employee%rowtype
  3    is select * from employee
  4        order by fk_department, last_name;
  5    function age (birth_date in date) return number is
  6      age number;
  7      begin
  8        age := trunc(months_between(sysdate, birth_date)/12, 0);
  9        return age;
 10      end;
 11    procedure total_employee_purchase
 12      (payroll_number in number, total_tools out number,
 13        total_glasses out number) is
 14      begin
 15        select count(tool_name) into total_tools
 16          from emp_tools
```

```
17          where fk_payroll_number = payroll_number;
18          select count(purchase_date) into total_glasses
19          from glasses
20          where fk_payroll_number = payroll_number;
21      end;
22  end employee_objects;
23  /

Package body created.
SQL>
```

End listing

At this point, other program units can use the package objects. The objects are called in the same manner as any other object of the same type, except that the name of the package qualifies the object name. The following is the statement used to call the procedure TOTAL_EMPLOYEE_PURCHASE:

Employee_objects.total_employee_purchase(100, glasses, emp_tools);

Listing 15.19 illustrates an anonymous procedure that uses the package objects. The procedure uses the cursor LIST_EMPLOYEES to list the employees. Each time an employee is fetched from the cursor, the function AGE and the procedure TOTAL_TOOL_PURCHASE are executed. A record is then output, listing the employee's name, age, and number of tool purchases. Notice the simplicity of the procedure.

Listing 15.19 *An Anonymous Procedure Using the Package Objects*

```
SQL> declare
  2     tools      number;
  3     glasses    number;
  4  begin
  5     for a in employee_objects.list_employees
  6     loop
  7  employee_objects.total_employee_purchase(a.payroll_number,
  8                                    tools, glasses);
```

```
 9
10 dbms_output.put_line (a.last_name||
11 ' '||to_char(employee_objects.age(a.birth_date))||
12       ' '||to_char(tools)||' '||to_char(glasses));
13 end loop;
14 end;
15 /
BUSH 87 3 0
COOLIDGE 126 2 1
EISENHOWER 107 3 1
FORD 85 3 1
ROOSEVELT 139 2 2
TRUMAN 114 0 1
CLINTON 58 0 0
JOHNSON 89 0 1
JOHNSON 189 2 1
KENNEDY 81 0 0
NIXON 89 2 1
ROOSEVELT 116 2 1
WILSON 141 3 1
ANTHONY 178 3 1
CARTER 84 0 2
HOOVER 123 2 0
REAGAN 73 3 1
ROOSEVELT 113 3 2
TAFT 140 1 1

PL/SQL procedure successfully completed.

SQL>

End listing
```

What's Next?

The next chapter concludes the PL/SQL coverage and is devoted to advanced developer topics, which include cursor variables, the processing of objects, and using Java classes.

▪ **PRACTICE**

1. Create a "division by zero" error. Trap the error, and display the appropriate message for the user.

2. Create a program that inserts a record into the Emp_tools table. The record should contain an employee ID that does not exist in the Employee table. Trap and handle this error.

3. Change the error handler in Question 2 to the OTHERS handler.

4. Use the OTHERS, SQLCODE, and SQLERRM methods to trap and display information about a "no data found" error.

5. Create a procedure that retrieves the State value for Clinton. If the value is not equal to *NJ*, use the exception section to display a message.

6. You need to create a listing that retrieves values from two tables. One of the tables has only a small number of values. Rather than joining the two tables, you have decided to put all of the records from the small table into a PL/SQL table. The integer identifier will be the ASCII value of the primary-key value. When you list the records from the larger table, you will identify the proper record from the PL/SQL record by determining the ASCII value of the table's foreign-key value and selecting the record from the PL/SQL table with the matching value.

For this exercise, perform the following:

a) Use the Department table as the small table. The ASCII value of the Department column values will be the integer identifier. The Department Name column values will be placed into the PL/SQL table.

b) Use the Employee table as the large table. Display the last names of each employee, along with his or her full department name from the PL/SQL table.

7. Create and save to the database a named procedure that outputs the words *I am soon to be a procedure-building guru*.

8. Create and save to the database a named procedure that displays the employees who were employed between two inputted dates.

9. Create and save to the database a named procedure that outputs the oldest employee for each department who was employed between two inputted dates. This procedure should use another stored procedure that determines the employee.

10. Modify the procedure in Question 9. The called procedure should be defined within the calling procedure.

11. Create a named procedure that is used to update the wages for the employees in a given department. The main procedure should retrieve the records for a given department and should contain the UPDATE statement. This procedure should call a second procedure that contains the wage-update rates (WEL: .07; INT: .06; POL: .15; OTHERS: .05).

12. Create a function that assigns the text string value *I am soon to be a PL/SQL function guru* to a calling application.

13. Create a function that determines the seniority based on the employment date. Use this function in a SELECT statement to determine each employee's years of seniority.

14. Create an anonymous procedure that lists the employees in the Employee table. The procedure should have two functions within it. The first function should determine the number of tool purchases for the employee, and the second function should determine the number of eyeglasses purchases for the employee. Display the number of tool and eyeglasses purchases for each employee.

15. Create a package of employee objects. The package should contain the following:

   - A cursor that retrieves the employee records
   - A function that computes an employee's years of seniority
   - A procedure that evaluates an employee's seniority and updates the Absences column in the Employee table by using the following algorithm:

Seniority years	Absences
+ 50	10
40–50	9
30–40	8
20–30	7
10–20	6
0–10	5

16. Create an anonymous procedure that uses the package objects created in Question 15 to update the Allowable Absences column in the employee table. The procedure should perform the following:

   - Retrieve each of the records from the Employee table
   - Compute the seniority of each employee
   - Update the Absences column in the Employee table based on the procedure created in Question 1

16

Advanced PL/SQL Topics

This chapter covers some advanced PL/SQL topics that are particularly of interest to the developer. I include coverage of these topics primarily to have more extensive coverage of PL/SQL. Power users sometimes request or attempt this functionality. When they have trouble, they will contact their first line of support: the data administrator or IT developer.

The first topic is cursor variables, which allow a procedure to pass a result set to a calling object. I have occasionally used cursor variables in an Oracle form and report. The second topic completes the coverage of objects first discussed in Chapter 3. This section discusses how to use PL/SQL to extract object attributes from the database. The final topic covers PL/SQL and Java. Oracle is moving toward the increased use of Java in its products.

Cursor Variables

Cursor variables are a special PL/SQL type that allows a procedure to return the rows from a cursor to a calling application. This can be useful when you want to switch cursors dynamically, as you will see in Listing 16.1, or to return multiple rows from a procedure. The cursor variable designates an area of memory that stores the returned rows from the procedure.

Two steps are needed to create a cursor variable:

- Declare the cursor as a REF CURSOR type.
- Define a cursor variable using the type.

Here is a syntax example of the declaration:

Type *type_name* is ref cursor return *return_type*;
Cursor_variable_name   *type_name*;

The return type can be a data type or a PL/SQL record. When the return data type is included, the cursor variable is constrained. When the return data type is omitted, the cursor variable is unconstrained and can therefore be used for any type of query.

A special command is used to launch the SELECT statement that populates the cursor variable. A syntax template of this command follows:

Open *cursor_variable_name* for *select_statement*;

To illustrate the use of a cursor variable, assume that your boss would like you to run a procedure twice a month. Your boss personally likes to congratulate the employees on their birthday. You are to develop a procedure that will identify the employee for your boss. You want the procedure to display employees who were born during the end of the current month, when the procedure is executed at the beginning of the month. You also want to display the employees who were born during the beginning of the next month, when the procedure is executed at the end of the current month.

This procedure requires two different queries: one that returns the former list of employees and the other the latter. Your boss wants only one procedure or report. This means that the procedure will need an OUT mode parameter that can handle the output of two different cursors. Cursor variables are perfect for this because they are used to designate an area of memory and do not have to be constrained (i.e., have the variables defined). Listing 16.1 illustrates a procedure that complies with your boss's needs.

Listing 16.1 *Listing Using a Cursor Variable to Display Employees with Birthdays*

```
SQL> create or replace procedure
  2  employee_birthday_list as
  3  -- This procedure will display a
  4  -- list of employees
  5  -- whose birthdays fall in the
```

```
 6   -- first or last part of
 7   -- the current month
 8   type names_ref is ref cursor;
 9   names      names_ref;
10   celebraters    employee%rowtype;
11   procedure find_names (employees out names_ref) as
12   begin
13     if to_number(substr(sysdate,1,2)) < 16 then
14        open employees for select * from employee
15          where to_number(substr(birth_date, 1, 2)) >= 16
16            and substr(birth_date, 4, 3) = substr(sysdate, 4, 3);
17     else
18        open employees for select * from employee
19          where to_number(substr(birth_date, 1, 2)) < 16
20            and substr(add_months(sysdate,1), 4, 3) =
21                substr(birth_date, 4, 3);
22     end if;
23     end;
24   begin
25     find_names(names);
26     fetch names into celebraters;
27     while names%found loop
28        dbms_output.put_line (celebraters.last_name);
29        fetch names into celebraters;
30     end loop;
31   end;
32   /
```

defines the type of cursor variable (It is unconstrained because it does not contain a return data type.)

defines the instances of the cursor variable

defines the OUT parameter as a cursor variable

uses the cursor variable to place the results of the procedure into memory

brings the records into the procedure

```
Procedure created.

SQL> exec employee_birthday_list;
TRUMAN

PL/SQL procedure successfully completed.

SQL>

End listing
```

Processing Objects

In Chapter 2, you saw that the Oracle9i database was able to contain objects. You can create an object type and use this same object type in many different tables. You can also create varrays, nested tables, and object tables. PL/SQL is normally used to process these database objects because a code block has the ability to employ types that are identical to the object types used in the various Oracle9i objects. These types can be used to accept the database object types and to process the individual components.

If you remember, objects are actually one record. The record does not contain columns as in a table. It actually consists of a set of segments that are known only when the object is processed using the object-type template.

Listing 16.2 illustrates the object-type template. The first DDL statement creates an object type that consists of a series of named segments. The object type is then used as the data type for one of the columns in the Student table. If you should want to select the various City values from the table, you cannot reference the City field in the SELECT statement. You may reference only the Addressing column, as shown in the final SELECT statement in the listing. As you can see, the segment values are returned as one overall value. In order to process the individual object-type segments, you must impress them into an object-type template.

Listing 16.2 *Object-Type Template*

```
create or replace type address_attr as object
(address          varchar2(20),
 city             varchar2(20),
 state            varchar2(2),
 zip              char(5),
 phone            char(12));

create table student
(ssn              number(9),
 first_name       varchar2(15),
 last_name        varchar2(15),
 addressing       address_attr);

SQL> select addressing from student;
```

```
ADDRESSING(ADDRESS, CITY, STATE, ZIP, PHONE)
----------------------------------------------------------------------
----------------------------------
ADDRESS_ATTR('100 RIVER ROAD', 'MT. VERNON', 'VA', '10234', '102-345-
9809')

SQL>

End listing
```

In order to break the Addressing value into multiple components, a function can be used. Listing 16.3 illustrates the function and how it is used. An IN mode parameter using the ADRESS_ATTR object-type template is used to create an object instance that is populated when the function is called. The function then returns the City segment of the object type. The following SELECT statement then uses the CITY function to return the City value.

Listing 16.3 *Using a Function to Return the City Segment of an Object Type*

```
SQL> create or replace function city (in_add in address_attr) return
varchar2 is
  2  begin
  3    return in_add.city;
  4  end;
  5  /

Function created

SQL> column city format a30
SQL> select last_name, city(addressing) city from student;

LAST_NAME       CITY
--------------- ------------------------------
WASHINGTON      MT. VERNON

SQL>

End listing
```

To summarize, segments of an embedded object can be returned by using a PL/SQL object such as a function to impress the value into the instance of the object type. An embedded object was used in the given examples. This same technique can be used with a varray.

Nested Object Tables

A nested object table is an Oracle9i object that is similar to an embedded-object type. It is a column in a table that is based on an object-type template. The difference is that the column can have numerous instances of its object type, thereby allowing the column to contain numerous records.

To select the values in the nested table, you must retrieve the nested object table from the database, place it into a table structure, and extract each of the records. When the nested object table is placed into the table structure, each of the records is referenced with an integer key beginning with a 1. You can then use any of the records based on this key. If you want to know how many records are in the nested table, you can use the PL/SQL table variable COUNT. In fact, you can use any of the PL/SQL table variables because the PL/SQL structure containing the nested object table is essentially a PL/SQL table.

Listing 16.4 illustrates the use of PL/SQL to extract nested object table values. A named procedure called CUSTOMER_READINGS was created. A PL/SQL table was defined by using %TYPE, which references the Customer table's nested object table: Readings. A record was selected, and the Readings values were placed into this PL/SQL table. A numeric FOR loop that used the COUNT variable to determine the high-range value was used to print each of the records from the nested table.

Listing 16.4 *Selecting Values From a Nested Object Table*

```
SQL> create or replace procedure customer_readings
  2                       (acct in number) is
  3     read_table          customer.readings%type;        ┌─ PL/SQL record
  4     cust                customer.acct_num%type;        │   definition
  5     cursor a is select acct_num,
  6              readings from customer                     ┌─ selecting the nested
  7                  where acct_num = acct;                 │   object table
  8   begin
  9     open a; fetch a into cust, read_table;
```

```
10     for cnt_var in 1..read_table.count
11     loop
12       dbms_output.put_line (read_table(cnt_var).reading_date
13       ||' '||read_table(cnt_var).reading);
14     end loop;
15     close a;
16   end;
17   /
```

> determines the number of records in the table

> outputting the record value

```
Procedure created.

SQL> exec customer_readings(1);
01-JAN-00 1000
01-FEB-00 1900
01-MAR-00 2400
01-APR-00 3300
01-MAY-00 3900
01-JUN-00 4900
01-JUL-00 5600
01-AUG-00 6800
01-SEP-00 7500
01-OCT-00 8300
01-NOV-00 8765
01-DEC-00 9500

PL/SQL procedure successfully completed.

SQL>

End listing
```

PL/SQL and Java

Java has been growing in popularity in recent years because of its ability to run on any machine, as well as its openness. The Java philosophy closely matches Oracle's approach of running on all platforms. This makes Java and Oracle a good match. Oracle has embraced Java from the start. It was available in previous versions, but beginning with Oracle8i, Oracle has embedded a Java environment called JServer within the database. This includes Enterprise JavaBeans (EJB) server software, 100-pure JVM, a CORBA 2.0 architecture, and built-in support for Java Database Connectivity (JDBC), SQLJ, and XML. Don't get worried; this means that you can use Java with PL/SQL.

Creating and Using a Java Class within PL/SQL

Java classes can be used within PL/SQL stored procedures. The following are the steps needed to create a Java class and place it into the Oracle database:

1. Create the Java source file external to Oracle.
2. Create a Java class by compiling the source file.
3. Load the Java class into the Oracle9i database.
4. Build a PL/SQL call spec or Wrapper program.

Some of the following steps will require Java Development Kit (JDK) 1.1.5 or later. This product comes with Oracle9i. You may also download it from the Sun Microsystems Java Web site (http://java.sun.com/products/jdk/ 1.2/docs/index.html).

To illustrate, I will describe how to develop a Java class that generates a random number. Listing 16.5 contains a source Java script for the random-number generator. This source code file is compiled with the Java executable JAVAC.

Listing 16.5 *Java Script for a Random-Number Generator*

```java
import java.util.Random;

public class Random_number {

  public Random_number() {
  }

  public static int getRandomInt() {
    Random random = new Random();
    return random.nextInt();
  }

  public static int getStringLength(java.lang.String s) {
    return s.length();
  }
}
end listing
```

To compile the script, execute the following command from the MS-DOS prompt. You may have to enter full file path names on the executable and source files. You may also create and compile the file by using Oracle's JBuilder.

Javac random_number.java

To load the class into the Oracle9i database, execute the following command:

Loadjava –user scott/tiger –oci9 – resolve random_number.class

Executing the statement will cause the Java class to be placed into the database as an object. The User_objects data dictionary view can be used to review whether the object is in the database. Listing 16.6 illustrates a SELECT statement that identifies Java classes within the database. It lists the RANDOM_NUMBER class created using the above statement.

Listing 16.6 *Using the User_object View to Identify Java Objects*

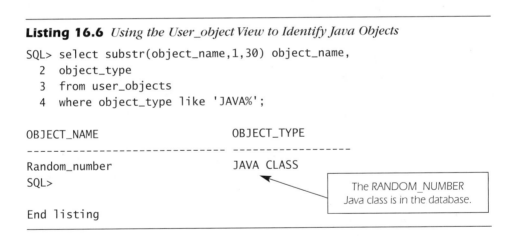

```
SQL> select substr(object_name,1,30) object_name,
  2   object_type
  3   from user_objects
  4   where object_type like 'JAVA%';


OBJECT_NAME                        OBJECT_TYPE
------------------------------     ------------------
Random_number                      JAVA CLASS
SQL>
```

The RANDOM_NUMBER Java class is in the database.

```
End listing
```

The last step in using a Java class is to create a call spec or a PL/SQL Wrapper. This essentially consists of a PL/SQL header for the procedure that launches the Java class. Listing 16.7 illustrates the call spec used to execute the RANDOM_NUMBER Java class. It also shows how to execute the call spec.

Listing 16.7 *Creating and Using a Call Spec*

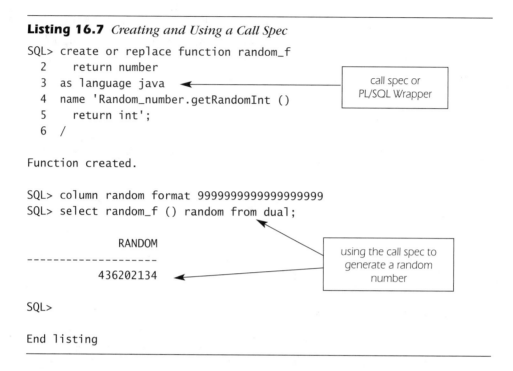

```
SQL> create or replace function random_f
  2     return number
  3  as language java
  4  name 'Random_number.getRandomInt ()
  5     return int';
  6  /

Function created.

SQL> column random format 9999999999999999999
SQL> select random_f () random from dual;

                  RANDOM
--------------------
               436202134

SQL>

End listing
```

Java classes can also be dropped from the database. The following script will delete the RANDOM_NUMBER class from the database:

Dropjava –user scott/tiger random_number;

Loading the Java Source Code into the Database

In the previous section, the Java class was loaded into the Oracle9i database. The class is the compiled version of the Java script. If you wanted to see the source code for the class, you would have to locate the Java file external to the Oracle9i database. Oracle, however, has provided a mechanism to load the Java source code into the database: the CREATE JAVA command, shown in Listing 16.8.

Listing 16.8 *Creating a Java Source Code Object*

```
SQL>create or replace java source named "Random_number"
  2  as
  3  public class Random_number {
```

```
 4     public Random_number() {
 5     }
 6     public static int getRandomInt() {
 7       Random random = new Random();
 8       return random.nextInt();
 9     }
10     public static int getStringLength(java.lang.String s) {
11       return s.length();
12     }
13   };
14   /

Operation 160 succeeded.

SQL>

End listing
```

Semicolons in a script normally tell Oracle to process statement. When loading a Java source file, you do not want Oracle to execute statements whenever it encounters a semicolon. Java source files are loaded with them. Before loading a Java script, change the character that causes Oracle to process statements. This can be done with the SQLTERMINATOR environmental variable: Setting it to OFF will cause Oracle to ignore the semicolons; setting it to ON will reactivate the character.

What's Next?

This chapter completes the book. Now it's time for you to use whatever skills you have acquired from this book. SQL is a powerful and complex tool. It takes a great deal of practice and patience to be an expert in the language. When I wrote my first SQL statement 16 years ago, I was amazed at the power. I am continually finding new tools that Oracle has incorporated into the database. I enjoy writing SQL, and I hope you will too.

Appendix A

Glossary

attribute   A fact or piece of information about a real-world thing such as a car, person, or customer.

cardinality   An ERD relationship property that describes the number of related instances an entity may have. For example, a student may take many courses. *Many* identifies the cardinality.

Cartesian join   A join procedure that matches each of the records in the first table to each of the records in the second table. This type of join is caused by the omission of the join condition(s) in the WHERE clause.

cluster   A method of storing tables that are related and that are often used together. It can increase performance.

column   One of the attributes that are stored in a table. Database tables are comprised of records that consist of one or more columns. Each column represents an attribute, such as gender or hair color.

column alias   Another name for an expression in the SELECT clause. It is defined by placing the alias name after the expression.

commit   An SQL command that permanently saves any pending data-modification transactions in the database.

composite key   Two or more values that make a record different from any other record in a table. It is also a primary key (or identifier) for the record.

concatenated key   See *composite key*.

concatenation   A technique whereby two sets of character values are combined into one value.

concurrency   Database property whereby two or more users try to modify the same record at the same time. Database record locking prevents this from occurring.

connect string   A set of characters that identifies an Oracle installation. These characters follow a table name.

constraint   A database device that is placed on a table. It ensures a particular type of data integrity.

correlated subquery   A SELECT statement that is used as an argument for the EXISTS and NOT EXISTS operators. The statement is executed once for each record that the master SELECT statement returns.

cursor   An area of memory that accepts the results of a SELECT statement. Records in the cursor are retrieved one at a time for processing.

data   A value that is stored in a database.

database   A series of tables that represent a subject or object.

database link   A database definition that can be used to access a remote database. The data link passes the user ID and password to the remote database.

data control language (DCL)   A series of SQL commands that are used for maintaining which users can access the Oracle database and its various objects.

data definition language (DDL)   A series of SQL commands that are used for establishing and maintaining the objects in the Oracle database.

data dictionary   A series of views/tables that Oracle has created that identify existing database elements such as tables, constraints, indexes, or synonyms.

data flow   A data flow diagram symbol that represents a set of attributes or data that a process moves.

data flow diagram (DFD)   A diagram that represents the flow, storage, and processing of data within a system.

data manipulation language (DML)   A series of SQL commands that are used to maintain the records within the database.

data stores   A data flow diagram symbol. It represents data at rest.

date picture   Describes how a date is to be formatted.

DCL   See *Data Control Language.*

DDL   See *Data Definition Language.*

DELETE   A DML command that is used to remove records from a table.

derived table   See *inline view.*

DESCRIBE   A command used to view the columns in a table or view.

DFD   See *Data Flow Diagram.*

DML   See *Data Manipulation Language.*

dual   A psuedotable that can be used in the FROM clause of a SELECT statement when no other table is needed. It is useful for generating sequence number or calculated values based on a function.

encapsulation   An object-oriented property whereby data and the applications (methods) that access the data are placed in the same object.

enterprise resource planning system (ERP)   A purchased system that documents, controls, and plans the tasks within a company.

entity   A data modeling object that represents something about which attribute values are to be kept. Examples of attributes are cars, planes, customers, or students.

entity relationship drawing (ERD)   A diagram that describes the entities, attributes, and relationships among various entities. This is a tool that is useful for designing and understanding a database.

equijoin   A join condition whereby records from two tables are matched when a value in one table record equals a value in the other table. This is the most common type of join.

ERD   See *entity relationship drawing.*

ERP   See *entity resource planning system.*

exception handler   A statement that is in the exception section of a PL/SQL code block and is executed when a specific error occurs.

expression   A value in a SELECT statement. This value can be a column, function, text literal, or a combination of the three.

field   A synonym for *table column.*

foreign key   A table column that contains values that are primary-key values in another table. This column is used to match records with the other table.

function   A named PL/SQL procedure that returns a value to the calling object.

grant   A DCL command that enables the target user to perform a database task.

identifier   An attribute that uniquely identifies an entity instance.

index   A database object that is related to one or more columns in a table. An index is used to identify table records quickly and to ensure the uniqueness of a column's values.

inline view   A SELECT statement that is placed in the FROM clause of a SELECT statement. The inline view creates a virtual table for the outer Select statement.

INSERT   A DML command that is used to add records to a table.

instance   One occurrence of an entity.

item   See *field*.

join   A relational database technique whereby a record from one table is matched to one or more records in another table.

looping structure   A PL/SQL construct that causes Oracle to repeat a set of instructions. There are three types of looping structures: LOOP, WHILE, and FOR.

materialized view   See *snapshot*.

metadata   A description of the content, quality, condition, availability, and other characteristics of data.

model   A graphical representation of a database.

nonequijoin   A join condition where the record from one table does not match a record from the second.

normalization   A process of reducing a relational database to its most efficient and effective size.

null   A blank or unknown value.

object privileges   A set of privileges that allow the user to maintain or view a table's records. The privileges are INSERT, UPDATE, DELETE, and SELECT.

OLAP   See *on-line analytical processing*.

OLTP   See *on-line transaction processing*.

On-line analytical processing (OLAP)   A type of system that is used to generate business information.

On-line transaction processing (OLTP)   A type of system that is used to conduct business tasks.

operator   A symbol that is placed between two expressions and causes an action or evaluation to occur. Examples are the plus sign (+) operator that adds two values and the equal sign (=) operator that evaluates the two expressions.

ordinality   An ERD relationship property that describes whether an entity instance is mandatory.

outer join   A join procedure that allows a record to be displayed even though it does not have a matching value in the joined table.

overloading   A technique that allows multiple named procedures to have the same name. The procedure parameter lists differentiate the various procedures.

package   A PL/SQL database object that holds cursors, procedures, functions, and variables that are related in some way.

PL/SQL   Oracle's proprietary programming language.

primary key   Same as an identifier except that it pertains to one or more columns that uniquely identify a record in a table.

privilege   The ability to perform a database task. Users must be granted a privilege for each task that is to be performed.

procedure   A PL/SQL code block. It can also be considered a program.

profile   User ID settings that limit the use of database resources. The settings affect database settings such as CPU per session, connect time, idle time, and passwords.

qualify   A technique that is used to identify a specific database object such as a table. The technique consists of preceding an object such as a column name with a period and the name of the parent object. This technique is generally used with table columns that have similar names.

relationship   A symbol on an ERD, describing how one entity is related to another. The relationship shows ordinality and cardinality.

REVOKE   A DCL command that takes one or more privileges away from the designated user.

role   A database designation that can be granted privileges and can then be granted to individual users. Roles dramatically reduce the time needed to maintain user privileges.

ROLLBACK   A DML command that restores the database to the state it was in when the last COMMIT command was performed.

rowid   A psuedocolumn on all records. It identifies the physical location of the record within the Oracle database.

segment   An area of reserved disk space within a tablespace.

selfjoin   A join procedure where records from the same table are matched. This type of join occurs when a unary relationship exists.

sequence   A database object that generates a new sequential number.

set operator   A symbol that causes Oracle to combine the result sets of two distinct SELECT statements in a particular manner.

snapshot   A database tool that copies or replicates portions of a remote database.

spooling   A process that captures screen output and places it into an external file. The file can then be modified or printed.

SQL   See *Structured Query Language*.

SQL*Loader   An Oracle tool that is used to load external-file data into the Oracle tables.

string   A series of alphanumeric characters.

Structured Query Language   An ANSI standard language that is used to interact with a relational database.

subquery   A SELECT statement that resides in the WHERE clause of another SELECT statement. A subquery returns one or more values that are used as an argument.

subselect   See *subquery*.

substitution variable   A variable that will cause Oracle to prompt the user for a value. The entered value is then substituted for the original variable.

synonym   A database designation that documents another name for a target database object.

system privileges   A set of privileges that allows the user to maintain the database objects.

table   A database object that stores records.

table relationship diagram   A diagram that display tables and their relationships to each other.

text literal Sets of characters that can be used as expressions and arguments.

TRUNCATE A DCL command that removes all records from a table without saving them.

UPDATE A DML command that is used to modify an existing record.

user account The Oracle ID that allows a user to access the database.

user ID See *user account*.

view A SELECT statement that is stored in the database. This object will return a derived or virtual table.

wildcard character A character symbol (e.g., % or _) that can be placed in a text literal argument. The character will cause Oracle to ignore sets of characters and to focus on the positions of characters when matching arguments.

Appendix B

Answers

CHAPTER 1

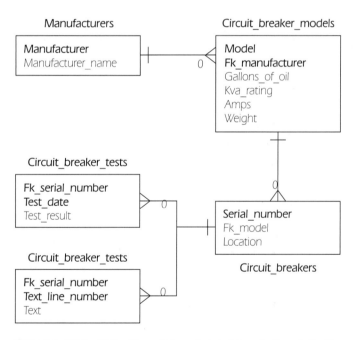

Figure App. B.1 *Circuit breaker table relationship diagram*

■ CHAPTER 2

1. n/a

2. n/a

3. n/a

4. 1

5. 11

6. 11
c/last_name/first_name
13
c/last_name/first_name

7. Save c:/prob7.sql

8. Start c:/prob7.sql

9. Create table manufacturers
(manufacturer   char(3),
 manufacturer_name   varchar2(20));
Create table circuit_breaker_models
(model   varchar2(20),
 fk_manufacturer   char(3),
 gallons_of_oil   number(4,0),
 kva_rating   number(4,1),
 amps   number(4,0),
weight   number(6,0));
create table circuit_breakers
(serial_number   varchar2(20),
 fk_model   varchar2(20),
 location   varchar2(30));
create table circuit_breaker_tests
(fk_serial_number   varchar2(20),
 test_date   date,
 test_result   number(5,1));
create table circuit_breaker_text
(fk_serial_number   varchar2(20),
 text_line_number   number,
 text   varchar2(300));

10. Drop table manufacturers;
Drop table circuit_breaker_models;
Drop table circuit_breakers;
Drop table circuit_breaker_tests;
Drop table circuit_breaker_text;
Drop table circuit_breaker_text;

11. Create table manufacturers
(manufacturer   char(3) primary key,
 manufacturer_name   varchar2(20) not null);
Create table circuit_breaker_models
(model   varchar2(20) primary key,
 fk_manufacturer   char(3) references manufacturers,
 gallons_of_oil   number(4,0),
 kva_rating   number(4,1),
 amps   number(4,0),
 weight   number(6,0) default (0));
create table circuit_breakers
(serial_number   varchar2(20) primary key,
 fk_model   varchar2(20) references circuit_breaker_models,
 location   varchar2(30));
create table circuit_breaker_tests
(fk_serial_number   varchar2(20),
 test_date   date,
 test_result   number(5,1),
 check (test_result > 50 and test_result < 100),
 primary key (fk_serial_number, test_date),
 foreign key (fk_serial_number) references circuit_breakers);
create table circuit_breaker_text
(fk_serial_number   varchar2(20),
 text_line_number   number,
 text   varchar2(300),
primary key (fk_serial_number, text_line_number),
foreign key (fk_serial_number) references circuit_breakers);

12. Create synonym employee_tool_purchases for emp_tools;
Select * from employee_tool_purchases;
Drop synonym employee_tool_purchases;

13. Create or replace trigger upper_case
Before insert on employee
Referencing new as new
For each row
begin
:New.last_name := upper(:new.last_name);
:New.first_name := upper(:new.first_name);
:New.state := upper(:new.state);
End;
/

■ CHAPTER 3

1. Insert into employee (last_name, first_name, payroll_number,
fk_department, Social_security_number, gender, current_position,
wages, birth_date,
   Employment_date, phone, state, street, city)
Values ('QUAYLE', 'DAN', 50, 'INT', 312-33-9089, 'M',
   'CHIEF EXECUTIVE', 50000, '09-MAR-42',
   to_date('20-JAN-2001', 'DD-MON-YYYY'),
   '712-345-9876', 'IN', '1234 WESTERN', 'INDIANAPOLIS');

2. Insert into glasses (fk_payroll_number, purchase_date, optician,
cost) select payroll_number, '07-MAY-2001', 'Pearl Optical', 78
from employee
where fk_department = 'WEL';

3. Update employee set wages = (wages*1.03);
Update employee set wages = wages + 900
   where fk_department = 'WEL';

4. delete from glasses;

5. rollback;

■ CHAPTER 4

1. Select tname from tab;

2. Desc employee or describe employee

3. Select fk_department, last_name, first_name, current_position
From employee;

4. select fk_department, 'Mr. ' || first_name || ' ' || last_name, current_position
from employee;

5. Select last_name, first_name, wages, (wages*1.06)+2300-250
From employee;

6. Select fk_department, first_name, last_name
From employee order by fk_department;

7. Select fk_department, first_name, last_name
from employee
order by fk_department desc, last_name, first_name;

8. Select fk_department, last_name, nvl(wages,0)/52
from employee
order by 1, 3;

9. Select first_name, last_name from employee where first_name = 'JOHN';

10. Select first_name, last_name, wages from employee where wages is null;

11. Select first_name, last_name, state
from employee
where state = 'OH' or state = 'IA' or state = 'TX';
or
select first_name, last_name, state
from employee
where state in ('OH', 'IA', 'TX');

12. Select first_name, last_name, employment_date
from employee
where employment_date >= '01-JAN-1950'
and employment_date <= '01-JAN-1979';
or
Select first_name, last_name, employment_date
from employee
where employment_date between '01-JAN-1950' and '01-JAN-1979';

13. Select first_name, last_name, state
from employee
where state != 'OH' and state != 'IA' and state != 'TX';
or
select first_name, last_name, state

from employee
where state not in ('OH','IA','TX');

14. Select first_name, last_name, gender, wages, birth_date
from employee
where gender = 'M'
   and wages >= 10000
   and birth_date > '01-JAN-1920';

15. Select first_name, last_name, gender, wages, birth_date
from employee
where gender = 'M'
   or wages >= 10000
   or birth_date > '01-JAN-1920';

16. Select first_name, last_name, gender, wages, birth_date
from employee
where (gender = 'M'
   and wages >= 10000)
   or birth_date > '01-JAN-1920';

■ CHAPTER 5

1. Select last_name, first_name, purchase_date, optician
from employee, glasses
where payroll_number = fk_payroll_number;

2. Select last_name, first_name, purchase_date, optician
from employee, glasses
where payroll_number = fk_payroll_number(+);

3. Select department_name, last_name, first_name, purchase_date, optician
from department, employee, glasses
where department = fk_department
   and payroll_number = fk_payroll_number;

4. Select department_name, last_name, first_name, purchase_date, optician
from department d, employee e, glasses g
where d.department = e.fk_department
   and e.payroll_number = g.fk_payroll_number;

5. Select min(wages) from employee;

6. Select max(wages) from employee;

7. Select min(street), max(street) from employee;

8. Select department_name, count(last_name)
from department, employee
where department = fk_department(+)
group by department_name;

9. Select department_name, sum(cost)
from department, employee, glasses
where department = fk_department(+)
   and payroll_number = fk_payroll_number(+)
group by department_name;

10. select last_name, first_name, count(cost), sum(cost), avg(nvl(cost,0))
from employee, glasses
where payroll_number = fk_payroll_number(+)
group by last_name, first_name;

■ CHAPTER 6

1. Select lower(department_name), upper(last_name), initcap(first_name)
from department, employee
where department = fk_department;

2. Select lpad(department_name, 20,'#'), rpad(last_name, 25,'-')
From department, employee
Where department = fk_department;

3. Select first_name||''||last_name, length(first_name||''||last_name)
from employee;

4. Select first_name, substr(first_name, 2,2) from employee;

■ CHAPTER 7

1. Select last_name, first_name, employment_date
from employee
where mod(to_number(to_char(employment_date, 'yy')), 3) = 0;

2. Select last_name, first_name, avg(nvl(cost,0))
from employee, glasses
where payroll_number = fk_payroll_number(+)
group by last_name, first_name;

3. Select fk_department, avg(nvl(cost,0)), round(avg(nvl(cost,0)), –1)
from employee, glasses
where payroll_number = fk_payroll_number(+)
group by fk_department;

4. Select fk_department, sum(cost), trunc(sum(cost),–2)
from employee, glasses
where payroll_number = fk_payroll_number(+)
group by fk_department;

5. Select last_name, first_name, to_char(add_months(birth_date, 21*12), 'Month
yyyy')
From employee;

6. Select last_name, first_name, next_day(add_months(birth_date, 21*12), 'Saturday')
From employee;

7. Select last_name, first_name, to_char(birth_date, 'dd-MON-YYYY')
from employee
where birth_date < to_date('01-JAN-1890', 'DD-MON-YYYY');

8. Select last_name, first_name,
Round((months_between(min(purchase_date), birth_date))/12,0) age
From employee, glasses
Where payroll_number = fk_payroll_number
Group by last_name, first_name, birth_date;

9. Select to_char(to_date('01-JAN-2000', 'DD-MON-YYYY'), 'DAY
                                    DD-MON-YYYY')
From dual;

■ CHAPTER 8

1. Select last_name, first_name
from employee
where first_name = 'JOHN'
union
select last_name, first_name
from employee
where first_name = 'HAROLD'
union

```
    select last_name, first_name
    from employee
    where first_name = 'WILLIAM';
```

2.
```
Select last_name, first_name
from employee, emp_tools
where payroll_number = fk_payroll_number
minus
select last_name, first_name
from employee, glasses
where payroll_number = fk_payroll_number;
```

3.
```
Select 'Born Before 1920', last_name, first_name,
        to_char(birth_date, 'DD-MON-YYYY')
from employee
where birth_date < '01-JAN-1920'
union
select 'Born After 1920', last_name, first_name,
        to_char(birth_date, 'DD-MON-YYYY')
from employee
where birth_date >= '01-JAN-1920'
order by 1 desc, 2;
```

4.
```
Select 'Born Before 1920', last_name, first_name,
        to_char(birth_date, 'DD-MON-YYYY')
from employee, emp_tools
where birth_date < '01-JAN-1920'
   and payroll_number = fk_payroll_number
union
select 'Born After 1920', last_name, first_name,
        to_char(birth_date, 'DD-MON-YYYY')
from employee, glasses
where birth_date >= '01-JAN-1920'
   and payroll_number = fk_payroll_number
order by 1 desc, 2;
```

5.
```
select department_name
from department
where not exists (select * from employee
                    where fk_department = department.department);
```

6. select department_name, tool_name, tool_cost
from department, employee, emp_tools
where department = fk_department
  and payroll_number = fk_payroll_number
  and department = upper('&department_code');

7. select department_name, tool_name, tool_cost
from department, employee, emp_tools
where department = fk_department
  and payroll_number = fk_payroll_number
  and department = upper('&department_code')
union
select department_name, optician, cost
from department, employee, glasses
where department = fk_department
  and payroll_number = fk_payroll_number
  and department = upper('&department_code');

8. accept department_code prompt 'Enter Department Code: ';
select department_name, tool_name, tool_cost
from department, employee, emp_tools
where department = fk_department
  and payroll_number = fk_payroll_number
  and department = upper('&department_code')
union
select department_name, optician, cost
from department, employee, glasses
where department = fk_department
  and payroll_number = fk_payroll_number
  and department = upper('&department_code');

■ CHAPTER 9

1. select gender, current_position, sum(tool_cost) "Tool Cost"
from employee, emp_tools
where payroll_number = fk_payroll_number
group by rollup (gender, current_position)
order by 1,2;

2. select last_name||',`||first_name name,
   tool_cost + cost "Equipment_cost",
   rank () over (order by tool_cost+cost asc nulls first)
   from employee,
   (select fk_payroll_number, sum(tool_cost) tool_cost
   from employee, emp_tools
   where payroll_number = fk_payroll_number(+)
   group by fk_payroll_number) t,
   (select fk_payroll_number, sum(cost) cost
   from employee, glasses
   where payroll_number = fk_payroll_number(+)
   group by fk_payroll_number) g
   where payroll_number = t.fk_payroll_number(+)
     and payroll_number = g.fk_payroll_number(+);

3. select *
   from (select department, last_name||',`||first_name,
     sum(cost) eyeglass_cost,
     rank() over (partition by department
     order by sum(cost) asc nulls first) Lowest_eyeglass_cost_rank
   from department, employee, glasses
   where department = fk_department
     and payroll_number = fk_payroll_number(+)
   group by department, last_name, first_name)
   where lowest_eyeglass_cost_rank <= 2;

4. select purchase_date, last_name||',`||first_name,
     cost eyeglass_cost,
     sum(cost) over (order by purchase_date
     rows unbounded preceding) balance
   from employee, glasses
   where payroll_number = fk_payroll_number;

5. select department, sum(cost) "Total Eyeglass Cost",
     ratio_to_report (sum(cost)) over () as cost_ratio
   from department, employee, glasses
   where department = fk_department(+)
     and payroll_number = fk_payroll_number
   group by department;

6. select tool_name, purchase_date, tool_cost,
　　tool_cost - lag(tool_cost, 1) over
　　(partition by tool_name order by purchase_date) diff
　from emp_tools;
　select (case when cost <= 100
　　then 'Less than 100'
　when cost >= 100 and cost <= 125
　　then '100 to 125'
　when cost > 126 and cost <= 150
　　then '126 to 150'
　when cost > 30 then 'Above 150' end)
　"Eyeglass cost categories", count(*) as amount
　from glasses
　group by (case when cost <= 100
　　then 'Less than 100'
　when cost >= 100 and cost <= 125
　　then '100 to 125'
　when cost > 126 and cost <= 150
　　then '126 to 150'
　when cost > 30 then 'Above 150' end);

▪ CHAPTER 10

1. create or replace view mailing_list as
　select decode(gender, 'M', 'Mr.', 'F', 'Ms.')||first_name||' '||last_name name, street,
　city, state
　from employee;

2. create or replace view employee_wages as
　select fk_department, last_name, first_name, city, wages
　from employee
　where fk_department = 'WEL'
　with check option;
　update employee_wages set fk_department = 'INT'
　where city = 'PLAINS';

■ CHAPTER 11

```
set linesize 132
column sysdate noprint new_val day
column last_name hea 'Last Name' for a15
column first_name hea 'First Name' for a10
column employment_date hea 'Employment| Date' jus center format a10
column current_position hea 'Current Position' format a18
column wages hea 'Wages' format $999,999.99
column purchase_date hea 'Tool|Purchase| Date' format a10 jus center
column tool_name hea 'Tool Name'
column tool_cost hea 'Cost of|Tool' format $999.99 jus right
column department_name hea 'Department Name'
break on department_name on last_name on first_name -
     on employment_date on current_position on wages
compute sum label 'Dept Total' of tool_cost on department_name
ttitle left day center 'Departmental Tool Purchases'
btitle right sql.pno
select department_name, last_name, first_name, employment_date,
     current_position, wages, purchase_date, tool_name, tool_cost, sysdate
from department, employee, emp_tools
where department = fk_department
     and payroll_number = fk_payroll_number
order by 1,2,3,7;
clear columns
clear computes
clear breaks
ttitle off
btitle off
```

■ CHAPTER 14

```
1. begin
      dbms_output.put_line ('I am soon to be a PL/SQL expert');
   end;
   /
```

2. begin <<sections>>
    goto section3;
    <<section1>>
    dbms_output.put_line ('Section 1');
    goto section4;
    <<section2>>
    dbms_output.put_line ('Section 2');
    goto section1;
    <<section3>>
    dbms_output.put_line ('Section 3');
    goto section2;
    <<section4>>
    dbms_output.put_line ('Section 4');
  end b_label;
  /

3. declare
    retirement_date   date;
    emp_var   employee%rowtype;
  begin
    select max(birth_date)
    into emp_var.birth_date
    from employee;
    select last_name, first_name
    into emp_var.last_name, emp_var.first_name
    from employee
    where birth_date = emp_var.birth_date;
    retirement_date := add_months(emp_var.birth_date, 12*65);
    dbms_output.put_line (emp_var.first_name||''||emp_var.last_name||' Retires On');
    dbms_output.put_line (to_char(retirement_date));
  end;
  /

4. declare
    retirement_date   date;
    working_days   number;
    emp_var   employee%rowtype;
  begin

```
    select max(birth_date)
    into emp_var.birth_date
    from employee;
    select last_name, first_name
    into emp_var.last_name, emp_var.first_name
    from employee
    where birth_date = emp_var.birth_date;
    retirement_date := add_months(emp_var.birth_date, 12*65);
    working_days := trunc(retirement_date - sysdate, 0);
    dbms_output.put_line (emp_var.first_name||''||emp_var.last_name||'Retires
    On');
    dbms_output.put_line (to_char(retirement_date));
    dbms_output.put_line ('He has '||to_char(working_days)||' days left to work');
  end;
  /
```

5.
```
  declare
     bush_tool_purchases      number;
     truman_tool_purchases    number;
  begin
     select count(*) into bush_tool_purchases
     from employee, emp_tools
     where employee.payroll_number = emp_tools.fk_payroll_number
        and last_name = 'BUSH';
     select count(*) into truman_tool_purchases
     from employee, emp_tools
     where employee.payroll_number = emp_tools.fk_payroll_number
        and last_name = 'TRUMAN';
     if bush_tool_purchases > truman_tool_purchases then
     dbms_output.put_line ('Bush has '||to_char(bush_tool_purchases-
        truman_tool_purchases)||' more than Truman');
  else
     dbms_output.put_line ('Truman has '||to_char(truman_tool_purchases-
        bush_tool_purchases)||' more than Bush');
  end if;
  end;
  /
```

6. declare
    bush_tool_purchases   number;
    truman_tool_purchases   number;
  begin
   select count(*) into bush_tool_purchases
   from employee, emp_tools
   where employee.payroll_number = emp_tools.fk_payroll_number
     and last_name = 'BUSH';
   select count(*) into truman_tool_purchases
   from employee, emp_tools
   where employee.payroll_number = emp_tools.fk_payroll_number
     and last_name = 'TRUMAN';
   if bush_tool_purchases > truman_tool_purchases then
   dbms_output.put_line ('Bush has '||to_char(bush_tool_purchases-
     truman_tool_purchases)||' more than Truman');
   if bush_tool_purchases-truman_tool_purchases >= 2 then
     dbms_output.put_line ('Bush has more than 2 more purchases than Truman');
   end if;
  else
   dbms_output.put_line ('Truman has '||to_char(truman_tool_purchases-
     bush_tool_purchases)||' more than Bush');
   if truman_tool_purchases-bush_tool_purchases >= 2 then
     dbms_output.put_line ('Truman has more than 2 more purchases than Bush');
   end if;
  end if;
  end;
  /

7. declare
    decade   number;
  begin
   select to_number(substr(birth_date, 8, 2)) into decade
   from employee
   where last_name = 'CLINTON';
   if decade between 0 and 9 then
    dbms_output.put_line ('Clinton was born in the 1st decade');
   elsif decade between 10 and 19 then
    dbms_output.put_line ('Clinton was born in the 2nd decade');

```
      elsif decade between 20 and 29 then
        dbms_output.put_line ('Clinton was born in the 3rd decade');
       elsif decade between 30 and 39 then
         dbms_output.put_line ('Clinton was born in the 4th decade');
        elsif decade between 40 and 49 then
          dbms_output.put_line ('Clinton was born in the 5th decade');
         elsif decade between 50 and 59 then
           dbms_output.put_line ('Clinton was born in the 6th decade');
          elsif decade between 60 and 69 then
            dbms_output.put_line ('Clinton was born in the 7th decade');
           elsif decade between 70 and 79 then
             dbms_output.put_line ('Clinton was born in the 8th decade');
            elsif decade between 80 and 89 then
              dbms_output.put_line ('Clinton was born in the 9th decade');
             elsif decade between 90 and 99 then
               dbms_output.put_line ('Clinton was born in the 10th decade');
     end if;
   end;
   /
```

8.
```
   declare
   avg_age                        number;
   cursor a_age is select trunc(avg(months_between(employment_date,
                  birth_date)/12),0)
                     from employee;
   begin
     open a_age;
     fetch a_age into avg_age;
     close a_age;
     dbms_output.put_line ('This average starting age is '||to_char(avg_age));
   end;
   /
```

9.
```
   declare
     h_day                       employee.employment_date%type;
     lname                       employee.last_name%type;
     fname                       employee.first_name%type;
   cursor start_day is select min(employment_date) from employee
                 where fk_department = 'WEL';
```

```
        cursor emp_name is select first_name, last_name from employee
                    where employment_date = h_day;
    begin
      open start_day;
      fetch start_day into h_day;
      close start_day;
      open emp_name;
      fetch emp_name into fname, lname;
      close emp_name;
      dbms_output.put_line (fname||''||lname||' was the first employee hired');
    end;
    /
```

10.
```
    declare
      b_day                        employee.birth_date%type;
      cursor a is select max(birth_date) from employee;
    begin
      open a;
      fetch a into b_day;
      dbms_output.put_line (to_char(b_day));
      open a;
      close a;
    end;
    /
```

11.
```
    declare
      b_day        employee.birth_date%type;
      cursor a is select max(birth_date) from employee;
    begin
      open a;
      fetch a into b_day;
      dbms_output.put_line (to_char(b_day));
      if not a%isopen then open a; end if;
      close a;
    end;
    /
```

12.
```
    declare
      cursor a is select * from employee
                where last_name = 'REAGAN';
```

```
   a_var      a%rowtype;
   cursor b is select count(*) t_cnt from emp_tools
            where fk_payroll_number = a_var.payroll_number;
   b_var      b%rowtype;
   cursor c is select count(*) g_cnt from glasses
            where fk_payroll_number = a_var.payroll_number;
   c_var      c%rowtype;
 begin
   open a; fetch a into a_var; close a;
   open b; fetch b into b_var; close b;
   open c; fetch c into c_var; close c;
   dbms_output.put_line ('Reagan was hired on '||a_var.employment_date);
   dbms_output.put_line ('Tool purchases equal '||to_char(b_var.t_cnt));
   dbms_output.put_line ('Glasses purchases equal '||to_char(c_var.g_cnt));
 end;
 /
```

13.
```
 declare
   cursor a is select * from emp_tools;
   a_var      a%rowtype;
   counter    number := 0;
 begin
   open a;
   loop
    fetch a into a_var;
    counter := counter + 1;
    dbms_output.put_line (to_char(counter)||''||a_var.purchase_date||'
     '||a_var.tool_name);
    exit when counter = 12;
   end loop;
 end;
 /
```

14.
```
 declare
   cursor a is select * from emp_tools;
   a_var    a%rowtype;
   counter  number := 0;
 begin
   open a;
```

```
   loop
    fetch a into a_var;
    counter := counter + 1;
    dbms_output.put_line (to_char(counter)||''||a_var.purchase_date||'
     '||a_var.tool_name);
    if counter = 12 then exit; end if;
   end loop;
  end;
  /
```

15.
```
 declare
   cursor a is select first_name||''||last_name name
            from employee
            where fk_department = 'INT';
   a_var     a%rowtype;
  begin
   open a;
   fetch a into a_var;
   while a%found loop
    dbms_output.put_line (a_var.name);
    fetch a into a_var;
   end loop;
   close a;
  end;
  /
```

16.
```
 declare
   cursor a is select payroll_number, first_name||''||last_name name
            from employee;
   a_var     a%rowtype;
   cursor b is select count(*) t_cnt from emp_tools
            where fk_payroll_number = a_var.payroll_number;
   b_var     b%rowtype;
   cursor c is select count(*) g_cnt from glasses
            where fk_payroll_number = a_var.payroll_number;
   c_var     c%rowtype;
  begin
   open a;
   fetch a into a_var;
```

```
      while a%found loop
         open b; fetch b into b_var; close b;
         open c; fetch c into c_var; close c;
         dbms_output.put_line (to_char(a%rowcount)||''||a_var.name);
         dbms_output.put_line ('   Tool purchases '||to_char(b_var.t_cnt));
         dbms_output.put_line ('   Glass purchases '||to_char(c_var.g_cnt));
         fetch a into a_var;
       end loop;
    end;
    /
```

17.
```
    declare
       cursor a is select payroll_number, first_name||''||last_name name
                 from employee;
       a_var    a%rowtype;
       cursor b is select count(*) t_cnt from emp_tools
                 where fk_payroll_number = a_var.payroll_number;
       b_var    b%rowtype;
       cursor c is select count(*) g_cnt from glasses
                 where fk_payroll_number = a_var.payroll_number;
       c_var    c%rowtype;
    begin
      open a;
      fetch a into a_var;
      while not a%notfound loop
         open b; fetch b into b_var; close b;
         open c; fetch c into c_var; close c;
         dbms_output.put_line (to_char(a%rowcount)||''||a_var.name);
         dbms_output.put_line ('   Tool purchases '||to_char(b_var.t_cnt));
         dbms_output.put_line ('   Glass purchases '||to_char(c_var.g_cnt));
         fetch a into a_var;
       end loop;
    end;
    /
```

18.
```
    declare
       cursor a is select * from employee
                 for update of absences;
       a_var    a%rowtype;
```

```
begin
  open a;
  fetch a into a_var;
  while a%found loop
    update employee set absences = 0
    where current of a;
    fetch a into a_var;
  end loop;
  close a;
end;
/
```

19.
```
declare
    cursor a is select first_name||''||last_name name,
            to_char(birth_date,'DD-MON-YYYY') bday
            from employee
            order by 1;
    a_var    a%rowtype;
begin
  open a;
  for cnt_var in 1..5 loop
    fetch a into a_var;
    dbms_output.put_line (to_char(cnt_var)||''||a_var.name||''||a_var.bday);
  end loop;
  close a;
end;
/
```

20.
```
declare
    cursor a is select first_name||''||last_name name,
            to_char(birth_date,'DD-MON-YYYY') bday
            from employee
            order by 1;
    a_var    a%rowtype;
begin
  open a;
  for cnt_var in reverse 1..5 loop
    fetch a into a_var;
    dbms_output.put_line (to_char(cnt_var)||''||a_var.name||''||a_var.bday);
```

```
    end loop;
    close a;
end;
/
```

21.
```
declare
    cursor a is select fk_department, first_name||''||last_name name
            from employee
            where fk_department in ('INT','POL')
            order by 1;
begin
    for cnt_var in a loop
    dbms_output.put_line (cnt_var.fk_department||''||cnt_var.name);
    end loop;
end;
/
```

22.
```
begin
    for cnt_var in (select fk_department, first_name||''||last_name name
            from employee
            where fk_department in ('INT','POL')
            order by 1)
    loop
    dbms_output.put_line (cnt_var.fk_department||''||cnt_var.name);
    end loop;
end;
/
```

23.
```
declare
    t   emp_tools%rowtype;
    g   glasses%rowtype;
begin
    for a in (select * from employee) loop
    t.tool_cost := null;  t.tool_name := null; t.purchase_date := null;
    g.cost := null; g.purchase_date := null;
      for b in (select * from emp_tools
            where fk_payroll_number = a.payroll_number)
    loop
      if t.tool_cost is null or b.tool_cost > t.tool_cost then
      t.tool_cost := b.tool_cost;
```

```
      t.tool_name := b.tool_name;
      t.purchase_date := b.purchase_date;
    end if;
  end loop;
  for c in (select * from glasses
            where fk_payroll_number = a.payroll_number)
  loop
    if g.cost is null or c.cost > g.cost then
      g.cost := c.cost;
      g.purchase_date := c.purchase_date;
    end if;
  end loop;
  dbms_output.put_line (a.last_name||' purchased');
  dbms_output.put_line ('Tool: '||t.purchase_date||''||t.tool_name||''
                          ||to_char(t.tool_cost));
  dbms_output.put_line ('Glasses: '||g.purchase_date||''||to_char(g.cost));
  end loop;
end;
/
```

CHAPTER 15

1.
```
declare
  a    number;
begin
  a := 10 / 0;
exception
  when zero_divide then
  dbms_output.put_line ('YOU HAVE ATTEMPTED TO DIVIDE A NUMBER
                         BY ZERO');
end;
/
```

2.
```
declare
  bad_payroll_number        exception;
  pragma exception_init (bad_payroll_number,-02291);
```

```
      begin
         insert into tools (fk_payroll_number, tool_name, purchase_date)
         values (987, 'PLIERS', '08-APR-98');
      exception
         when bad_payroll_number then
         dbms_output.put_line ('You have violated the payroll number constraint');
      end;
      /
```

3. bcgin
```
         insert into emp_tools (fk_payroll_number, tool_name, purchase_date)
         values (987, 'PLIERS', '08-APR-98');
      exception
         when others then
            dbms_output.put_line ('You have violated the payroll number constraint');
      end;
      /
```

4. declare
```
      lname       employee.last_name%type;
      begin
         select last_name into lname from employee
         where last_name = 'PALINSKI';
      exception
         when others then
         dbms_output.put_line (to_char(sqlcode));
         dbms_output.put_line (sqlerrm);
      end;
      /
```

5. declare
```
      clintons_state          employee.state%type;
      wrong_state             exception;
      begin
         select state into clintons_state
         from employee
         where last_name = 'CLINTON';
         if clintons_state != 'NJ' then
            raise wrong_state;
         end if;
```

```
exception
  when wrong_state then
  dbms_output.put_line ('Clinton has the wrong state value');
end;
/
```

6.
```
declare
    type dept_name_table is table of varchar2(30)
      index by binary_integer;
    dept_name    dept_name_table;
begin
  for a in (select * from department)
  loop
   dept_name(ascii(a.department)) := a.department_name;
  end loop;
  for b in (select * from employee)
  loop
   dbms_output.put_line(dept_name(ascii(b.fk_department))||''||b.last_name);
  end loop;
end;
/
```

7.
```
Create or replace procedure answer7 is
Begin
    Dbms_output.put_line ('I am soon to be a procedure-building guru');
End;
/
Execute answer7;
Drop procedure answer7;
```

8.
```
Create or replace procedure answer8 (beg_date in date, end_date in date) is
    Begin
      For a in (select * from employee where birth_date between beg_date
                                and end_date) Loop
      Dbms_output.put_line (a.last_name||''||a.birth_date);
    End loop;
    End;
/
Execute answer8('01-JAN-1901','01-JAN-1999');
Drop procedure answer8;
```

9. *Called Procedure*

```
create or replace procedure answer9a
    (dept in varchar2, beg_date in date, end_date in date,
    lname out employee.last_name%type)
is
begin
    select min(last_name) into lname
    from employee
    where fk_department = dept
        and birth_date between beg_date and end_date
        and birth_date = (select min(birth_date)
                        from employee
                        where fk_department = dept
                            and birth_date between beg_date and end_date);
end;
/
```

Calling Procedure

```
Create or replace procedure answer9 (beg_date in date, end_date in date) is
    lname    employee.last_name%type;
Begin
    For a in (select * from department)
    Loop
        Answer9a(a.department, beg_date, end_date, lname);
        Dbms_output.put_line (a.department||''||lname);
    End loop;
End;
/
Execute answer9('01-JAN-1901','01-JAN-1999');
Drop procedure answer9;
Drop procedure answer9a;
```

10.
```
Create or replace procedure answer10 (beg_date in date, end_date in date) is
    lname      employee.last_name%type;
    procedure answer10a
        (dept in varchar2, beg_date in date, end_date in date,
        lname out employee.last_name%type)
    is
```

```
begin
    select min(last_name) into lname
    from employee
    where fk_department = dept
      and birth_date between beg_date and end_date
      and birth_date = (select min(birth_date)
                        from employee
                        where fk_department = dept
                          and birth_date between beg_date and end_date);
end;
Begin
    For a in (select * from department)
    Loop
        Answer10a(a.department, beg_date, end_date, lname);
        Dbms_output.put_line (a.department||''||lname);
    End loop;
End;
/
Execute answer10('01-JAN-1901', '01-JAN-1999');
Drop procedure answer10;
```

11.
```
Create or replace PROCEDURE answer11a (dept in varchar2, rate out number) IS
BEGIN
  if dept = 'WEL' then rate := .07;
  elsif dept = 'INT' then rate := .06;
  elsif dept = 'POL' then rate := .15;
  else
                        rate := .05;
  end if;
END;
/
create or replace PROCEDURE answer11 (dept in varchar2) IS
  new_wages   number;
  rate        number;
begin
  for a in (select * from employee where fk_department = dept)
    loop
        problem11a(a.fk_department, rate);
```

```
        new_wages := a.wages * (1 + rate);
        update employee set wages = new_wages
            where payroll_number = a.payroll_number;
            dbms_output.put_line (a.last_name||''||to_char(a.wages)||
                            ''||to_char(new_wages));
    end loop;
end;
/
Execute answer11('WEL');
Drop procedure answer11a;

Drop procedure answer11;
```

12.
```
Create or replace function saying return varchar2 is
Begin
  Return 'I am soon to be a PL/SQL function guru';
End;
/
Begin
  Dbms_output.put_line (saying);
End;
/
Drop function saying.
```

Or

```
Declare
  function saying return varchar2 is
  Begin
    Return 'I am soon to be a PL/SQL function guru';
  End;
Begin
  Dbms_output.put_line (saying);
End;
/
```

13.
```
create or replace function seniority (employment_date in date) return number
is
 seniority   number;
```

```
begin
 seniority := trunc(months_between(sysdate, employment_date)/12, 1);
 return seniority;
end;
/
select last_name, seniority(employment_date) from employee;
drop function seniority;
```

14.
```
create or replace function tool_number (payroll_number in varchar2)
return number is
 tool_number   number;
begin
  select count(tool_name)
  into tool_number
  from emp_tools
  where fk_payroll_number = payroll_number;
  return tool_number;
end;
/
create or replace function glasses_number (payroll_number in varchar2)
  return number is
  glasses_number   number;
begin
  select count(optician)
  into glasses_number
  from glasses
  where fk_payroll_number = payroll_number;
  return glasses_number;
end;
/
begin
for a in (select * from employee)
loop
 dbms_output.put_line ('Name: '||a.last_name);
 dbms_output.put_line ('Tools  : '||to_char(tool_number(a.payroll_number)));
 dbms_output.put_line ('Glasses: '||to_char(glasses_number(a.payroll_number)));
 end loop;
end;
```

```
/
drop function tool_number;
drop function glasses_number;
```

15. Create or replace package personnel is
```
    Cursor list_emps return employee%rowtype;
    Function seniority (employment_date in date) return number;
    Procedure avail_absences (seniority in number, absences out number);
End;
/
Create or replace package body personnel is
    Cursor list_emps return employee%rowtype
    Is
    Select * from employee;
    Function seniority (employment_date in date) return number
    Is
      Seniority    number;
    Begin
      Seniority := trunc(months_between(sysdate, employment_date)/12, 0);
      Return seniority;
    End;
    Procedure avail_absences (seniority in number, absences out number)
    Is
    begin
      if seniority > 50 then absences := 10;
        elsif seniority > 40 then absences := 9;
        elsif seniority > 30 then absences := 8;
        elsif seniority > 20 then absences := 7;
        elsif seniority > 10 then absences := 6;
      else
          absences := 5;
      end if;
      end;
end personnel;
/
```

16. declare
```
    sen    number;
    abs    number;
```

```
begin
  for a in personnel.list_emps
  loop
    sen := personnel.seniority(a.employment_date);
    personnel.avail_absences(sen, abs);
    dbms_output.put_line(a.last_name||''||to_char(abs));
  end loop;
end;
/
```

Bibliography

Feuerstein, Steven. *Oracle PL/SQL Programming*. 2nd ed. O'Reilly & Associates, Sebastopol, CA: 1997.

Harrison, Guy. *Oracle SQL: High-Peformance Tuning*. 2nd ed. Prentice Hall PTR, Upper Saddle River: 2001.

Hoffer, Jeffery A., Joey F. George, and Joseph S. Valacich. *Modern Systems Analysis and Design*. 3rd ed. Prentice Hall, Upper Saddle River: 2002.

Koch, George, and Kevin Loney. *Oracle8: The Complete Reference*. Osborne/McGraw-Hill, Berkeley: 1997.

Oracle8i Concepts, Release 8.1.5: Schema Objects http://technet.oracle.com/doc/server.815/a67781/c08schem.htm#18096

Oracle8i Concepts Release 8.1.5: SQL for Analysis http://technet.oracle.com/doc/oracle8i_816/server.816/a76994/analysis.htm

Oracle9i Database http://technet.oracle.com/products/oracle9i/content.html

SQL*Plus User's Guide and Reference, Release 8.1.5 http://technet.oracle.com/doc/server.815/a66736/toc.htm

Index

A

ABS function, 172
ACCEPT (user variable) commands, 209, 211–212
Access paths, cost-based optimizers, 302–303, 322
ADD constraint, ALTER command, 49, 59
Addition (+) function, 172
Addition operators (+), 108
ADD_MONTHS date function, 181–182, 252
ADTs (abstract data types)
    collection types
       object-type tables, 70, 72–73
       varrays, 70–72
    defined, 68
    object types, 69–70
Aggregate variables, 346–347
    cursors, 357–358
ALL evaluation operator, 198, 200, 201
ALL keyword, with evaluation operators, 114–115
All-objects view, data dictionary, 96
ALL_ROWS mode, cost-based optimizers, 302
ALTER commands
    ALTER SESSION, 313, 315
    ALTER TABLE, 49–50
    ALTER TABLESPACE, 42–43
    ALTER TRIGGER, 67
    object privileges, 87
    system privileges, 82–83
Analytical functions
    basics, 215
    CUBE, 218–219
    CUME_DIST, 229–230
    data warehouses, viewing data, 215–216
    DENSE-RANK

    basics, 225
    Top-N and Bottom-N queries, 226–227
    GROUPING, 220–222
    LAG, 239–243
    LEAD, 239–243
    NTITLE, 230–231
    PERCENT-RANK, 227–228
       versus CUME_DIST, 229–230
    RANK, 222–225
    ROLLUP, 216–218
    ROW_NUMBER, 231–232
    statistical functions, 243–245
    windowing functions
       BETWEEN ... AND, 234
       cumulative aggregate functions, 234–238
       CURRENT ROW, 234
       ORDER BY, 233
       OVER, 233
       PARTITION BY, 233
       ROWS | RANGE, 233
       UNBOUNDED FOLLOWING, 234
       UNBOUNDED PRECEDING, 234–235
ANALYZE commands, 301
    system privileges, 83
AND keyword
    clauses
       HAVING, 148–149
       WHERE, 120, 121–122
    cumulative aggregate functions, 237
    evaluation operators, 114–115
    performance tuning, 322
Anonymous block procedures, 339
ANY evaluation operator, 198, 200–202

Arithmetic operators, 107–109
Arrays, 389–392
Ascending/descending order, ORDER BY clauses,
    124–125
ASCII function, 152
Assignment operator (:=), 347
Attributes, entities, 3–5
AUDIT commands, system privileges, 83
AVG group function, 143, 145
AVG keyword, COMPUTE command, 277

B
B-Tree indexes, 293, 295, 296, 297
BACKUP ANY TABLE command, 83
Baseline tools, SQL*Plus, 31
BECOME USER command, 83
BETWEEN ... AND windowing functions, 234
BETWEEN evaluation operator, 110, 115–116
   cumulative aggregate functions, 237
BFILE data type, 48
Binary relationship, entities, 8
Bitmap indexes, 295–296
BLOB data type, 48
Block labels, code blocks, 341–342
Boolean variables, 345
Bottom-N and Top-N queries, 226–227
BREAK command, 274–277
   with COMPUTE command, 277–280
Breaks, report-writing tools (SQL*Plus), 274–277
BTITLE command, 267–269
Business objects
   basics, 325–329
   multidimensional tables, 329–331
   normalization inapplicable, 326
   object tables, 324
BY keyword, CREATE USER command, 78

C
Cardinality database relationship, 9–10
   ERDs, 14–15
Cartesian joins, 135, 141
CASCADE keyword, DROP USER command, 78
Case-changing functions
   LOWER, 155
   UPPER, 164–165
CASE statements, 167–169
CEIL function, 172
CHAR data type, 47
   LENGTH function, 154
Character functions
   ASCII, 152

CHR, 152
DECODE, 165–167
INITCAP, 151, 152, 153, 169
INSTR, 152, 153–154
LENGTH, 152, 154–155
LOWER, 152, 155
LPAD, 152, 156
LTRIM, 152, 156–157
REPLACE, 152, 157–158
RPAD, 152, 158–159
RTRIM, 152, 159
SOUNDEX, 152, 160–161
TO_CHAR, 153, 162
TRANSLATE, 153, 162–163
TRIM, 153, 163–164
UPPER, 153, 164–165
Character variables, 344
CHECK constraint, 54–55, 62
Child tables, 11, 12
CHOOSE_ROWS mode, cost-based optimizers, 302
CHR function, 152
CLEAR BREAKS command, 276
CLOB data type, 48
CLOSE command, 355–356
Clustering, 303
Code blocks, looping structures
   FOR, 360
   LOOP, 360, 361–363
   WHILE, 360, 363–366
      with %FOUND cursor attribute, 364–366
Code blocks (PL/SQL)
   arrays, 389–392
   comments, 343
   cursors
      with aggregate variables, 357–358
      attributes, 358
      basics, 354
      commands, 355–356
      defining, 354–355
      versus SELECT/INTO statements, 360
   declaration section, 340–341
   ELSEIF structures, 349, 353
   exception handling, 381–388
   exception section, 340–341, 388–389
   executable section, 340–341
   executing programs, 339, 341
   functions, 407–412
   header section, 340–341
   IF-THEN-ELSE structures, 349, 350–354
   labels and block labels, 341–342
   locking records, 367–370

looping structures
  FOR, 372–377
    cursors, 375–377
    nested loops, 366–367, 377–378
  marking records, 370–371
  named procedures, 396–407
  packages, 412–418
  table attributes, 392–395
  table records, 389–392
    deleting, 395–396
  variables, 343–349
  writing programs, 337–339
Collection types, ADTs (abstract data types)
  object-type tables, 70, 72–73
  varrays, 70–72
COLUMN command, 273–274
  formatting options, 269–272
Columns
  aliases, 105
  defined, 4
  formatting options, 270–272
  indexing, 293–294
  joins, columns with same names, 133–134
  PLAN_TABLE tables, 306–307
  qualifying, 133
COMMENT ANY TABLE command, 83
Comments, code blocks, 343
COMMIT commands, 88, 93
Comparison operators. *See* Evaluation operators
Complex database views, 252–253, 256–257
Composite indexes. *See* Concatenated indexes
Composite keys. *See* Concatenated keys
COMPUTE command, with BREAK command,
      277–280
Concatenated indexes, 294–295, 322
Concatenated keys, 12
Concatenation operators (||), 106–107
Concurrency control, 367–368
Connect strings, 32, 78
CONSTANT constraint, variables, 345–346
Constraints
  ADD, 59
  basics, 53–54
  CHECK, 54–55, 62
  DEFAULT option, 55
  DISABLE, 60
  DROP, 59
  ENABLE, 60
  FOREIGN KEY, 58–59, 61
  MODIFY, 59, 60
  NOT NULL, 55–56, 61

NOVALIDATE, 60
PRIMARY KEY, 57–58, 61
UNIQUE, 56, 62
VALIDATE, 60
variables, 345–346
when to use, 61–62
Correlated subqueries, 203–204
Correlation, statistical functions, 243–245
COS function, 172
COSH function, 172
Cost-based optimizers
  access paths, 322
  clustering, 303
COUNT attribute, PL/SQL tables, 393–395
COUNT group function, 143–144
COUNT keyword, COMPUTE command,
      277
Covariance, statistical functions, 243–245
COVAR_POP statistical function, 243
COVAR_SAMP statistical function, 243
CREATE commands
  CREATE DATABASE LINK, 63–64
  CREATE INDEX, 51–52, 298
  CREATE ROLE, 80–81
  CREATE/SELECT TABLE (copying), 49
  CREATE SEQUENCE, 64–65
  CREATE SYNONYM, 62–63
  CREATE TABLE, ADTs
    collection type, 70–73
    nested objects, 73
    object type, 68–70
  CREATE TABLESPACE, 41–42
  CREATE USER, 78–79
  CREATE VIEW, 248–251
  system privileges, 83–85
CUBE function, 218–219
CUME_DIST function, *versus* PERCENT-RANK
      function, 229–230
Cumulative aggregate functions, 234–238
CURRENT ROW windowing function, 234
Cursor variables, PL/SQL, 421–423
Cursors
  with aggregate variables, 357–358
  attributes, 358
    %FOUND with looping structures, 364–366
  basics, 354
  commands, 355–356
  defining, 354–355
  FOR looping structure, 375–377
  versus SELECT/INTO statements, 360
CURVAL keyword, 64

D

Data, defined, 1
Data Control Language. *See* DCL
Data Definition Language. *See* DDL
Data dictionary, 94
    prefixes and levels of information, 94
    views, 96-99
Data flow diagrams. *See* DFDs
Data flows, 7
Data Manipulation Language. *See* DML
Data schema diagrams, based on ERDs, 22-23
Data stores, 7
Data types, 47-48
Data warehouses
    analytical functions, viewing data, 215-216
    business objects
        basics, 325-329
        multidimensional tables, 329-331
        normalization inapplicable, 326
        tables, 324
    versus database production systems, 323-324
    historic tables, 324
    materialized views, 262
    summary tables, 324
Database administrators (DBAs), 39
Database management software. *See* DBMS
Database objects
    nested tables, 426-427
    processing, 424-426
Database production systems, *versus* data warehouses, 323-324
Database relationships
    cardinality, 9-10
    Many-to-Many, 18-19, 20
    One-to-Many, 9-10, 18-19
    One-to-One, 18
    ordinality, 9-10
Database schema diagrams, necessity, 6-7
Database view
    administering, 248-251
    WITH CHECK OPTION clause, 253-254
    defined, 247
    INSTEAD OF trigger, UPDATE command alternative, 255-258
    WITH READ ONLY clause, 254-255
    reasons to use, 258
    simple and complex, 252-253. 256-257
Databases
    defined, 1
    desk analogy, 39-40
    integrity, 53-62

optimizing (*See* Performance optimization; Performance tuning)
    SQL retrieval info required, 5
    tablespaces, 40
    types, 40-41
DATE data type, 47
Dates
    date functions
        ADD_MONTHS, 181-182
        basics, 181
        GREATEST, 182
        LAST_DAY, 182, 183
        MONTHS_BETWEEN, 182, 183-184
        NEXT_DAY, 182, 184-185
        ROUND, 185-186, 187
        TO_CHAR, 182
        TO_DATE, 182, 186, 188
        TRUNC, 185-186, 187
    date pictures, 178-181
    date values, 177-178
    variables, 345
DBAs (database administrators), 39
DBMS (database management software), defined, 1
DBMS_STATS package, 301
DCL (Data Control Language), user accounts
    commands, CREATE USER, 78-79
    commands, DROP USER, 78-79
    default accounts, SYS and SYSTEM, 77
    host IDs, 78
    manager, default ID, 77
    passwords, 78
    privileges
        commands, 79-88
        granting/revoking, 77, 80, 81-82
        object privileges, 79, 87-88
        roles, 80-81
        system privileges, 79
        system privileges (list), 82-86
    profiles, 78
    usernames, 78
DDL (Data Definition Language), ?
DECIMAL data type, 47
Declaration section, code blocks, 340-341
    PL/SQL tables, 390-391
DECLARE keyword, code blocks, 340
DECODE function, 165-167
DEFAULT option, constraints, 55
DEFINE (user variable) command, 209, 210-211
DELETE ANY TABLE command, system privileges, 85
DELETE attribute, PL/SQL tables, 393-395

DELETE commands
  manipulating records, 88, 92
  object privileges, 87
DENSE-RANK function
  basics, 225
  Top-N and Bottom-N queries, 226–227
Derived table view, 258, 260–261
  defined, 247
DESC command. *See* DESCRIBE command
Descending/ascending order, ORDER BY clauses,
      124–125
Descending indexes, 295
DESCRIBE command, 101, 102–103
Designer6i (Oracle), 22
Developer-defined processing, 388–389
DFDs (data flow diagrams), 7
Dictionaries. *See* Data dictionary
Dictionary view, data dictionary, 95–96
DISABLE constraint, ALTER command, 50, 60
Discoverer 4.0 (Oracle), 334–336
DISTINCT keyword
  COUNT function, 144
  GROUP BY clause, 252
  performance tuning, 322
Division (/) function, 172
Division operators (/), 108
DML (Data Manipulation Language)
  commands
    COMMIT, 88, 93
    DELETE, 88, 92
    INSERT, 88–91
    ROLLBACK, 88, 93
    TRUNCATE, 93–94
    UPDATE, 88, 91–92
  database views
    WITH CHECK OPTION clause, 253–254
    simple and complex, 252–253. 256–257
Double ampersand (&&) variable, 207–209
Drilling down, 331–333
DROP commands
  DROP COLUMN option, ALTER command, 50
  DROP INDEX, 52–53
  DROP PROCEDURE, 397–398
  DROP ROLE, 80–81
  DROP SYNONYM, 63
  DROP TABLE, 51
  DROP TABLESPACE, 44
  DROP TRIGGER, 67
  DROP USER, 78–79
  system privileges, 85–86
DROP constraint, ALTER command, 50, 59

DUAL keyword, FROM clause, 153
Dynamic performance views, V$SQL_PLAN, 312

E
Edit menu commands, SQL*Plus Editor, 38
Editing software, 36–39
ELSEIF structures, 349, 353
ENABLE constraint, 60
  ALTER command, 50, 60
Encapsulation, 412–413
END keyword, code blocks, 340, 341
Entities. *See also* ERDs
Entity relationship diagrams. *See* ERDs
Environmental variables, 282–288
Equal to (=) evaluation operator, 110, 111
  subqueries, 198
Equijoins, 134, 135
  performance tuning, 322
Error handling. *See* Exception handling
ESCAPE keyword, evaluation operators, 119
Evaluation operators
  BETWEEN, 110, 115–116
  IN, 110, 113–114
  equal to (=), 110, 111
  greater than (>), 110, 112–113
    single-row subqueries, 198
  greater than or equal to (>=), 110
    single-row subqueries, 198
  IS NULL, 111
  less than (<), 110, 112–113
    subqueries, 198
  less than or equal to (I<=), 110
    subqueries, 198
  LIKE
    basics, 111, 116–117
    ESCAPE keyword, 119
    wildcard characters, 117–119
  not equal to (), 198
  not qual to (), single-row subqueries, 198
Exception handling, 381–388
EXCEPTION keyword, code blocks, 340
Exception reporting, 331–333
Exception section, 388–389
  code blocks, 340–341
Exceptions, variables, 345
Executable section, code blocks, 340–341
EXECUTE ANY PROCEDURE command, system
      privileges, 86
EXECUTE commands, object privileges, 87
EXISTS attribute, PL/SQL tables, 393–395
EXISTS operator, 203

performance tuning, 322
EXP function, 172
EXPLAIN PLAN command
  basics, 305
  PLAN_TABLE tables, 305–308, 312
  reading results, 308–312
  trace statistics, 318
  versus V$SQL_PLAN view, 312
Expressions
  CASE, 167–169
  ORDER BY clauses
    expression numbers, 126–127
    multiple expressions, 125–126
  SELECT clauses, 104–106
EXTERNALLY keyword, CREATE USER command,
  78

F

FETCH/INTO command, 355–356
File menu commands, SQL*Plus Editor, 37–38
FIRST attribute, PL/SQL tables, 393–395
First normal form, 20--21
FIRST_ROWS mode, cost-based optimizers, 302
FLOAT data type, 47
FLOOR function, 172
FOLLOWING keyword, cumulative aggregate func-
  tions, 236–238
Footer and title settings, report-writing tools
  (SQL*Plus), 267–269
FOR looping structure, 360
  cursors, 375–377
  nested loops, 377–378
  numeric loops, 372–375
FOR UPDATE and FOR UPDATE OF keywords,
  locking records, 367–370
FOR UPDATE OF keyword, locking records,
  369–370
FORCE ANY TRANSACTION command, 86
FOREIGN KEY constraint, 58–59, 61
Foreign keys, 11
Formatting databases
  columns, 270–271
  footers, 268
  headers, 268
%FOUND cursor attribute, 358
  WHILE looping structure, 364–366
FROM clauses, SELECT commands, 103
  joins
    Cartesian joins, 135, 141
    columns with same names, 133–134
    equijoins, 134, 135

multiple tables, 131–133
    nonequijoins, 135, 138–139
    outer joins, 135–138
    self joins, 135, 139–140
FROM keyword
  SELECT clauses, 106
  TRIM function, 163
Full table scans, 292
Function-based indexes, 295, 298
Functions. *See* Analytical functions; Character
      functions; Dates, date functions; Group
      functions; Numeric functions
  PL/SQL, 407–412

G

GRANT commands, 80, 81
  GRANT SELECT command, 251
  object privileges, 87–88
  system privileges, 86
Greater than (>) evaluation operator, 110, 112–113
  subqueries, 198
Greater than or equal to (>=) evaluation operator,
      110
  subqueries, 198
GREATEST date function, 182
GROUP BY clauses, SELECT commands, 103
Group functions
  AVG, 143, 145
  basics, 142
  COUNT, 143–144
  HAVING clauses, 148–149
  MAX, 143, 146
  MIN, 143, 145–146
  small groups, 146–148
  STDDEV, 143
  SUM, 143, 144
  VARIANCE, 143
GROUPING function, 220–222

H

Handling errors. *See* Exception handling
Hash joins, 304–305
HAVING clause, SELECT commands, 103
  limiting selected records, 148–149
Header section
  code blocks, 340–341
  named procedures, 398–399
    parameter modes, 399–404
Hierarchical databases, 1
Hints, 318–320, 322
  performance tuning, 322

Historic tables, 324
Host IDs, user accounts, 78

I
IDENTIFIED keyword, CREATE USER command, 78
Identifiers, entities, 7-8
  ERDs, creating, 14
  primary keys, 8
IF-THEN-ELSE structures, 349, 350-354
IN evaluation operator, 110, 113-114, 198, 199
IN named procedure parameter mode, 399, 400, 401-402
IN OUT named procedure parameter mode, 399, 400
INCREMENT setting, CREATE SEQUENCE command, 64-65
Index-organized tables, 295, 297-298
Indexes, 321-322
  B-Tree, 293, 295, 296, 297
  basics, 292-293
  bitmap, 295-296
  columns, selecting to index, 293-294
  commands
    CREATE INDEX, 51-52
    DROP INDEX, 52-53
    UNIQUE INDEX, 52-53
  concatenated, 294-295, 322
  descending, 295
  function-based, 295, 298
  index-organized tables, 295, 297-298
  reverse-key, 295, 297
INITCAP function, 151, 152, 153, 169
Inline view, 258, 260-261
  defined, 247
INSERT commands
  INSERT ANY TABLE, 86
  manipulating records, 88-91
  object privileges, 87
Instances, entities, 3
INSTEAD OF trigger, DML statement alternative for views, 255-258
INSTR function, 152, 153-154
Integer identifiers, 389-390
INTERSECT set operator, 196
INTO operator, 347-349
IS NULL evaluation operator, 111
%ISOPEN cursor attribute, 358, 359

J
Java, and PL/SQL, 427-431
Joins, 10-12

Cartesian, 135, 141
columns with same names, 133-134
equijoins, 134, 135
  performance tuning, 322
multiple tables, 131-133
nonequijoins, 135, 138-139
outer, 10, 135-138
performance optimization
  hash joins, 304-305
  nested-loop joins, 303-304
  sort-merge joins, 304
self, 135, 139-140

L
Labels, code blocks, 341-342
LAG function, 239-243
LAST attribute, PL/SQL tables, 393-395
LAST_DAY date function, 182, 183
LEAD function, 239-243
LENGTH function, 152, 154-155
Less than (<) evaluation operator, 110, 112-113
  subqueries, 198
Less than or equal to (<=) evaluation operator, 110
  subqueries, 198
LIKE evaluation operator
  basics, 111, 116-117
  ESCAPE keyword, 119
  performance tuning, 322
  wildcard characters, 117-119
Linear regression, statistical functions, 243-245
LINESIZE setting, printing, 127-128
Links, databases, 63-64
LIST command, 34
LN function, 172
Local installations, 33
LOCK ANY TABLE command, system privileges, 86
Locking records, 367-370
LOG function, 172
LONG data type, 47
LONG VARCHAR data type, 47
LOOP looping structure, 360, 361-363
Looping structures
  FOR, 360
  LOOP, 360, 361-363
  WHILE, 360, 363-364
    with %FOUND cursor attribute, 364-366
    nested loops, 366-367
LOWER function, 152, 155
LPAD function, 152, 156
LTRIM function, 152, 156-157

M

MANAGE TABLESPACE command, 86
Management information systems
   business objects, 325–331
   data warehouses, *versus* database production
      systems, 323–324
   drilling down, 331–333
   exception reporting, 331–333
   OLAP, 334–336
Manager ID, user accounts, 77
Many-to-Many database relationship, 18–19, 20
Many-to-Many Not Optional table relationship, 25
Many-to-Many Optional table relationship, 25
Many-to-Many with Link Table table relationship,
   25
Materialized view, 262–265
   defined, 247
MAX group function, 143, 146
MAXIMUM keyword, COMPUTE command, 277
Metadata, defined, 1
MIN group function, 143, 145–146
MINIMUM keyword, COMPUTE command, 277
MINUS set operator, 195
MISLABEL data type, 47
MOD function, 171, 172, 173
Models. *See* Relational database models
MODIFY constraint, ALTER command, 49, 59, 60
MONTHS_BETWEEN date function, 182, 183–184
Multicolumn indexes. *See* Concatenated indexes
Multiplication (*) function, 172
Multiplication operators (*), 108

N

Named procedures, 396–407
Nested-loop joins, 303–304
Nested looping structures, 366–367
Nested tables in database objects, 426–427
Network databases, 1
   pointers, 2
NEXT attribute, PL/SQL tables, 393–395
NEXT_DAY date function, 182, 184–185
NEXTVAL keyword, 64
Nonequijoins, 135, 138–139
Normalization
   basics, 19–22
   inapplicable for business objects, 326
Not equal to () evaluation operator, subqueries,
   198
NOT EXISTS operator, 203
NOT IN operator, performance tuning, 322
NOT NULL constraint, 55–56, 61

   variables, 345–346
NOT operator, performance tuning, 322
%NOTFOUND cursor attribute, 358
   FOR loops, 375
NOVALIDATE constraint, 60
NTITLE function, 230–231
Null values, 109
NULLIF function, 172
NULLS FIRST | NULLS LAST clause, RANK func-
   tion, 223–225
NUMBER data type, 47
NUMBER keyword, COMPUTE command, 277
Numeric FOR loops, 372–375
Numeric functions
   ABS, 172
   addition (+), 172
   CEIL, 172
   COS, 172
   COSH, 172
   division (/), 172
   EXP, 172
   FLOOR, 172
   LN, 172
   LOG, 172
   MOD, 171, 172, 173
   multiplication (*), 172
   NULLIF, 172
   NVL, 172, 173–174
   NVL2, 172, 173–175
   POWER, 172
   ROUND, 172, 175–176
      with dates, 185–186, 187
   SIGN, 172
   SIN, 172
   SINH, 172
   SQRT, 173
   subtraction (-), 172
   TAN, 173
   TANH, 173
   TO_NUMBER, 171, 173
   TRUNC, 173, 176–177
      with dates, 185–186, 187
Numeric variables, 344–345
NVL function, 147–148, 172, 173–174
NVL2 function, 172, 173–175

O

Object privileges, user accounts, 79, 87–88
Object-relational databases, defined, 1
Object technology, 1–2
   ADTs

collection types
   object-type tables, 70, 72–73
   varrays, 70–72
  defined, 68
  object types, 69–70
  versus relational databases, 68
Object types, ADTs (abstract data types), 69–70
OLAP, Oracle Discoverer 4.0, 334–336
OLTP (on-line transaction processing), data warehouses
  analytical functions, 215
  versus database production systems, 323–324
  materialized views, 262
ON DELETE CASCADE option, FOREIGN KEY constraint, 58, 59
ON keyword, COMPUTE command, 277
On-line analytical tools. *See* OLAP
On-line transaction processing. *See* OLTP
One-to-Many database relationship, 9–10, 18–19
One-to-Many Not Optional table relationship, 24
One-to-Many Optional table relationship, 25
One-to-One database relationship, 18
One-to-One Not Optional table relationship, 24
One-to-One Optional table relationship, 24
OPEN command, 355–356
Optimizing databases. *See* Performance optimization
Option menu commands, SQL*Plus Editor, 39
OR keyword
  clauses
   HAVING, 148–149
   WHERE, 121–122
  performance tuning, 322
Oracle
  Designer6i, 22
  Discoverer 4.0, 334–336
ORDER BY clauses, SELECT commands, 103, 123–127
ORDER BY windowing function, 233
Ordinality database relationship, 9–10
  ERDs (entity relationship diagrams), 14–15
OTHERS exception, 386–387
OUT named procedure parameter mode, 399, 400, 402–404
Outer joins, 10, 135–138
OVER windowing function, 233
Overloading procedures, 405–407

P
Packages
  PL/SQL, 412–418

  procedures, 338
PAGESIZE setting, printing, 128
Parent tables, 11, 12
PARTITION BY windowing function, 233
PARTITION clause
  analytical functions, 222
  CREATE TABLE command, 48
  Top-N and Bottom-N queries, 226–227
Passwords, user accounts, 78
PERCENT-RANK function, 227–228
  versus CUME_DIST function, 229–230
Performance optimization. *See also* Performance tuning
  cost-based optimizers, 301
   access paths, 302–303, 322
   clustering, 303
   modes, 302
   settings, 302
  joins
   hash, 304–305
   nested-loop, 303–304
   sort-merge, 304
  rule-based optimizers, 299–301
Performance tuning. *See also* Performance optimization
  basics, 291
  dynamic performance views, V$SQL_PLAN, 312
  EXISTS operator, 322
  EXPLAIN PLAN command
   basics, 305
   PLAN_TABLE tables, 305–308, 312
   reading results, 308–312
  guidelines, 321–322
  hints, 318–320, 322
  indexes, 321–322
   B-Tree, 293, 295, 296, 297
   basics, 292–293
   bitmap, 295–296
   columns, selecting to index, 293–294
   concatenated, 294–295, 322
   descending, 295
   function-based, 295, 298
   index-organized tables, 295, 297–298
   reverse-key, 295, 297
  joins, equijoins, 322
  keywords
   AND, 322
   DISTINCT, 322
   OR, 322
   UNION, 322
   WHERE CURRENT OF, 370

Performance tuning *(continued)*
  operators
    LIKE, 322
    NOT, 322
    NOT IN, 322
  SET TIMING ON command, 321
  SUBSTR function, 322
  trace statistics
    ALTER SESSION commands, 313, 315
    basics, 313
    running and viewing, 313–318
    TKPROF command, 314–318
      options, 314–315
PL/SQL, database view, INSTEAD OF trigger,
    255–258
PL/SQL (Procedure Language SQL)
  code blocks
    arrays, 389–392
    comments, 343
    ELSEIF structures, 349, 353
    exception handling, 381–388
    exception section, 388–389
    functions, 407–412
    IF-THEN-ELSE structures, 349, 350–354
    locking records, 367–370
    marking records, 370–371
    named procedures, 396–407
    packages, 412–418
    sections, 340–341
    stored procedures, 97–99
    table attributes, 392–395
    table records, 389–392
      deleting, 395–396
    triggers, 65–67
    variables, 343–349
  cursor variables, 421–423
  database objects
    nested tables, 426–427
    processing, 424–426
  executing programs, 339, 341
  and Java, 427–431
  writing programs, 337–339
PLAN_TABLE tables, 305–308
  scripts, 312
Pointers, network databases, 2
POWER function, 172
PRAGMA EXCEPTION_INIT keyword, 385
PRECEDING keyword, cumulative aggregate func-
    tions, 236–238
PRIMARY KEY constraint, 57–58, 61
Primary keys, 8, 10–12

Printing reports, 280–281
  query results, 127–128
PRIOR attribute, PL/SQL tables, 393–395
PRIVATE keyword, synonyms, 62, 63
Privileges, user accounts, 77
  commands, 79–88
  granting/revoking, 80, 81–82
  object privileges, 79, 87–88
  roles, 80–81
  system privileges, 79
  system privileges (list), 82–86
Procedure Language SQL. *See* PL/SQL
Procedures, 338
Profiles, user accounts, 78
PS/SQL (Procedure Language SQL), code blocks
  cursors, 354–360, 364–366
  looping structures, 360–366
    nested FOR loops, 377–378
    nested loops, 366–367
  looping structures, FOR, 372–377
PUBLIC keyword
  database links, 64
  synonyms, 62, 63
Public or private synonyms, 62, 63

Q
Queries, printing results, 127–128
Quest software, TOAD, 73
QUOTA keyword, CREATE USER command, 78

R
RANGE INTERVAL keyword, cumulative aggregate
    functions, 236
RANK function, 222–225
Ranking functions
  CUME_DIST, *versus* PERCENT-RANK analytical
    function, 229–230
  DENSE-RANK
    basics, 225
    Top-N and Bottom-N queries, 226–227
  NTITLE, 230–231
  PERCENT-RANK, *versus* CUME_DIST analytical
    function, 229–230
  RANK, 222–225
  ROW_NUMBER, 231–232
RATIO_TO_REPORT function, 238–239
RAW data type, 48
RAW MISLABEL data type, 48
READUP command, system privileges, 86
Records in databases, commands, manipulating
    values, 88–94

REFERENCES command, object privileges, 87
Regression (linear), statistical functions, 243–245
Relational database models, 3
  converting from ERDs
    basics, 17–18
    normalization, 19–22
    process steps, 18–19
Relational databases. *See also* RDBMS
  defined, 1–3
  versus object technology, 68
  tables, entity attribute values, 4–7
Relationships
  databases (*See also* Table relationship diagrams)
    cardinality, 9–10
    Many-to-Many, 18–19, 20
    One-to-Many, 18–19
    One-to-One, 18
    ordinality, 9–10
  entity types, 8
Remote installations, 32–33
RENAME TABLE command, 50
REPLACE function, 152, 157–158
Report-writing tools (SQL*Plus)
  breaks, 274–277
  environmental variables, 282–288
  formatting columns, 269–274
  printing reports, 280–281
  SET commands, 282, 287–288
  subtotals, 277–280
  title and footer settings, 267–269
RESTRICTED SESSION command, system privileges, 86
Reverse-key indexes, 295, 297
REVERSE keyword, FOR loops, 372, 374
REVOKE commands, 81–82
REVOKE commandsobject privileges, 87–88
Roles, user accounts, 80–81
ROLLBACK commands, manipulating records, 88, 93
ROLLUP function, 216–218
ROUND function, 172, 175–176
  with dates, 185–186, 187
%ROWCOUNT cursor attribute, 358
  FOR loops, 375–376
ROWID keyword, SELECT clause, 299
ROW_NUMBER function, 231–232
ROWS | RANGE windowing function, 233
%ROWTYPE keyword, 346
  cursors, 357–358
RPAD function, 152, 158–159

RTRIM function, 152, 159
RUN command, 34

S
SAMLLINT data type, 47
SAVEPOINT command, manipulating records, 93
Search menu commands, SQL*Plus Editor, 39
Second normal form, 20--21
SELECT clauses
  PL/SQL functions, 410–411
  SELECT commands, 103
    character functions, 151–169
      arithmetic operators, 107–109
      concatenation operator, 106–107
SELECT commands. *See also* Subqueries
  basics, 33–34
  FROM clauses, 103
    character functions, 165–167
  data dictionary contents display, 95–96
  database queries, 103–106
  entering commands on multiple lines, 35
  GROUP BY clauses, 103
  GROUP BY clauses, functions
    AVG, 143, 145
    basics, 142
    COUNT, 143–144
    HAVING clause, 148–149
    MAX, 143, 146
    MIN, 143, 145–146
    small groups, 146–148
    STDDEV, 143
    SUM, 143, 144
    VARIANCE, 143
  HAVING clauses, 103
  identifying table and column names, 101–103
  object privileges, 87
  ORDER BY clauses, 103, 123–127
  SELECT clauses, 103
    arithmetic operators, 107–109
    concatenation operator, 106–107
  system privileges, 86
  WHERE clauses, 103
    AND, SOME, and ALL keywords, with evaluation operators, 114–115
    basics, 109–110
    character functions, 169
    evaluation operators, 110–116
    joins, 141
    LIKE operators, 116–119
    AND and OR keywords, 120–123
SELECT/INTO statements, *versus* cursors, 360

SELECT statement. *See* SELECT command
Self joins, 135, 139–140
Sequences, CREATE SEQUENCE command, 64–65
Sequential databases, 1
SET commands, 282, 287–288
   SET TIMING ON, 321
Set operators
   basics, 191–192
   INTERSECT, 196
   MINUS, 195
   rules, 192
   UNION, 192–194
   UNION ALL, 194–195
SET UNUSED option, ALTER command, 50
SIGN function, 172
Simple database views, 252–253. 256–257
SIN function, 172
Single ampersand (&) variable, 205–207
SINH function, 172
SOME keyword, with evaluation operators,
   114–115
Sort-merge joins, 304
SOUNDEX function, 152, 160–161
SPOOL commands, 127, 280–281
Spooling, printing reports, 280–281
SQL, retrieval info required, 5
SQLCODE variable, 387–388
SQLERRM variable, 387–388
SQL*Plus
   commands, 33–34
      entering on multiple lines, 35
   defined, 31
   log on, basics, 32–33
   report-writing tools
      breaks, 274–277
      environmental variables, 282–288
      formatting columns, 269–274
      printing reports, 280–281
      SET commands, 282, 287–288
      subtotals, 277–280
      title and footer settings, 267–269
SQL*Plus Editor
   basics, 37
   editing commands (list), 36
   menu commands, 38–39
SQRT function, 173
START WITH setting, CREATE SEQUENCE command, 64–65
Statistical functions, 243–245
STD keyword, COMPUTE command, 277
STDDEV group function, 143

STDDEV_POP statistical function, 243
STDDEV_SAMP statistical function, 243
Stored procedures, PL/SQL code, 97–99
Structured query language. *See* SQL
Subqueries
   basics, 196–197
   correlated, 203–204
   multiple-column, 202
   multiple-row, 198–201
   single-row, 197–198
Substitution variables, 205–207
SUBSTR function, 252
   performance tuning, 322
Subtotals, report-writing tools (SQL*Plus), 277–280
Subtraction operators (–), 108, 172
SUM group function, 143, 144
SUM keyword, COMPUTE command, 277
Summary tables, 324
Synonyms, commands
   CREATE SYNONYM, 62–63
   DROP SYNONYM, 63
SYS user account, 77
   data dictionary, 94
      All-objects view, 96
      Dictionary view, 95–96
      prefixes and levels of information, 94
      User-objects view, 96–97
      User_source view, 97–99
System privileges, 79
   list, 82–86
SYSTEM user account, 77

T
Table relationship diagrams
   elements, 23
   example, 26–28
   symbols and relationships, 23–26
Tables. *See also* Child tables; Parent tables
   collection types, 70–73
   defined, 4
   entity attribute values, 4–7
   object types, 69–70
   removing (*See* DROP command)
Tablespaces
   commands, 41–44
   types, 40–41
TAN function, 173
TANH function, 173
Ternary relationship, entities, 8
Text literals, 105, 106
Third normal form, 20––21

Title and footer settings, report-writing tools (SQL*Plus), 267–269
TKPROF command, 314–318
TOAD (Quest), 73
TO_CHAR function, 153, 162, 182
TO_DATE date function, 182, 186, 188
TO_NUMBER function, 171, 173
Top-N and Bottom-N queries
   DENSE-RANK function, 226–227
   PARTITION clause, 226–227
Trace statistics, 313– 318
TRANSLATE function, 153, 162–163
Triggers, 65–67
   INSTEAD OF, 255–258
TRIM function, 153, 163–164
TRUNC function, 173, 176–177
   with dates, 185–186, 187
TRUNCATE command, manipulating records, 93–94
TTITLE command, 267–269
%TYPE keyword, 346

U
Unary relationship, entities, 8
UNBOUNDED FOLLOWING windowing function, 234
UNBOUNDED PRECEDING windowing function, 234–235
UNDEFINE (user variable) command, 211
UNION ALL set operator, 194–195, 203–204
UNION operator, performance tuning, 322
UNION set operator, 192–194
UNIQUE constraint, 56, 62
UNIQUE INDEX command, 52–53
UNLIMITED TABLESPACE command, system privileges, 86
UPDATE commands
   WITH CHECK OPTION clause, 253–254
   INSTEAD OF trigger alternative, 255–258
   manipulating records, 88, 91–92
   object privileges, 87
   WITH READ ONLY clause, 254–255
UPPER function, 153, 164–165
User accounts
   commands, CREATE/DROP USER, 78–79
   default accounts, SYS and SYSTEM, 77
   host IDs, 78
   manager, default ID, 77
   passwords, 78
   privileges
      commands, 79–88

      granting/revoking, 77
      object privileges, 79, 87–88
      system privileges, 79
      system privileges (list), 82–86
   profiles, 78
   usernames, 78
User-defined data types. *See* ADTs
User variable commands
   ACCEPT, 209, 211–212
   DEFINE, 209, 210–211
   UNDEFINE, 211
Usernames, user accounts, 78
User-objects view, data dictionary, 96–97
User_source view, data dictionary, stored procedures, PL/SQL code, 97–99
UTLPLS.SQL script, 312
UTLXPLP.SQL script, 312

V
VALIDATE constraint, 60
VAL_POP statistical function, 243
VARCHAR data type, 48
   LENGTH function, 154
Variables
   assigning values, 347–349
   basics, 205
   cursor variables, PL/SQL, 421–423
   definitions
      aggregate, 346–347
      basics, 343
      Boolean, 345
      characters, 344
      constrained, 345–346
      dates, 345
      exceptions, 345
      numbers, 344–345
   double ampersand (&&), 207–209
   environmental, 282–288
   single ampersand (&), 205–207
   user variable commands
      ACCEPT, 209, 211–212
      DEFINE, 209, 210–211
      UNDEFINE, 211
VARIANCE group function, 143
VARIANCE keyword, COMPUTE command, 277
VAR_SAMP statistical function, 243
Views
   basics, 247–248
   database, 247, 258
      administering, 248–251
      WITH CHECK OPTION clause, 253–254

Views *(continued)*
   INSTEAD OF trigger, 255-258
   WITH READ ONLY clause, 254-255
   simple and complex, 252-253. 256-257
 derived table, 247, 258, 260-261
 dynamic performance, V$SQL_PLAN, 312
 inline, 247, 258, 260-261
 materialized, 247, 262-265
 reasons to use, 258-262
V$SQL_PLAN dynamic performance view, 312

W
WHERE clauses
 performance tuning, 321-322
 SELECT commands, 103
   AND, SOME, and ALL keywords, with evalua-
       tion operators, 114-115
   basics, 109-110
   evaluation operators, 110-116
   joins, 141

   LIKE operators, 116-119
   AND and OR keywords, 120-123
WHERE CURRENT OF keyword, marking records,
       370-371
WHILE looping structure, 360, 363-364
   with %FOUND cursor attribute, 364-366
   nested loops, 366-367
Wildcard characters, evaluation operators, 117-119
Windowing functions, 233-235
   cumulative aggregate functions, 234-235
   moving averages, 236-238
WITH CHECK OPTION clause, database view,
       253-254
WITII READ ONLY clause, database view, 254-255
WRITEDOWN commands, system privileges, 86
WRITEUP commands, system privileges, 86

Z
Zero normal form, 20--21

Also Available from Addison-Wesley

0-201-74129-6

0-201-43336-2

0-201-69471-9

0-201-70309-2

0-201-61638-6

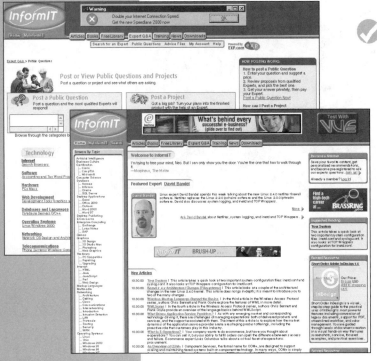

CD-ROM Warranty

Addison-Wesley warrants the enclosed disc to be free of defects in materials and faulty workmanship under normal use for a period of ninety days after purchase. If a defect is discovered in the disc during this warranty period, a replacement disc can be obtained at no charge by sending the defective disc, postage prepaid, with proof of purchase to:

Editorial Department
Addison-Wesley Professional
Pearson Technology Group
75 Arlington Street, Suite 300
Boston, MA   02116
Email: AWPro@awprofessional.com

Addison-Wesley makes no warranty or representation, either expressed or implied, with respect to this software, its quality, performance, merchantability, or fitness for a particular purpose. In no event will Addison-Wesley, its distributors, or dealers be liable for direct, indirect, special, incidental, or consequential damages arising out of the use or inability to use the software. The exclusion of implied warranties is not permitted in some states. Therefore, the above exclusion may not apply to you. This warranty provides you with specific legal rights. There may be other rights that you may have that vary from state to state. The contents of this CD-ROM are intended for personal use only.

More information and updates are available at:
http://www.awprofessional/titles/0-201-75294-8